GRAVITATION

P9-DEP-737

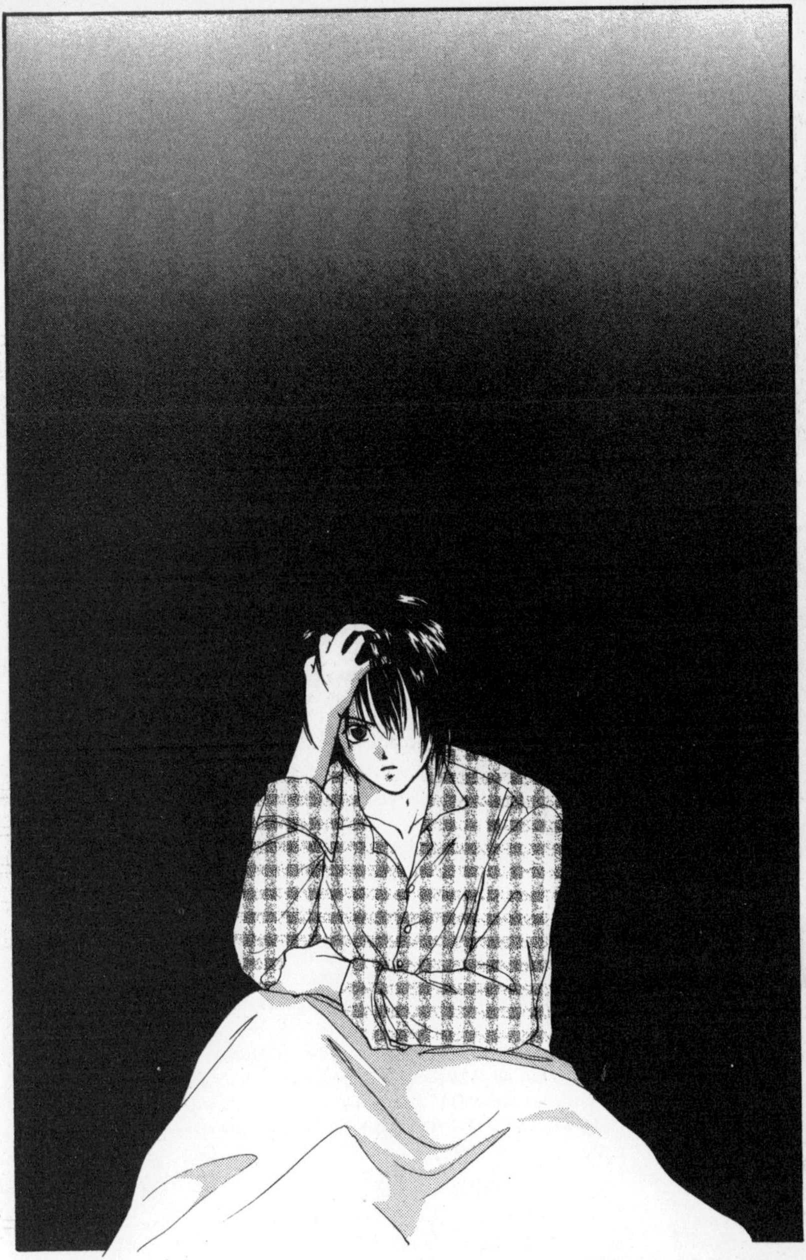

Gravitation

Translator - Ray Yoshimoto
English Adaptation - Jamie S. Rich
Copy Editor - Tim Beedle
Retouch and Lettering - Vicente Rivera, Jr.
Cover Layout - Raymond Makowski
Graphic Designer - Jose Macasocol, Jr.

Editor - Paul Morrissey
Managing Editor - Jill Freshney
Production Coordinator - Antonio DePietro
Production Managers - Jennifer Miller & Mutsumi Miyazaki
Art Director - Matt Alford
Editorial Director - Jeremy Ross
VP of Production - Ron Klamert
President & C.O.O. - John Parker
Publisher & C.E.O. - Stuart Levy

Email: editor@TOKYOPOP.com
Come visit us online at www.TOKYOPOP.com

A  Manga

TOKYOPOP Inc.
5900 Wilshire Blvd. Suite 2000
Los Angeles, CA 90036

Gravitation Vol. 4

ISBN: 1-59182-336-6

First TOKYOPOP printing: February 2004

10 9 8 7 6 5 4 3 2 1

Printed in the USA

Volume 4

By
Maki Murakami

Los Angeles • Tokyo • London

CONTENTS

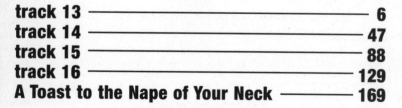

THE MEMBERS OF THE GRAVITATION BAND

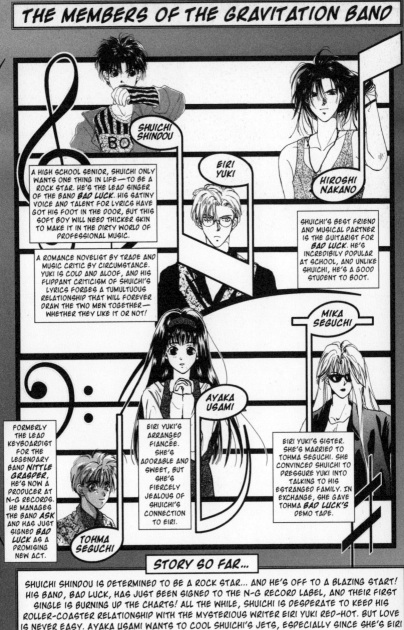

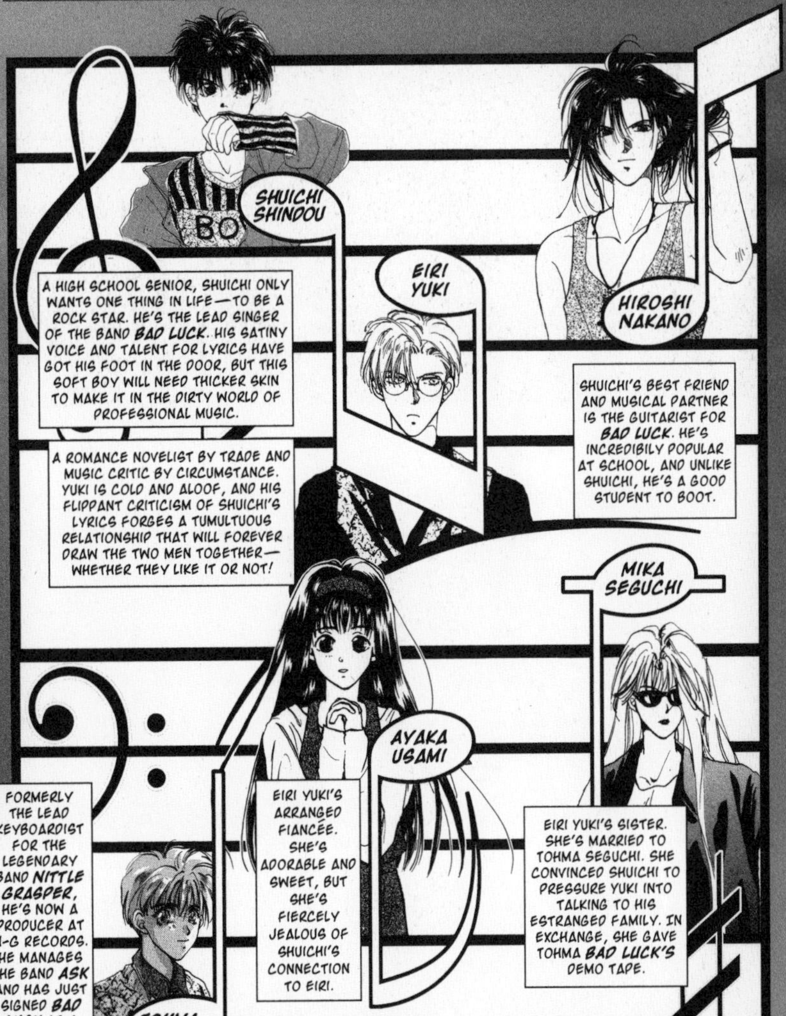
SHUICHI SHINDOU
A HIGH SCHOOL SENIOR, SHUICHI ONLY WANTS ONE THING IN LIFE—TO BE A ROCK STAR. HE'S THE LEAD SINGER OF THE BAND BAD LUCK. HIS SATINY VOICE AND TALENT FOR LYRICS HAVE GOT HIS FOOT IN THE DOOR, BUT THIS SOFT BOY WILL NEED THICKER SKIN TO MAKE IT IN THE DIRTY WORLD OF PROFESSIONAL MUSIC.
HIROSHI NAKANO
SHUICHI'S BEST FRIEND AND MUSICAL PARTNER IS THE GUITARIST FOR BAD LUCK. HE'S INCREDIBILY POPULAR AT SCHOOL, AND UNLIKE SHUICHI, HE'S A GOOD STUDENT TO BOOT.
EIRI YUKI
A ROMANCE NOVELIST BY TRADE AND MUSIC CRITIC BY CIRCUMSTANCE. YUKI IS COLD AND ALOOF, AND HIS FLIPPANT CRITICISM OF SHUICHI'S LYRICS FORGES A TUMULTUOUS RELATIONSHIP THAT WILL FOREVER DRAW THE TWO MEN TOGETHER—WHETHER THEY LIKE IT OR NOT!
MIKA SEGUCHI
EIRI YUKI'S SISTER. SHE'S MARRIED TO TOHMA SEGUCHI. SHE CONVINCED SHUICHI TO PRESSURE YUKI INTO TALKING TO HIS ESTRANGED FAMILY. IN EXCHANGE, SHE GAVE TOHMA BAD LUCK'S DEMO TAPE.
AYAKA USAMI
EIRI YUKI'S ARRANGED FIANCÉE. SHE'S ADORABLE AND SWEET, BUT SHE'S FIERCELY JEALOUS OF SHUICHI'S CONNECTION TO EIRI.
TOHMA SEGUCHI
FORMERLY THE LEAD KEYBOARDIST FOR THE LEGENDARY BAND NITTLE GRASPER, HE'S NOW A PRODUCER AT N-G RECORDS. HE MANAGES THE BAND ASK AND HAS JUST SIGNED BAD LUCK AS A PROMISING NEW ACT.

STORY SO FAR...

SHUICHI SHINDOU IS DETERMINED TO BE A ROCK STAR... AND HE'S OFF TO A BLAZING START! HIS BAND, BAD LUCK, HAS JUST BEEN SIGNED TO THE N-G RECORD LABEL, AND THEIR FIRST SINGLE IS BURNING UP THE CHARTS! ALL THE WHILE, SHUICHI IS DESPERATE TO KEEP HIS ROLLER-COASTER RELATIONSHIP WITH THE MYSTERIOUS WRITER EIRI YUKI RED-HOT. BUT LOVE IS NEVER EASY. AYAKA USAMI WANTS TO COOL SHUICHI'S JETS, ESPECIALLY SINCE SHE'S EIRI YUKI'S FIANCÉE! AND TAKI AIZAWA, THE LEADER OF THE RIVAL BAND ASK, WANTS TO EXPOSE SHUICHI'S HOMOEROTIC AFFAIR IN THE HOPES OF STOPPING BAD LUCK'S CAREER COLD. ARE SHUICHI AND YUKI DESTINED TO DRIFT APART, OR WILL THEY REMAIN INEXORABLY INTERTWINED, HELD TOGETHER BY A FORCE AS STRONG AS GRAVITY?

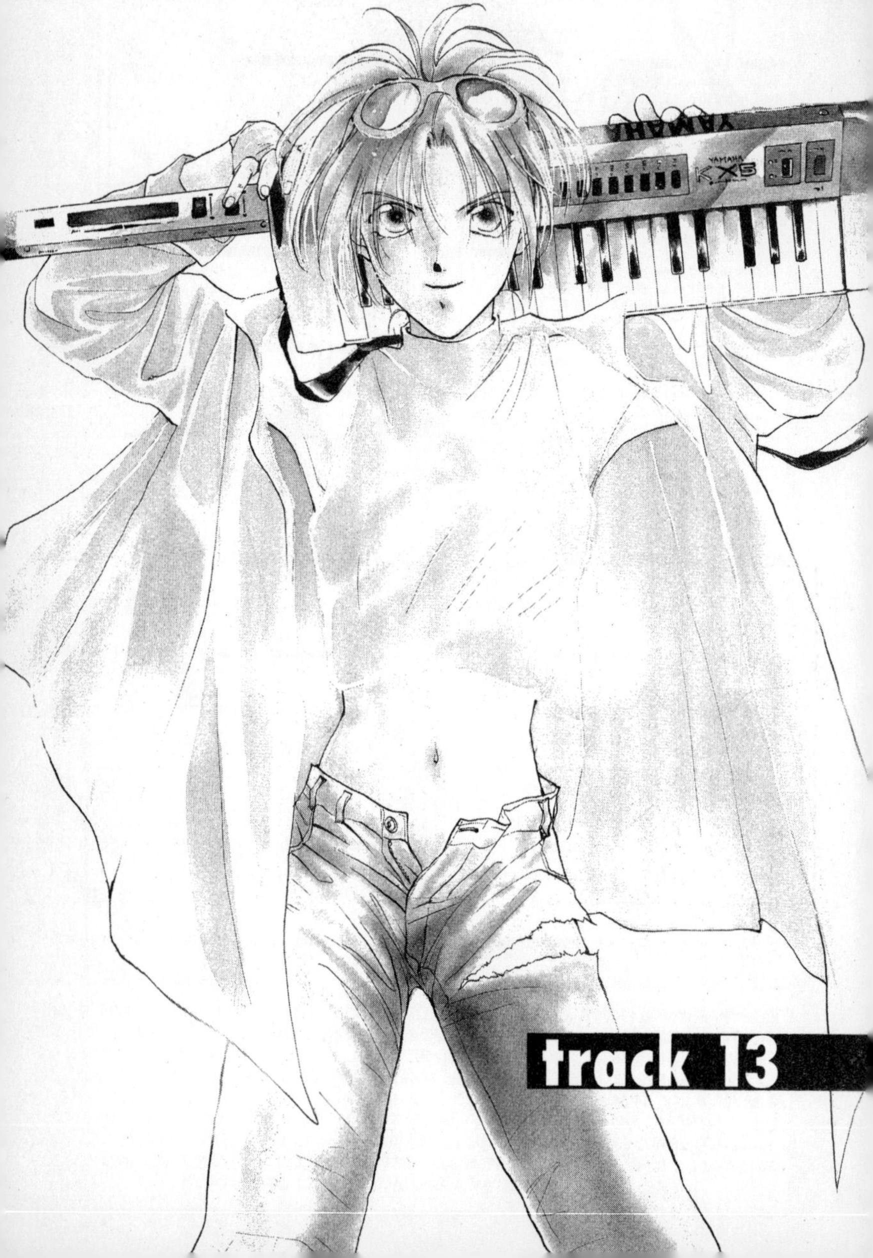
track 13

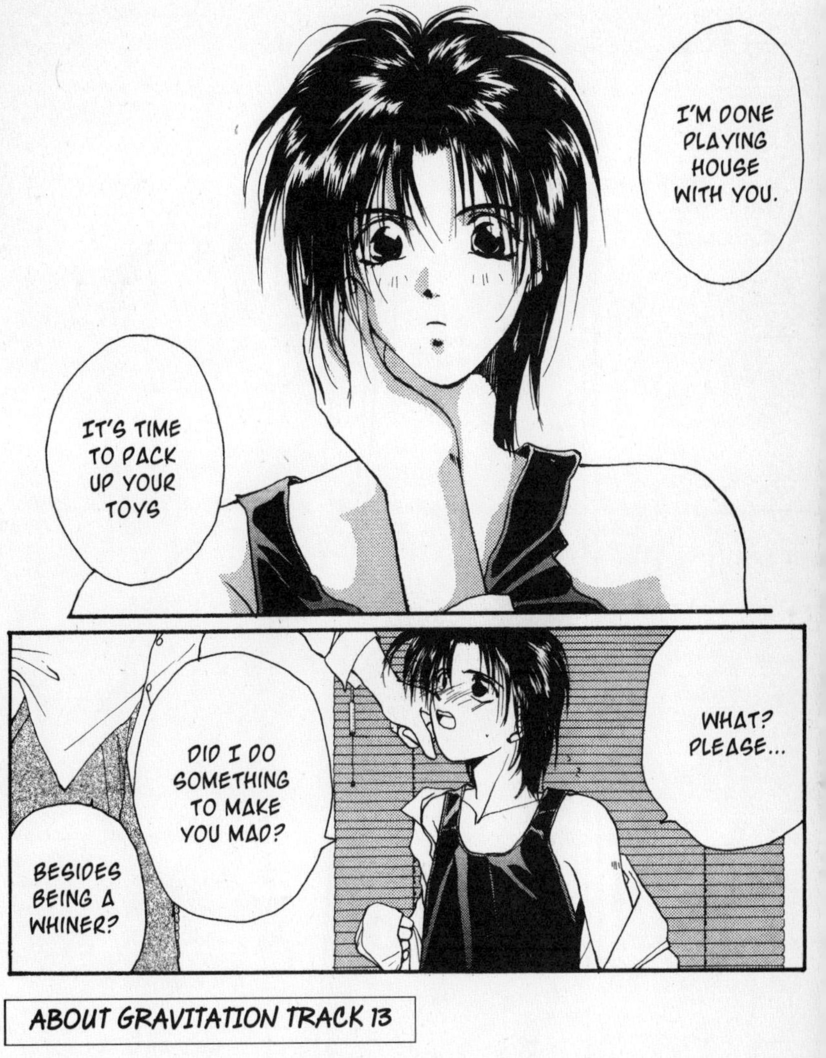
I'M DONE PLAYING HOUSE WITH YOU.
IT'S TIME TO PACK UP YOUR TOYS
WHAT? PLEASE...
DID I DO SOMETHING TO MAKE YOU MAD?
BESIDES BEING A WHINER?

ABOUT GRAVITATION TRACK 13

Hello. We're starting off book 4 with a bang, aren't we? Track 13 is just the beginning. I think you'll be surprised to see that this part of Gravitation is going to take some different twists and turns. Although it's been a pretty good time, I'm famous for missing deadlines. In order to avoid being late, I sank to a new low! I asked my mother to help me! With all the time it took to explain my process to her, everything from pasting screentones to finalizing the manuscript, it probably would've been faster if I had just done it myself. Then again, I'm probably exaggerating a little. Or maybe not.

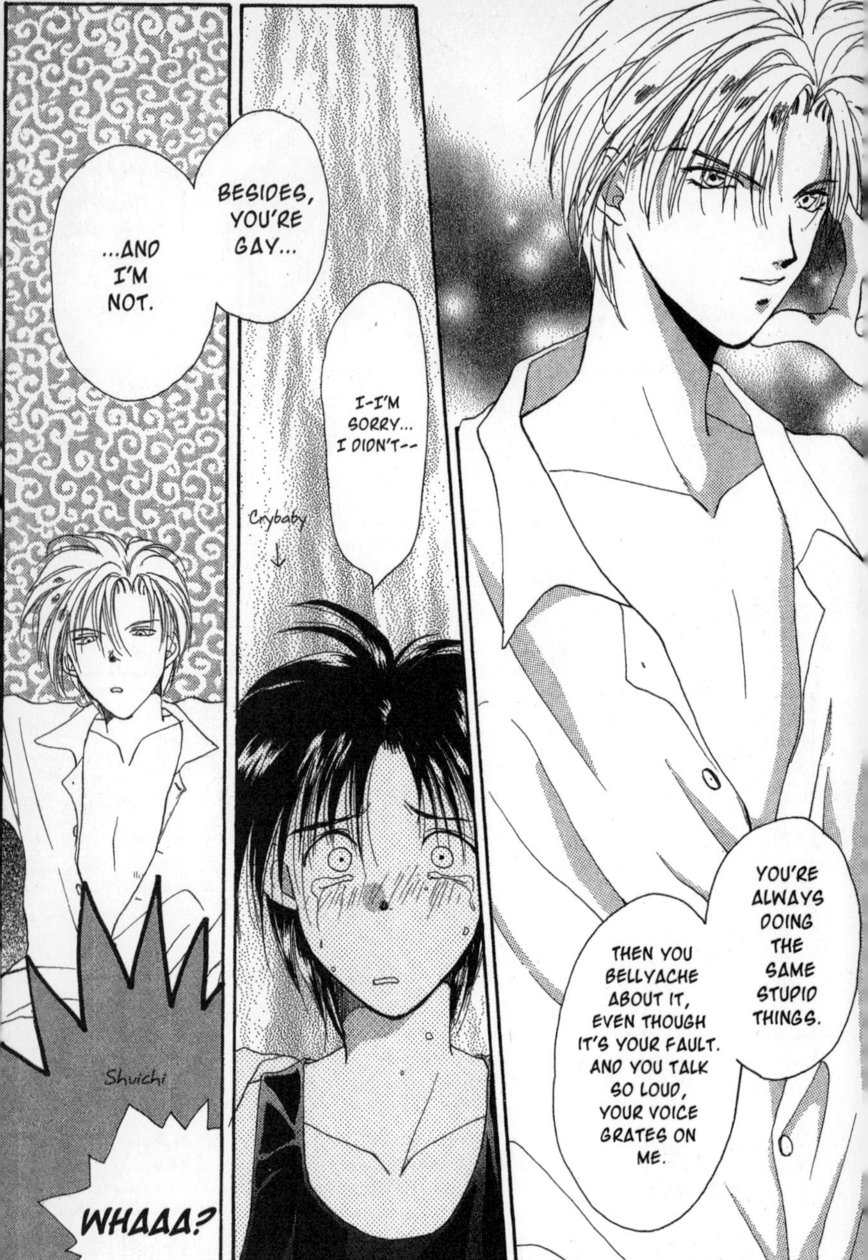
YOU'RE ALWAYS DOING THE SAME STUPID THINGS.
THEN YOU BELLYACHE ABOUT IT, EVEN THOUGH IT'S YOUR FAULT. AND YOU TALK SO LOUD, YOUR VOICE GRATES ON ME.
BESIDES, YOU'RE GAY...
I-I'M SORRY... I DIDN'T--
Crybaby
...AND I'M NOT.
Shuichi
WHAAA?

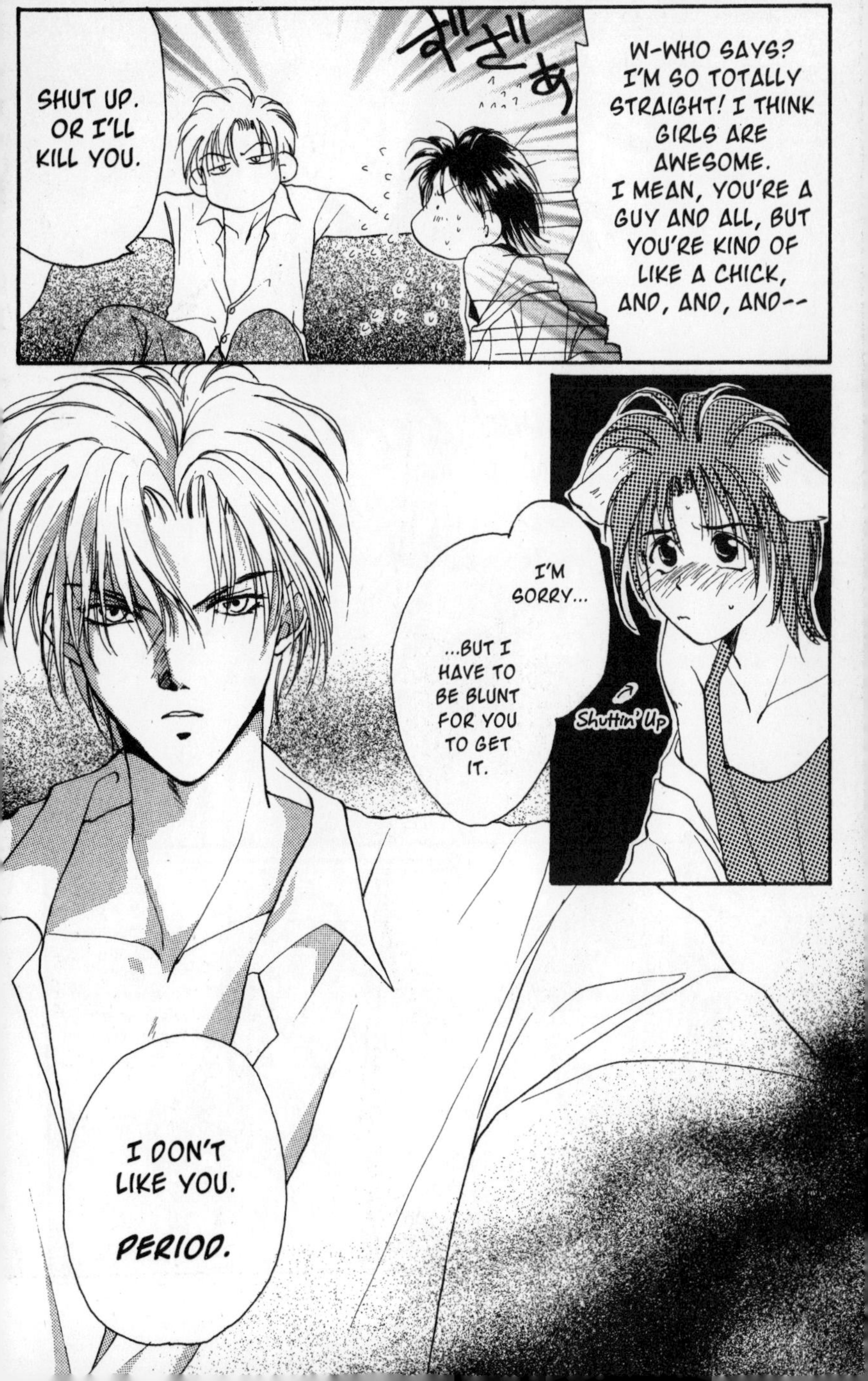
W-WHO SAYS? I'M SO TOTALLY STRAIGHT! I THINK GIRLS ARE AWESOME. I MEAN, YOU'RE A GUY AND ALL, BUT YOU'RE KIND OF LIKE A CHICK, AND, AND, AND--
ずざあ
SHUT UP. OR I'LL KILL YOU.
Shuttin' Up
I'M SORRY...
...BUT I HAVE TO BE BLUNT FOR YOU TO GET IT.
I DON'T LIKE YOU. PERIOD.

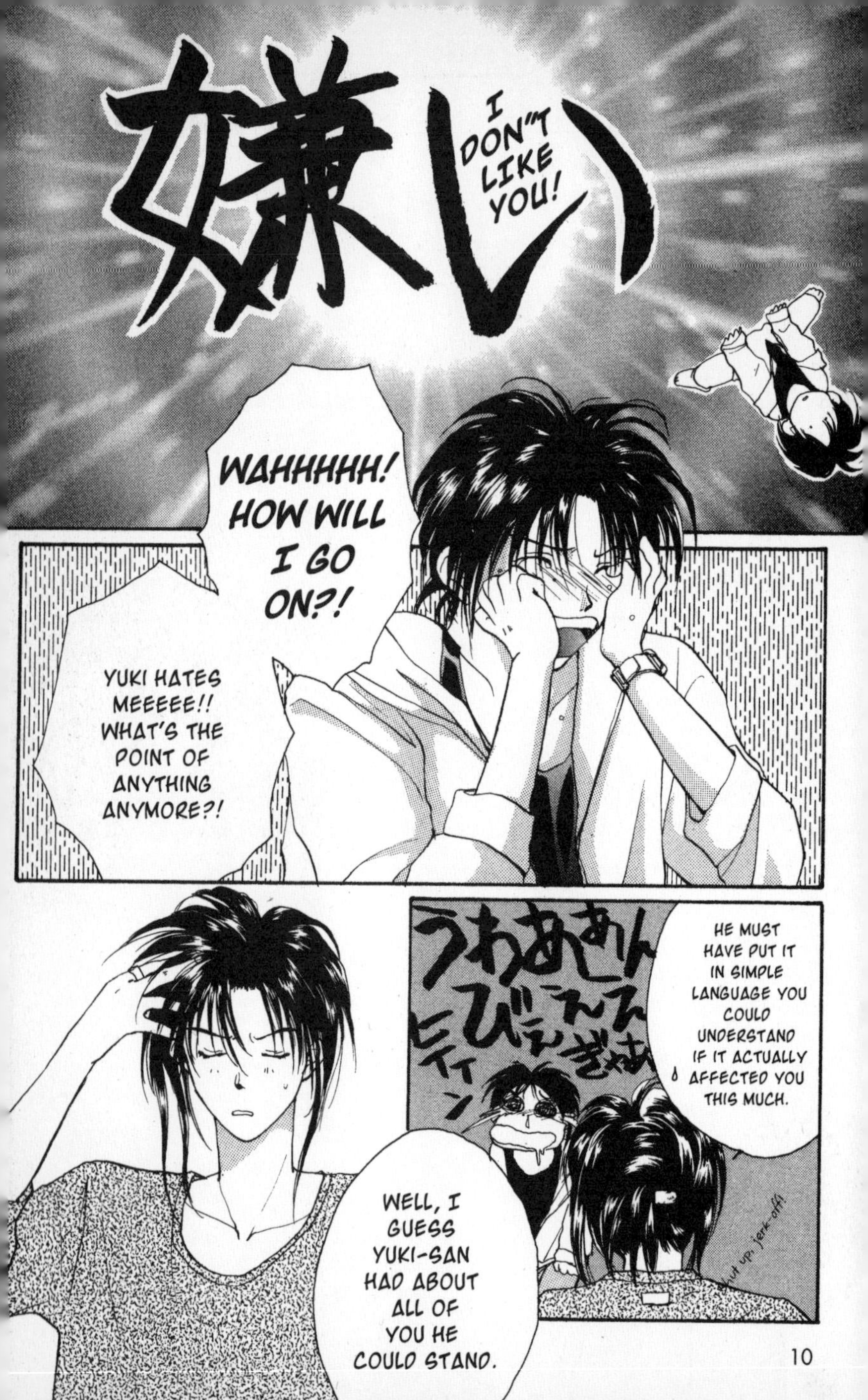
嫌い
I DON'T LIKE YOU!
WAHHHHH! HOW WILL I GO ON?!
YUKI HATES MEEEEE!! WHAT'S THE POINT OF ANYTHING ANYMORE?!
HE MUST HAVE PUT IT IN SIMPLE LANGUAGE YOU COULD UNDERSTAND IF IT ACTUALLY AFFECTED YOU THIS MUCH.
Shut up, jerk-off!
WELL, I GUESS YUKI-SAN HAD ABOUT ALL OF YOU HE COULD STAND.

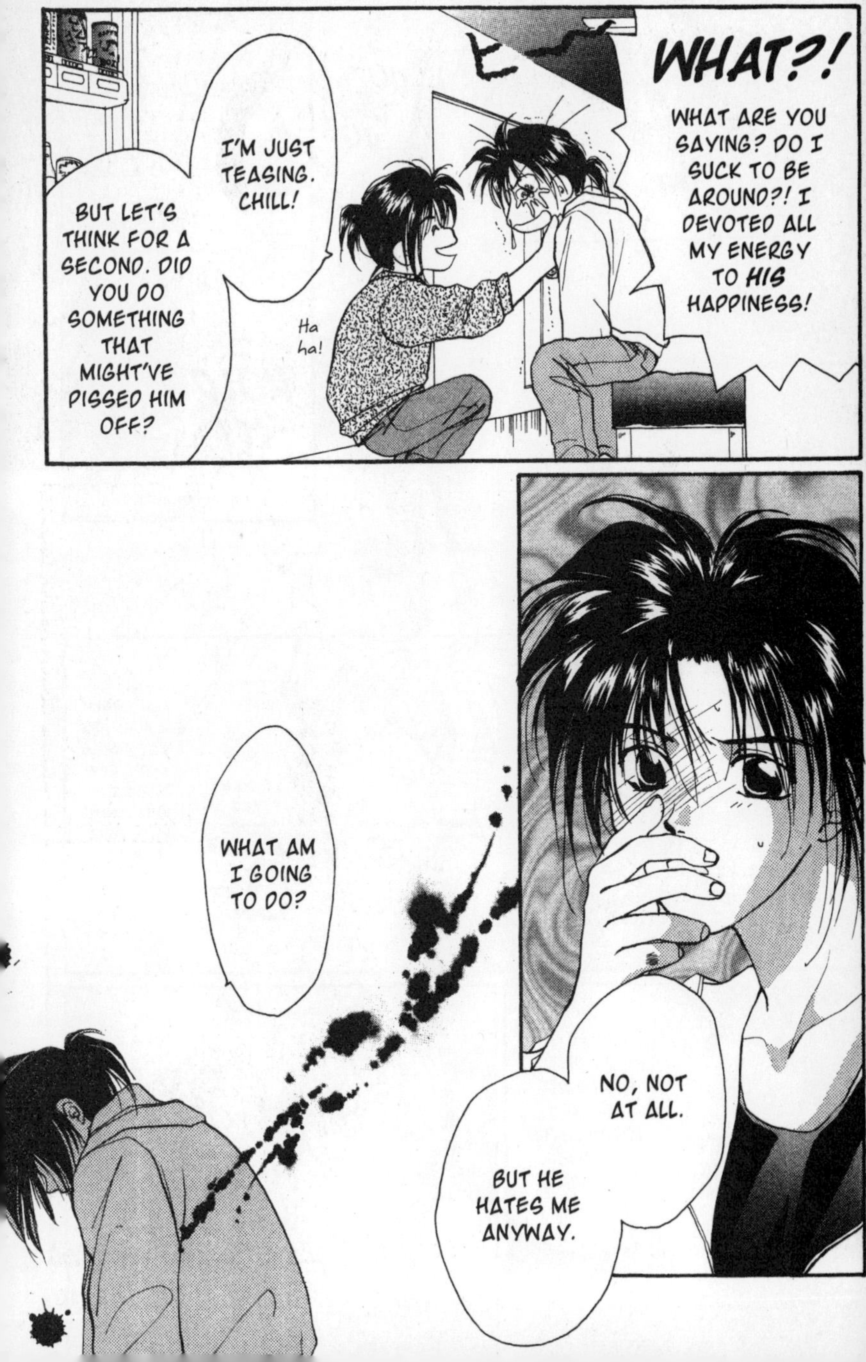
WHAT?!
WHAT ARE YOU SAYING? DO I SUCK TO BE AROUND?! I DEVOTED ALL MY ENERGY TO HIS HAPPINESS!
I'M JUST TEASING. CHILL!
Ha ha!
BUT LET'S THINK FOR A SECOND. DID YOU DO SOMETHING THAT MIGHT'VE PISSED HIM OFF?
NO, NOT AT ALL.
BUT HE HATES ME ANYWAY.
WHAT AM I GOING TO DO?

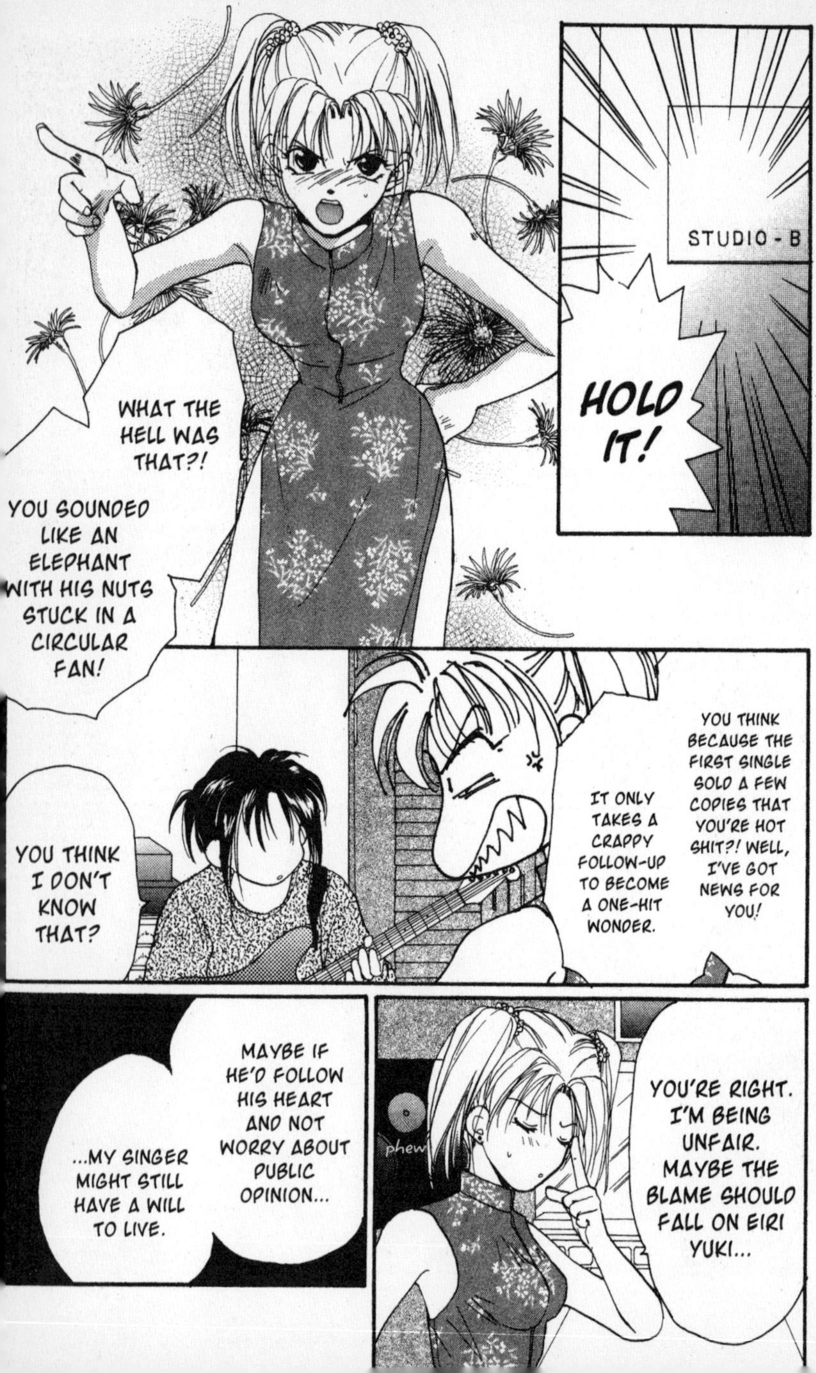
STUDIO - B
HOLD IT!
WHAT THE HELL WAS THAT?!
YOU SOUNDED LIKE AN ELEPHANT WITH HIS NUTS STUCK IN A CIRCULAR FAN!
YOU THINK BECAUSE THE FIRST SINGLE SOLD A FEW COPIES THAT YOU'RE HOT SHIT?! WELL, I'VE GOT NEWS FOR YOU!
IT ONLY TAKES A CRAPPY FOLLOW-UP TO BECOME A ONE-HIT WONDER.
YOU THINK I DON'T KNOW THAT?
YOU'RE RIGHT. I'M BEING UNFAIR. MAYBE THE BLAME SHOULD FALL ON EIRI YUKI...
phew
MAYBE IF HE'D FOLLOW HIS HEART AND NOT WORRY ABOUT PUBLIC OPINION...
...MY SINGER MIGHT STILL HAVE A WILL TO LIVE.

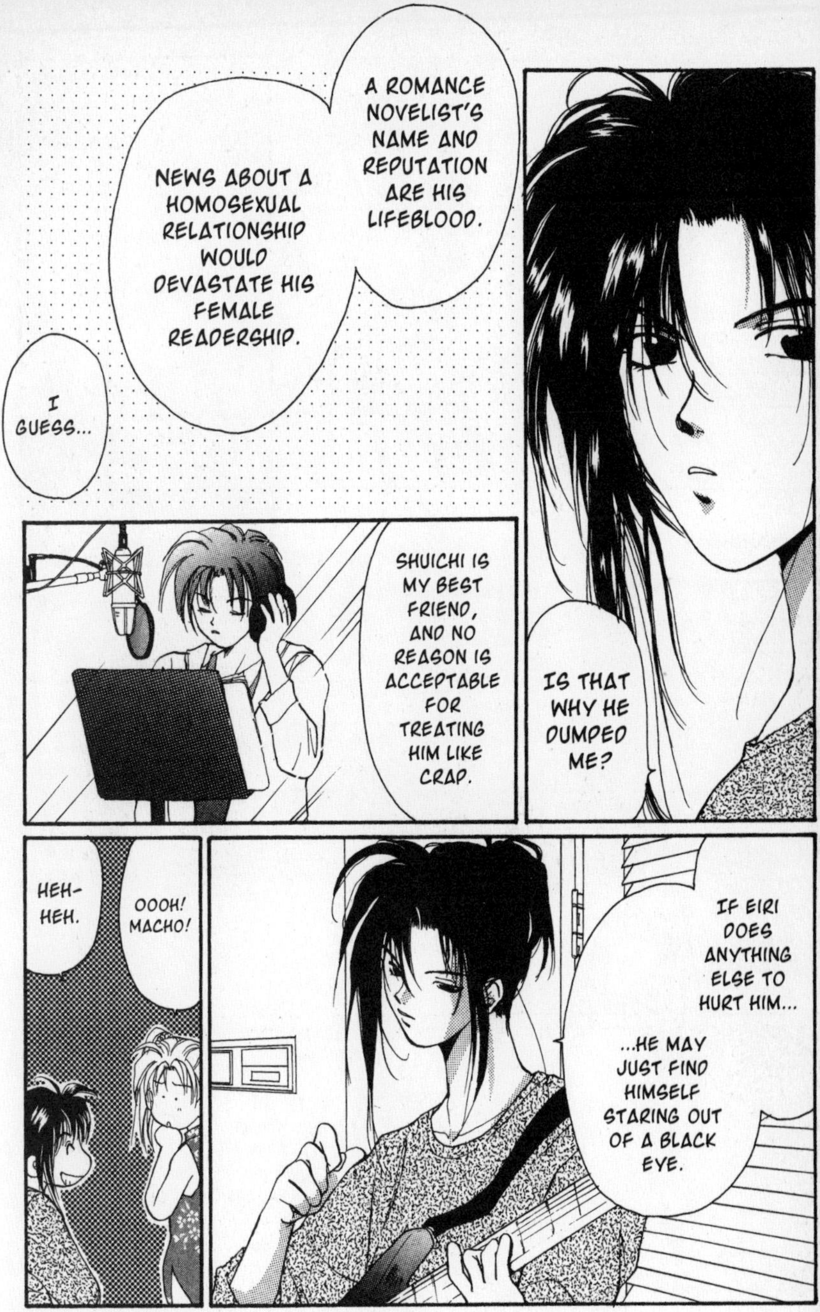
IS THAT WHY HE DUMPED ME?
A ROMANCE NOVELIST'S NAME AND REPUTATION ARE HIS LIFEBLOOD.
NEWS ABOUT A HOMOSEXUAL RELATIONSHIP WOULD DEVASTATE HIS FEMALE READERSHIP.
I GUESS...
SHUICHI IS MY BEST FRIEND, AND NO REASON IS ACCEPTABLE FOR TREATING HIM LIKE CRAP.
IF EIRI DOES ANYTHING ELSE TO HURT HIM...
...HE MAY JUST FIND HIMSELF STARING OUT OF A BLACK EYE.
OOOH! MACHO!
HEH-HEH.

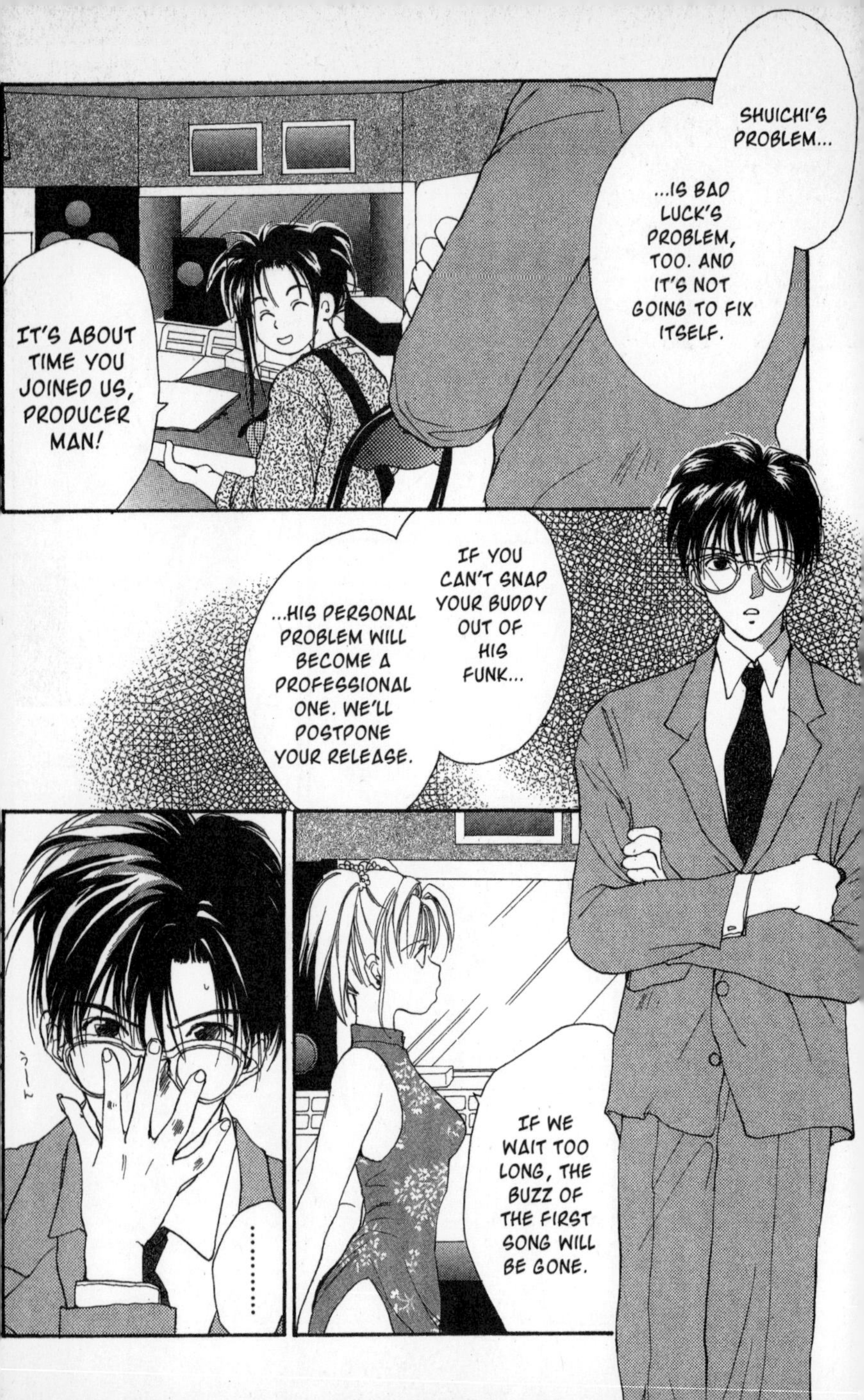
SHUICHI'S PROBLEM...
...IS BAD LUCK'S PROBLEM, TOO. AND IT'S NOT GOING TO FIX ITSELF.
IT'S ABOUT TIME YOU JOINED US, PRODUCER MAN!
IF YOU CAN'T SNAP YOUR BUDDY OUT OF HIS FUNK...
...HIS PERSONAL PROBLEM WILL BECOME A PROFESSIONAL ONE. WE'LL POSTPONE YOUR RELEASE.
IF WE WAIT TOO LONG, THE BUZZ OF THE FIRST SONG WILL BE GONE.
うーん
......

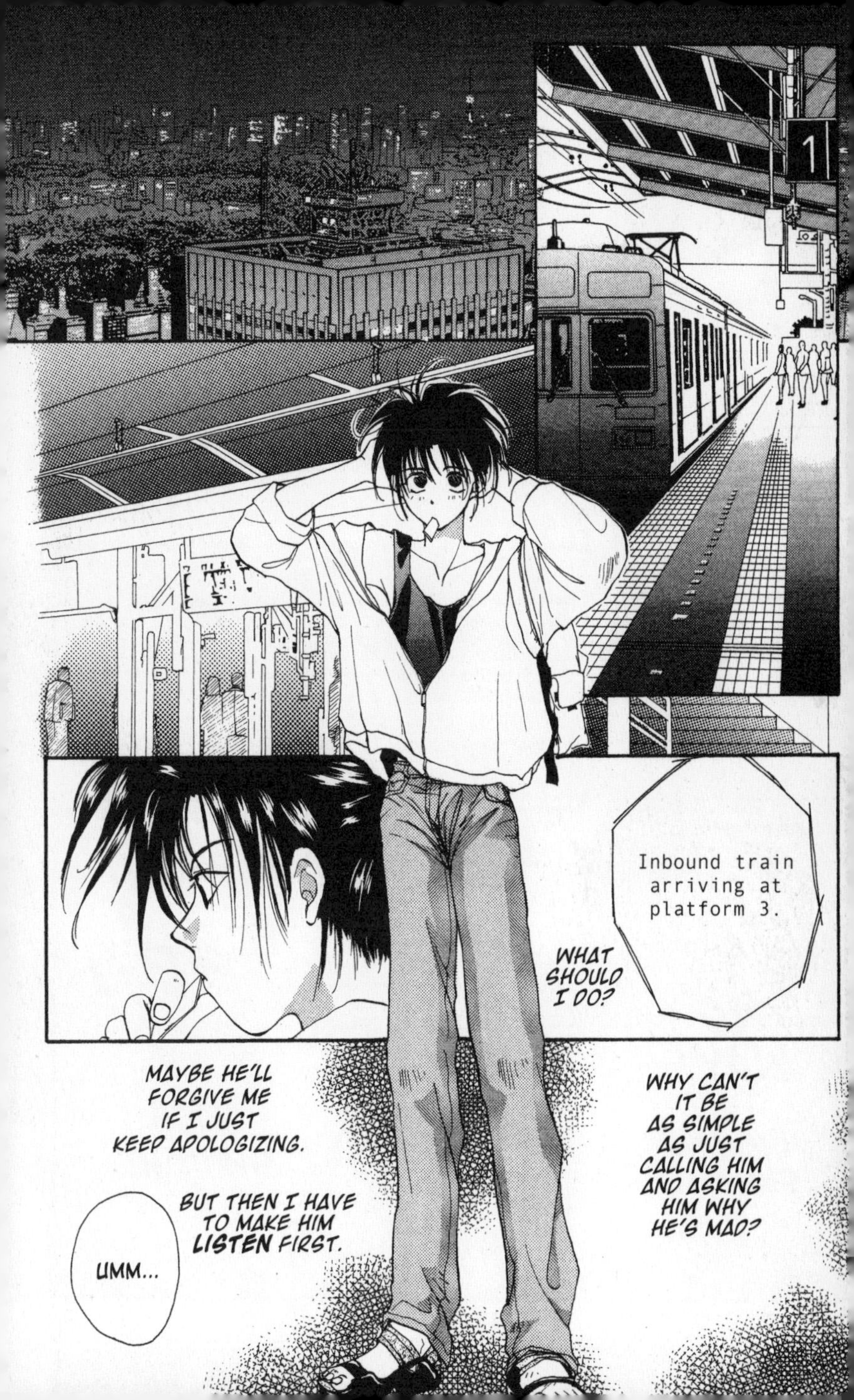
Inbound train arriving at platform 3.
WHAT SHOULD I DO?
WHY CAN'T IT BE AS SIMPLE AS JUST CALLING HIM AND ASKING HIM WHY HE'S MAD?
MAYBE HE'LL FORGIVE ME IF I JUST KEEP APOLOGIZING.
BUT THEN I HAVE TO MAKE HIM **LISTEN** FIRST.
UMM...

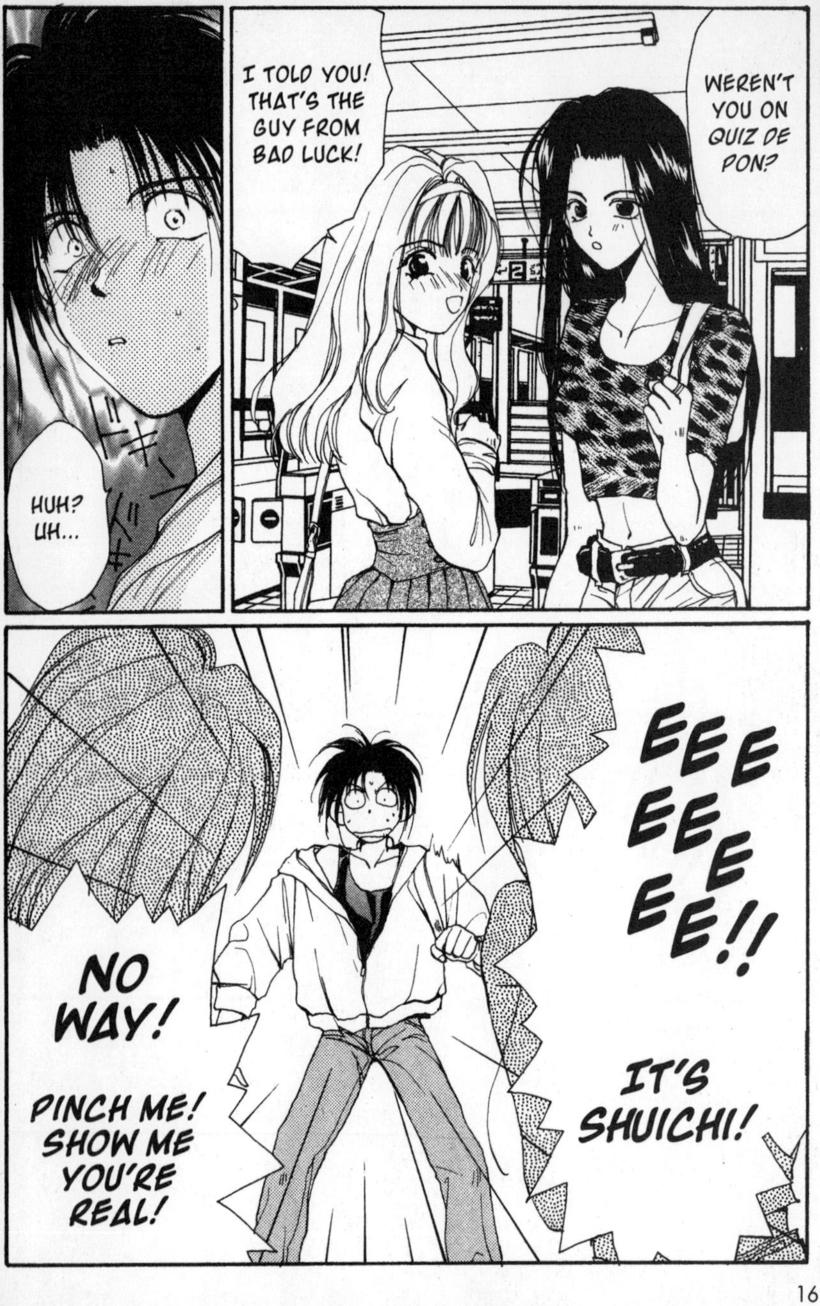
WEREN'T YOU ON QUIZ DE PON?
I TOLD YOU! THAT'S THE GUY FROM BAD LUCK!
HUH? UH...
EEEEEEEE!!
IT'S SHUICHI!
NO WAY!
PINCH ME! SHOW ME YOU'RE REAL!

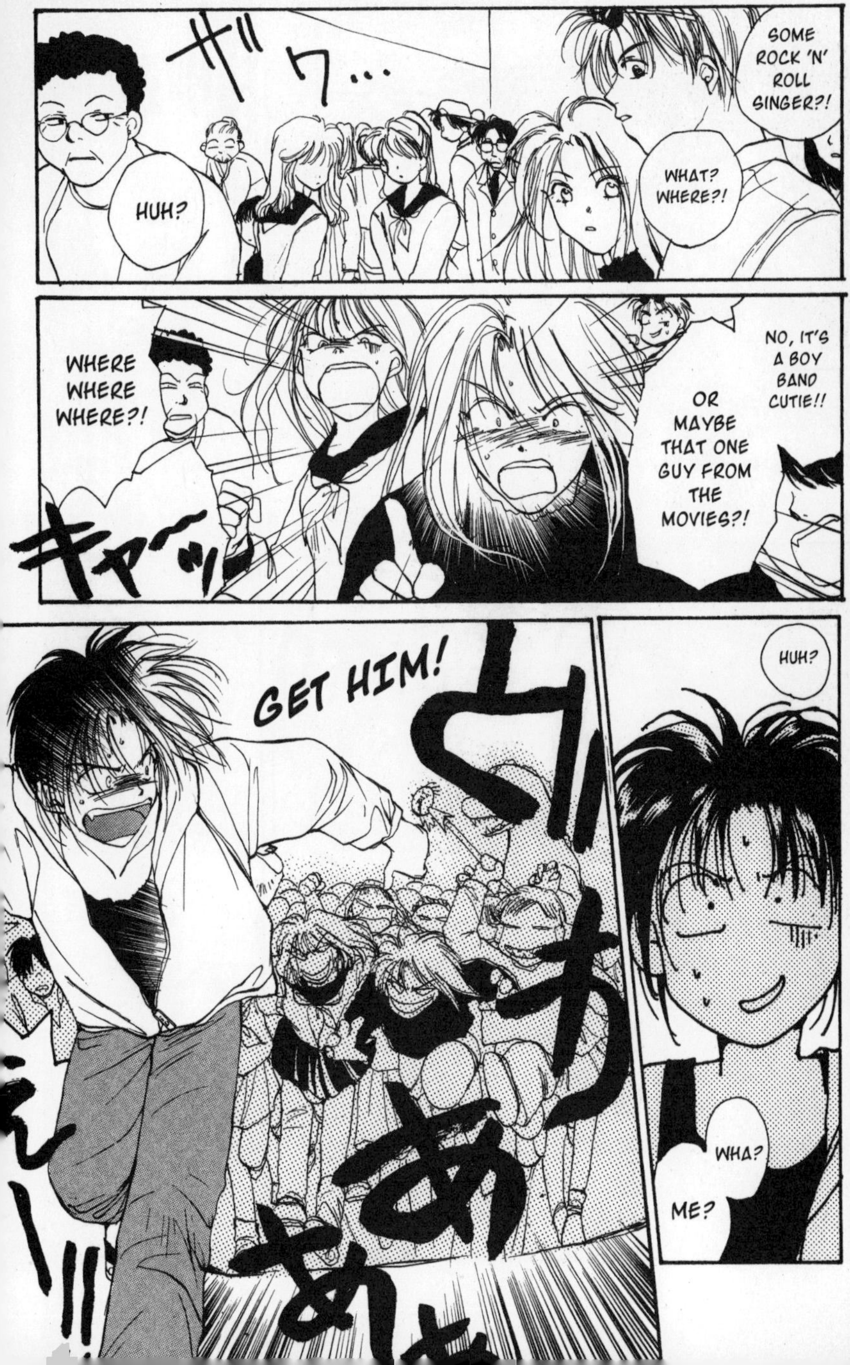
SOME ROCK 'N' ROLL SINGER?!
WHAT? WHERE?!
ザワ…
HUH?
NO, IT'S A BOY BAND CUTIE!!
OR MAYBE THAT ONE GUY FROM THE MOVIES?!
WHERE WHERE WHERE?!
キャーッ
HUH?
WHA?
ME?
GET HIM!

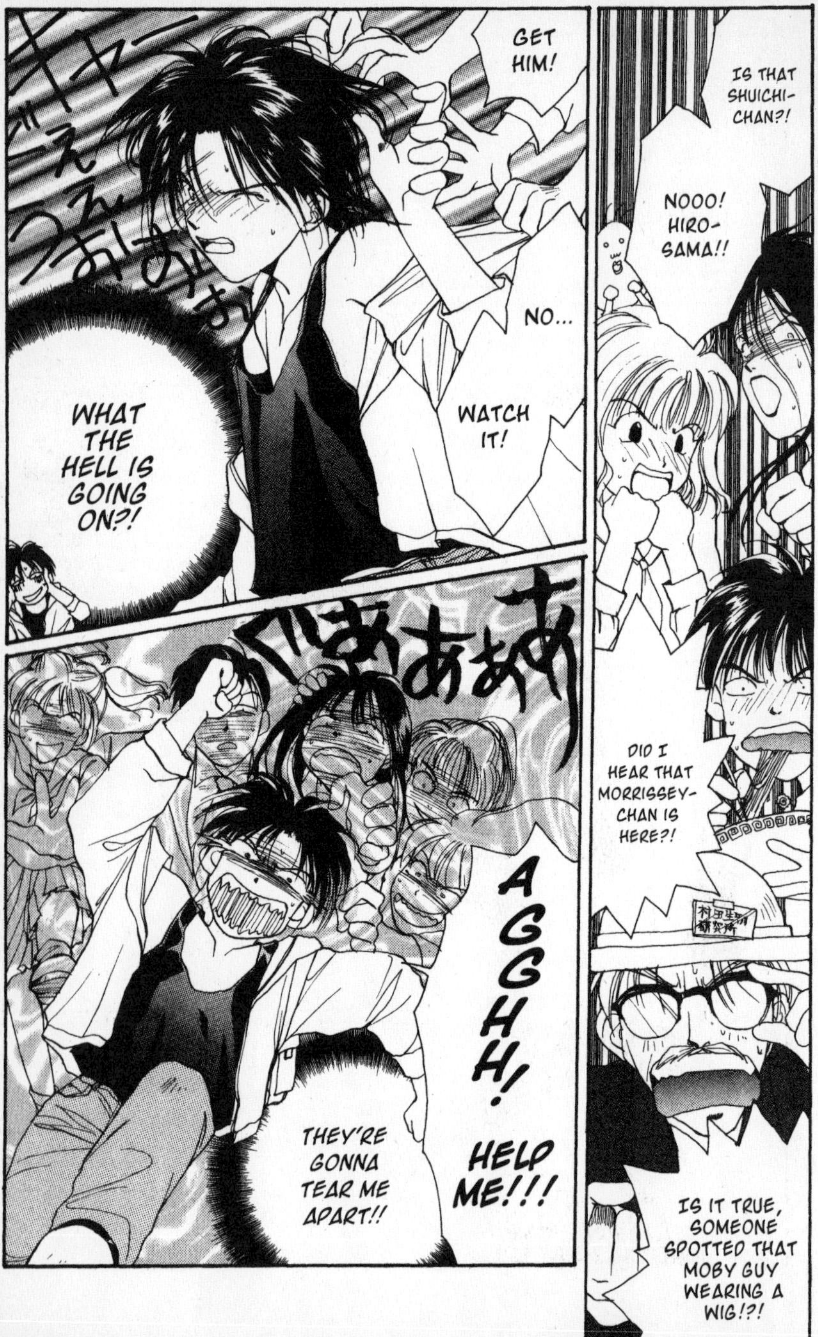
IS THAT SHUICHI-CHAN?!
NOOO! HIRO-SAMA!!
DID I HEAR THAT MORRISSEY-CHAN IS HERE?!
IS IT TRUE, SOMEONE SPOTTED THAT MOBY GUY WEARING A WIG!?!
GET HIM!
NO...
WATCH IT!
WHAT THE HELL IS GOING ON?!
AGGHH!
HELP ME!!!
THEY'RE GONNA TEAR ME APART!!

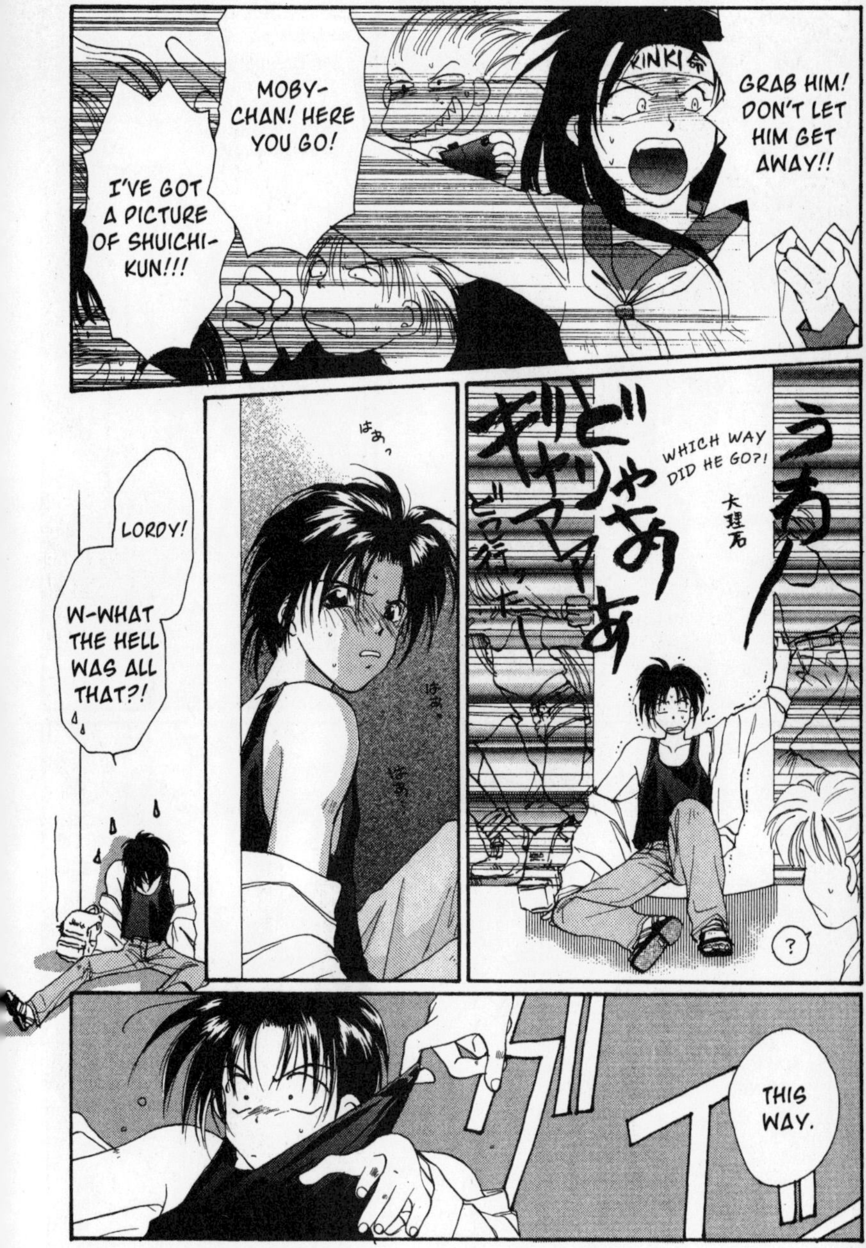
GRAB HIM! DON'T LET HIM GET AWAY!!
MOBY-CHAN! HERE YOU GO!
I'VE GOT A PICTURE OF SHUICHI-KUN!!!
WHICH WAY DID HE GO?!
?
LORDY!
W-WHAT THE HELL WAS ALL THAT?!
THIS WAY.

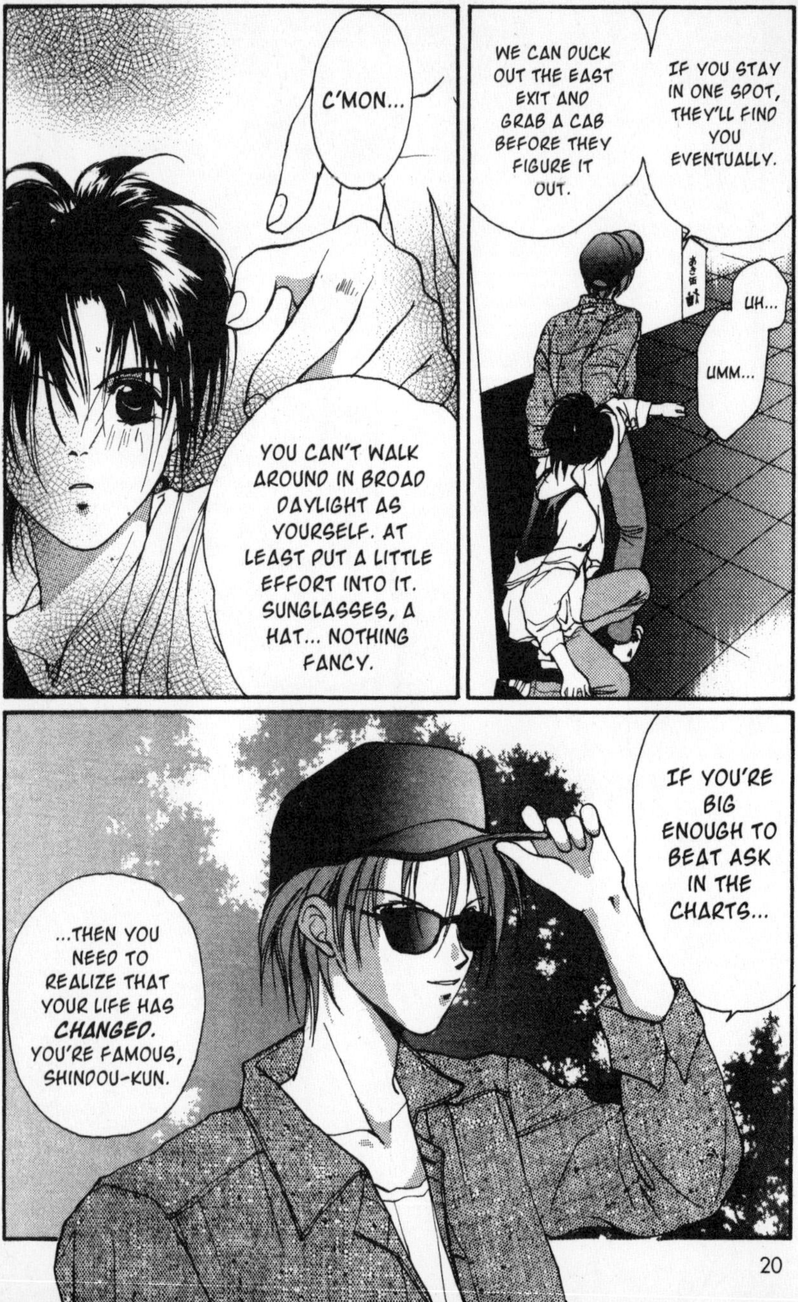
IF YOU STAY IN ONE SPOT, THEY'LL FIND YOU EVENTUALLY.
WE CAN DUCK OUT THE EAST EXIT AND GRAB A CAB BEFORE THEY FIGURE IT OUT.
UH...
UMM...
C'MON...
YOU CAN'T WALK AROUND IN BROAD DAYLIGHT AS YOURSELF. AT LEAST PUT A LITTLE EFFORT INTO IT. SUNGLASSES, A HAT... NOTHING FANCY.
IF YOU'RE BIG ENOUGH TO BEAT ASK IN THE CHARTS...
...THEN YOU NEED TO REALIZE THAT YOUR LIFE HAS CHANGED. YOU'RE FAMOUS, SHINDOU-KUN.

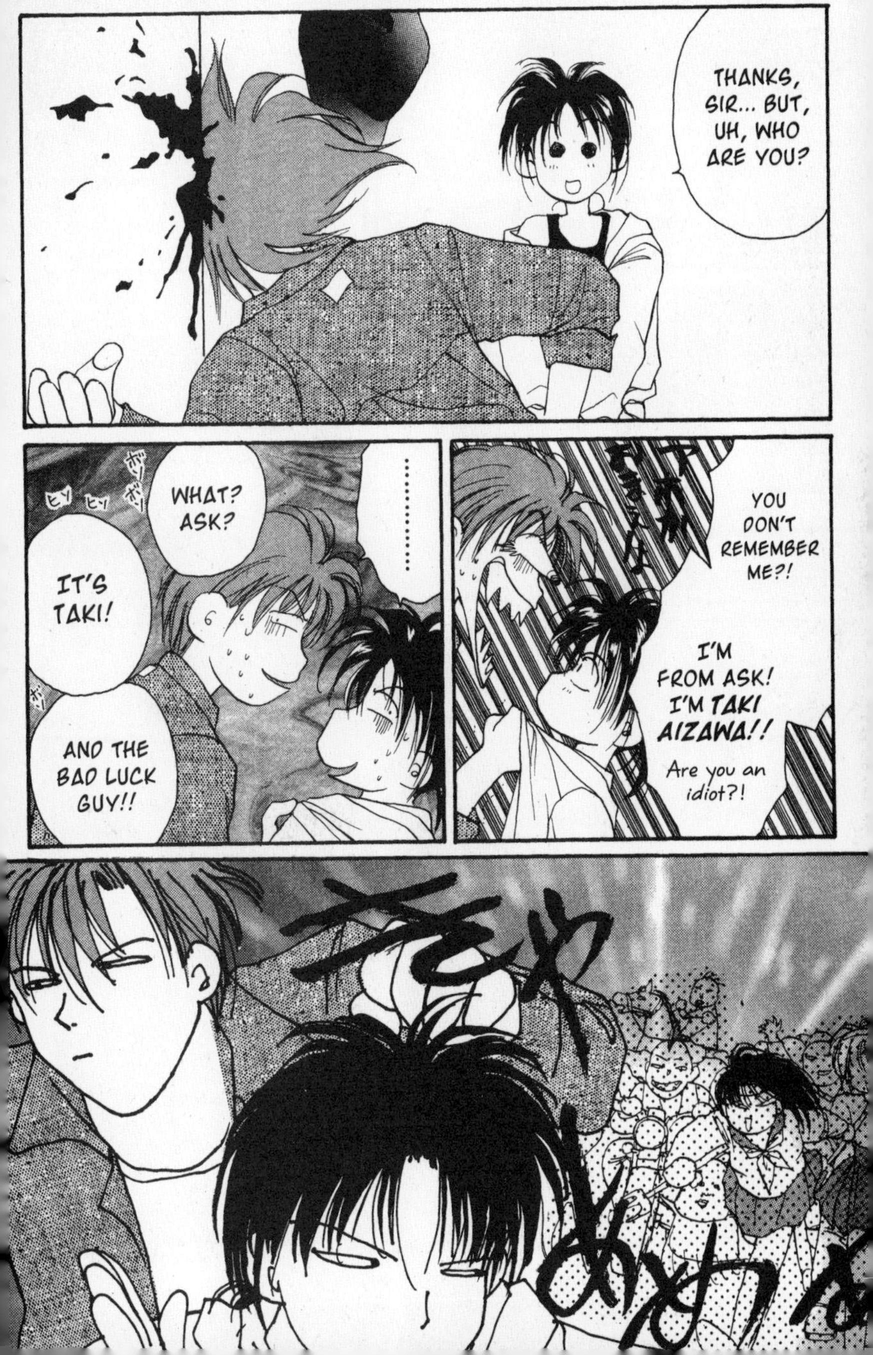
THANKS, SIR... BUT, UH, WHO ARE YOU?
YOU DON'T REMEMBER ME?!
I'M FROM ASK! I'M TAKI AIZAWA!!
Are you an idiot?!
......
WHAT? ASK?
IT'S TAKI!
AND THE BAD LUCK GUY!!

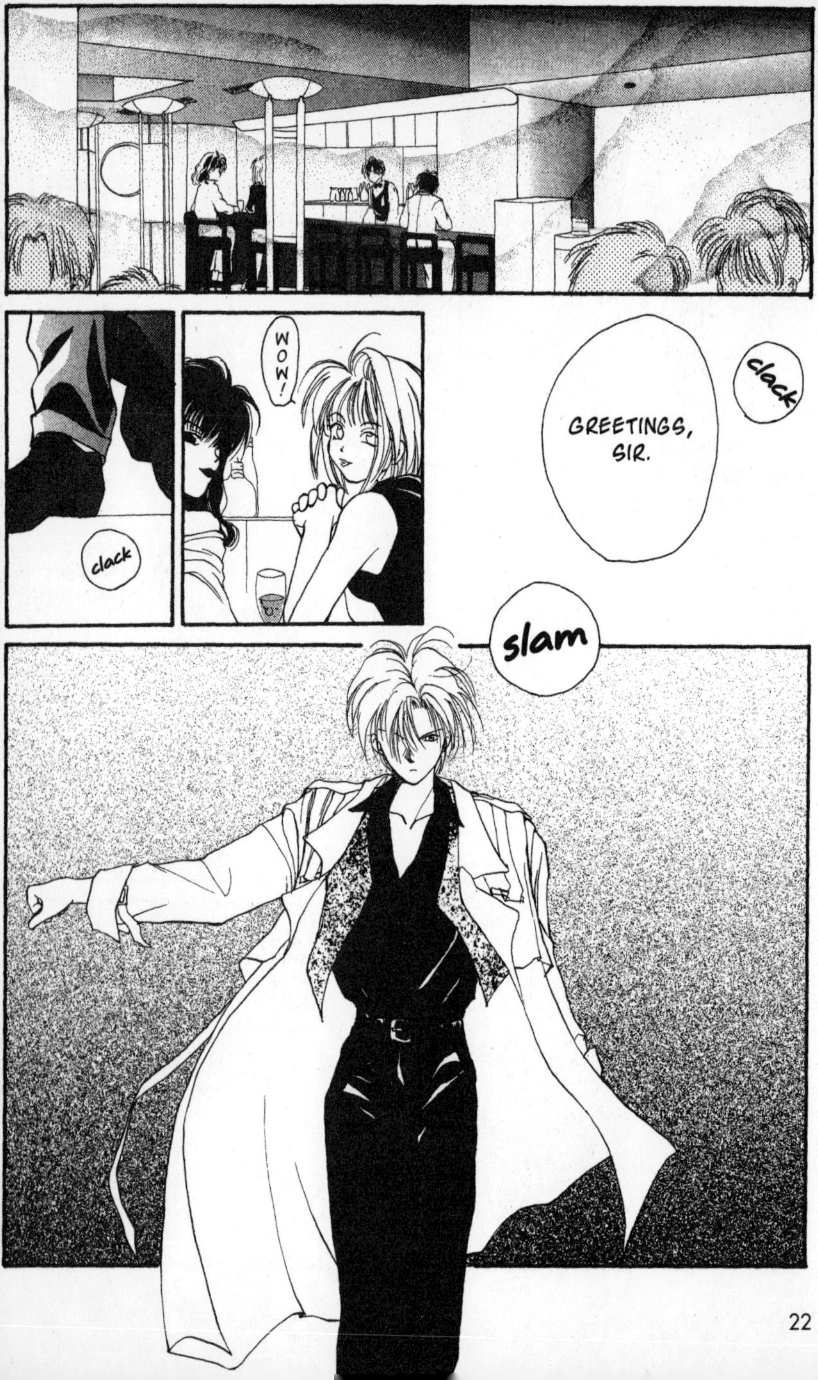
clack
GREETINGS, SIR.
WOW!
clack
slam

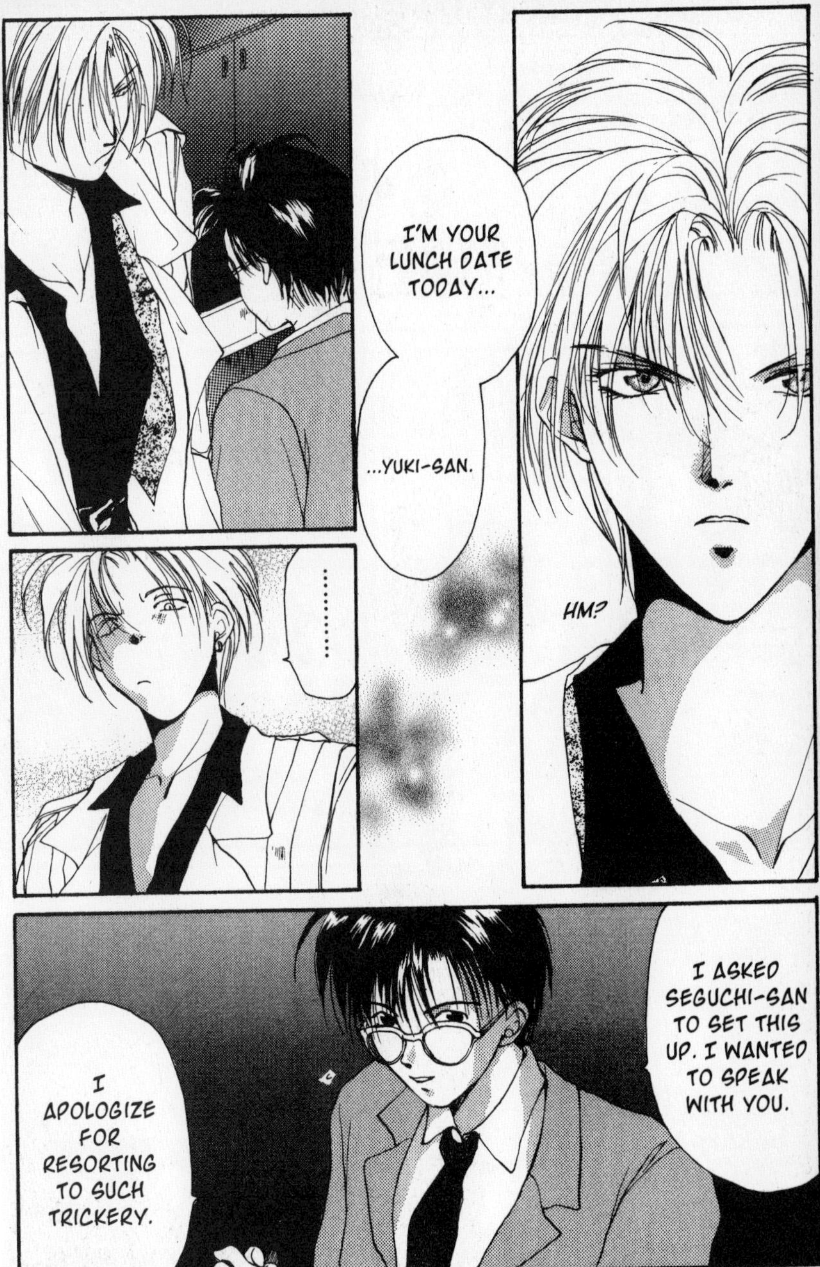
I'M YOUR LUNCH DATE TODAY...
...YUKI-SAN.
HM?
....
I ASKED SEGUCHI-SAN TO SET THIS UP. I WANTED TO SPEAK WITH YOU.
I APOLOGIZE FOR RESORTING TO SUCH TRICKERY.

A BIT PISSED OFF NOW... ↓

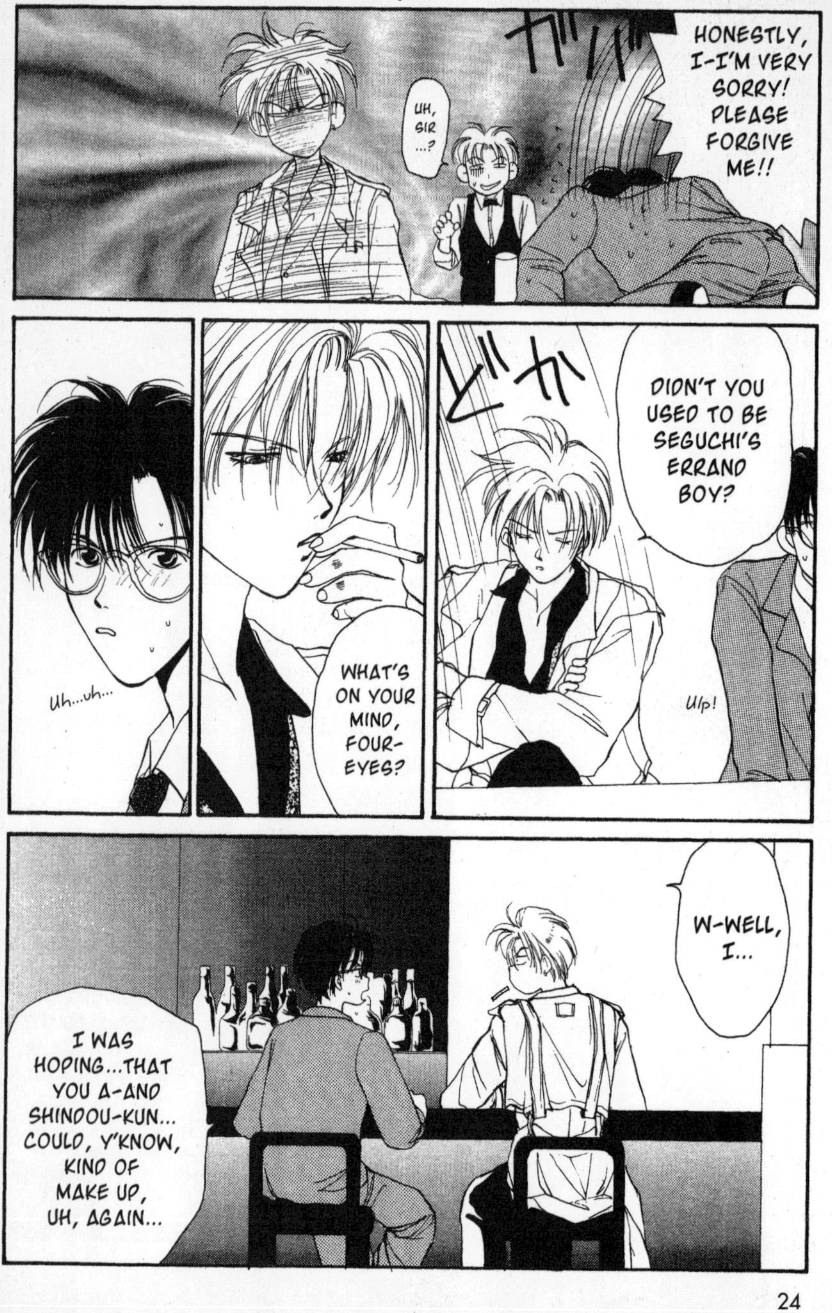
HONESTLY, I-I'M VERY SORRY! PLEASE FORGIVE ME!!
UH, SIR ...?
どか
DIDN'T YOU USED TO BE SEGUCHI'S ERRAND BOY?
Ulp!
WHAT'S ON YOUR MIND, FOUR-EYES?
Uh...uh...
W-WELL, I...
I WAS HOPING...THAT YOU A-AND SHINDOU-KUN... COULD, Y'KNOW, KIND OF MAKE UP, UH, AGAIN...

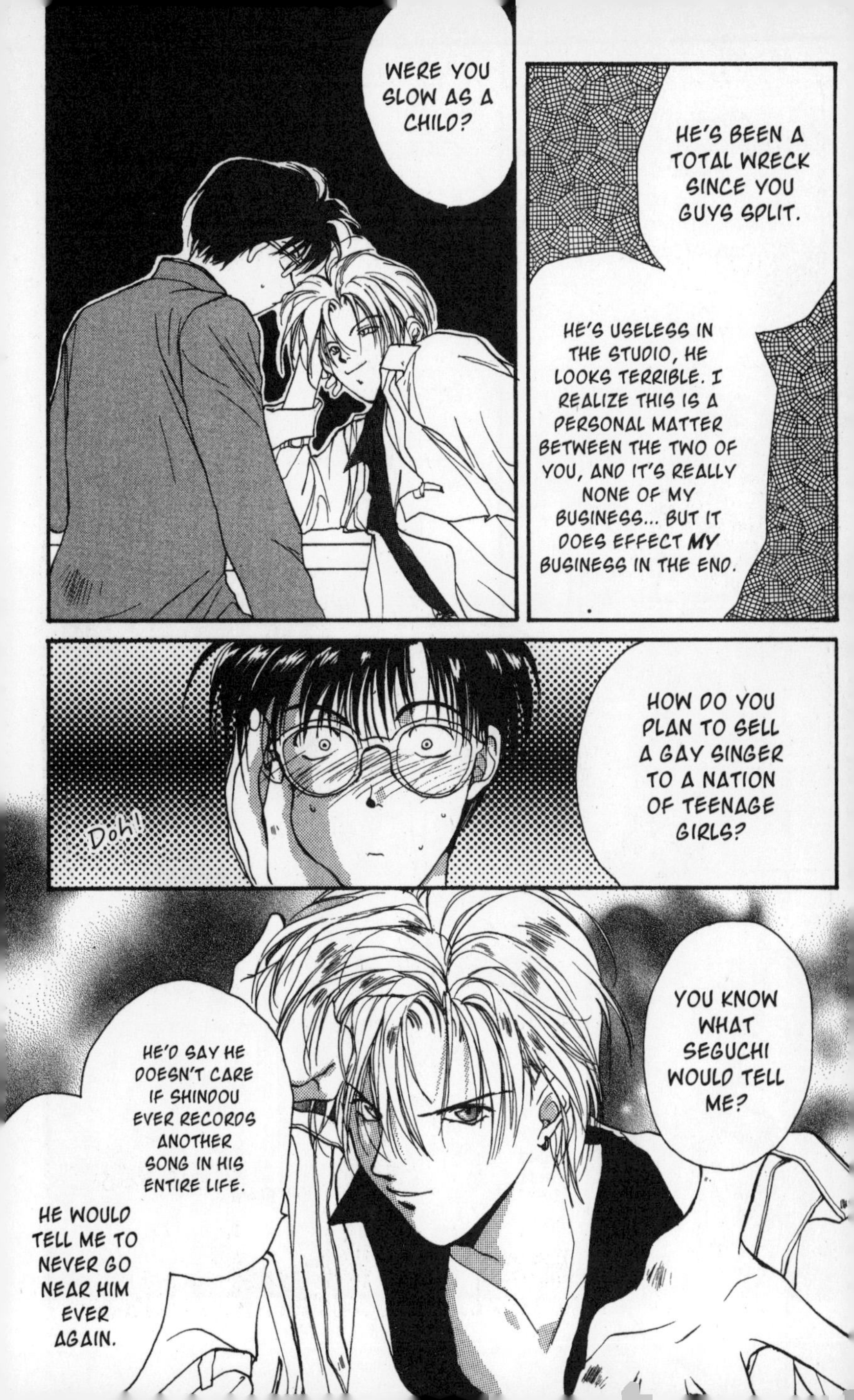
HE'S BEEN A TOTAL WRECK SINCE YOU GUYS SPLIT.
HE'S USELESS IN THE STUDIO, HE LOOKS TERRIBLE. I REALIZE THIS IS A PERSONAL MATTER BETWEEN THE TWO OF YOU, AND IT'S REALLY NONE OF MY BUSINESS... BUT IT DOES EFFECT MY BUSINESS IN THE END.
WERE YOU SLOW AS A CHILD?
HOW DO YOU PLAN TO SELL A GAY SINGER TO A NATION OF TEENAGE GIRLS?
Doh!
YOU KNOW WHAT SEGUCHI WOULD TELL ME?
HE'D SAY HE DOESN'T CARE IF SHINDOU EVER RECORDS ANOTHER SONG IN HIS ENTIRE LIFE.
HE WOULD TELL ME TO NEVER GO NEAR HIM EVER AGAIN.

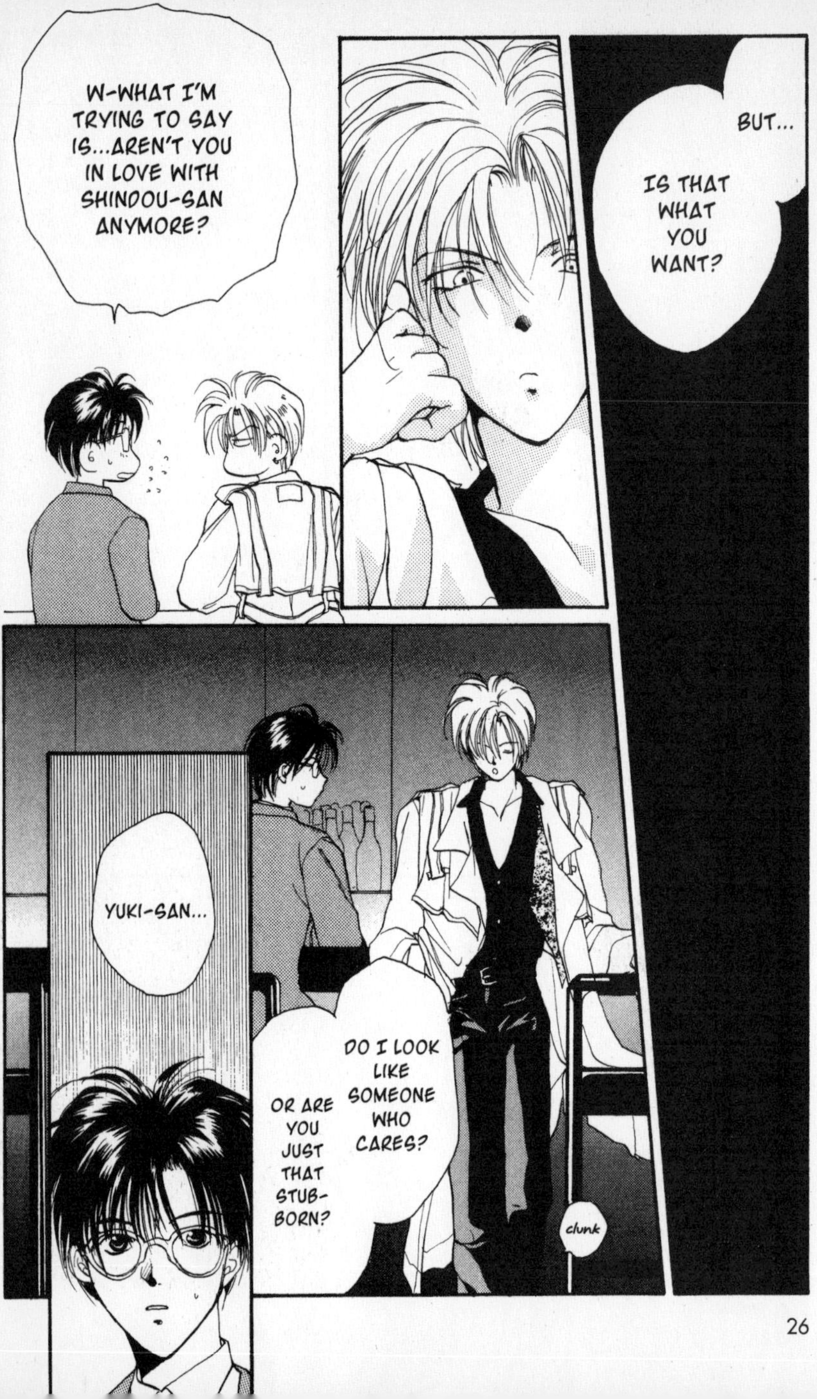

BUT...
IS THAT WHAT YOU WANT?
W-WHAT I'M TRYING TO SAY IS...AREN'T YOU IN LOVE WITH SHINDOU-SAN ANYMORE?
DO I LOOK LIKE SOMEONE WHO CARES?
OR ARE YOU JUST THAT STUB-BORN?
clunk
YUKI-SAN...

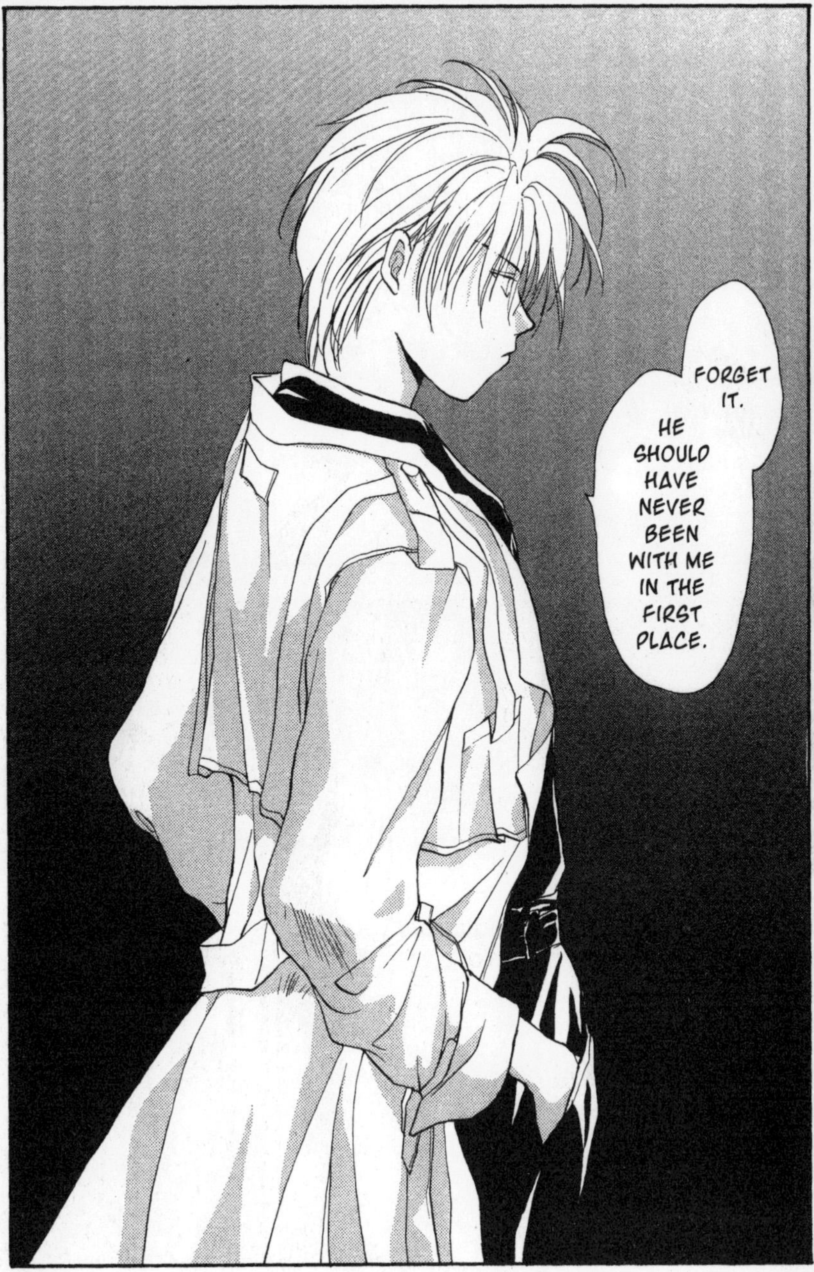
FORGET IT.
HE SHOULD HAVE NEVER BEEN WITH ME IN THE FIRST PLACE.

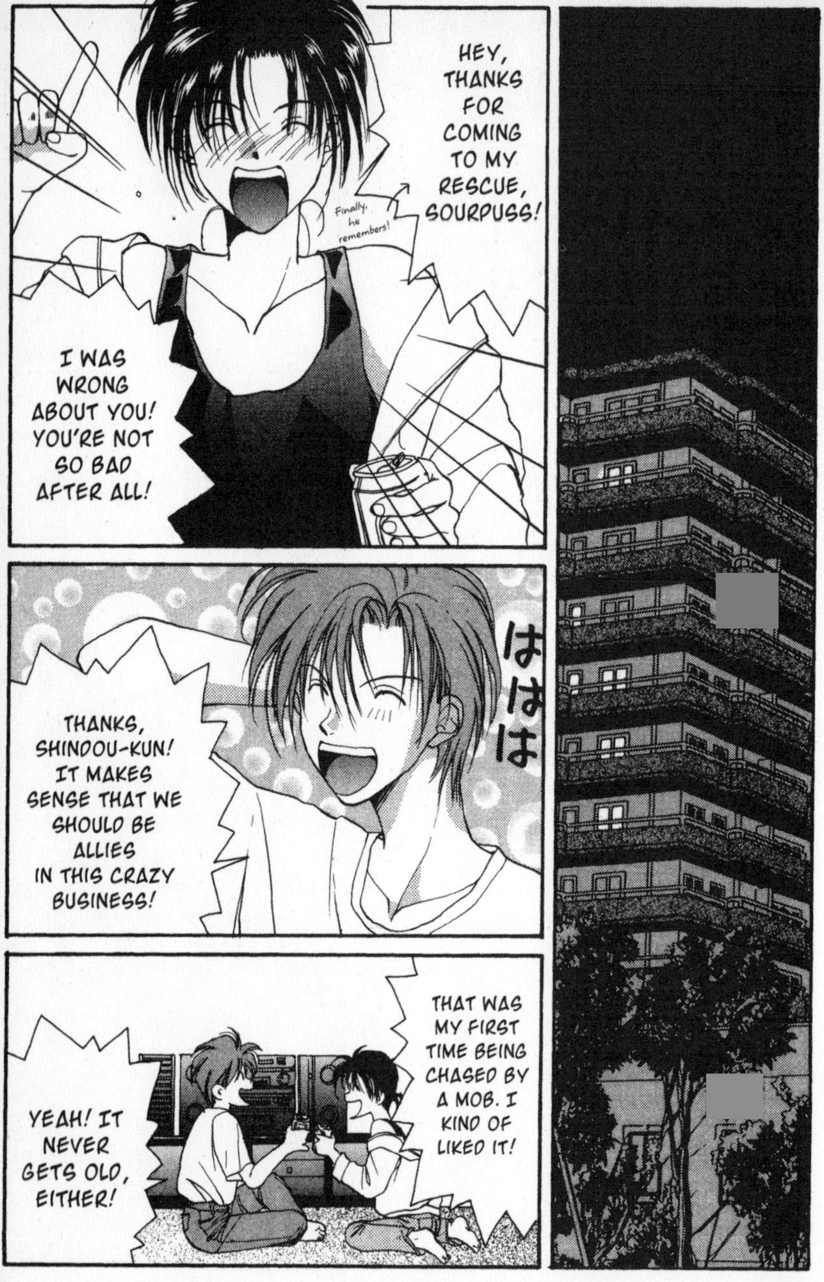
HEY, THANKS FOR COMING TO MY RESCUE, SOURPUSS!
Finally, he remembers!
I WAS WRONG ABOUT YOU! YOU'RE NOT SO BAD AFTER ALL!
ははは
THANKS, SHINDOU-KUN! IT MAKES SENSE THAT WE SHOULD BE ALLIES IN THIS CRAZY BUSINESS!
THAT WAS MY FIRST TIME BEING CHASED BY A MOB. I KIND OF LIKED IT!
YEAH! IT NEVER GETS OLD, EITHER!

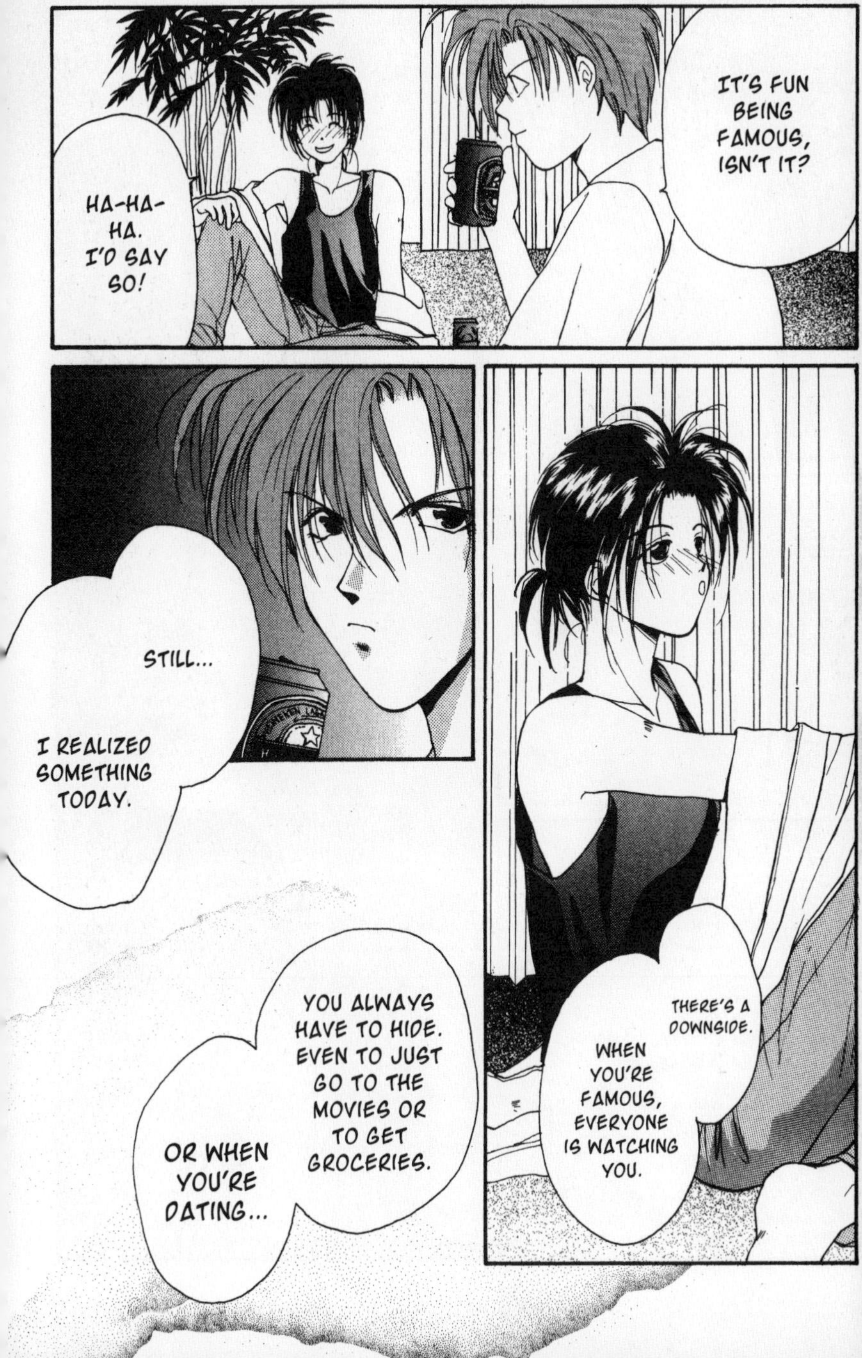
IT'S FUN BEING FAMOUS, ISN'T IT?
HA-HA-HA. I'D SAY SO!
THERE'S A DOWNSIDE.
WHEN YOU'RE FAMOUS, EVERYONE IS WATCHING YOU.
STILL...
I REALIZED SOMETHING TODAY.
YOU ALWAYS HAVE TO HIDE. EVEN TO JUST GO TO THE MOVIES OR TO GET GROCERIES.
OR WHEN YOU'RE DATING...

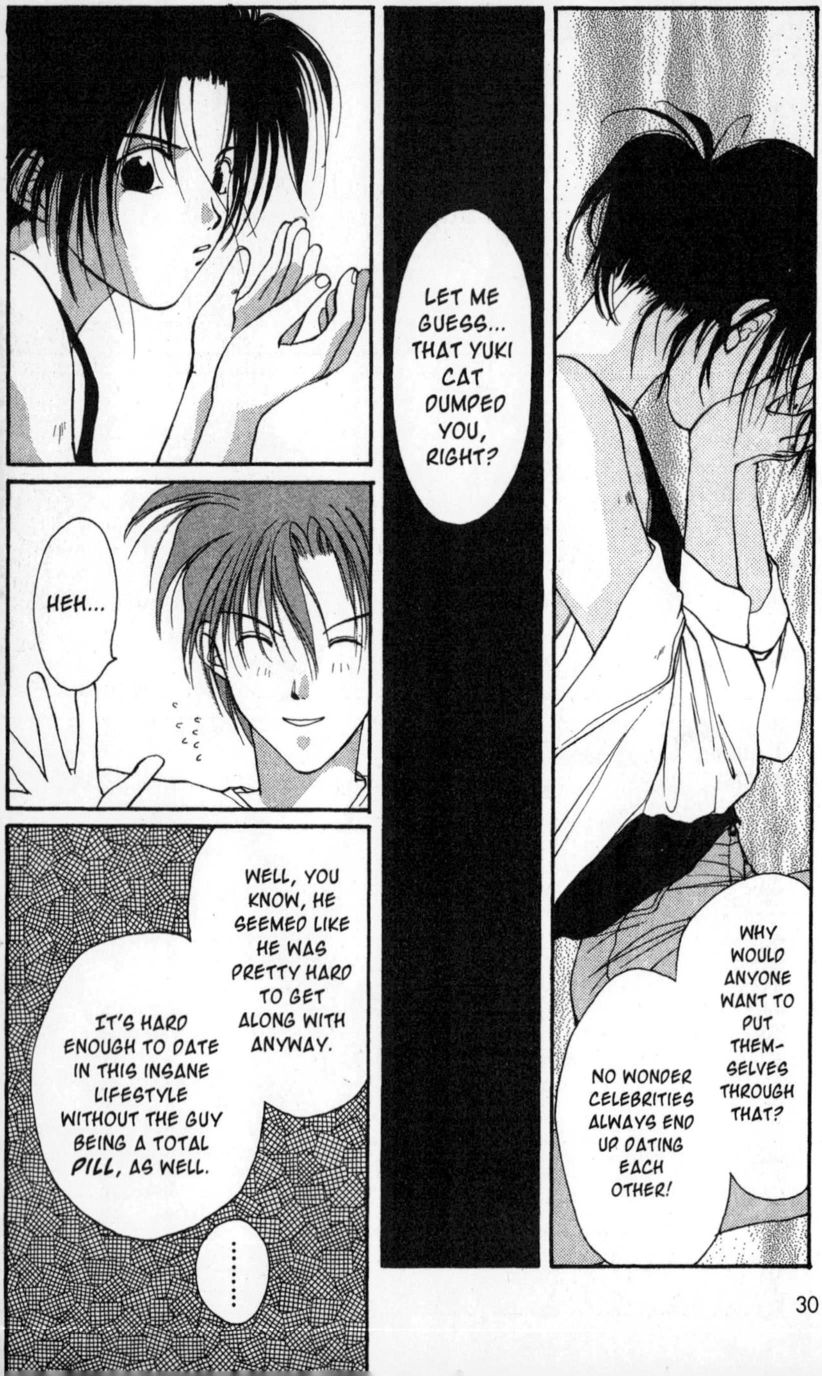
WHY WOULD ANYONE WANT TO PUT THEM-SELVES THROUGH THAT?
NO WONDER CELEBRITIES ALWAYS END UP DATING EACH OTHER!
LET ME GUESS... THAT YUKI CAT DUMPED YOU, RIGHT?
HEH...
WELL, YOU KNOW, HE SEEMED LIKE HE WAS PRETTY HARD TO GET ALONG WITH ANYWAY.
IT'S HARD ENOUGH TO DATE IN THIS INSANE LIFESTYLE WITHOUT THE GUY BEING A TOTAL *PILL*, AS WELL.
......

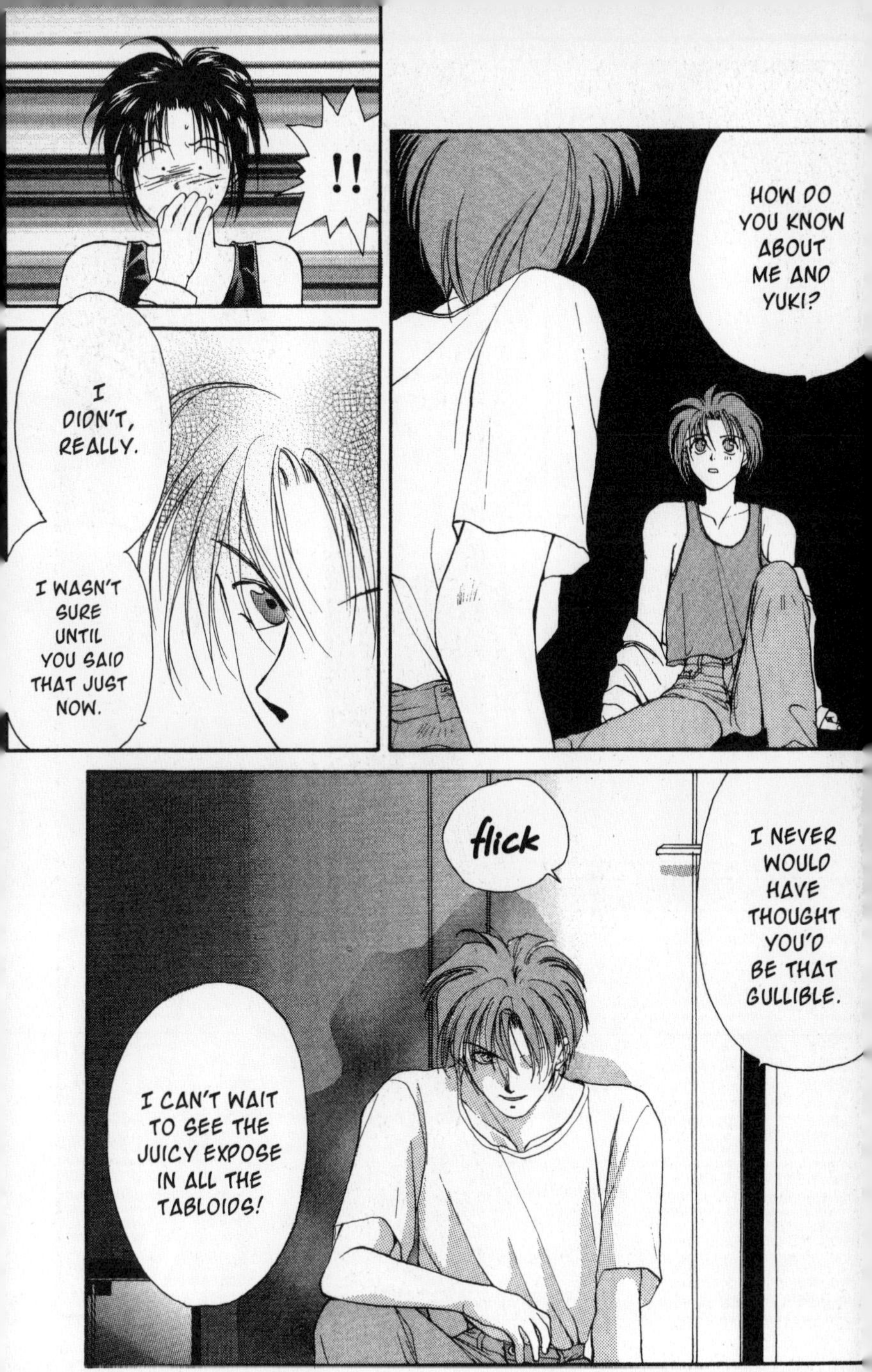
HOW DO YOU KNOW ABOUT ME AND YUKI?
!!
I DIDN'T, REALLY.
I WASN'T SURE UNTIL YOU SAID THAT JUST NOW.
I NEVER WOULD HAVE THOUGHT YOU'D BE THAT GULLIBLE.
flick
I CAN'T WAIT TO SEE THE JUICY EXPOSE IN ALL THE TABLOIDS!

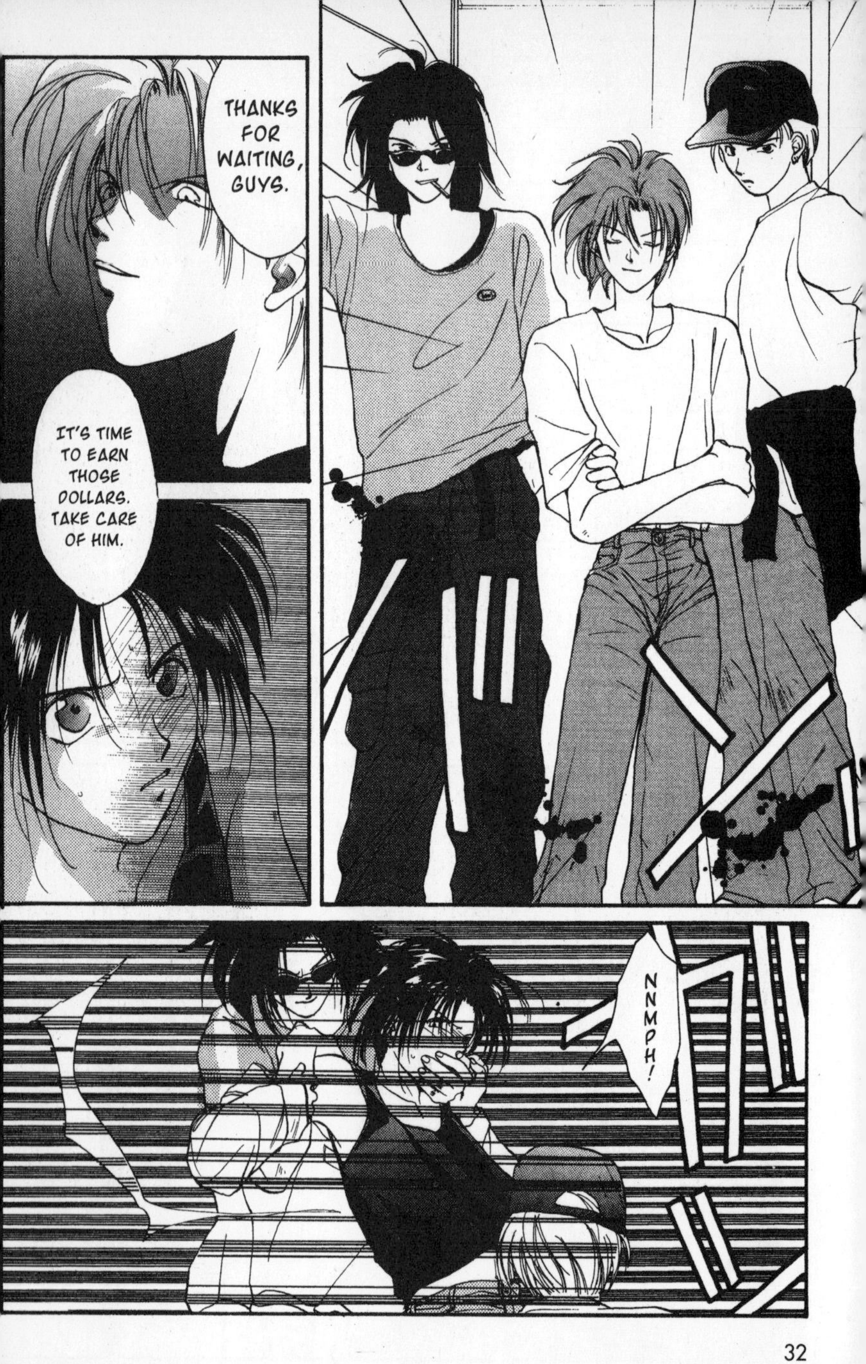
THANKS FOR WAITING, GUYS.
IT'S TIME TO EARN THOSE DOLLARS. TAKE CARE OF HIM.
NNMPH!

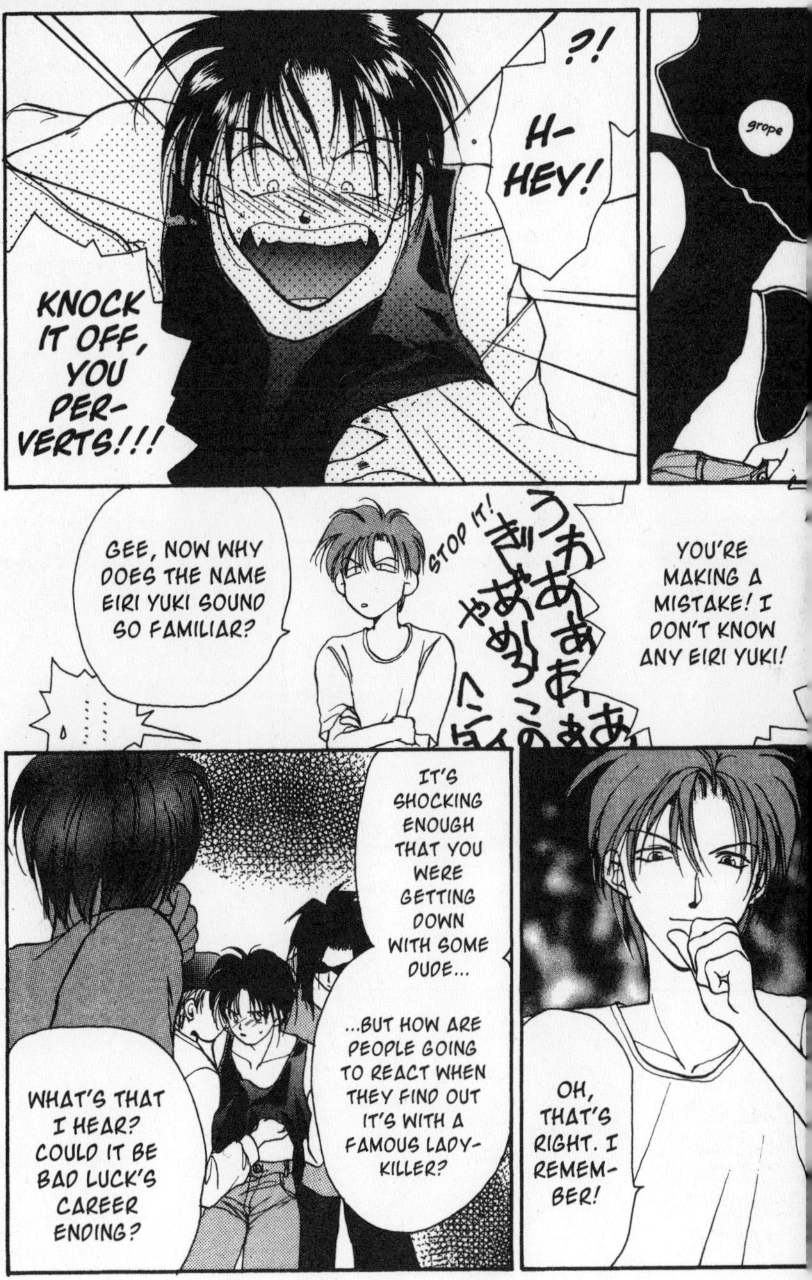
grope
?!
H-HEY!
KNOCK IT OFF, YOU PER-VERTS!!!
YOU'RE MAKING A MISTAKE! I DON'T KNOW ANY EIRI YUKI!
STOP IT!
GEE, NOW WHY DOES THE NAME EIRI YUKI SOUND SO FAMILIAR?
...
OH, THAT'S RIGHT. I REMEM-BER!
IT'S SHOCKING ENOUGH THAT YOU WERE GETTING DOWN WITH SOME DUDE...
...BUT HOW ARE PEOPLE GOING TO REACT WHEN THEY FIND OUT IT'S WITH A FAMOUS LADY-KILLER?
WHAT'S THAT I HEAR? COULD IT BE BAD LUCK'S CAREER ENDING?

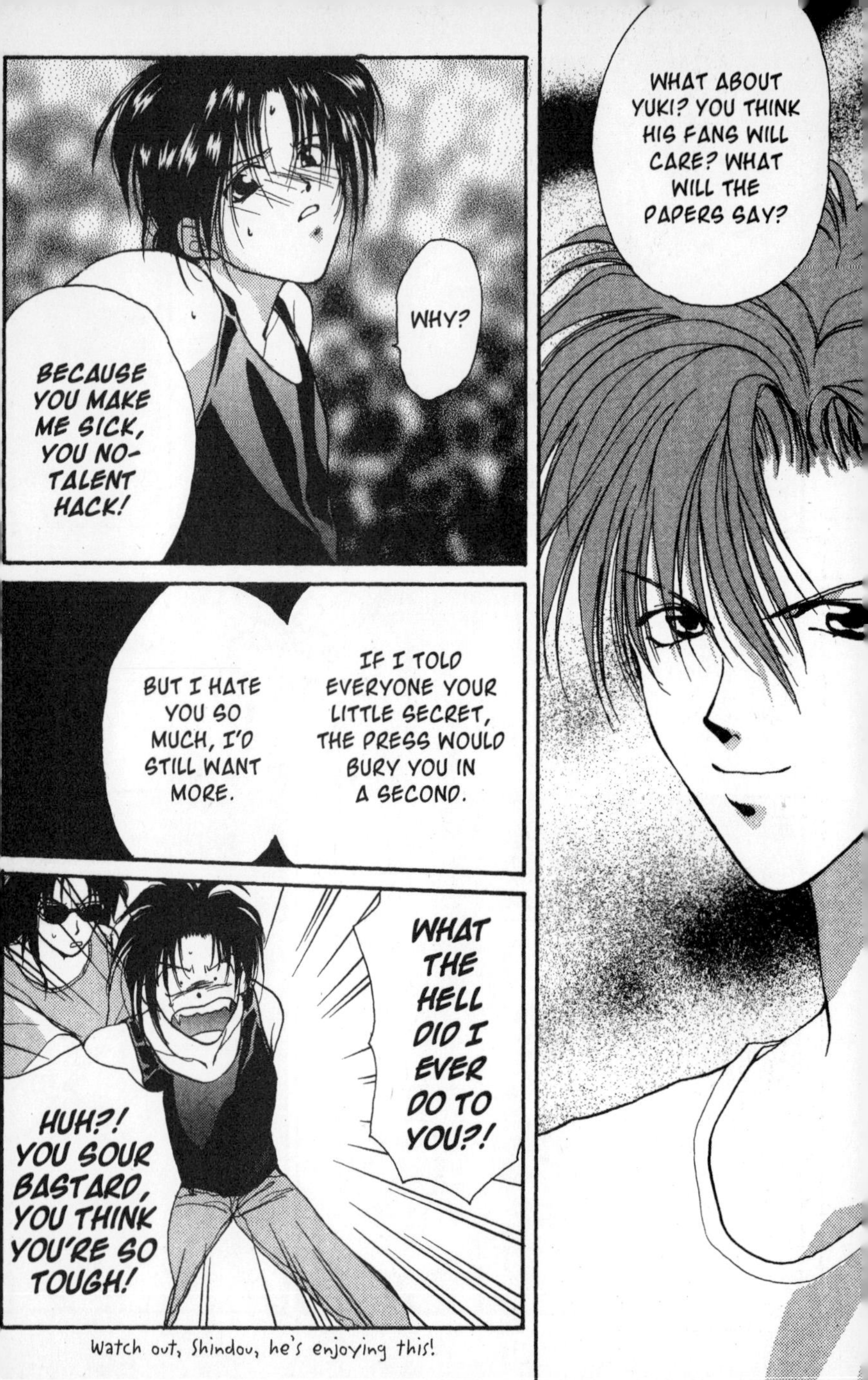
WHAT ABOUT YUKI? YOU THINK HIS FANS WILL CARE? WHAT WILL THE PAPERS SAY?
WHY?
BECAUSE YOU MAKE ME SICK, YOU NO-TALENT HACK!
IF I TOLD EVERYONE YOUR LITTLE SECRET, THE PRESS WOULD BURY YOU IN A SECOND.
BUT I HATE YOU SO MUCH, I'D STILL WANT MORE.
WHAT THE HELL DID I EVER DO TO YOU?!
HUH?! YOU SOUR BASTARD, YOU THINK YOU'RE SO TOUGH!
Watch out, Shindou, he's enjoying this!

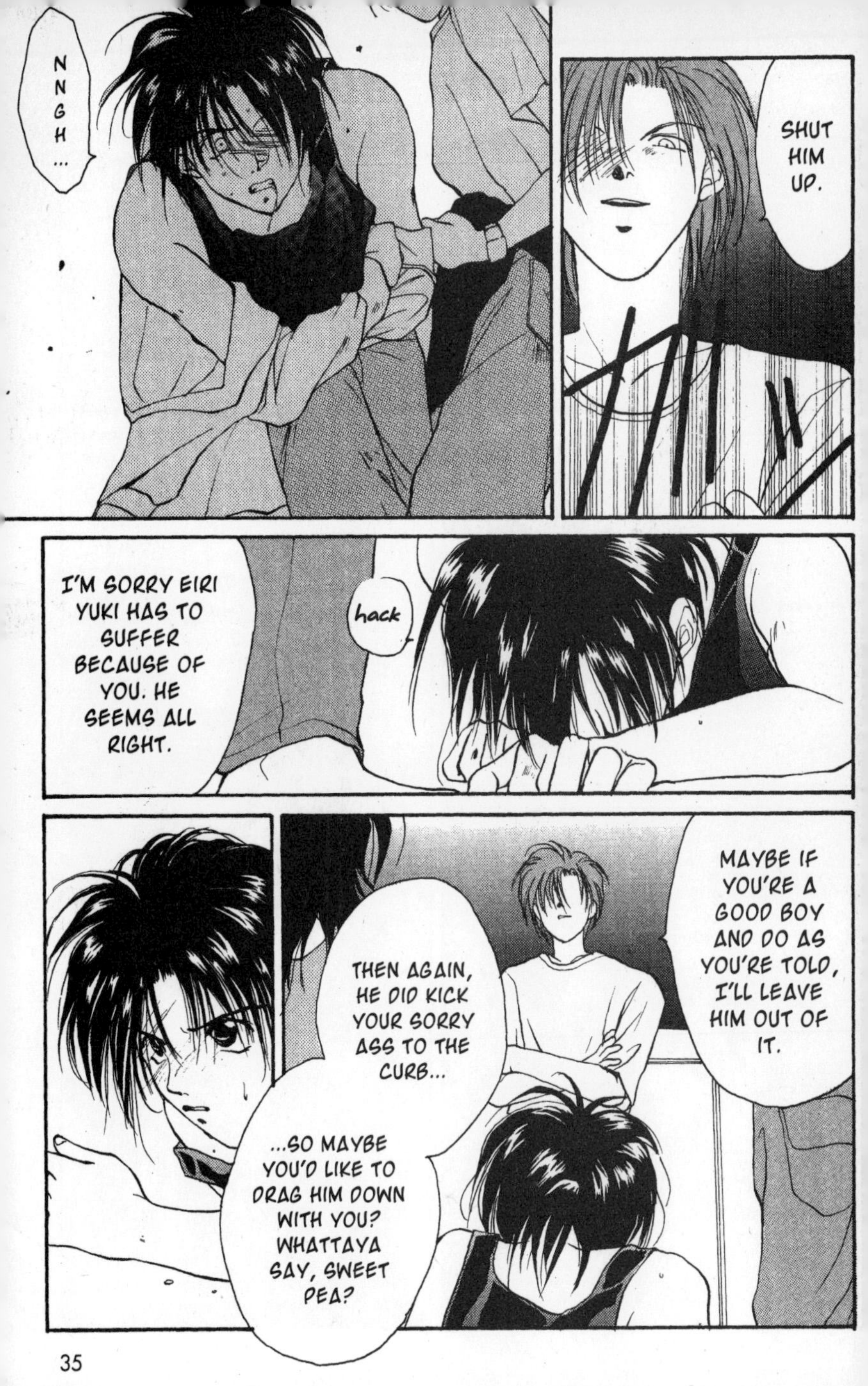
SHUT HIM UP.
NNGH...
hack
I'M SORRY EIRI YUKI HAS TO SUFFER BECAUSE OF YOU. HE SEEMS ALL RIGHT.
MAYBE IF YOU'RE A GOOD BOY AND DO AS YOU'RE TOLD, I'LL LEAVE HIM OUT OF IT.
THEN AGAIN, HE DID KICK YOUR SORRY ASS TO THE CURB...
...SO MAYBE YOU'D LIKE TO DRAG HIM DOWN WITH YOU? WHATTAYA SAY, SWEET PEA?

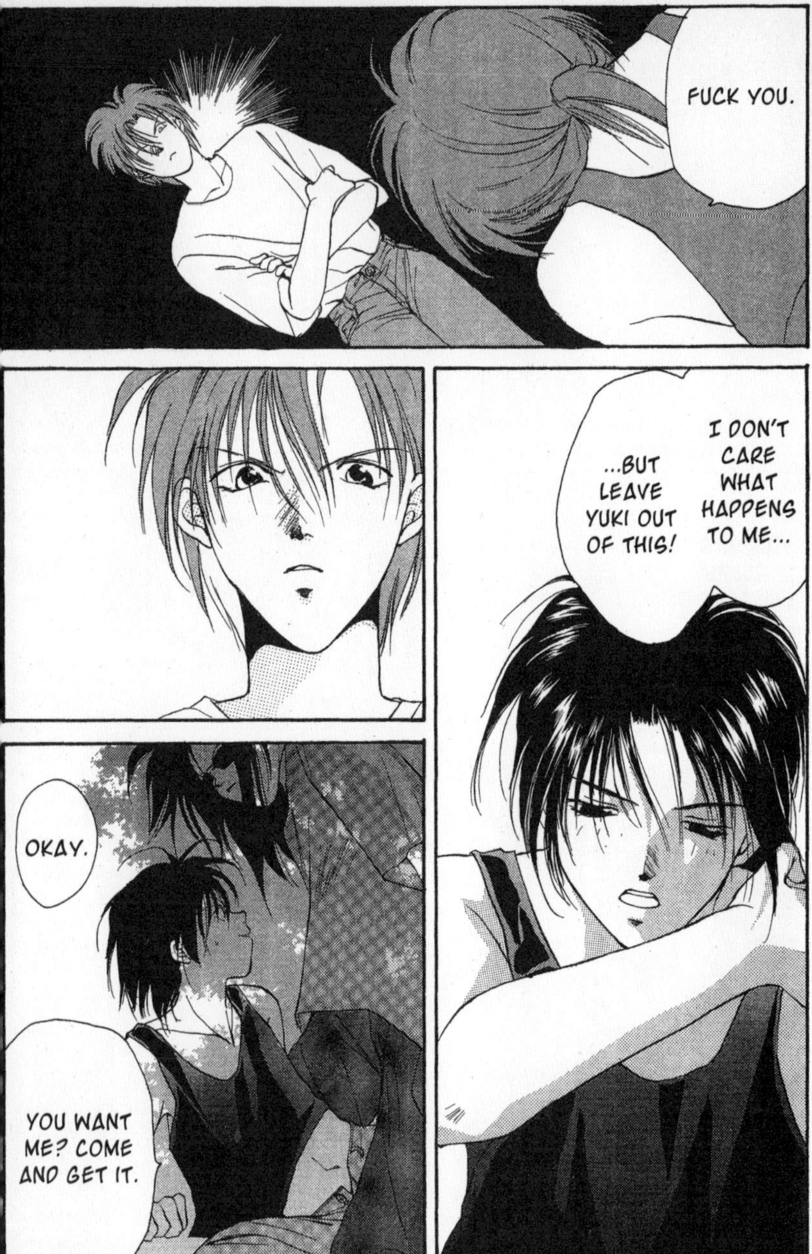
FUCK YOU.
I DON'T CARE WHAT HAPPENS TO ME...
...BUT LEAVE YUKI OUT OF THIS!
OKAY.
YOU WANT ME? COME AND GET IT.

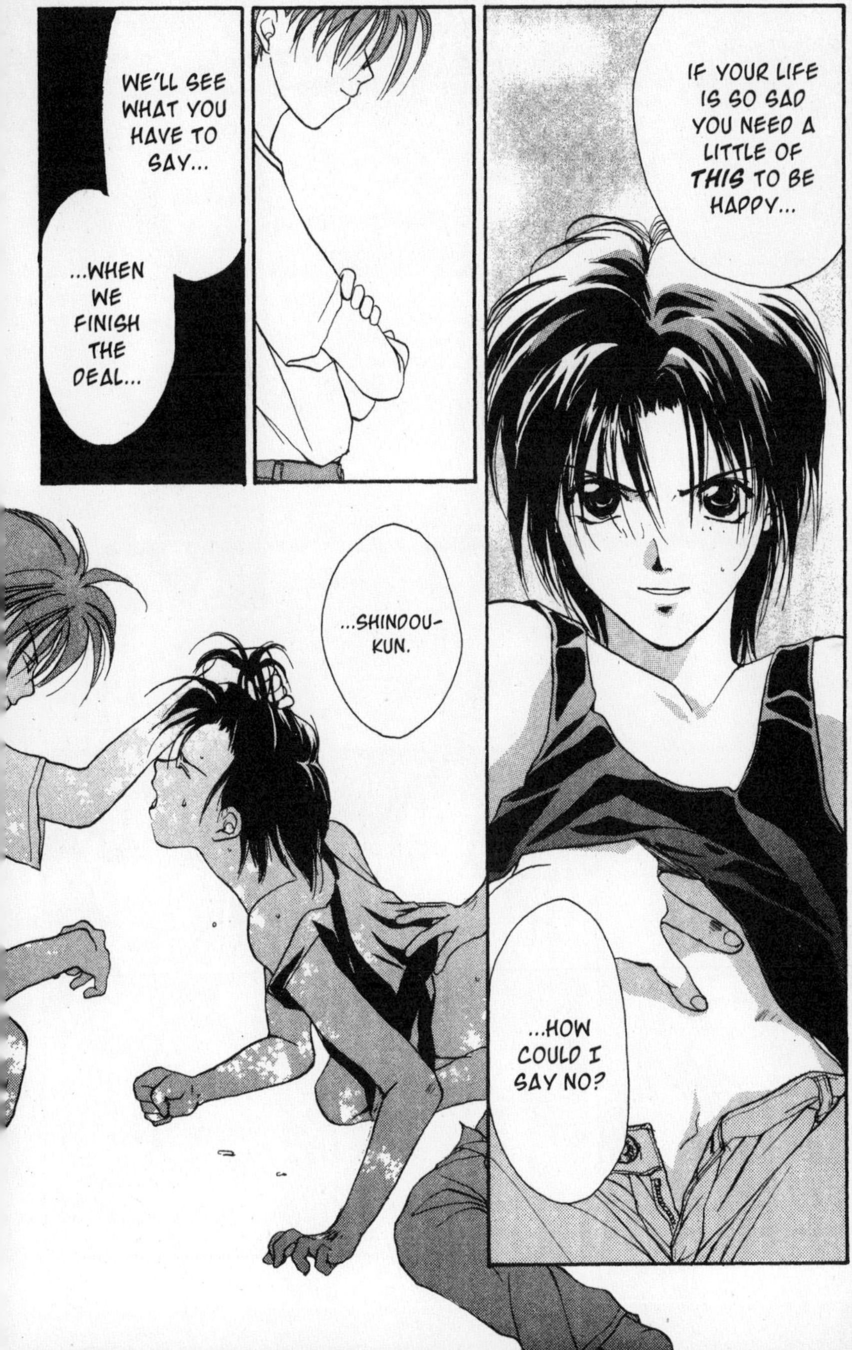
IF YOUR LIFE IS SO SAD YOU NEED A LITTLE OF **THIS** TO BE HAPPY...
...HOW COULD I SAY NO?
WE'LL SEE WHAT YOU HAVE TO SAY...
...WHEN WE FINISH THE DEAL...
...SHINDOU-KUN.

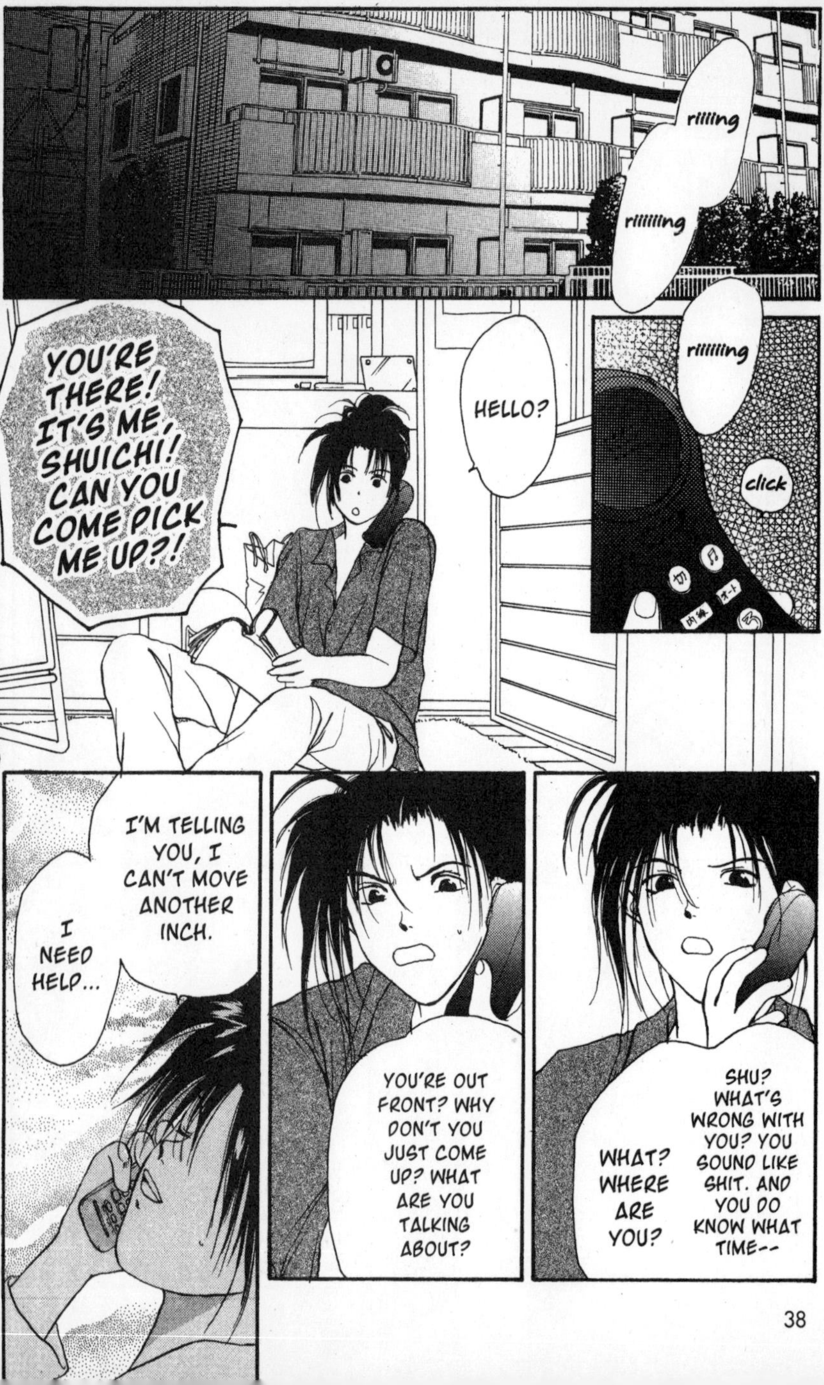
riiiing
riiiiiing
riiiiiing
click
HELLO?
YOU'RE THERE! IT'S ME, SHUICHI! CAN YOU COME PICK ME UP?!
SHU? WHAT'S WRONG WITH YOU? YOU SOUND LIKE SHIT. AND YOU DO KNOW WHAT TIME--
WHAT? WHERE ARE YOU?
YOU'RE OUT FRONT? WHY DON'T YOU JUST COME UP? WHAT ARE YOU TALKING ABOUT?
I'M TELLING YOU, I CAN'T MOVE ANOTHER INCH.
I NEED HELP...

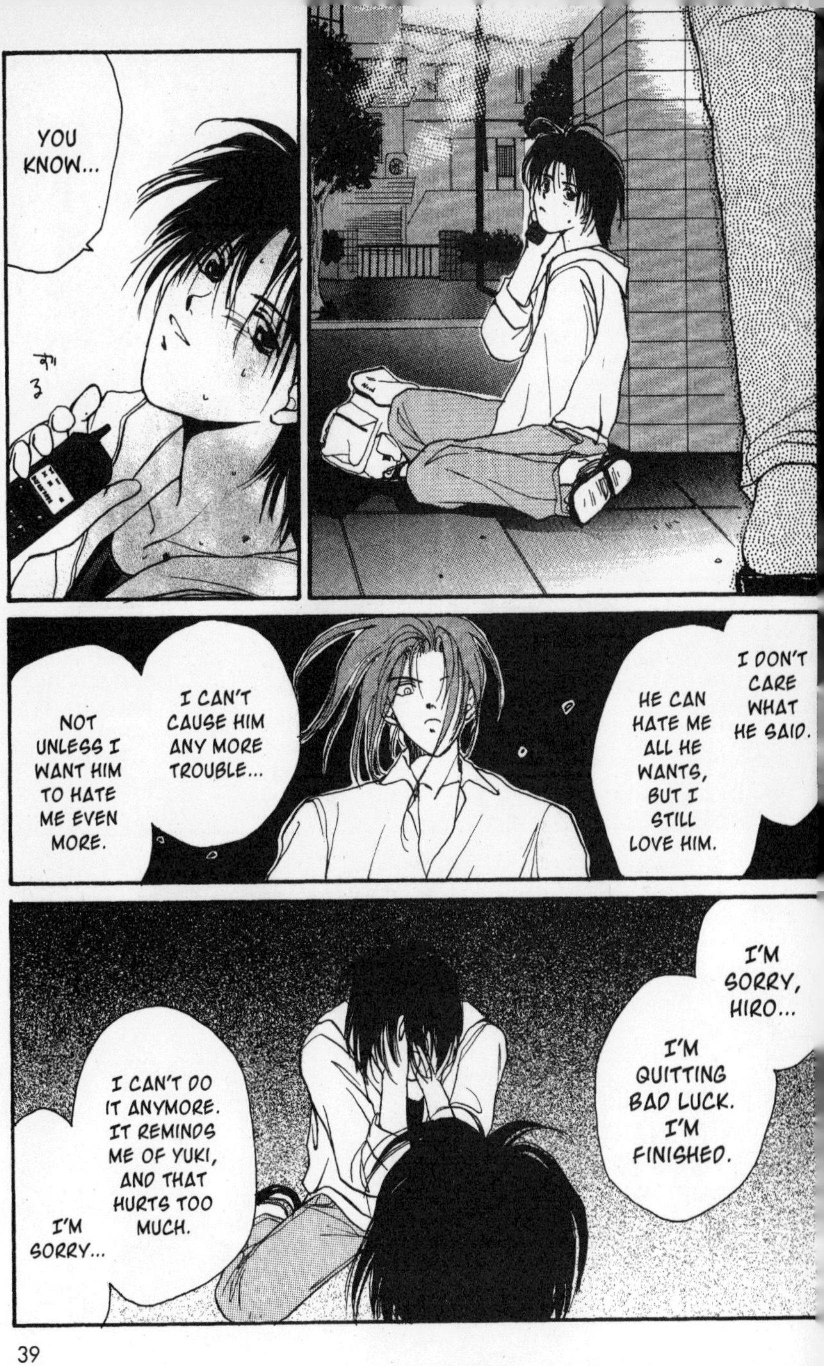
YOU KNOW...
I DON'T CARE WHAT HE SAID.
HE CAN HATE ME ALL HE WANTS, BUT I STILL LOVE HIM.
I CAN'T CAUSE HIM ANY MORE TROUBLE...
NOT UNLESS I WANT HIM TO HATE ME EVEN MORE.
I'M SORRY, HIRO...
I'M QUITTING BAD LUCK. I'M FINISHED.
I CAN'T DO IT ANYMORE. IT REMINDS ME OF YUKI, AND THAT HURTS TOO MUCH.
I'M SORRY...

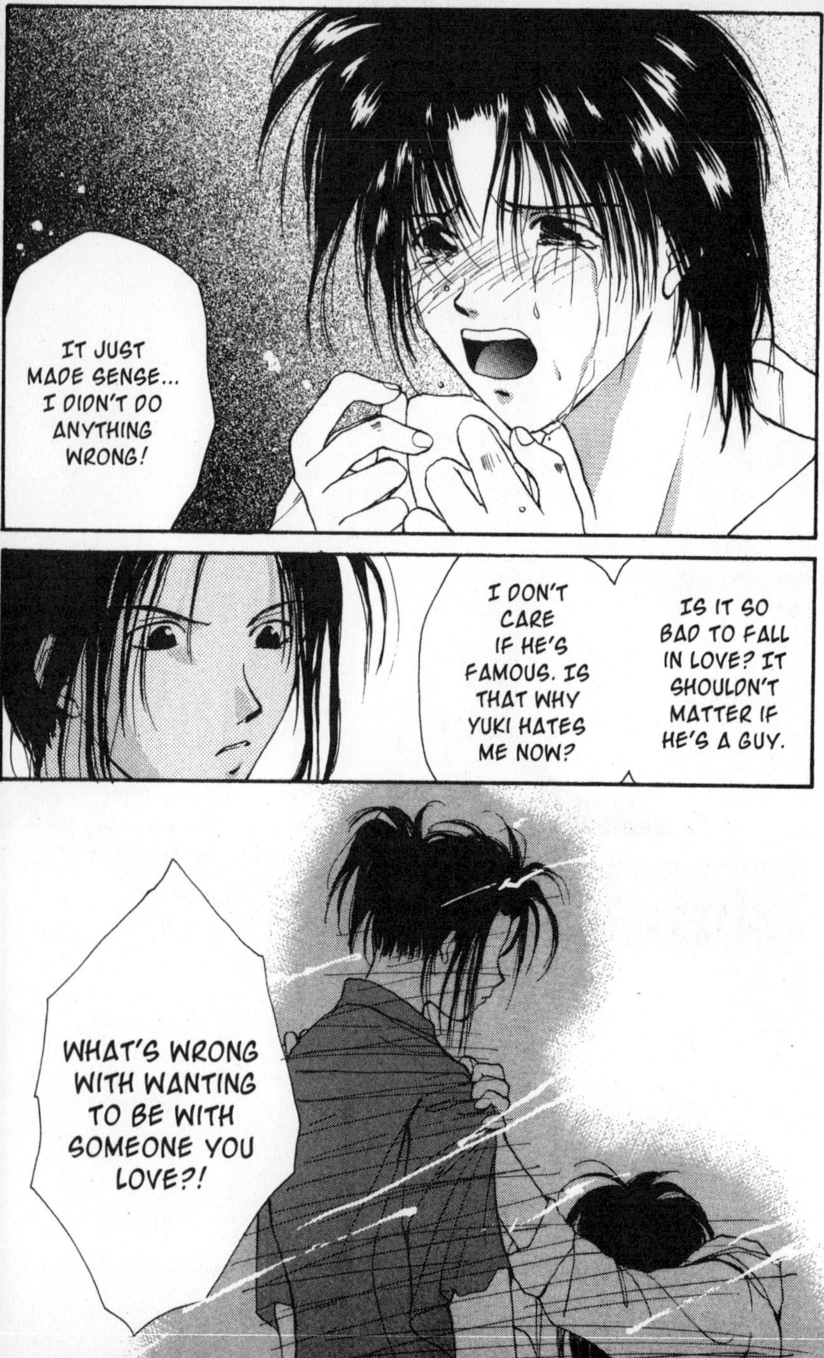
IT JUST MADE SENSE... I DIDN'T DO ANYTHING WRONG!
IS IT SO BAD TO FALL IN LOVE? IT SHOULDN'T MATTER IF HE'S A GUY.
I DON'T CARE IF HE'S FAMOUS. IS THAT WHY YUKI HATES ME NOW?
WHAT'S WRONG WITH WANTING TO BE WITH SOMEONE YOU LOVE?!

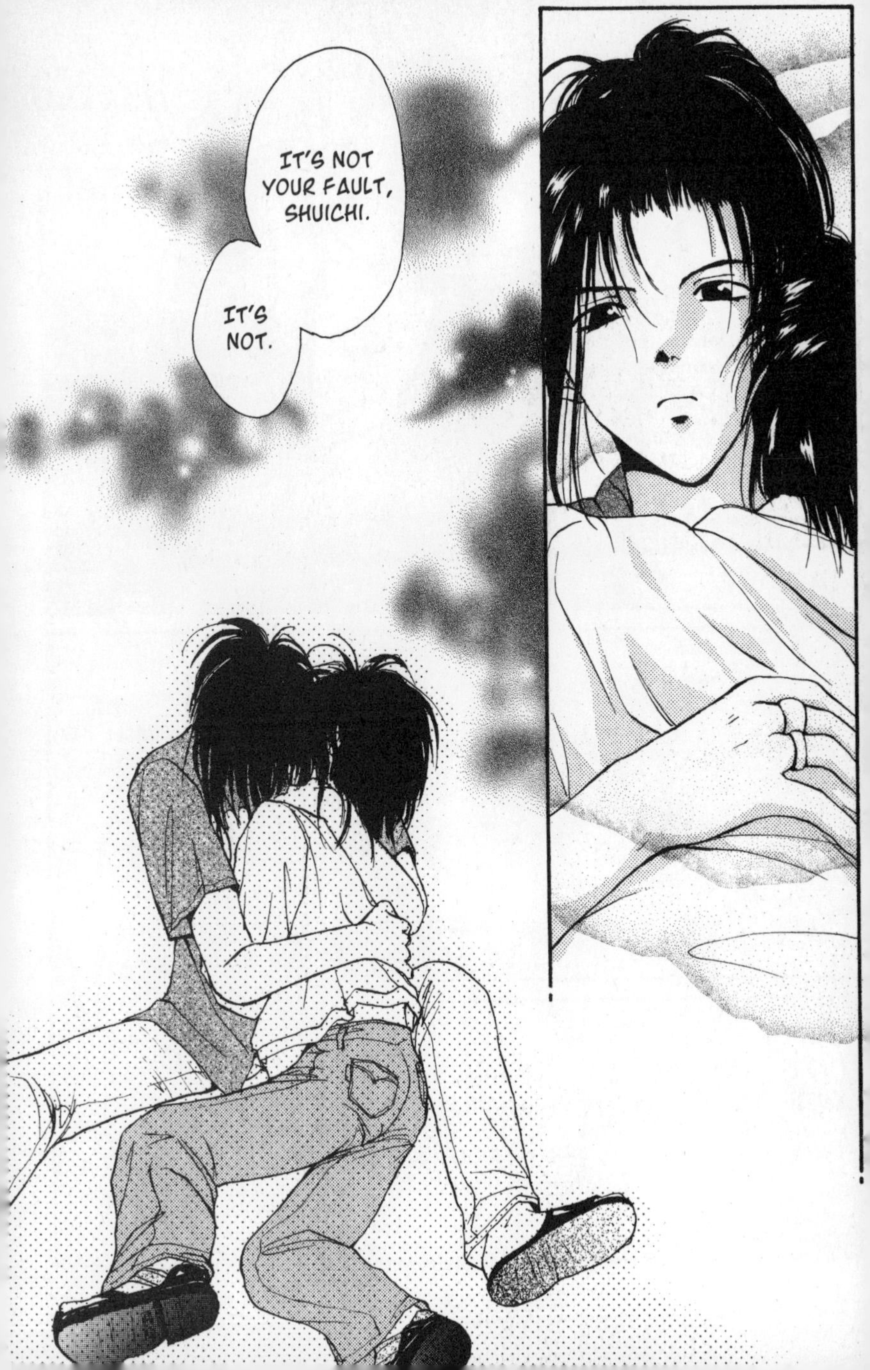
IT'S NOT YOUR FAULT, SHUICHI.
IT'S NOT.

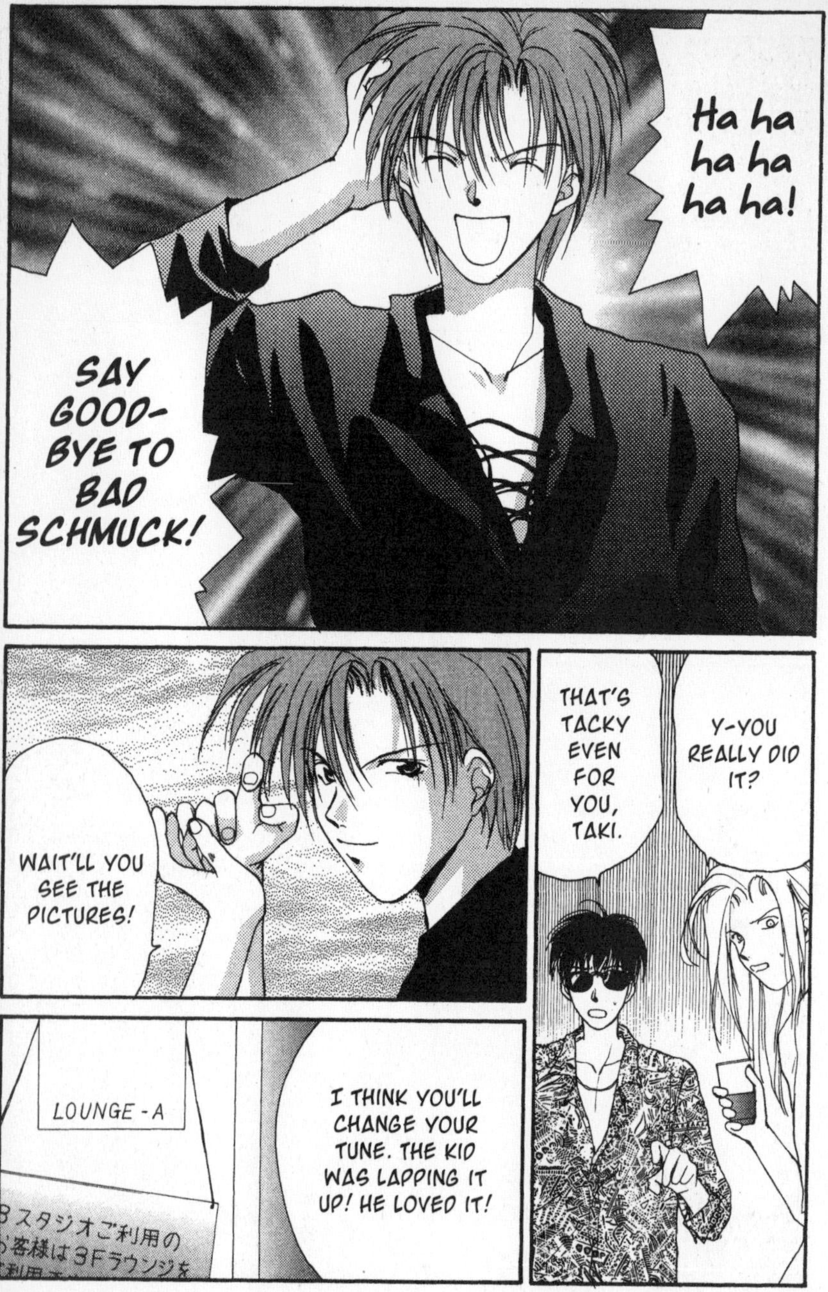
Ha ha ha ha ha ha!
SAY GOOD-BYE TO BAD SCHMUCK!
Y-YOU REALLY DID IT?
THAT'S TACKY EVEN FOR YOU, TAKI.
WAIT'LL YOU SEE THE PICTURES!
I THINK YOU'LL CHANGE YOUR TUNE. THE KID WAS LAPPING IT UP! HE LOVED IT!
LOUNGE - A
スタジオご利用の
お客様は3Fラウンジを

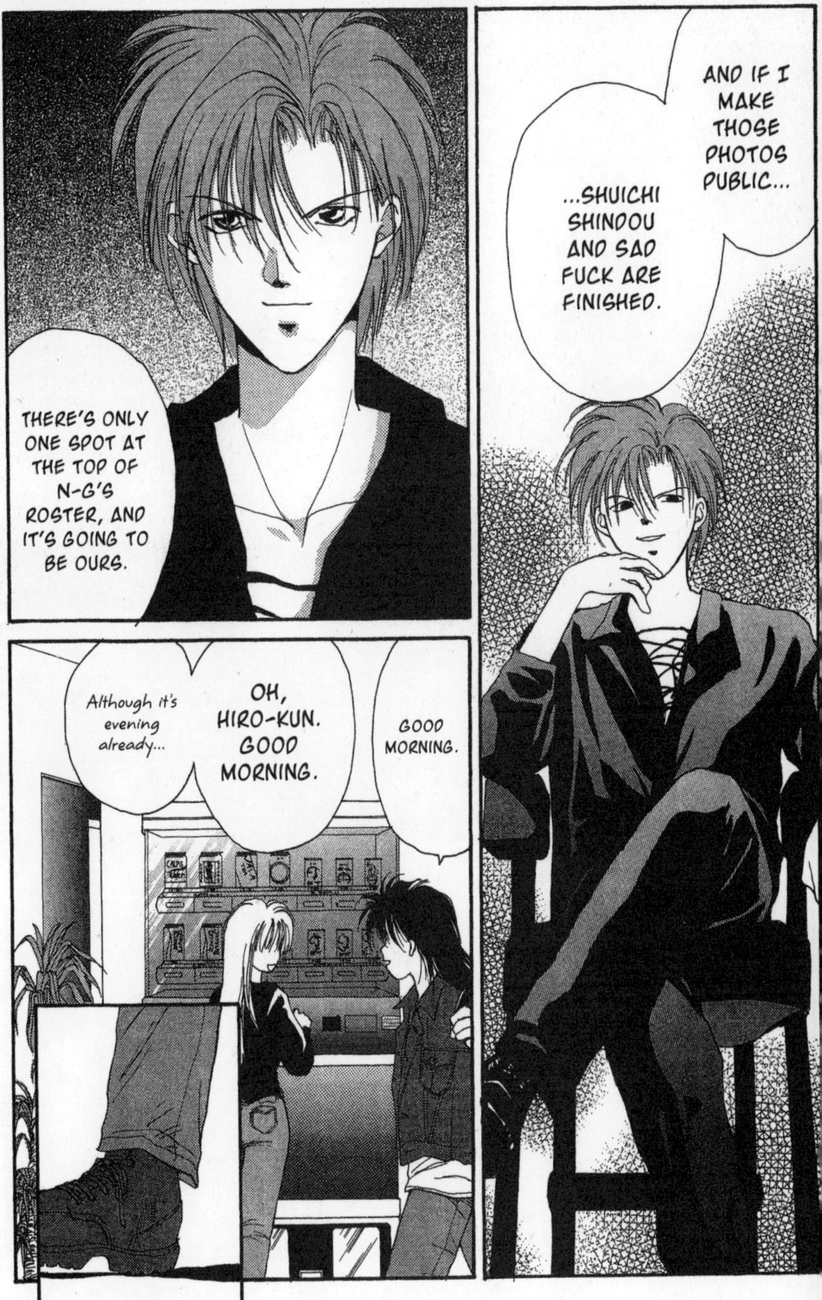
AND IF I MAKE THOSE PHOTOS PUBLIC...
...SHUICHI SHINDOU AND SAD FUCK ARE FINISHED.
THERE'S ONLY ONE SPOT AT THE TOP OF N-G'S ROSTER, AND IT'S GOING TO BE OURS.
GOOD MORNING.
OH, HIRO-KUN. GOOD MORNING.
Although it's evening already...

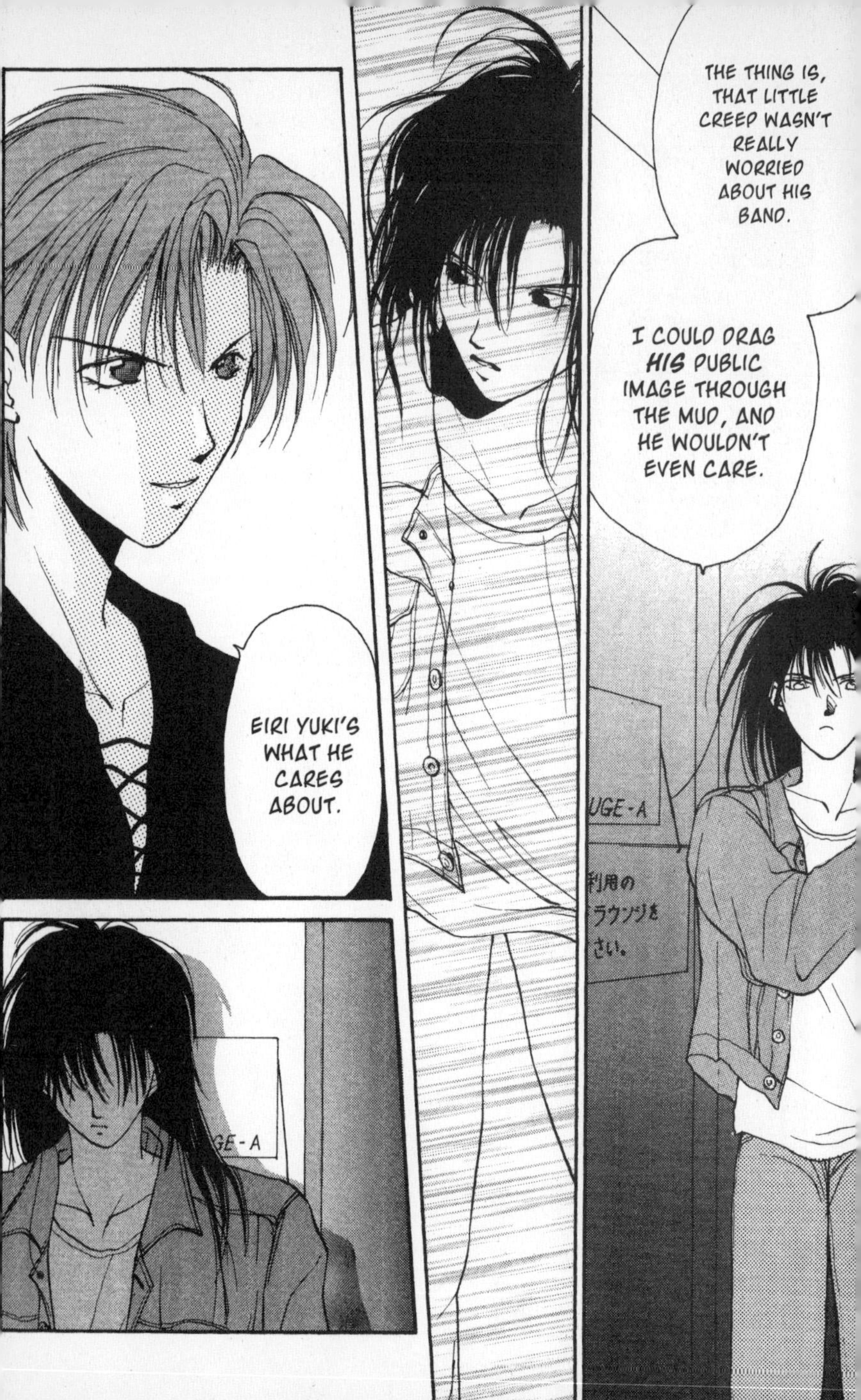
THE THING IS, THAT LITTLE CREEP WASN'T REALLY WORRIED ABOUT HIS BAND.
I COULD DRAG **HIS** PUBLIC IMAGE THROUGH THE MUD, AND HE WOULDN'T EVEN CARE.
EIRI YUKI'S WHAT HE CARES ABOUT.

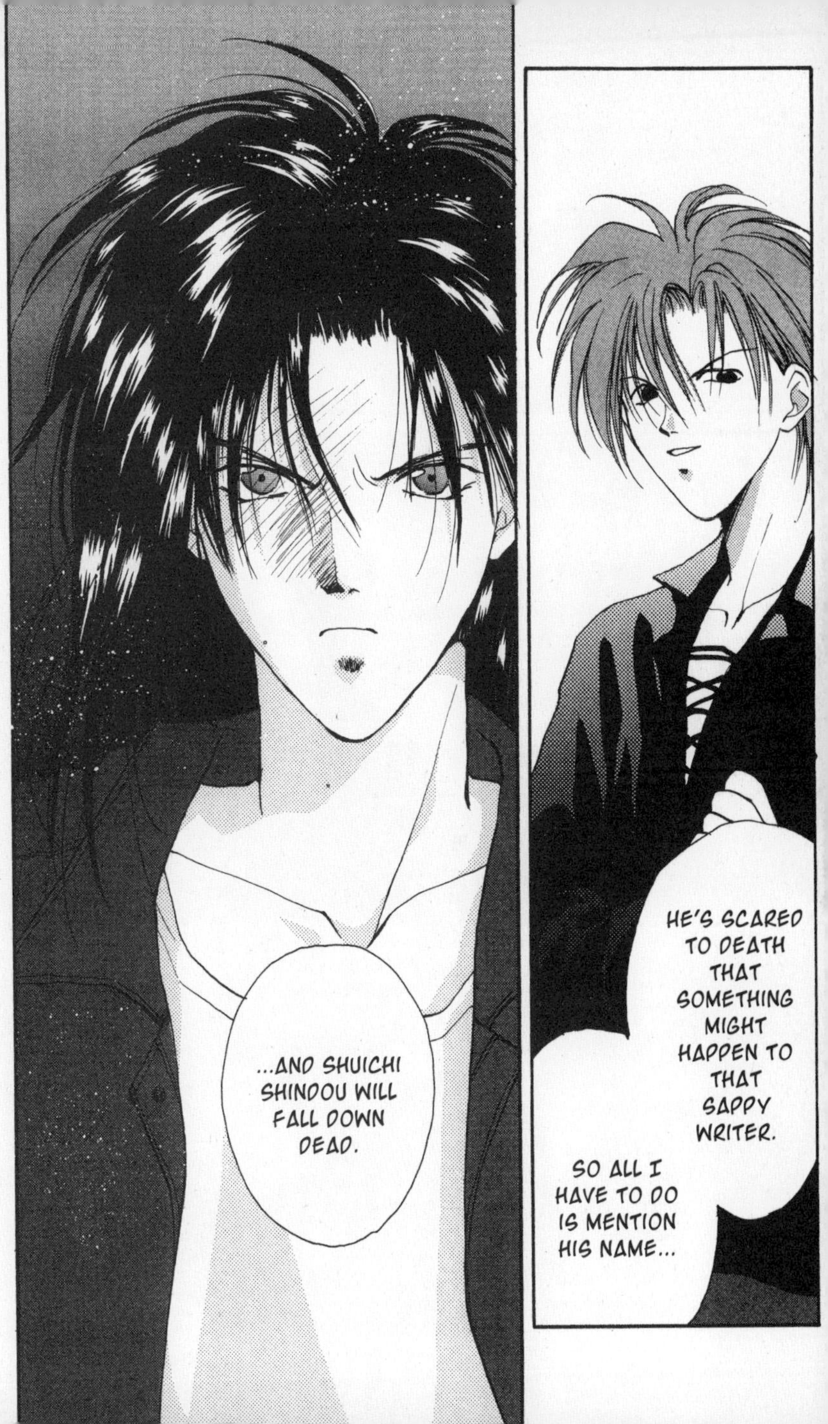
HE'S SCARED TO DEATH THAT SOMETHING MIGHT HAPPEN TO THAT SAPPY WRITER.
SO ALL I HAVE TO DO IS MENTION HIS NAME...
...AND SHUICHI SHINDOU WILL FALL DOWN DEAD.

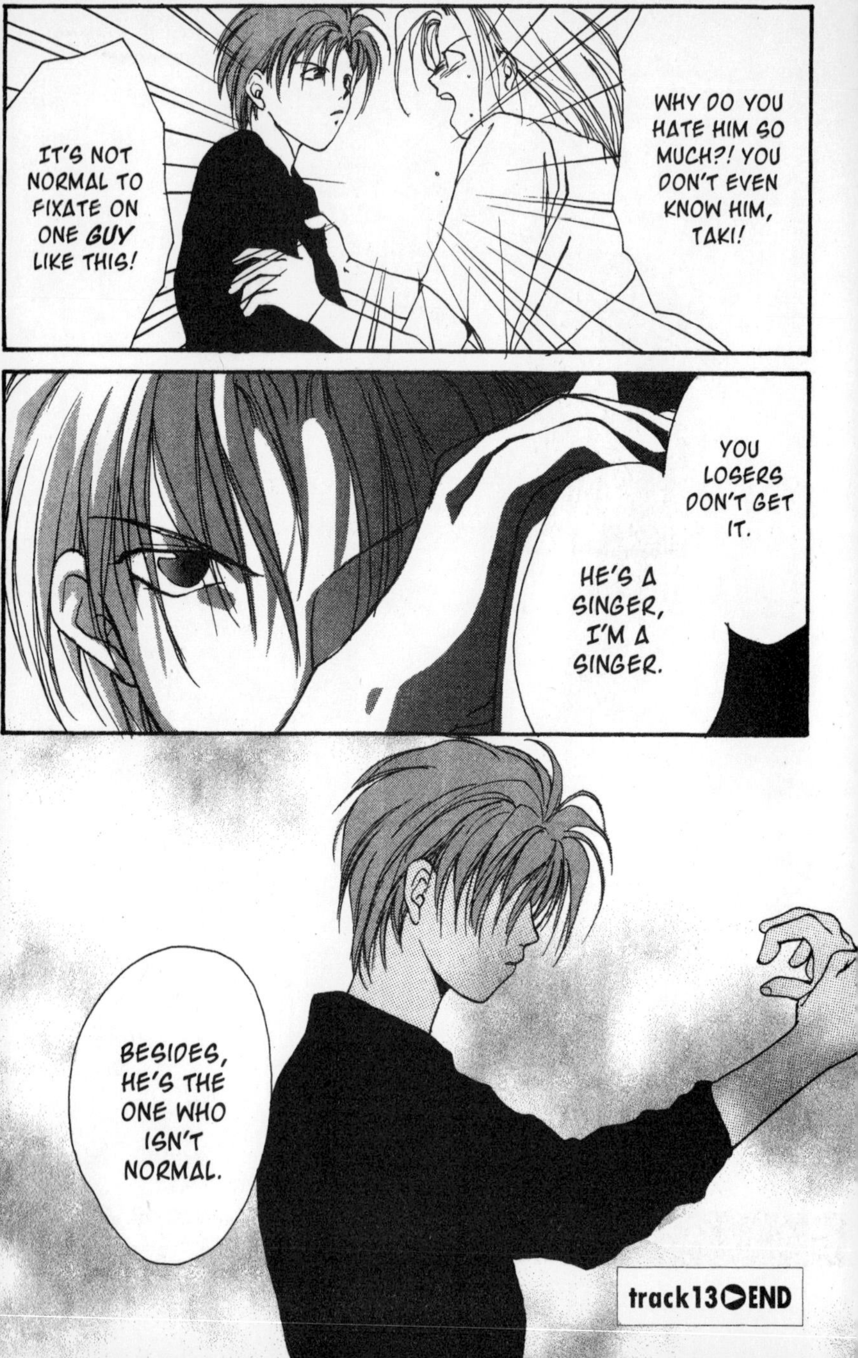
WHY DO YOU HATE HIM SO MUCH?! YOU DON'T EVEN KNOW HIM, TAKI!
IT'S NOT NORMAL TO FIXATE ON ONE *GUY* LIKE THIS!
YOU LOSERS DON'T GET IT.
HE'S A SINGER, I'M A SINGER.
BESIDES, HE'S THE ONE WHO ISN'T NORMAL.
track13 END

Gravitation

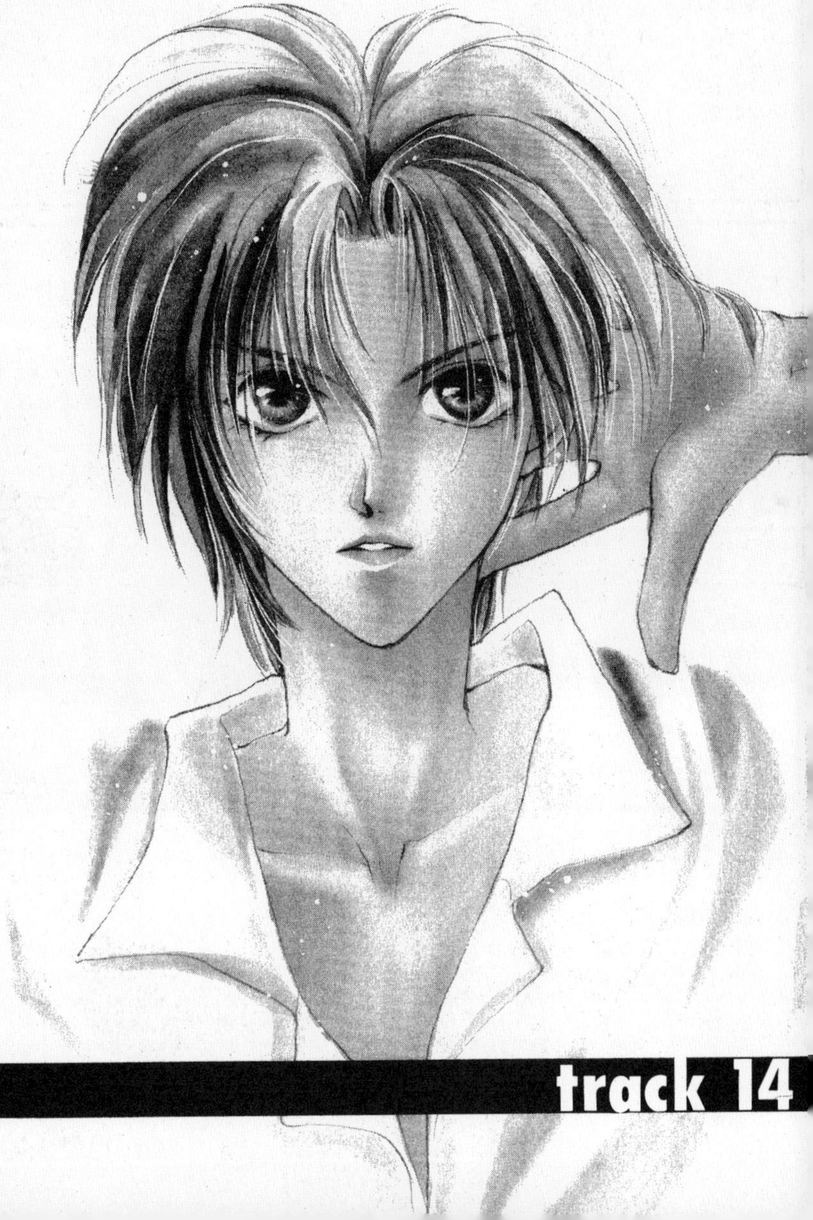

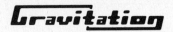

track 14

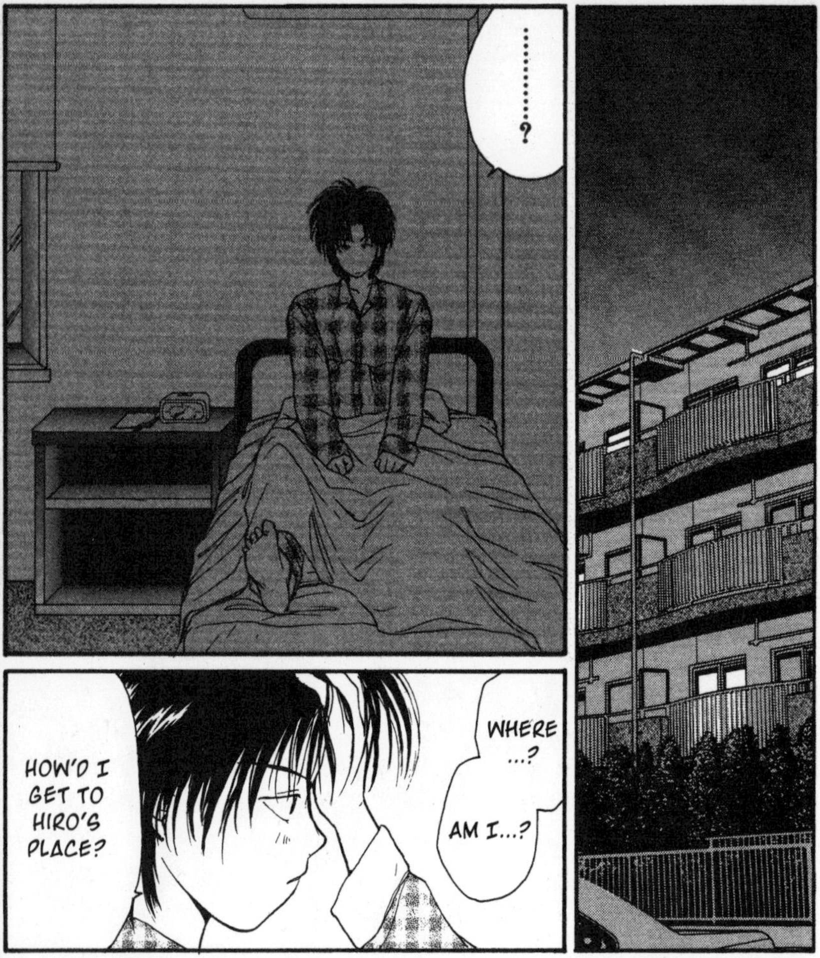
.........?
WHERE ...? AM I...?
HOW'D I GET TO HIRO'S PLACE?

ABOUT GRAVITATION TRACK 14

Yaaaa! Eeeek!

That droopy-eyed Taki had Shuichi gang-raped! How is he going to bounce back from that? What will he do? I can't believe I wrote such a crazy turn of events! I wonder what I was thinking? Starting with track 14, I'm going into a "what am I gonna do?" mode. Can you feel my intensity? Some highlights to watch for in this chapter: Shuichi and Hiro's deep friendship, and Eiri's emotionless reaction to everything—sometimes you gotta think, "Does this guy get it at all?" And, of course, the ever-changing hairstyles of Noriko!

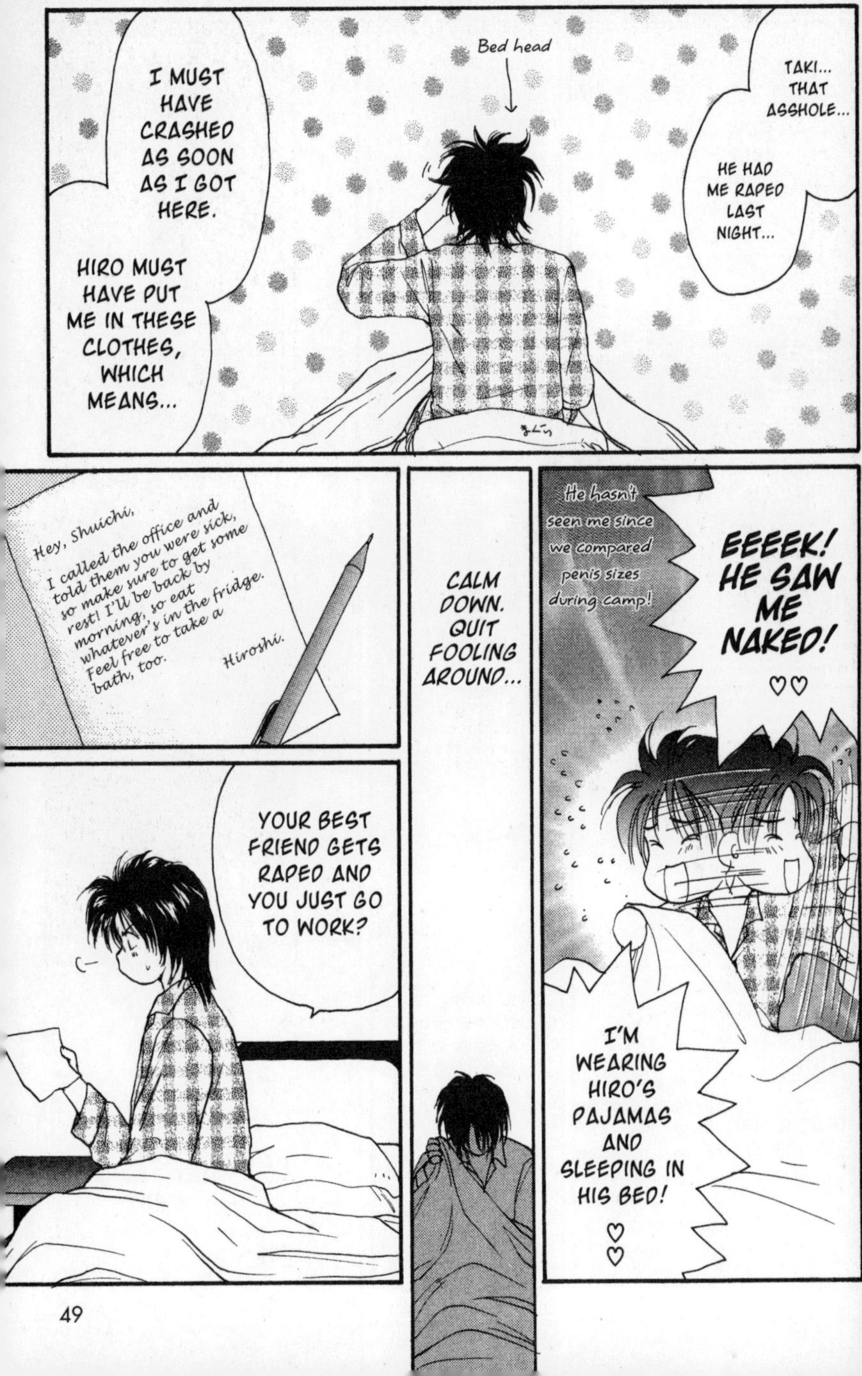
TAKI... THAT ASSHOLE...
HE HAD ME RAPED LAST NIGHT...
Bed head
I MUST HAVE CRASHED AS SOON AS I GOT HERE.
HIRO MUST HAVE PUT ME IN THESE CLOTHES, WHICH MEANS...
He hasn't seen me since we compared penis sizes during camp!
EEEEK! HE SAW ME NAKED!
I'M WEARING HIRO'S PAJAMAS AND SLEEPING IN HIS BED!
CALM DOWN. QUIT FOOLING AROUND...
Hey, Shuichi,
I called the office and told them you were sick, so make sure to get some rest! I'll be back by morning, so eat whatever's in the fridge. Feel free to take a bath, too.
Hiroshi.
YOUR BEST FRIEND GETS RAPED AND YOU JUST GO TO WORK?

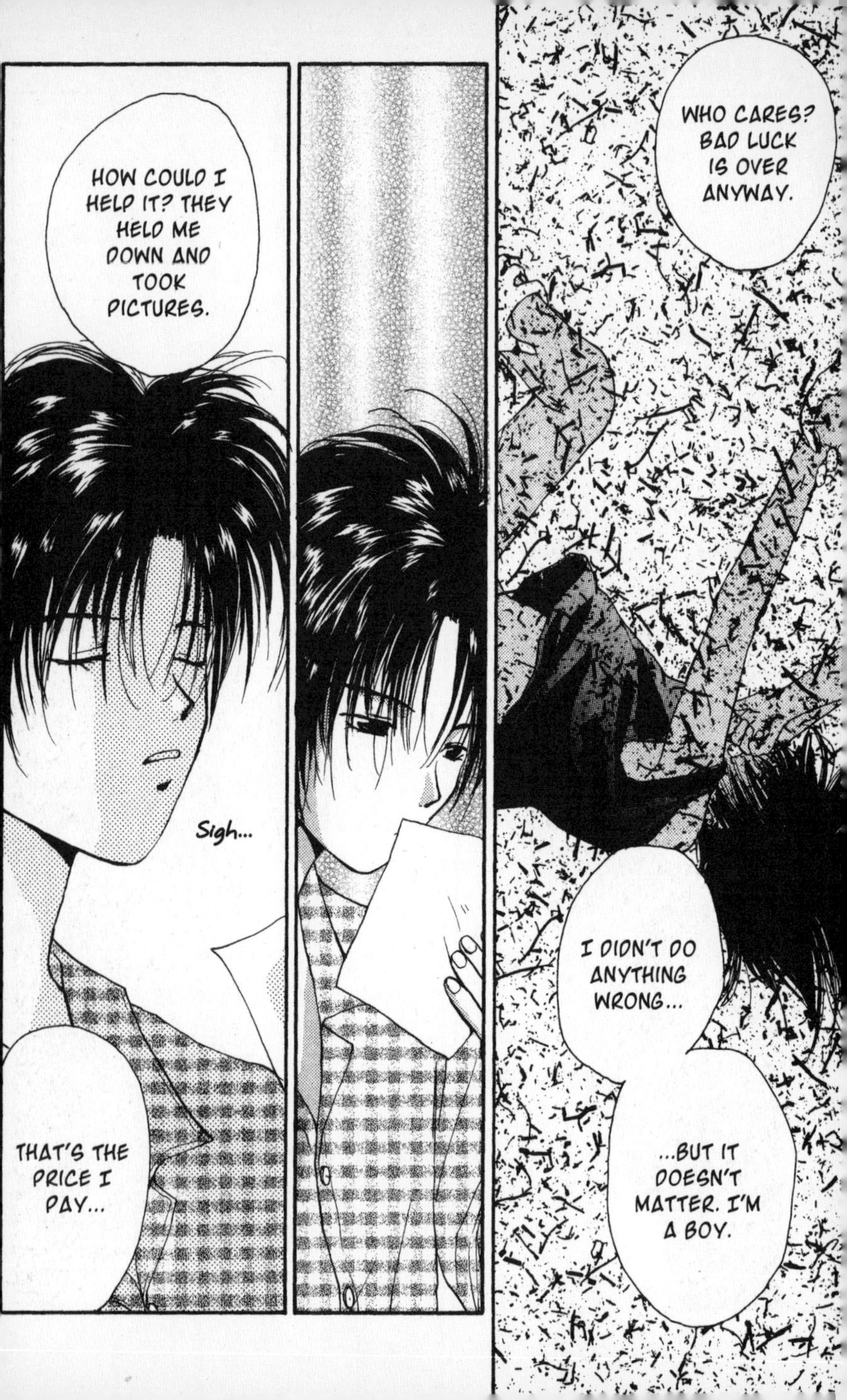
WHO CARES? BAD LUCK IS OVER ANYWAY.
I DIDN'T DO ANYTHING WRONG...
...BUT IT DOESN'T MATTER. I'M A BOY.
HOW COULD I HELP IT? THEY HELD ME DOWN AND TOOK PICTURES.
Sigh...
THAT'S THE PRICE I PAY...

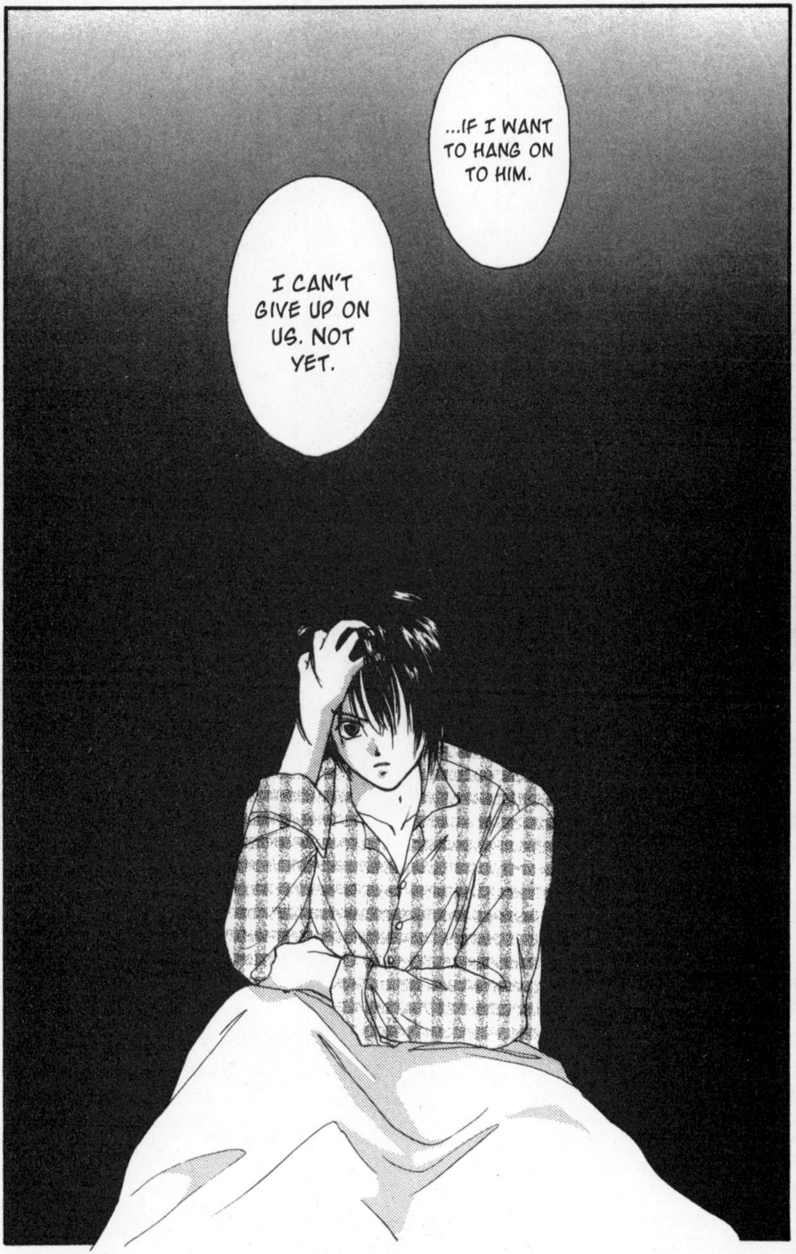
...IF I WANT TO HANG ON TO HIM.
I CAN'T GIVE UP ON US. NOT YET.

SO YOU'RE EIRI YUKI?
I REMEMBER COMING TO THIS NEIGHBORHOOD WITH MY SINGER...
...BUT WE GOT A BIT LOST LOOKING FOR THE ACTUAL ADDRESS.
slip
WELL, AT LEAST YOU'VE IMPROVED.

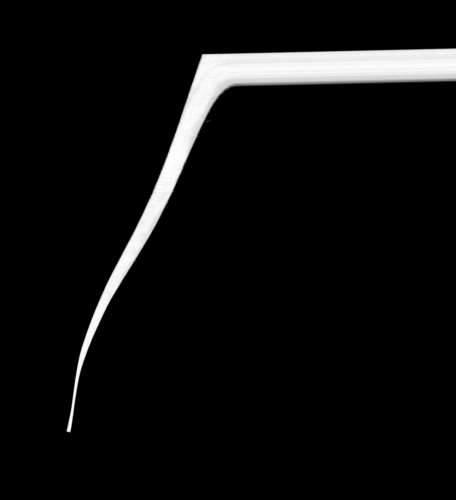

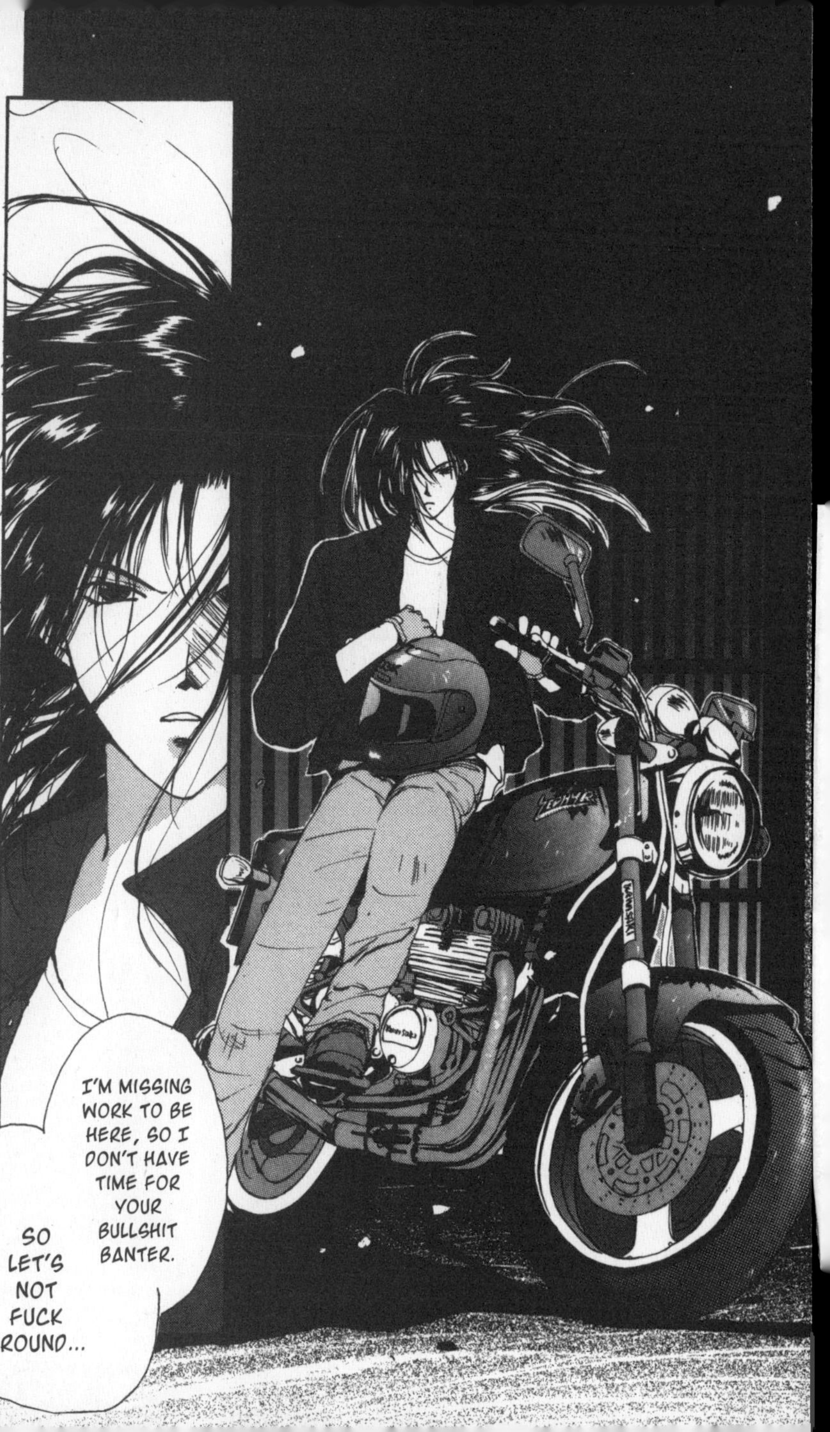
I'M MISSING WORK TO BE HERE, SO I DON'T HAVE TIME FOR YOUR BULLSHIT BANTER.
SO LET'S NOT FUCK AROUND...

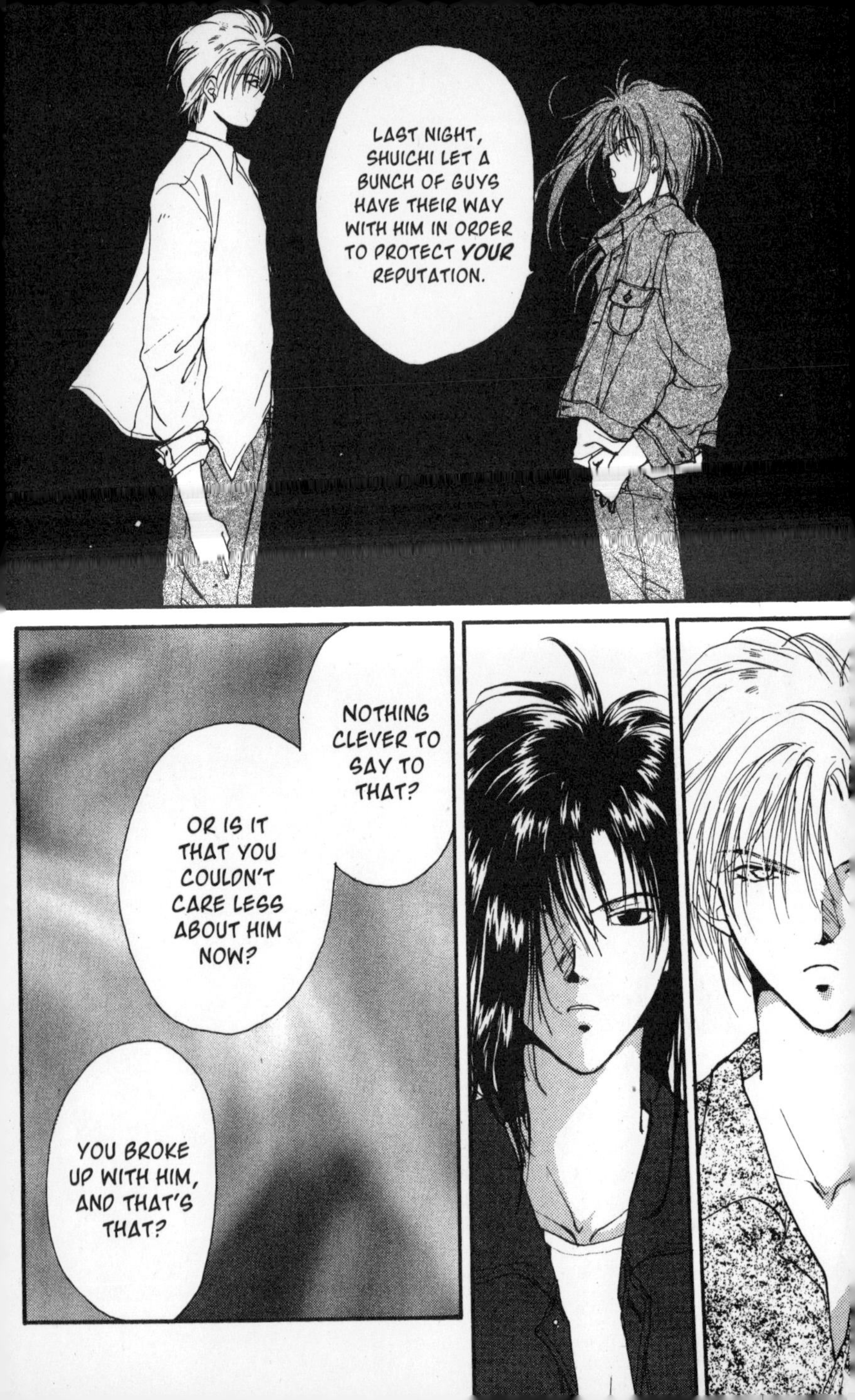
LAST NIGHT, SHUICHI LET A BUNCH OF GUYS HAVE THEIR WAY WITH HIM IN ORDER TO PROTECT *YOUR* REPUTATION.
NOTHING CLEVER TO SAY TO THAT?
OR IS IT THAT YOU COULDN'T CARE LESS ABOUT HIM NOW?
YOU BROKE UP WITH HIM, AND THAT'S THAT?

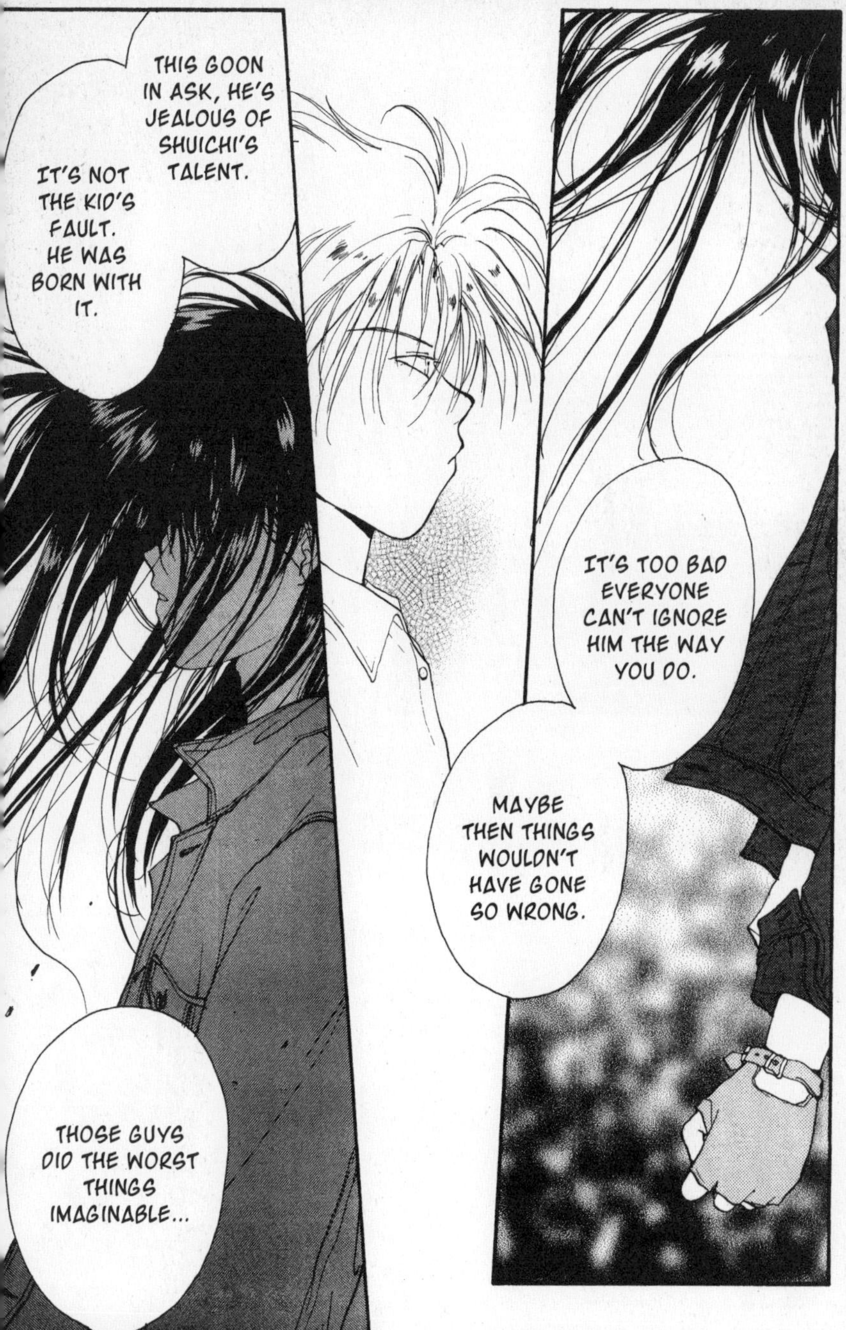
IT'S TOO BAD EVERYONE CAN'T IGNORE HIM THE WAY YOU DO.
MAYBE THEN THINGS WOULDN'T HAVE GONE SO WRONG.
THIS GOON IN ASK, HE'S JEALOUS OF SHUICHI'S TALENT.
IT'S NOT THE KID'S FAULT. HE WAS BORN WITH IT.
THOSE GUYS DID THE WORST THINGS IMAGINABLE...

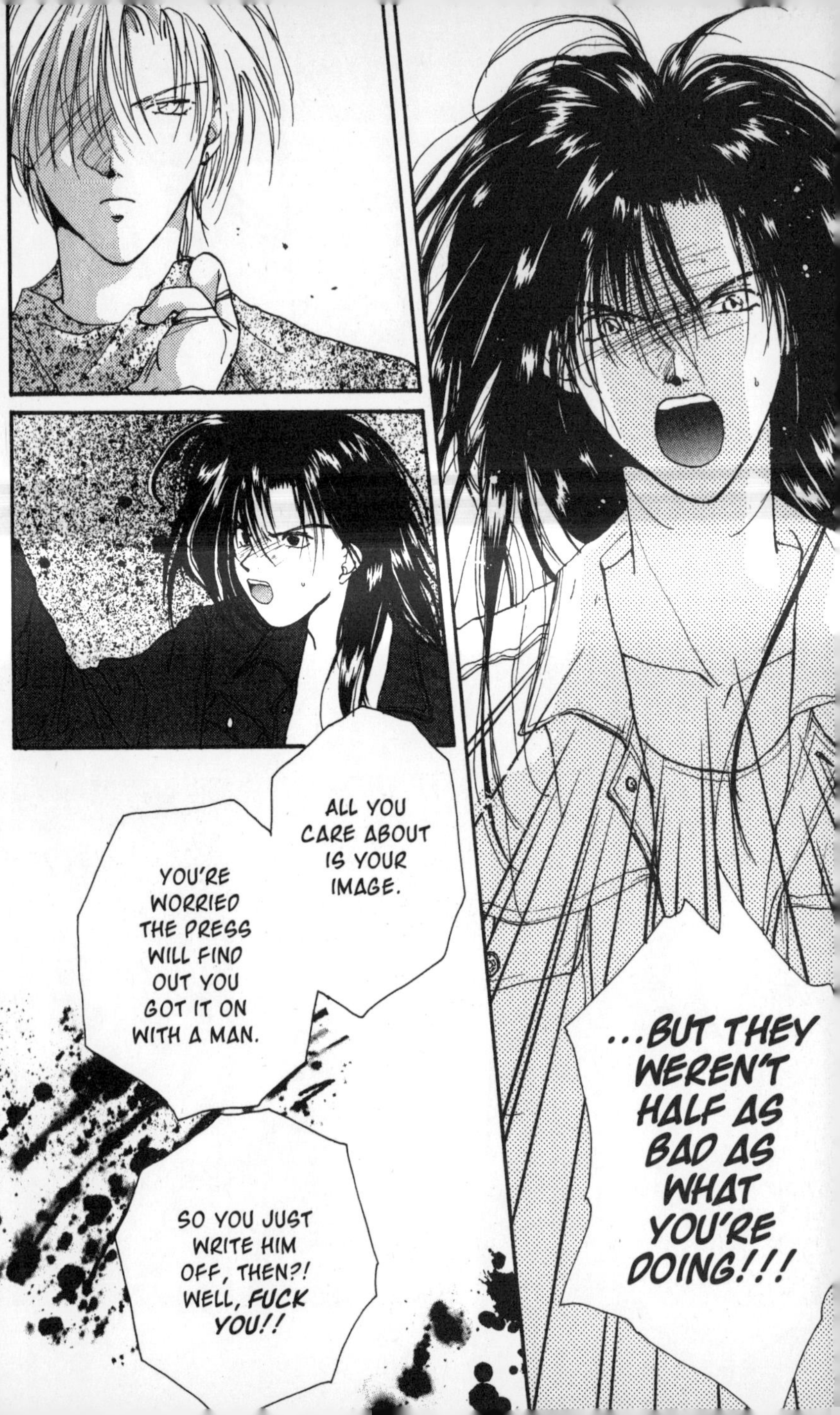
...BUT THEY WEREN'T HALF AS BAD AS WHAT YOU'RE DOING!!!
ALL YOU CARE ABOUT IS YOUR IMAGE.
YOU'RE WORRIED THE PRESS WILL FIND OUT YOU GOT IT ON WITH A MAN.
SO YOU JUST WRITE HIM OFF, THEN?! WELL, *FUCK YOU!!*

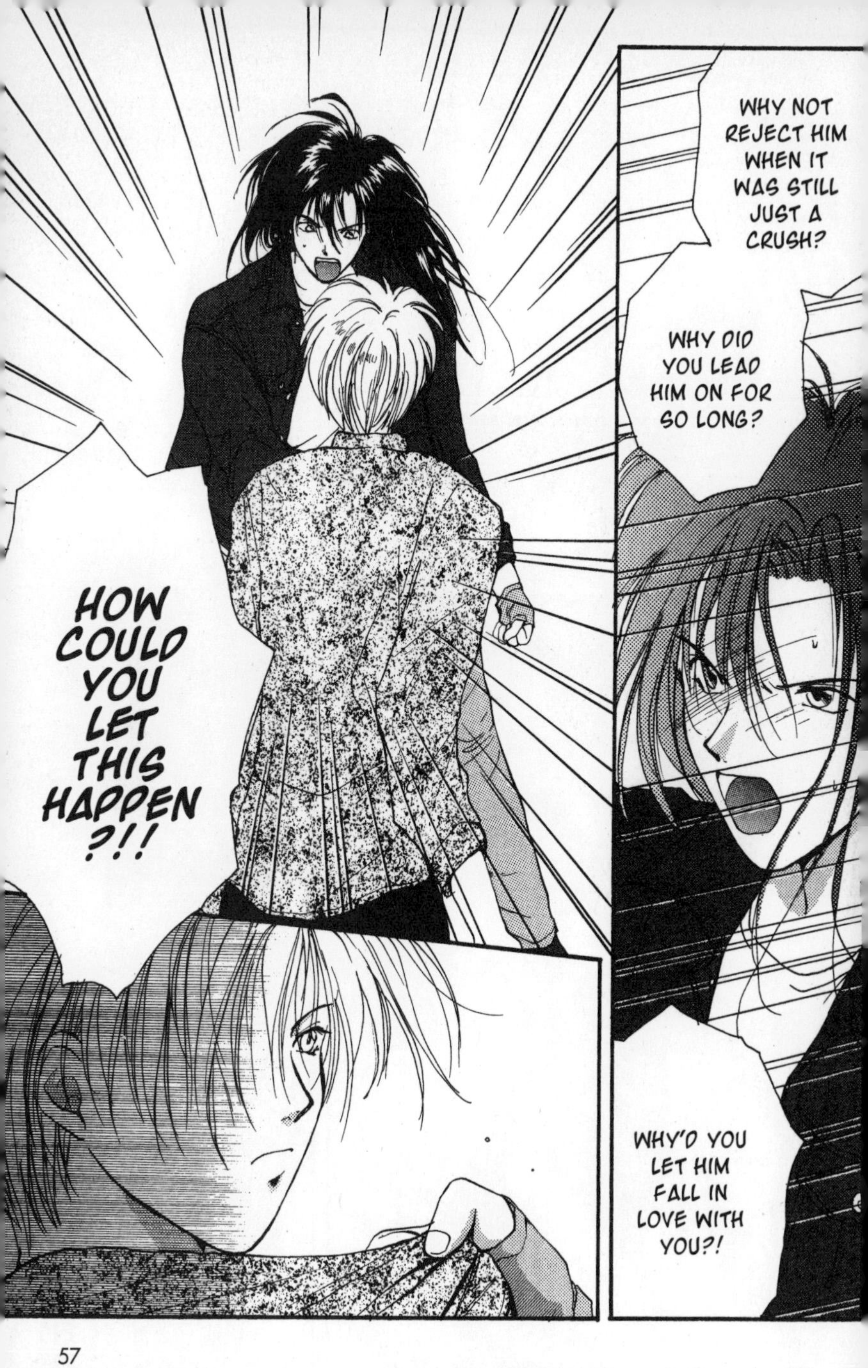
WHY NOT REJECT HIM WHEN IT WAS STILL JUST A CRUSH?
WHY DID YOU LEAD HIM ON FOR SO LONG?
WHY'D YOU LET HIM FALL IN LOVE WITH YOU?!
HOW COULD YOU LET THIS HAPPEN ?!!

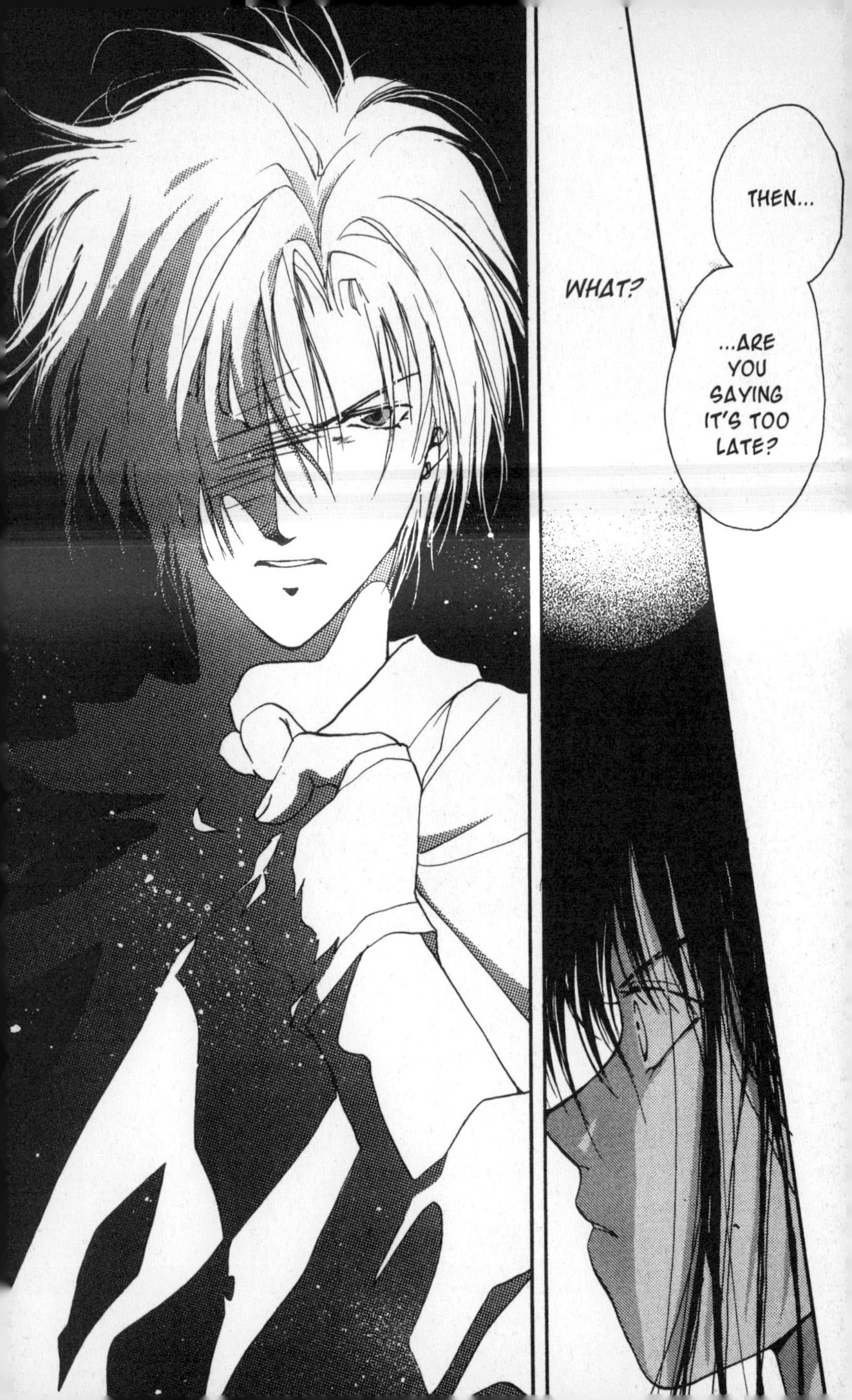
THEN... ...ARE YOU SAYING IT'S TOO LATE?
WHAT?

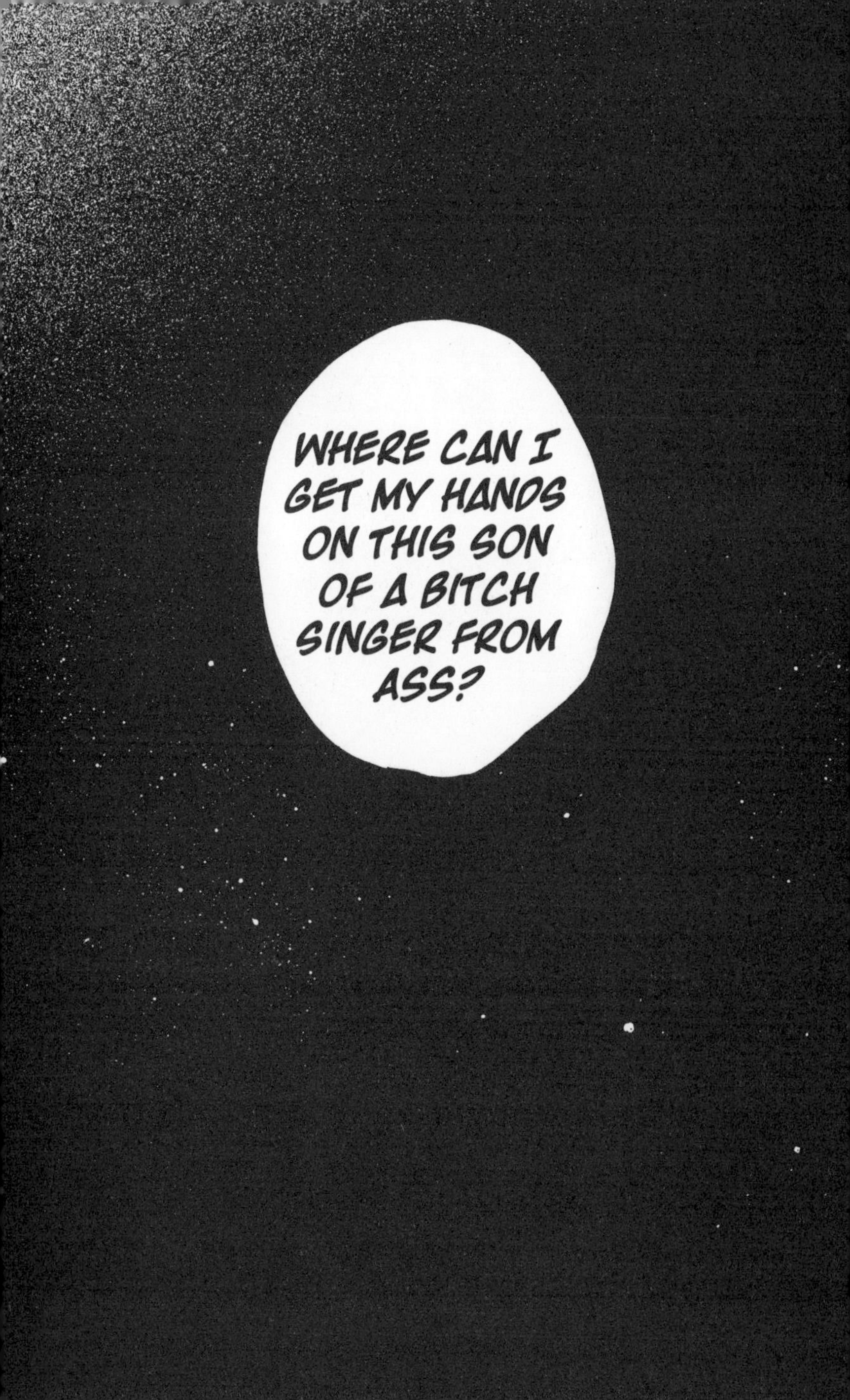
WHERE CAN I GET MY HANDS ON THIS SON OF A BITCH SINGER FROM ASS?

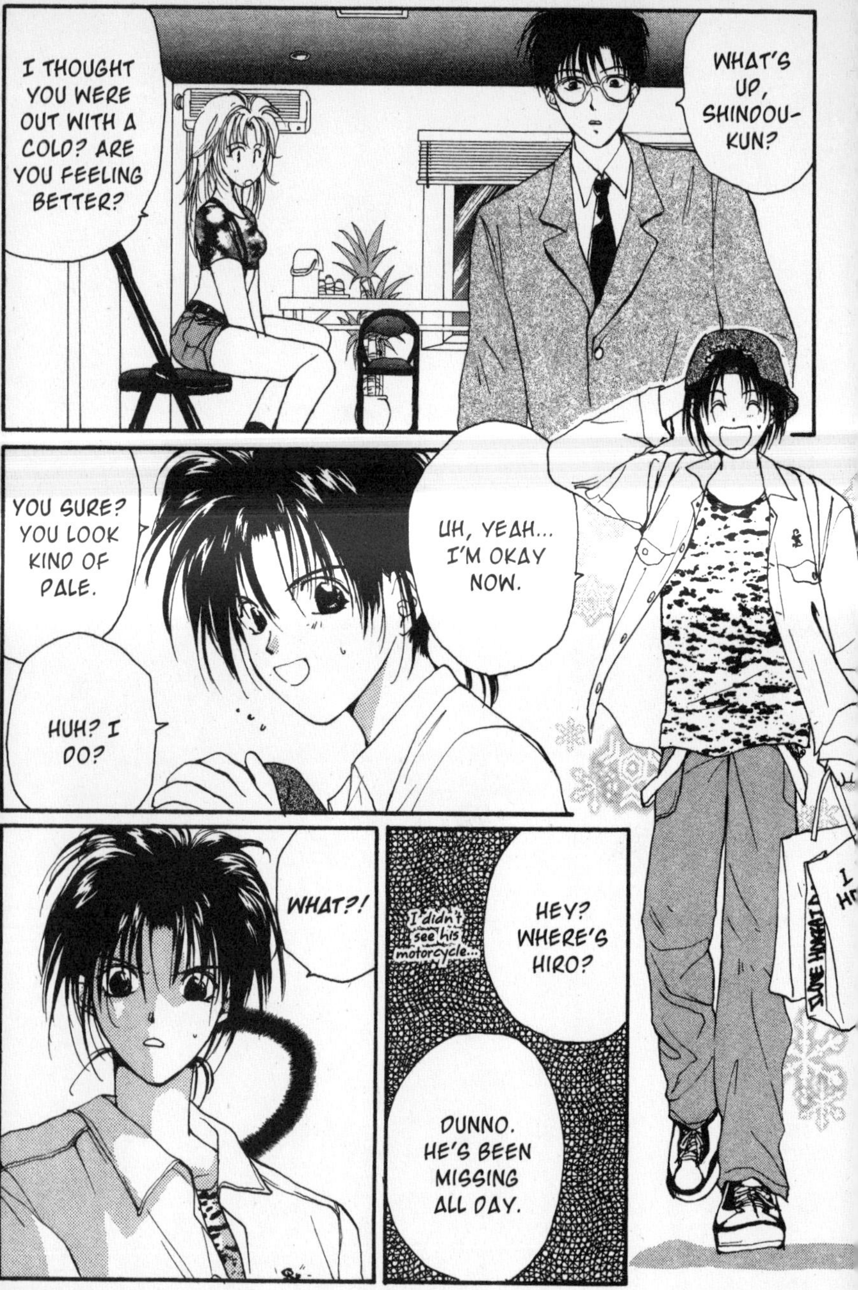
WHAT'S UP, SHINDOU-KUN?
I THOUGHT YOU WERE OUT WITH A COLD? ARE YOU FEELING BETTER?
UH, YEAH... I'M OKAY NOW.
YOU SURE? YOU LOOK KIND OF PALE.
HUH? I DO?
HEY? WHERE'S HIRO?
I didn't see his motorcycle...
DUNNO. HE'S BEEN MISSING ALL DAY.
WHAT?!

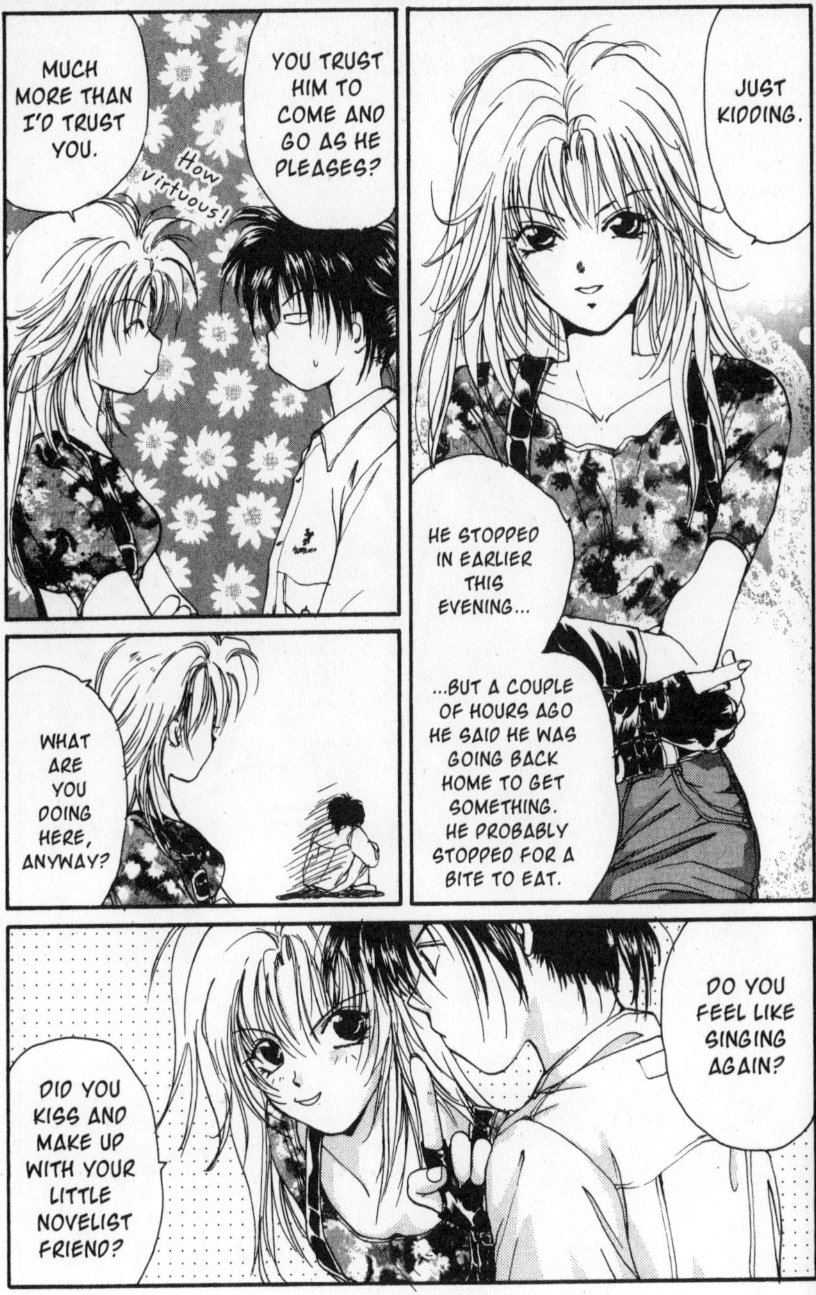
JUST KIDDING.
HE STOPPED IN EARLIER THIS EVENING...
...BUT A COUPLE OF HOURS AGO HE SAID HE WAS GOING BACK HOME TO GET SOMETHING. HE PROBABLY STOPPED FOR A BITE TO EAT.
YOU TRUST HIM TO COME AND GO AS HE PLEASES?
How virtuous!
MUCH MORE THAN I'D TRUST YOU.
WHAT ARE YOU DOING HERE, ANYWAY?
DO YOU FEEL LIKE SINGING AGAIN?
DID YOU KISS AND MAKE UP WITH YOUR LITTLE NOVELIST FRIEND?

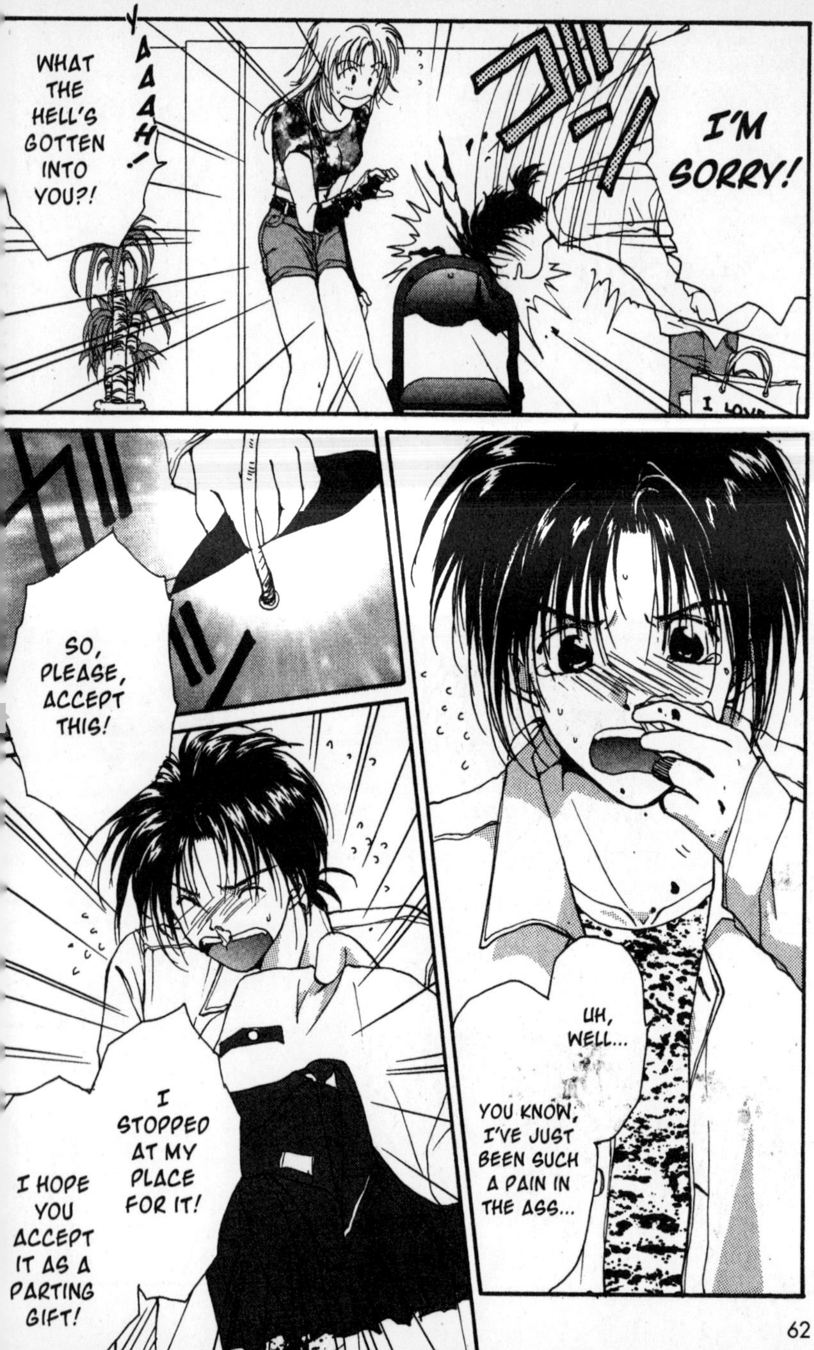
I'M SORRY!
YAAAAH!
WHAT THE HELL'S GOTTEN INTO YOU?!
UH, WELL...
YOU KNOW, I'VE JUST BEEN SUCH A PAIN IN THE ASS...
SO, PLEASE, ACCEPT THIS!
I STOPPED AT MY PLACE FOR IT!
I HOPE YOU ACCEPT IT AS A PARTING GIFT!

↓ Nosebleed

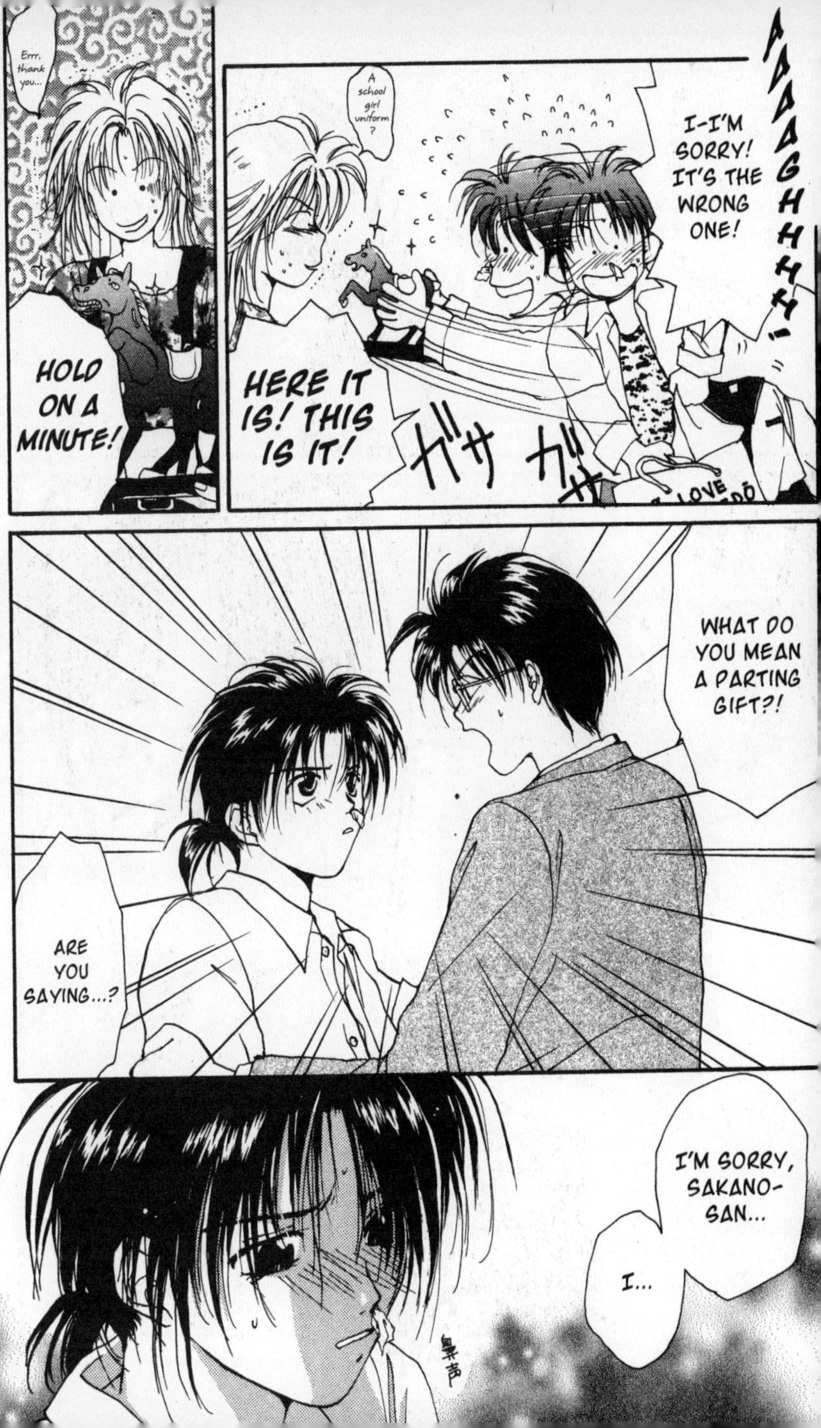
AAAAAGHHHHH!
I-I'M SORRY! IT'S THE WRONG ONE!
A school girl uniform?
HERE IT IS! THIS IS IT!
ガサ ガサ
Errr, thank you...
HOLD ON A MINUTE!
WHAT DO YOU MEAN A PARTING GIFT?!
ARE YOU SAYING...?
I'M SORRY, SAKANO-SAN...
I...
鼻声

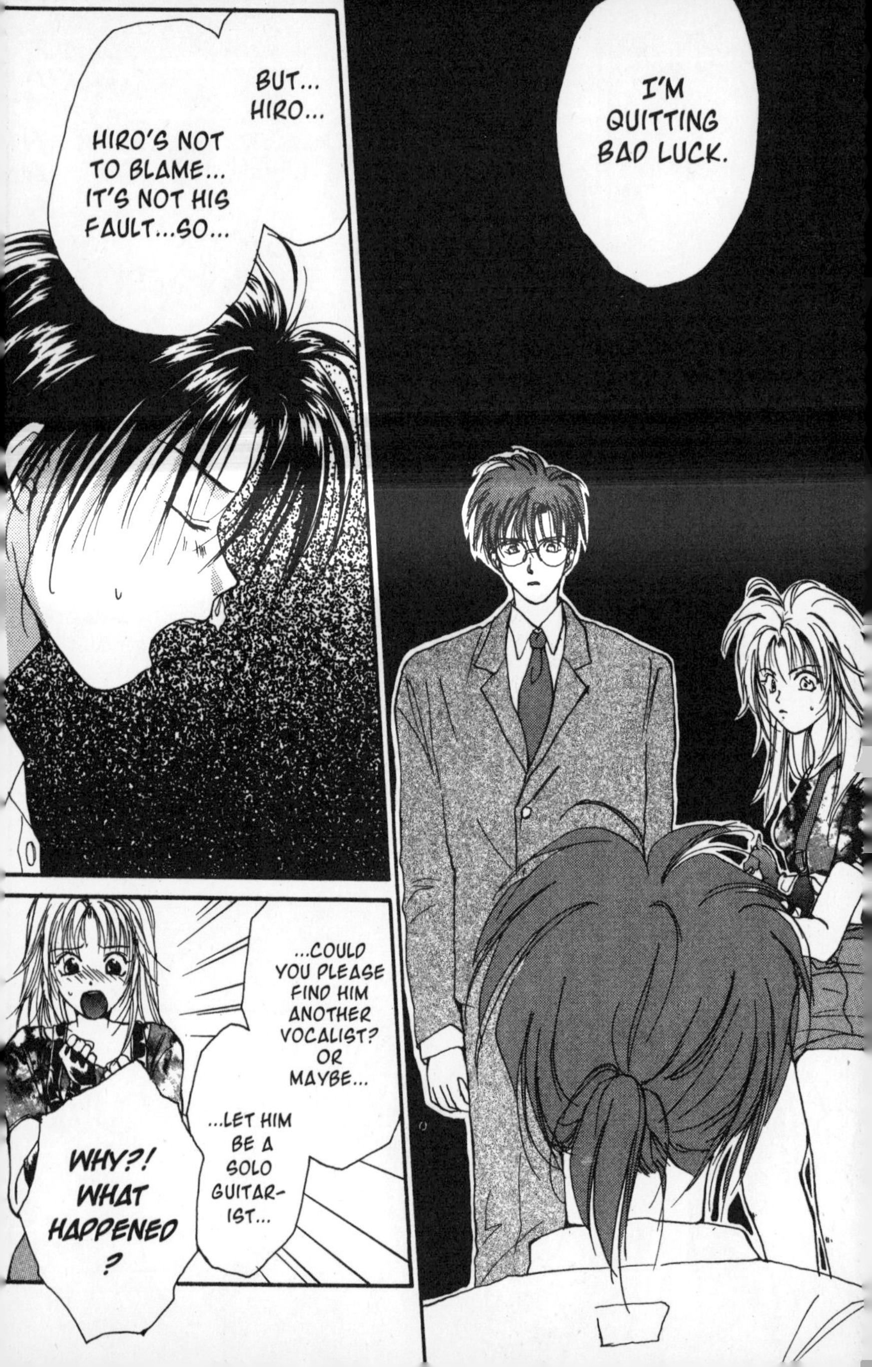
I'M QUITTING BAD LUCK.
BUT... HIRO...
HIRO'S NOT TO BLAME... IT'S NOT HIS FAULT...SO...
...COULD YOU PLEASE FIND HIM ANOTHER VOCALIST? OR MAYBE...
...LET HIM BE A SOLO GUITAR-IST...
WHY?! WHAT HAPPENED?

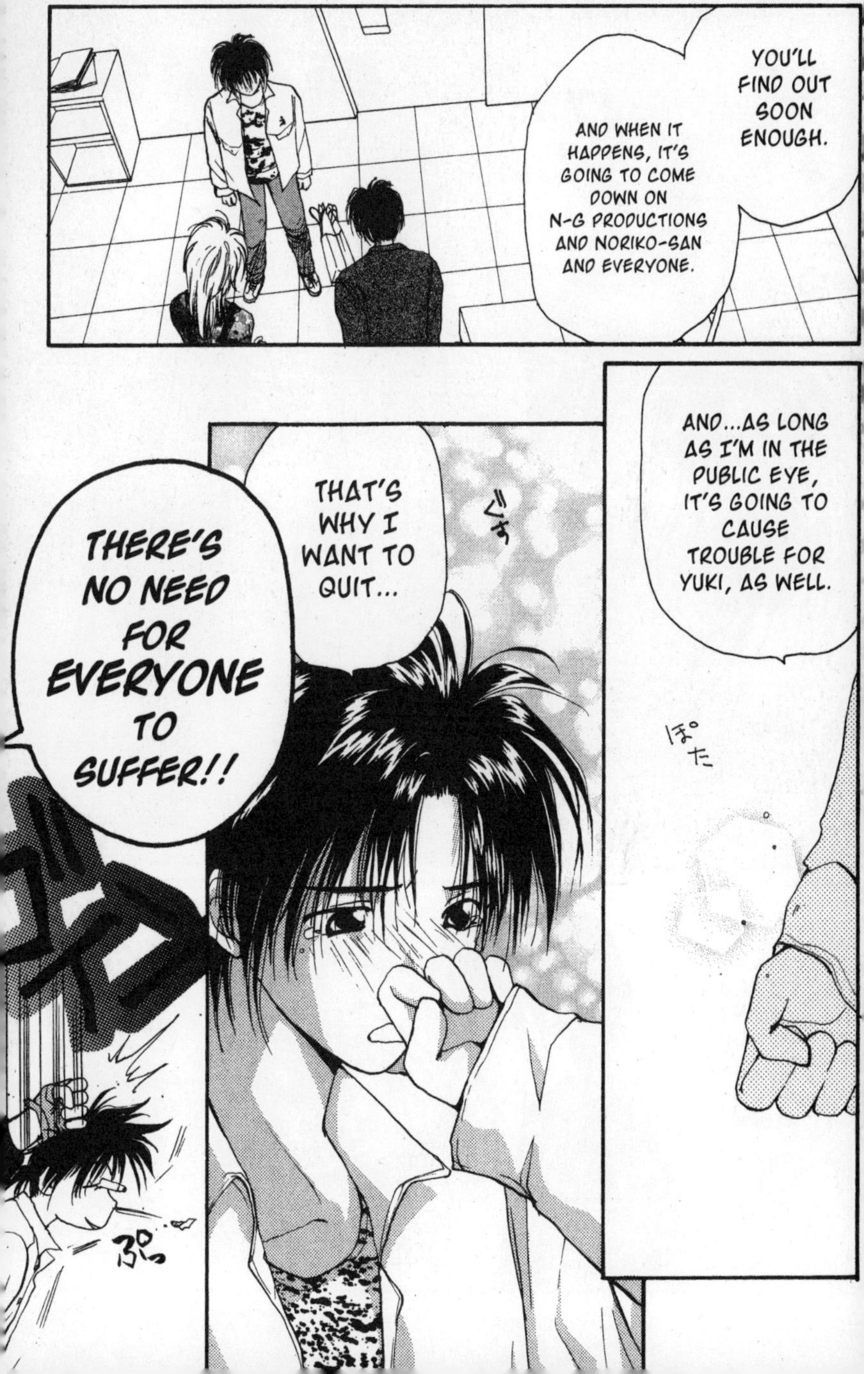
YOU'LL FIND OUT SOON ENOUGH.
AND WHEN IT HAPPENS, IT'S GOING TO COME DOWN ON N-G PRODUCTIONS AND NORIKO-SAN AND EVERYONE.
AND...AS LONG AS I'M IN THE PUBLIC EYE, IT'S GOING TO CAUSE TROUBLE FOR YUKI, AS WELL.
ぽた
ぐす
THAT'S WHY I WANT TO QUIT...
THERE'S NO NEED FOR EVERYONE TO SUFFER!!
ぷっ

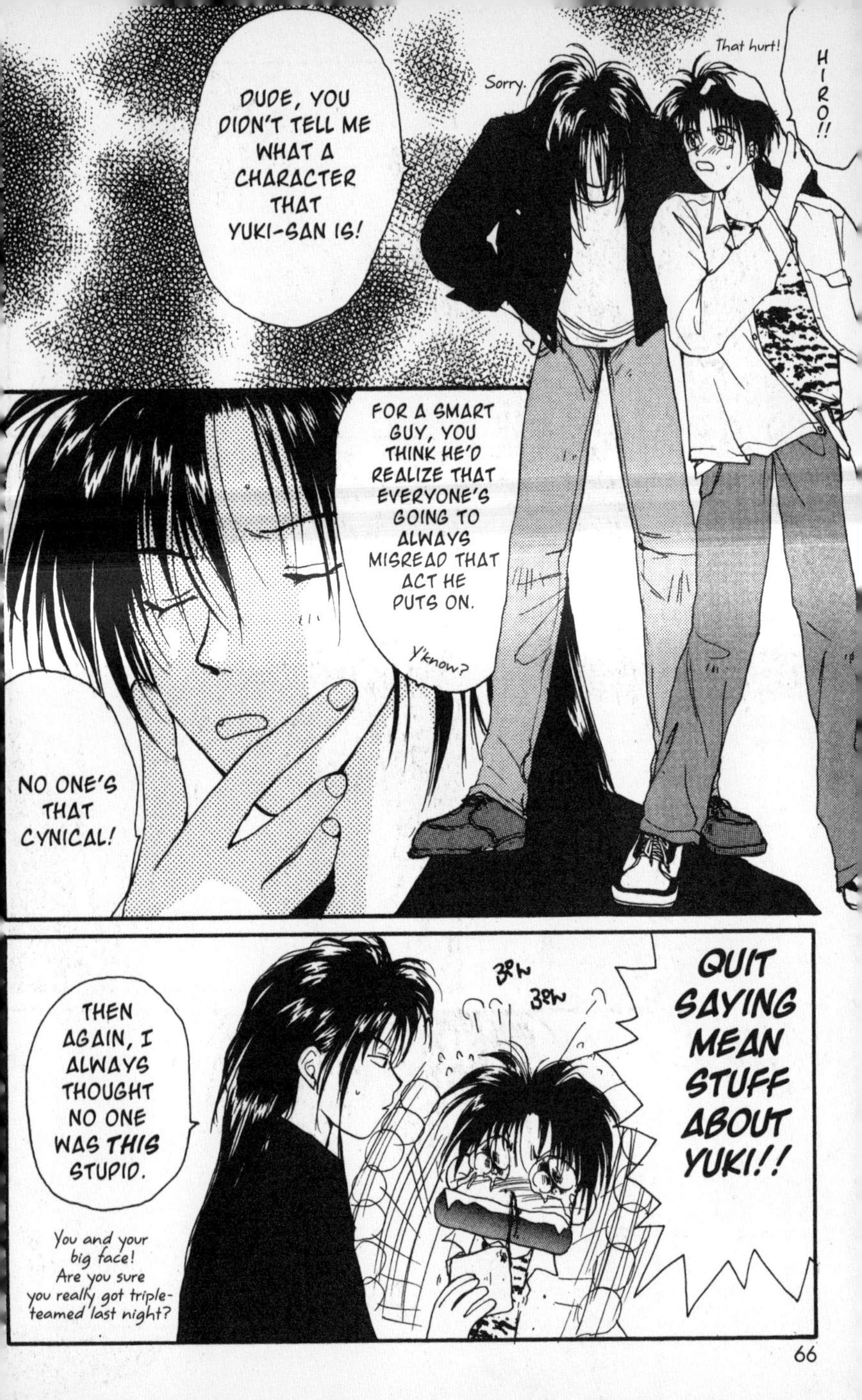
HIRO!!
That hurt!
Sorry.
DUDE, YOU DIDN'T TELL ME WHAT A CHARACTER THAT YUKI-SAN IS!
FOR A SMART GUY, YOU THINK HE'D REALIZE THAT EVERYONE'S GOING TO ALWAYS MISREAD THAT ACT HE PUTS ON.
Y'know?
NO ONE'S THAT CYNICAL!
QUIT SAYING MEAN STUFF ABOUT YUKI!!
THEN AGAIN, I ALWAYS THOUGHT NO ONE WAS THIS STUPID.
You and your big face! Are you sure you really got triple-teamed last night?

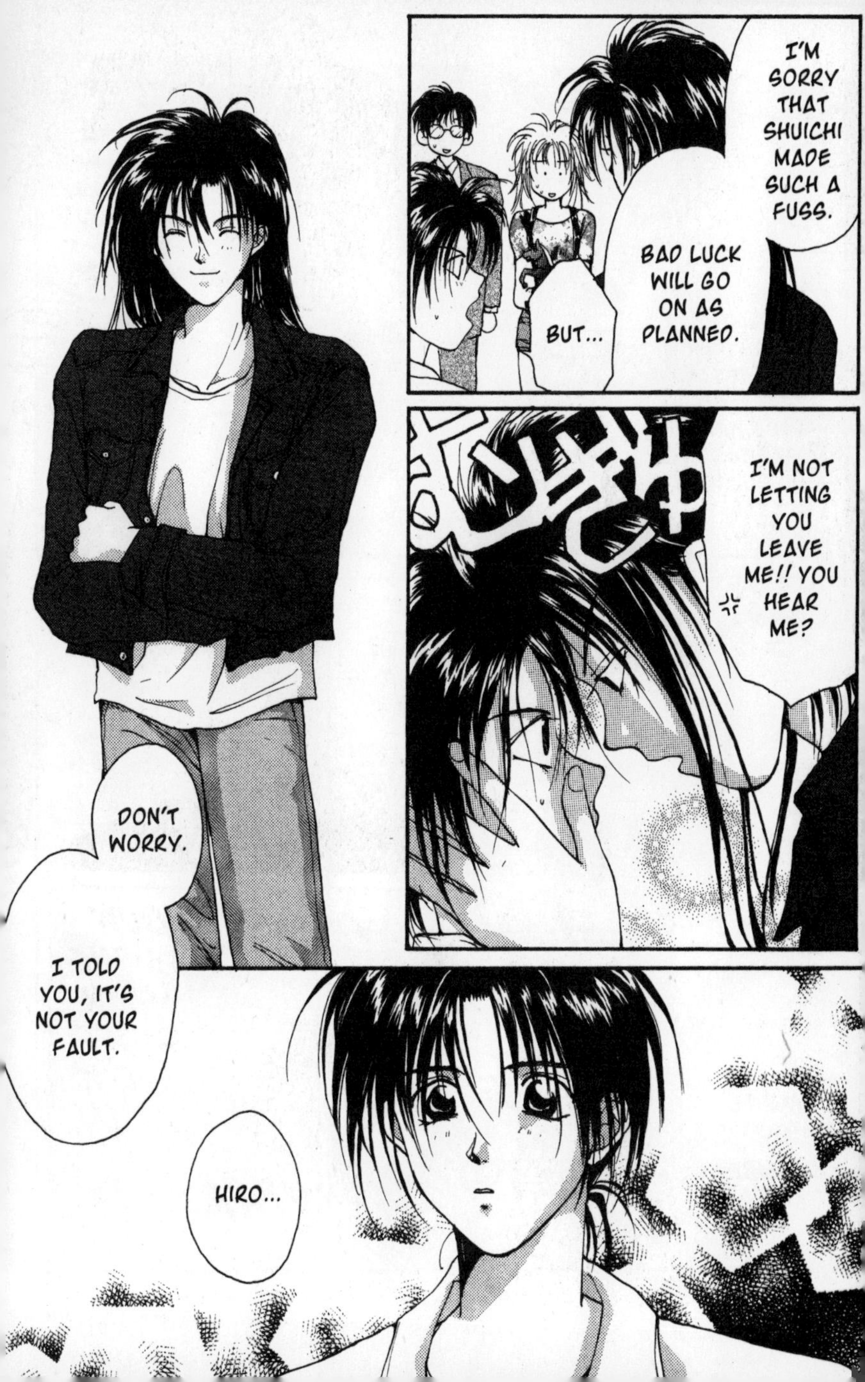
I'M SORRY THAT SHUICHI MADE SUCH A FUSS.
BAD LUCK WILL GO ON AS PLANNED.
BUT...
I'M NOT LETTING YOU LEAVE ME!! YOU HEAR ME?
DON'T WORRY.
I TOLD YOU, IT'S NOT YOUR FAULT.
HIRO...

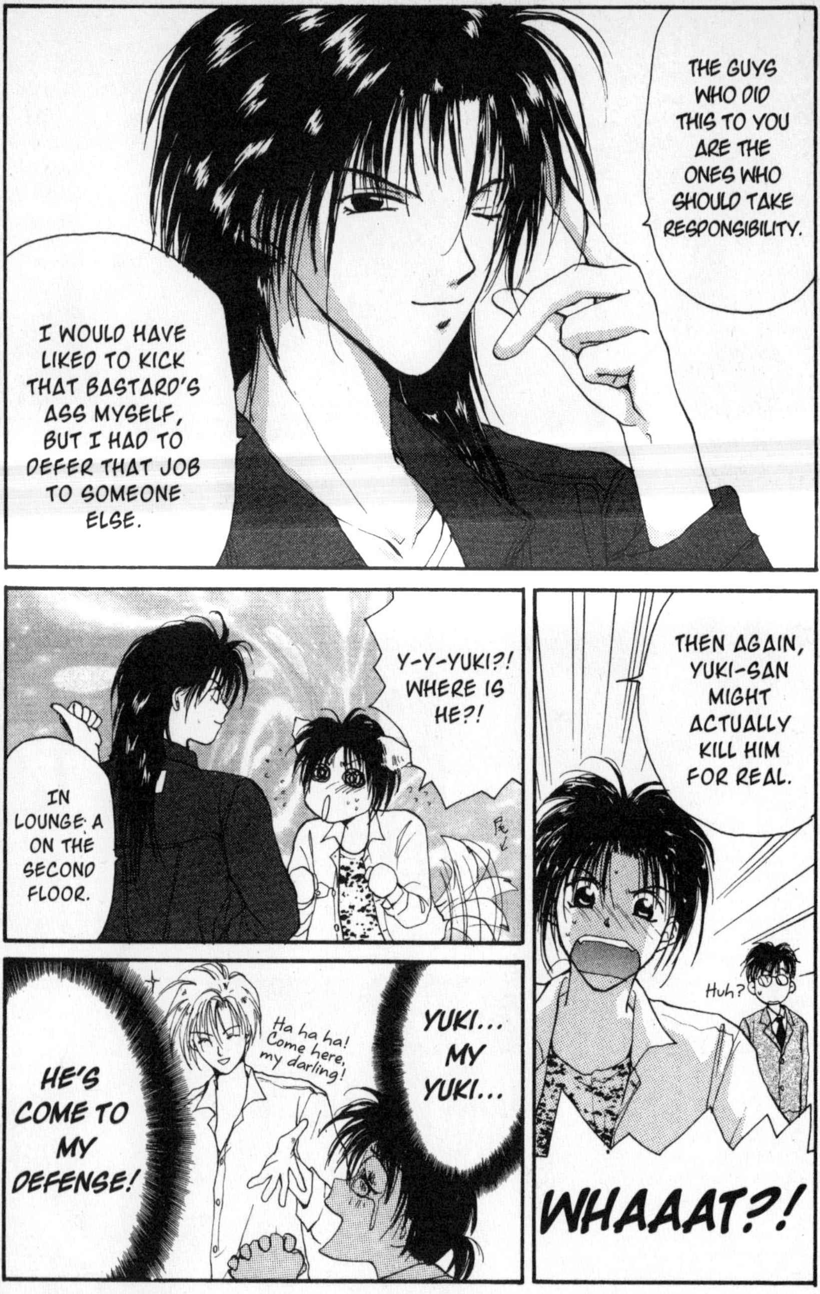
THE GUYS WHO DID THIS TO YOU ARE THE ONES WHO SHOULD TAKE RESPONSIBILITY.
I WOULD HAVE LIKED TO KICK THAT BASTARD'S ASS MYSELF, BUT I HAD TO DEFER THAT JOB TO SOMEONE ELSE.
THEN AGAIN, YUKI-SAN MIGHT ACTUALLY KILL HIM FOR REAL.
Huh?
WHAAAT?!
Y-Y-YUKI?! WHERE IS HE?!
IN LOUNGE A ON THE SECOND FLOOR.
YUKI... MY YUKI...
Ha ha ha! Come here, my darling!
HE'S COME TO MY DEFENSE!

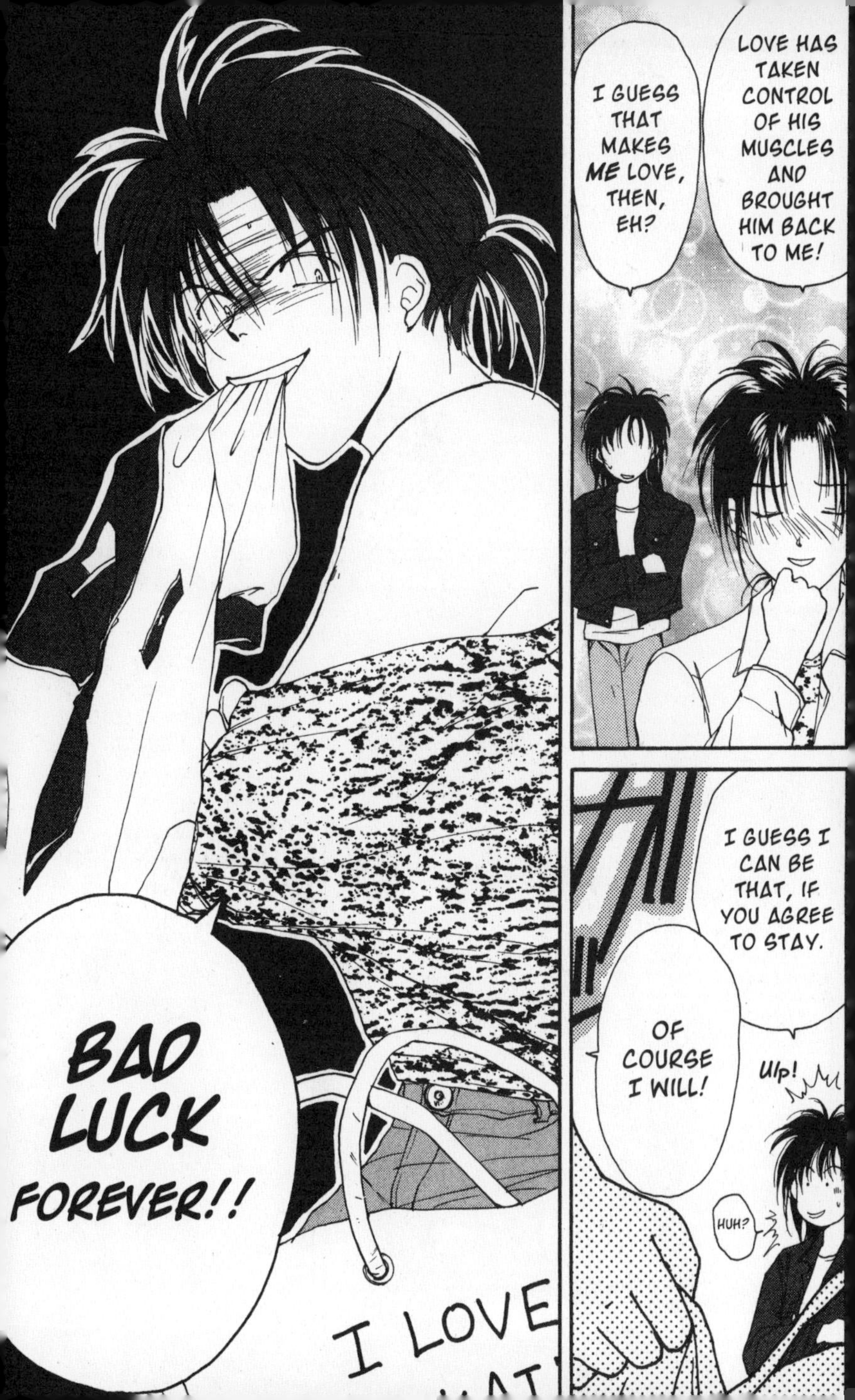
LOVE HAS TAKEN CONTROL OF HIS MUSCLES AND BROUGHT HIM BACK TO ME!
I GUESS THAT MAKES ME LOVE, THEN, EH?
I GUESS I CAN BE THAT, IF YOU AGREE TO STAY.
OF COURSE I WILL!
Ulp!
HUH?
BAD LUCK FOREVER!!
I LOVE

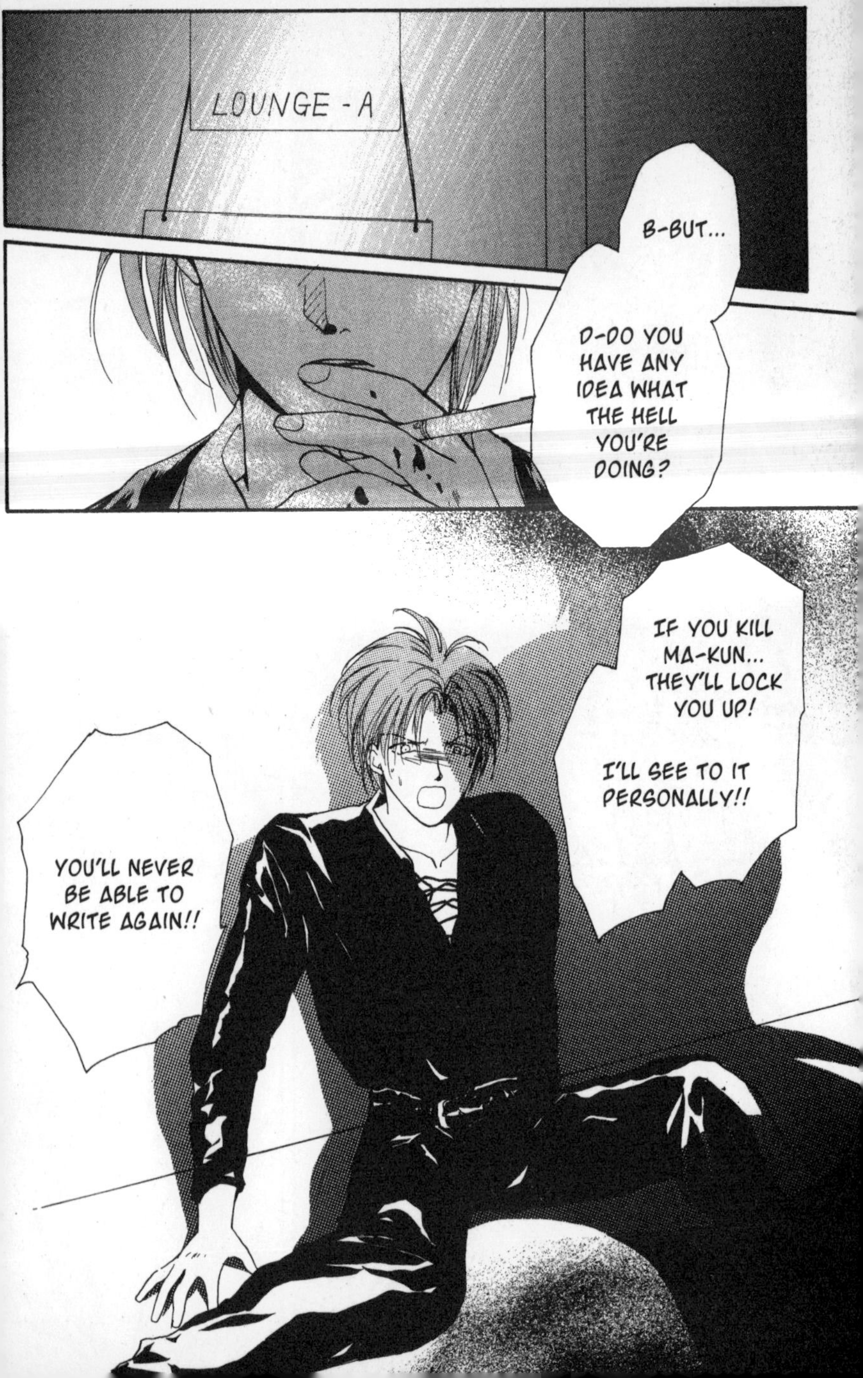
LOUNGE - A
B-BUT...
D-DO YOU HAVE ANY IDEA WHAT THE HELL YOU'RE DOING?
IF YOU KILL MA-KUN... THEY'LL LOCK YOU UP!
I'LL SEE TO IT PERSONALLY!!
YOU'LL NEVER BE ABLE TO WRITE AGAIN!!

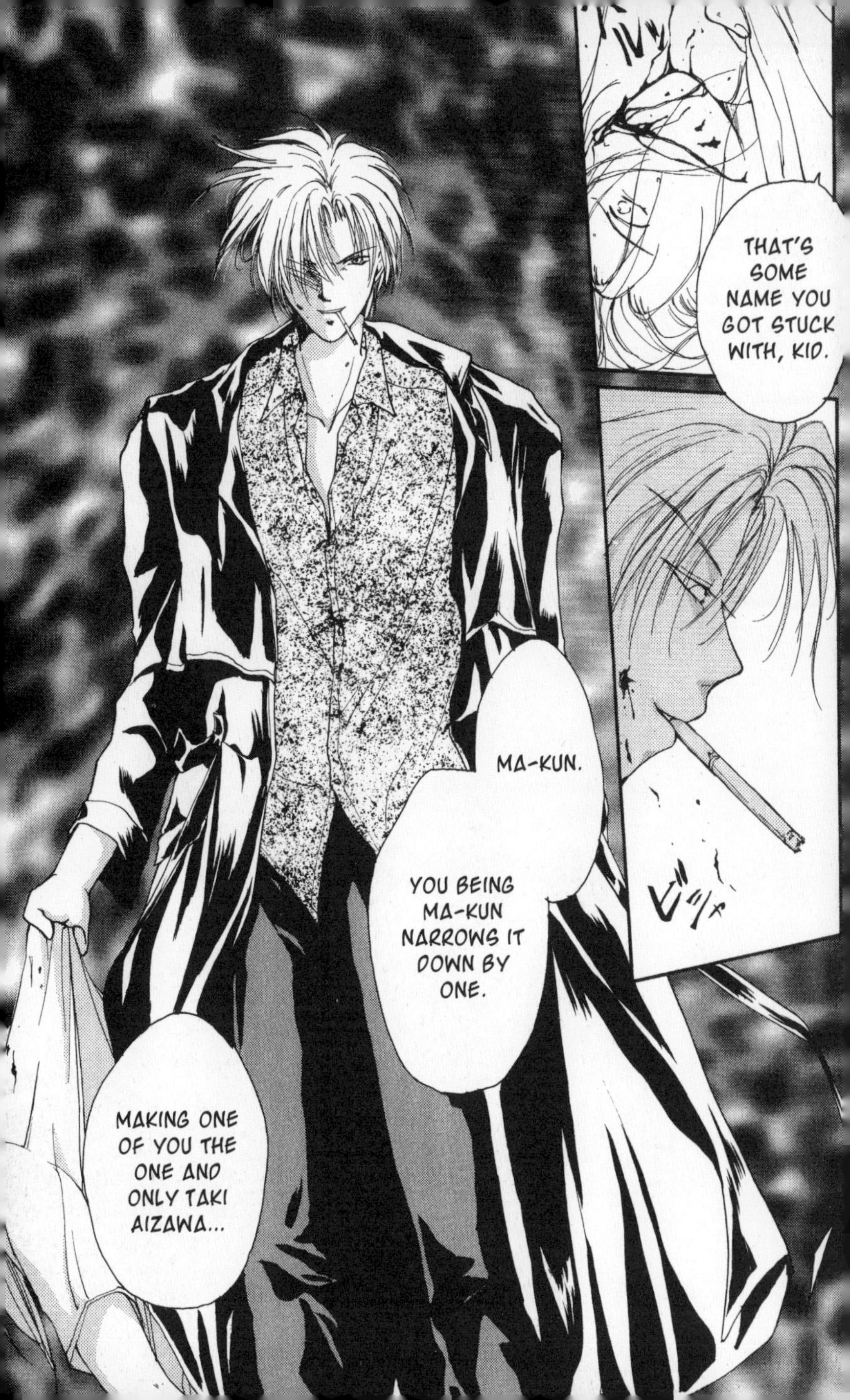
THAT'S SOME NAME YOU GOT STUCK WITH, KID.
MA-KUN.
YOU BEING MA-KUN NARROWS IT DOWN BY ONE.
MAKING ONE OF YOU THE ONE AND ONLY TAKI AIZAWA...

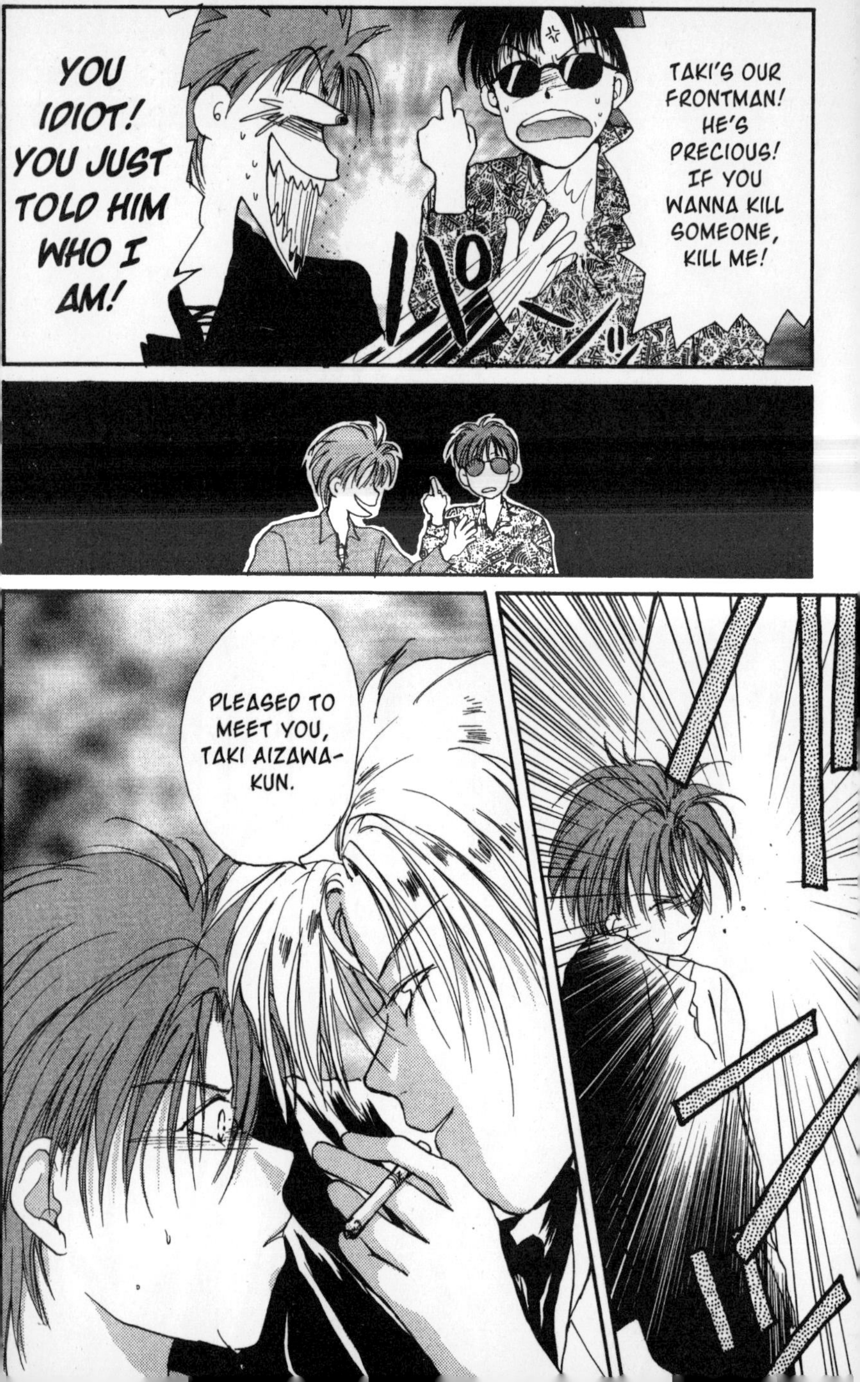
TAKI'S OUR FRONTMAN! HE'S PRECIOUS! IF YOU WANNA KILL SOMEONE, KILL ME!
YOU IDIOT! YOU JUST TOLD HIM WHO I AM!
PLEASED TO MEET YOU, TAKI AIZAWA-KUN.

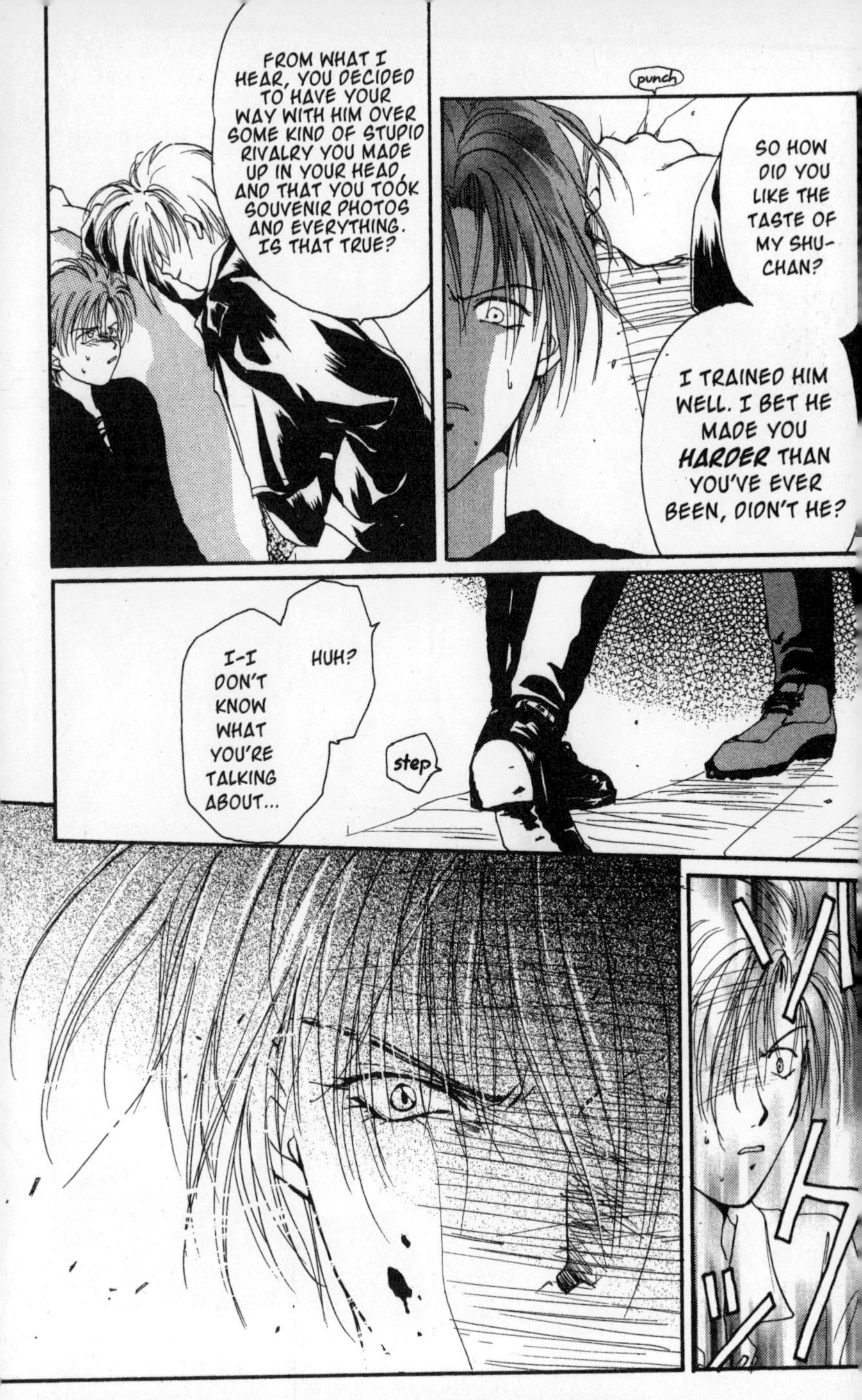
punch
SO HOW DID YOU LIKE THE TASTE OF MY SHU-CHAN?
I TRAINED HIM WELL. I BET HE MADE YOU HARDER THAN YOU'VE EVER BEEN, DIDN'T HE?
FROM WHAT I HEAR, YOU DECIDED TO HAVE YOUR WAY WITH HIM OVER SOME KIND OF STUPID RIVALRY YOU MADE UP IN YOUR HEAD, AND THAT YOU TOOK SOUVENIR PHOTOS AND EVERYTHING. IS THAT TRUE?
HUH?
I-I DON'T KNOW WHAT YOU'RE TALKING ABOUT...
step

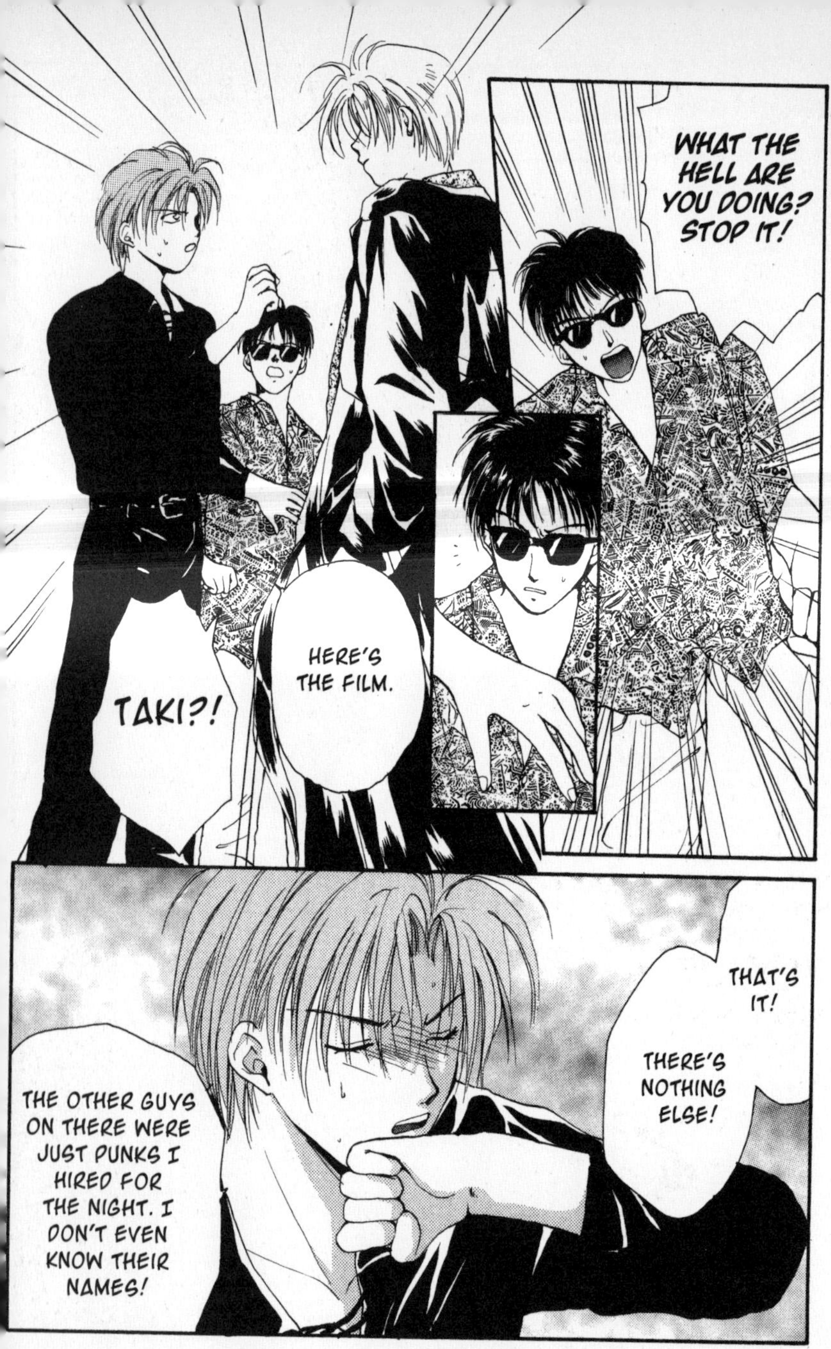
WHAT THE HELL ARE YOU DOING? STOP IT!
HERE'S THE FILM.
TAKI?!
THAT'S IT!
THERE'S NOTHING ELSE!
THE OTHER GUYS ON THERE WERE JUST PUNKS I HIRED FOR THE NIGHT. I DON'T EVEN KNOW THEIR NAMES!

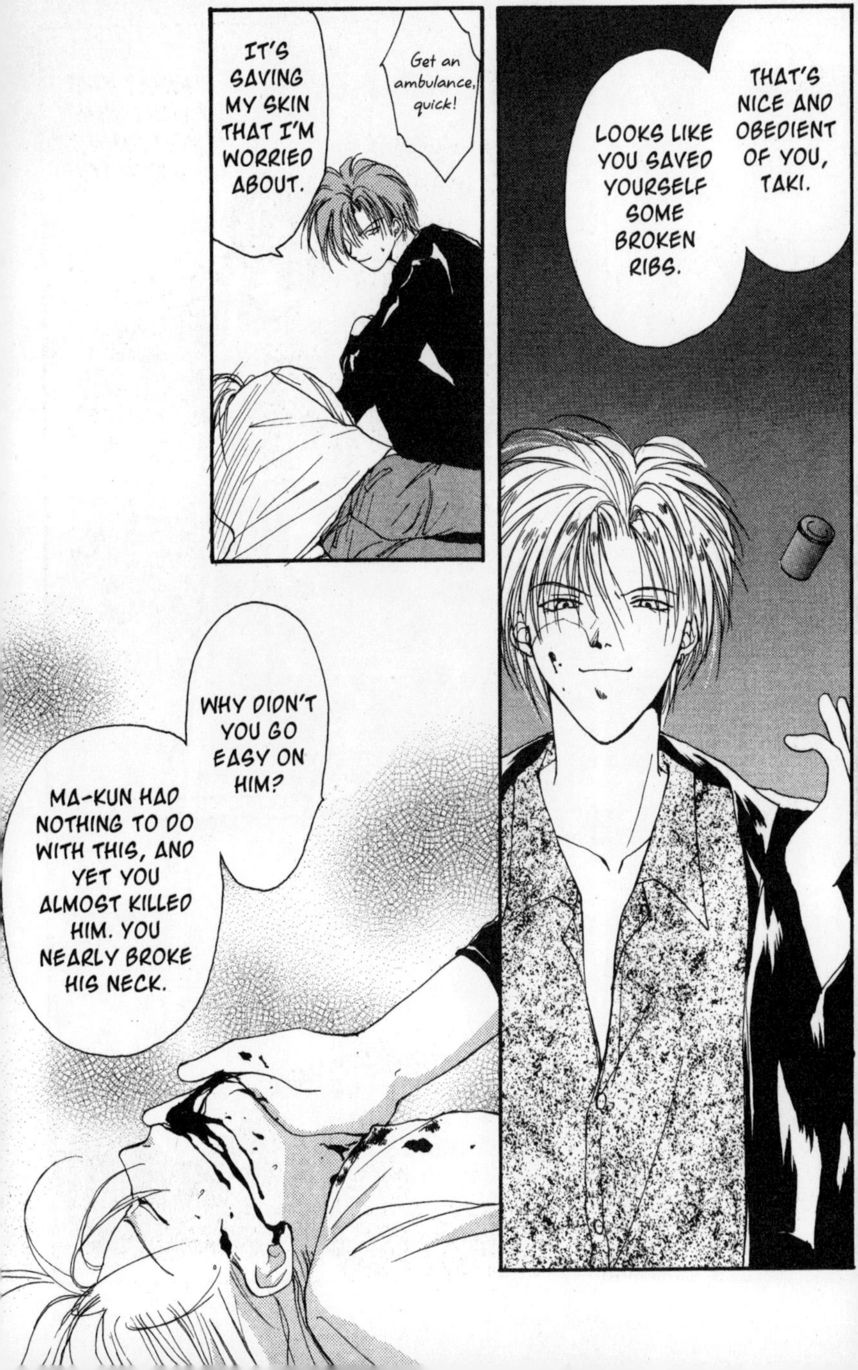
THAT'S NICE AND OBEDIENT OF YOU, TAKI.
LOOKS LIKE YOU SAVED YOURSELF SOME BROKEN RIBS.
Get an ambulance, quick!
IT'S SAVING MY SKIN THAT I'M WORRIED ABOUT.
WHY DIDN'T YOU GO EASY ON HIM?
MA-KUN HAD NOTHING TO DO WITH THIS, AND YET YOU ALMOST KILLED HIM. YOU NEARLY BROKE HIS NECK.

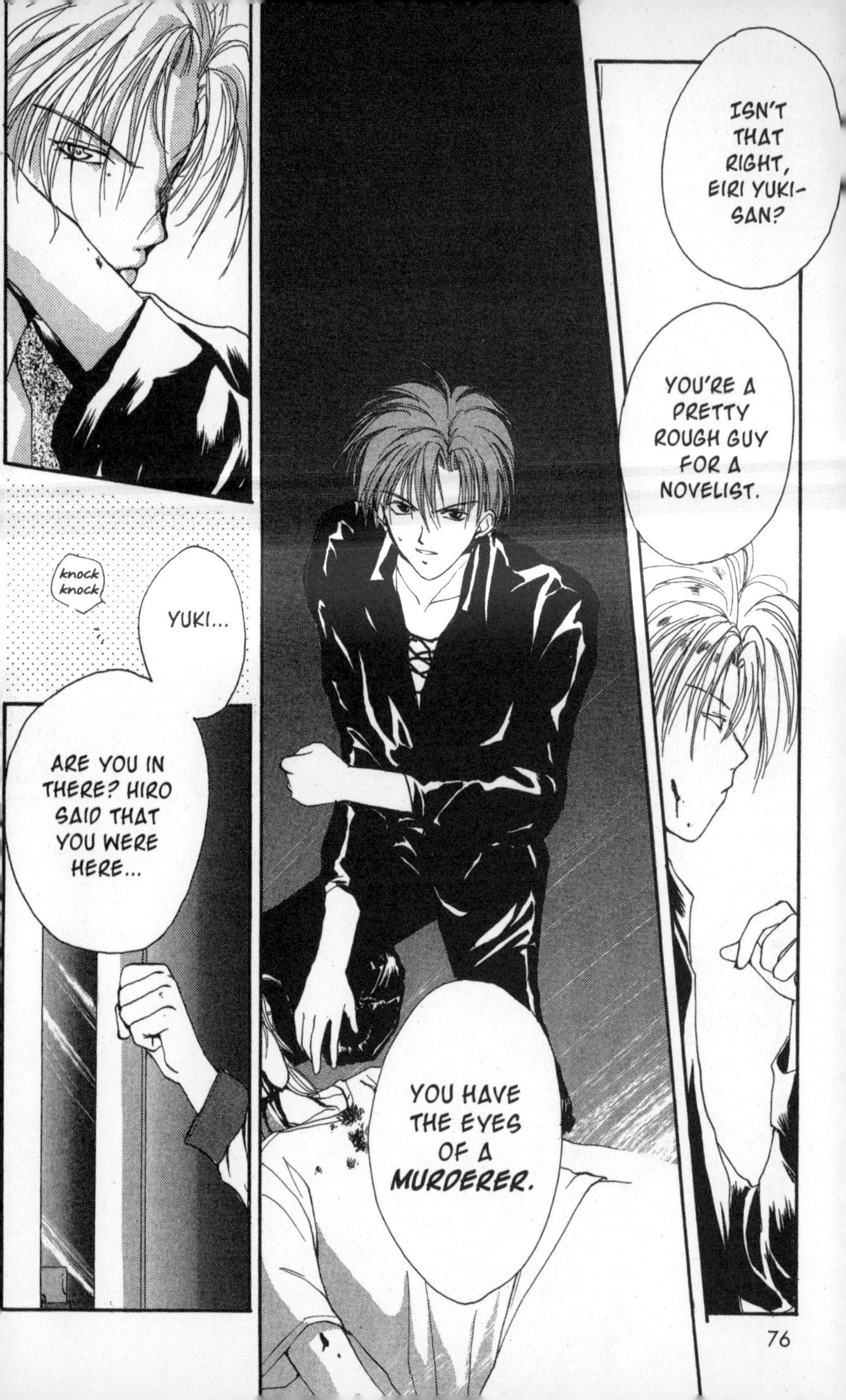
ISN'T THAT RIGHT, EIRI YUKI-SAN?
YOU'RE A PRETTY ROUGH GUY FOR A NOVELIST.
YOU HAVE THE EYES OF A MURDERER.
knock knock
YUKI...
ARE YOU IN THERE? HIRO SAID THAT YOU WERE HERE...

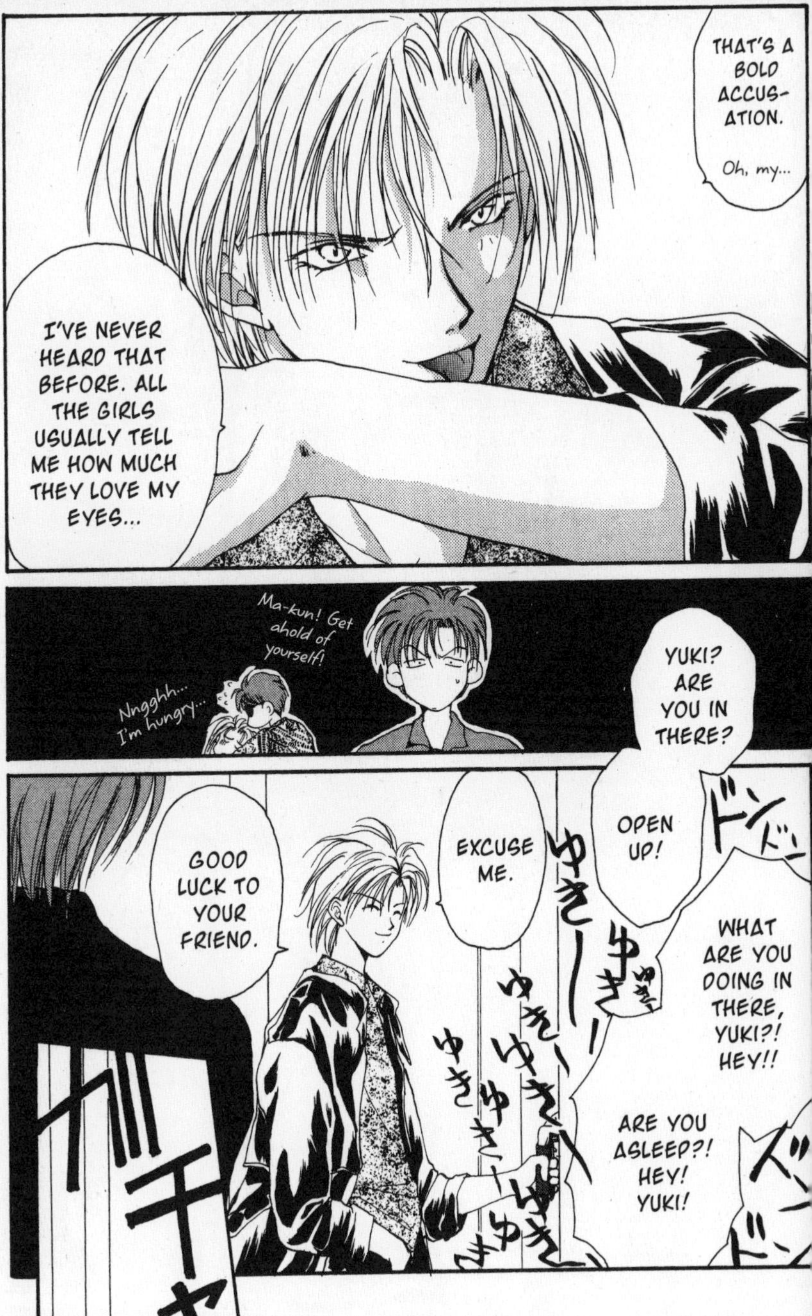
THAT'S A BOLD ACCUSATION.
Oh, my...
I'VE NEVER HEARD THAT BEFORE. ALL THE GIRLS USUALLY TELL ME HOW MUCH THEY LOVE MY EYES...
YUKI? ARE YOU IN THERE?
Ma-kun! Get ahold of yourself!
Nngghh... I'm hungry...
ドンドン
OPEN UP!
WHAT ARE YOU DOING IN THERE, YUKI?! HEY!!
EXCUSE ME.
ARE YOU ASLEEP?! HEY! YUKI!
GOOD LUCK TO YOUR FRIEND.
ガチャ

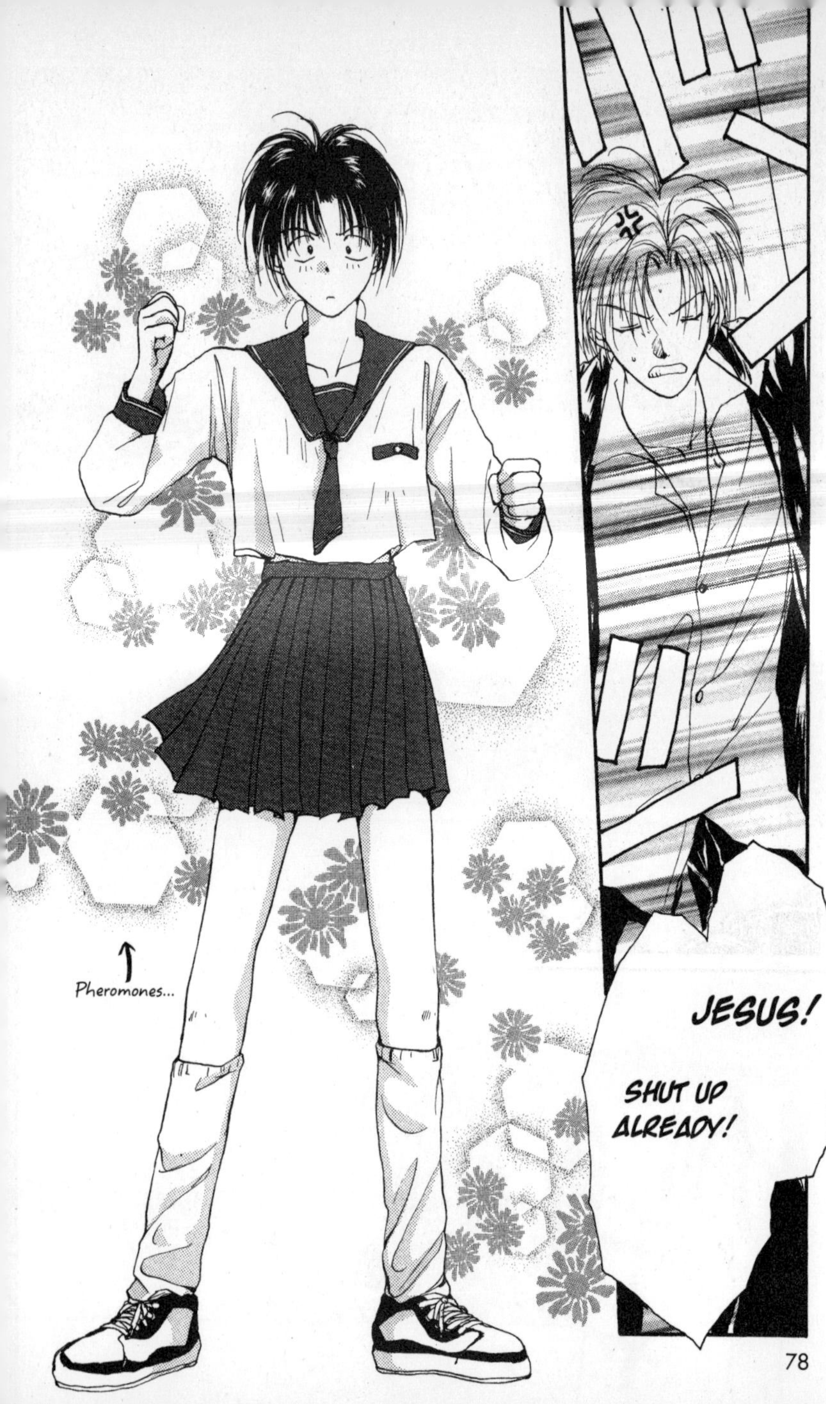
JESUS!
SHUT UP ALREADY!
Pheromones...

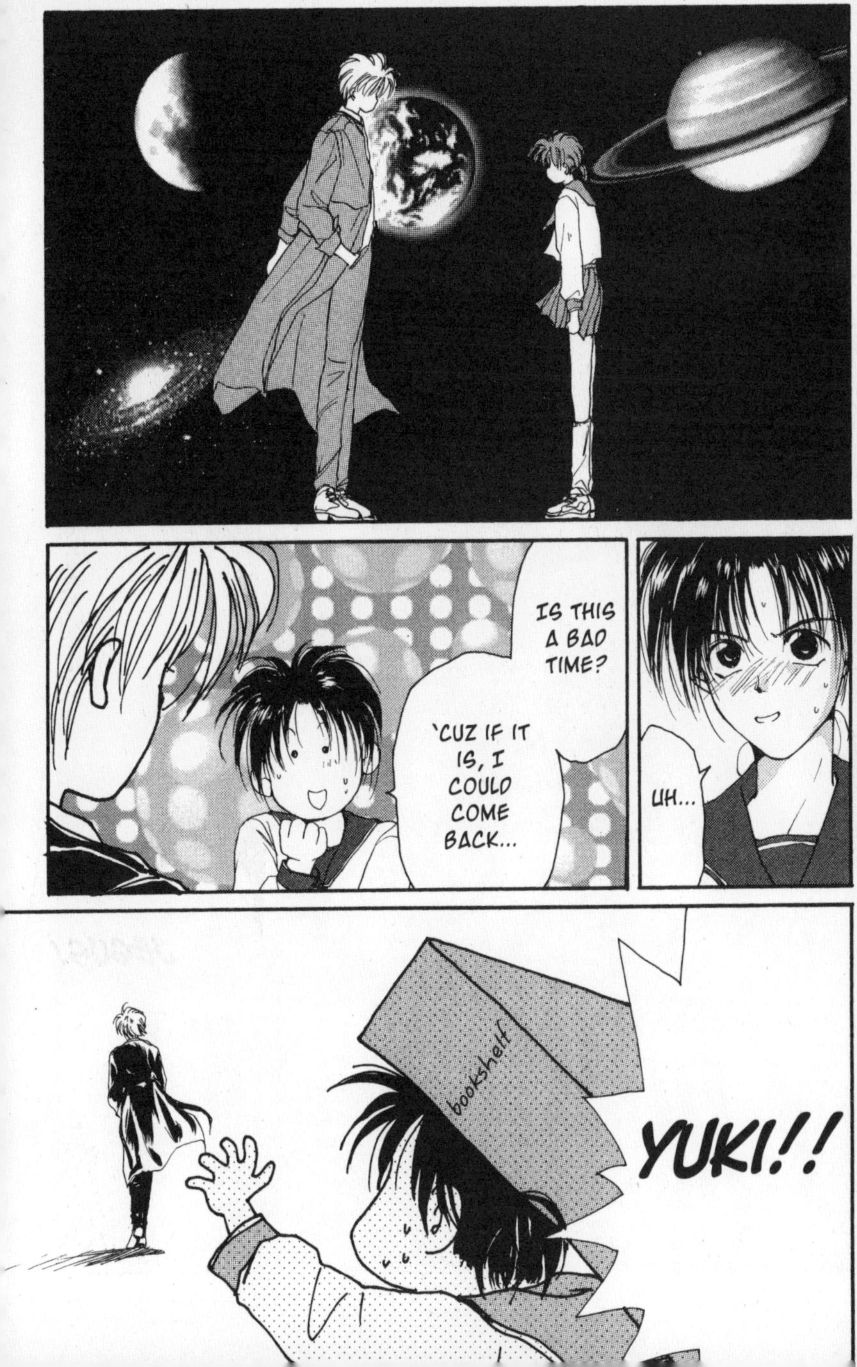
UH...
IS THIS A BAD TIME?
`CUZ IF IT IS, I COULD COME BACK...
YUKI!!
bookshelf

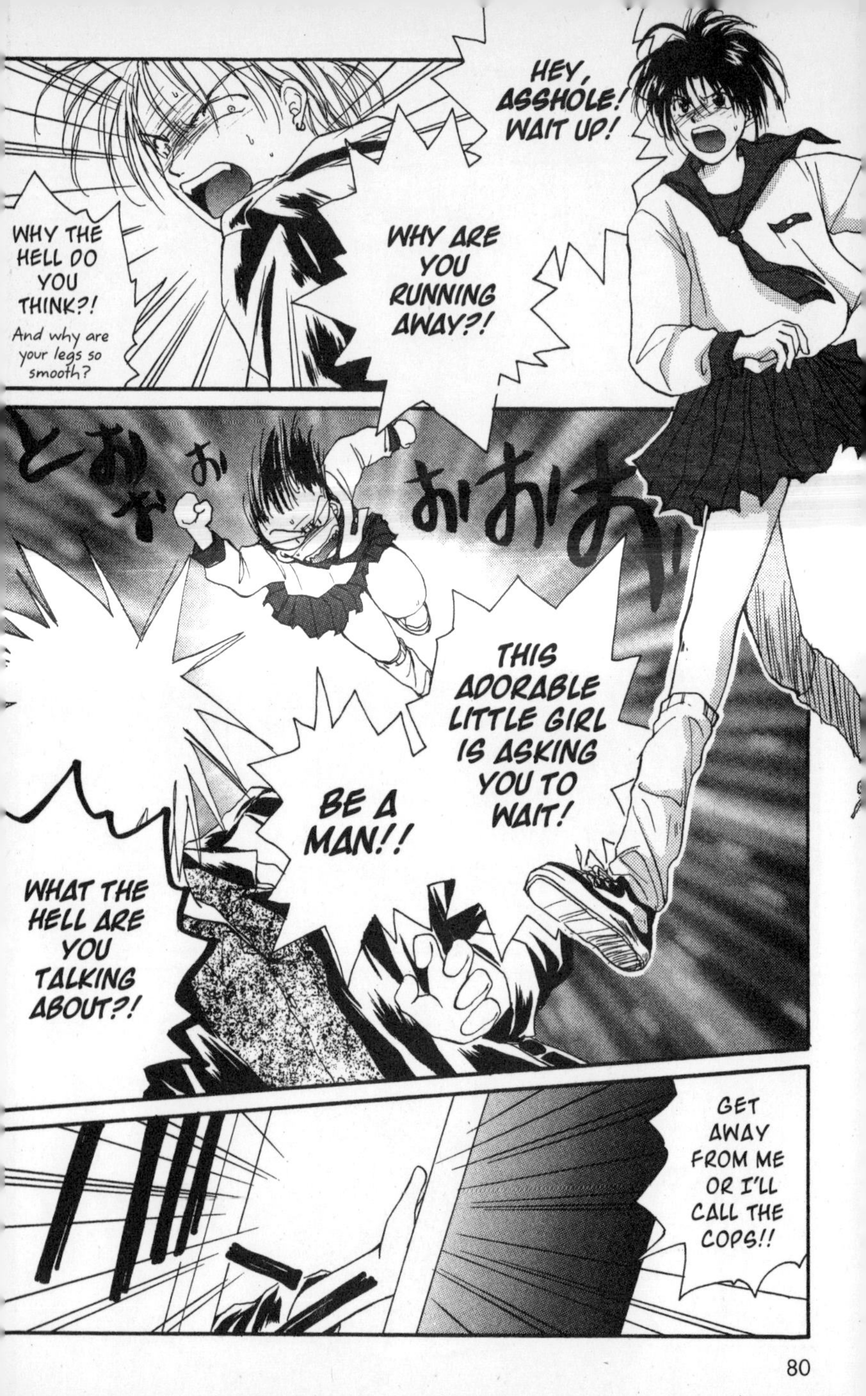
HEY, ASSHOLE! WAIT UP!
WHY ARE YOU RUNNING AWAY?!
WHY THE HELL DO YOU THINK?!
And why are your legs so smooth?
とおおおおお
THIS ADORABLE LITTLE GIRL IS ASKING YOU TO WAIT!
BE A MAN!!
WHAT THE HELL ARE YOU TALKING ABOUT?!
GET AWAY FROM ME OR I'LL CALL THE COPS!!

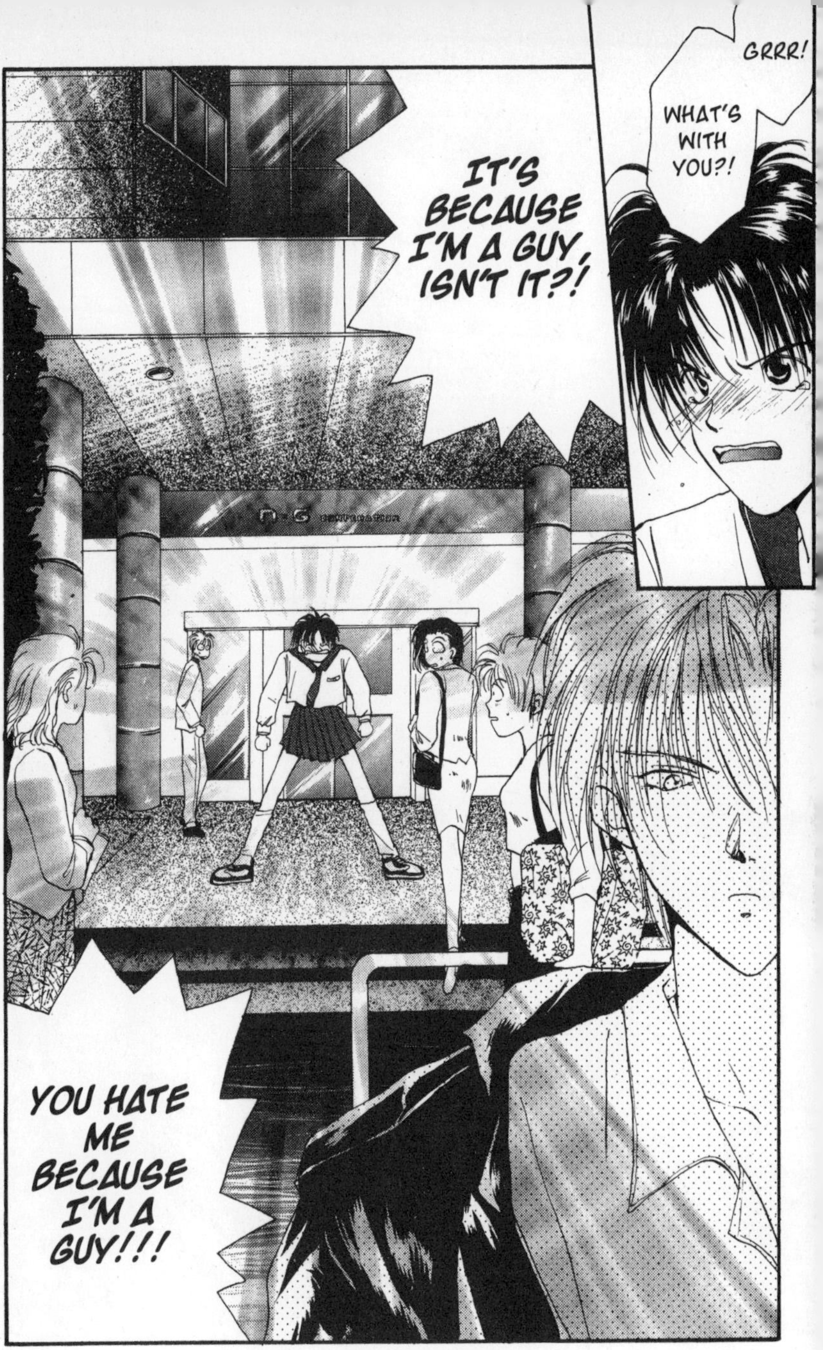
GRRR!
WHAT'S WITH YOU?!
IT'S BECAUSE I'M A GUY, ISN'T IT?!
YOU HATE ME BECAUSE I'M A GUY!!!

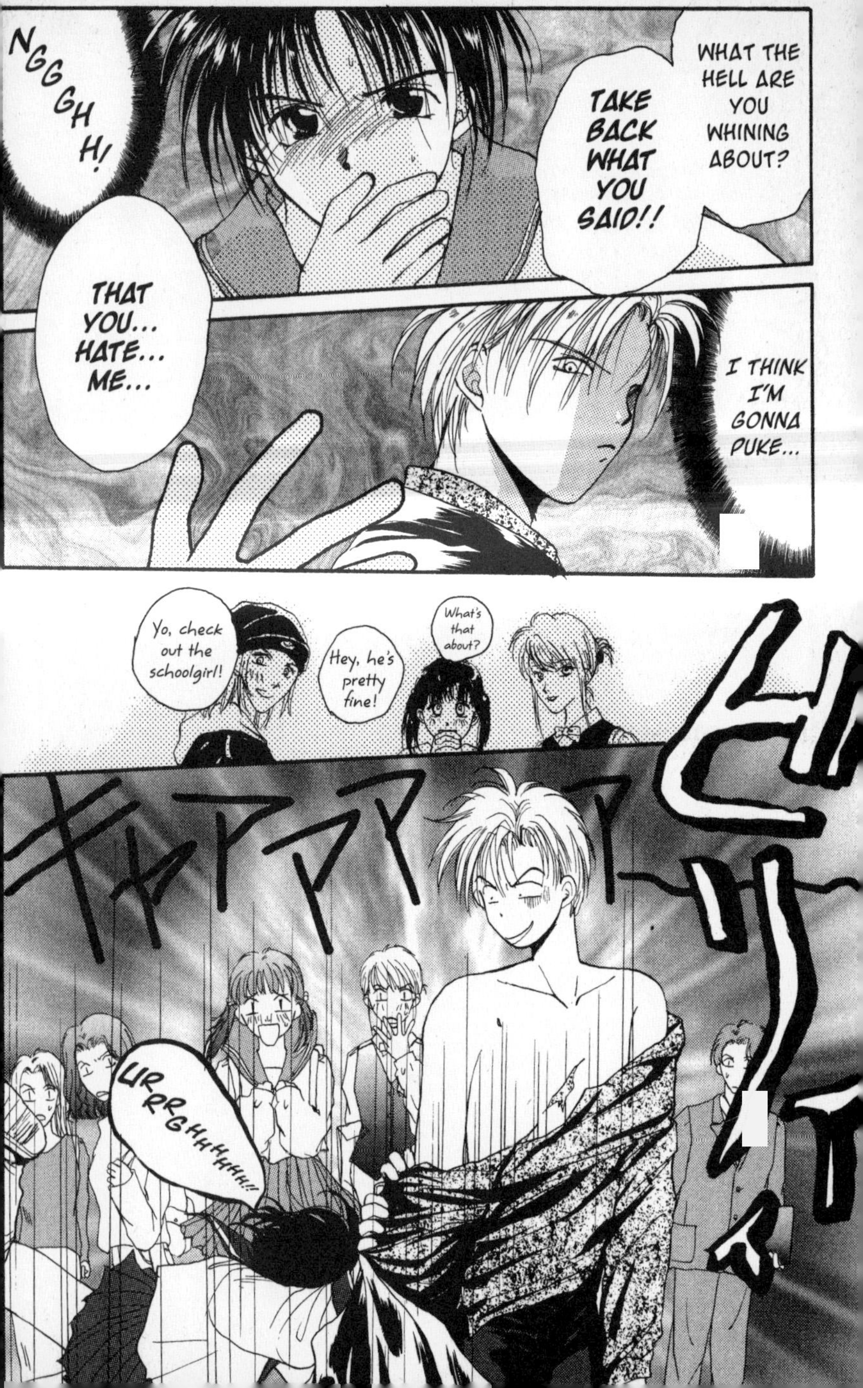
WHAT THE HELL ARE YOU WHINING ABOUT?
TAKE BACK WHAT YOU SAID!!
NGGGHH!
THAT YOU... HATE... ME...
I THINK I'M GONNA PUKE...
What's that about?
Hey, he's pretty fine!
Yo, check out the schoolgirl!
キャアアアー
URRRGHHHHHH!!

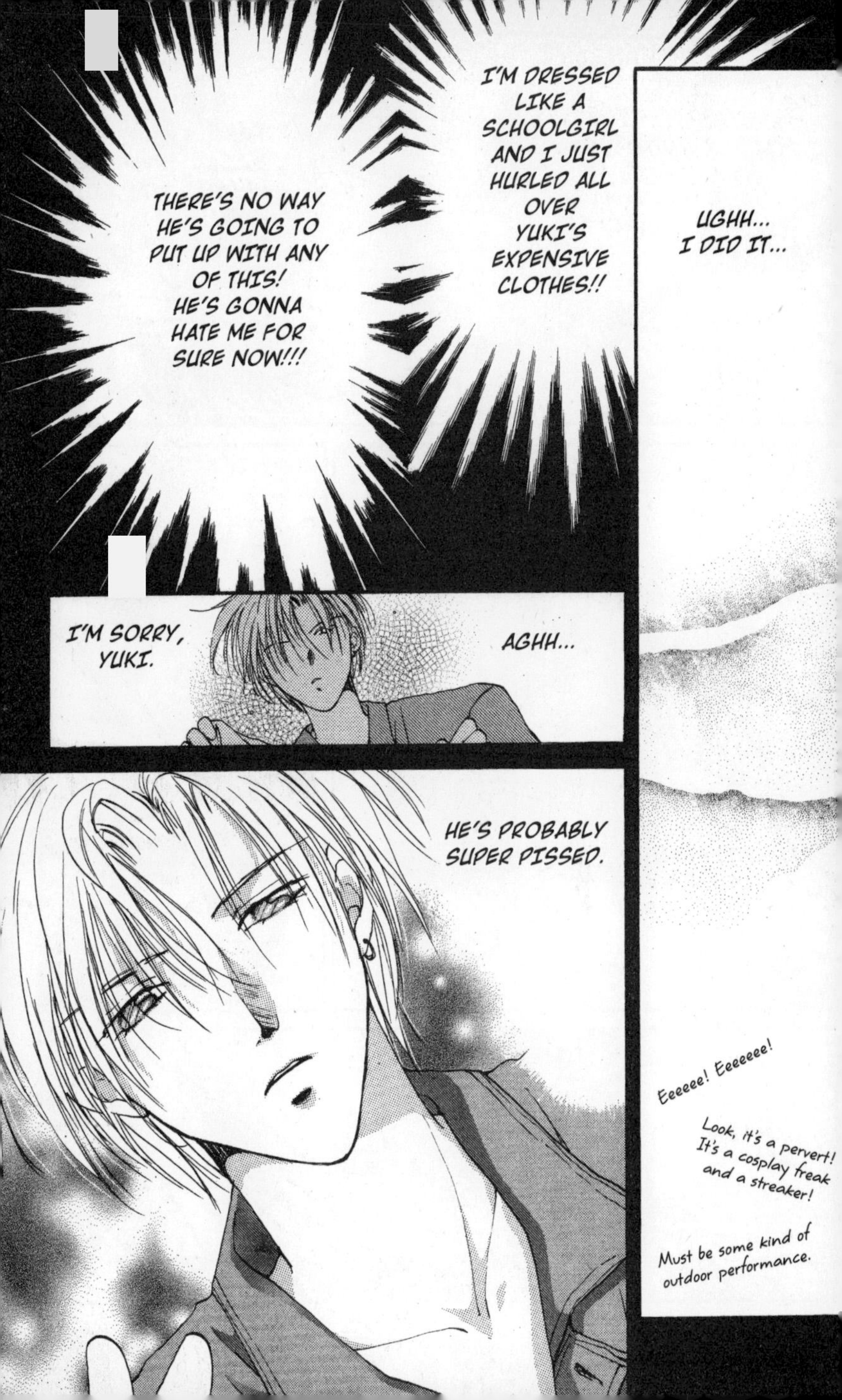
UGHH... I DID IT...
Eeeeee! Eeeeee!
Look, it's a pervert! It's a cosplay freak and a streaker!
Must be some kind of outdoor performance.
I'M DRESSED LIKE A SCHOOLGIRL AND I JUST HURLED ALL OVER YUKI'S EXPENSIVE CLOTHES!!
THERE'S NO WAY HE'S GOING TO PUT UP WITH ANY OF THIS! HE'S GONNA HATE ME FOR SURE NOW!!!
AGHH...
I'M SORRY, YUKI.
HE'S PROBABLY SUPER PISSED.

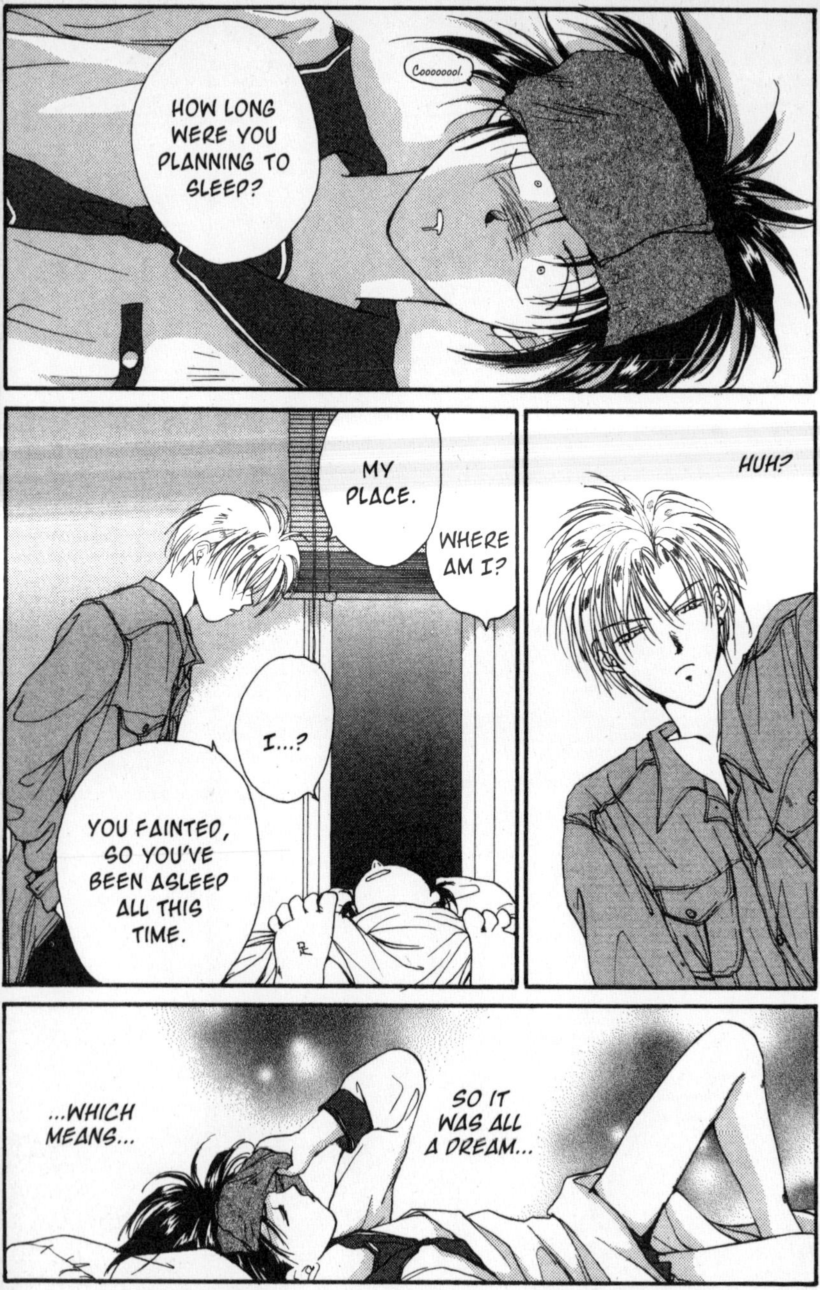
Cooooool.
HOW LONG WERE YOU PLANNING TO SLEEP?
HUH?
MY PLACE.
WHERE AM I?
I...?
YOU FAINTED, SO YOU'VE BEEN ASLEEP ALL THIS TIME.
SO IT WAS ALL A DREAM...
...WHICH MEANS...

Hey, I can see your panties!

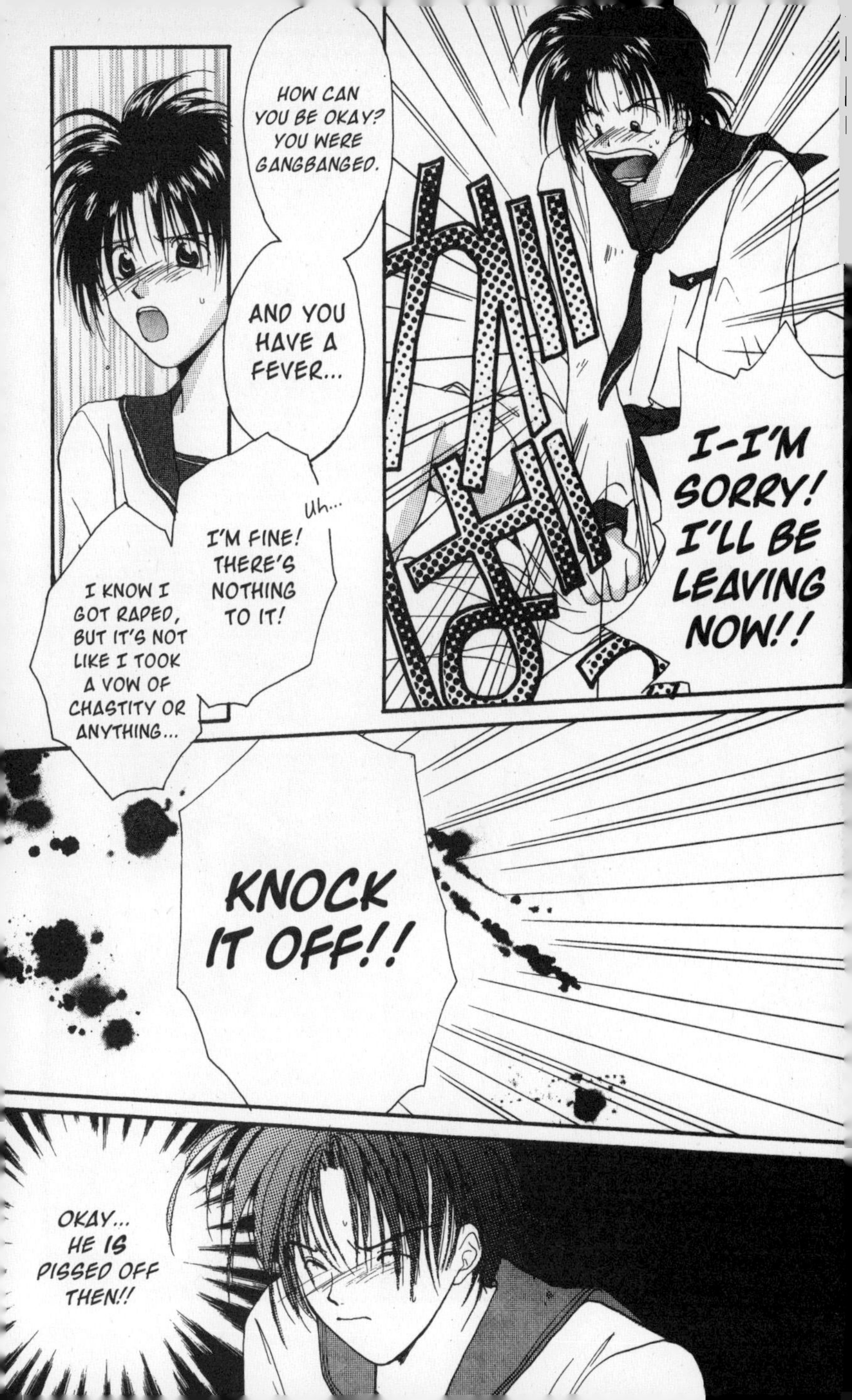
I-I'M SORRY! I'LL BE LEAVING NOW!!
HOW CAN YOU BE OKAY? YOU WERE GANGBANGED.
AND YOU HAVE A FEVER...
Uh...
I'M FINE! THERE'S NOTHING TO IT!
I KNOW I GOT RAPED, BUT IT'S NOT LIKE I TOOK A VOW OF CHASTITY OR ANYTHING...
KNOCK IT OFF!!
OKAY... HE IS PISSED OFF THEN!!

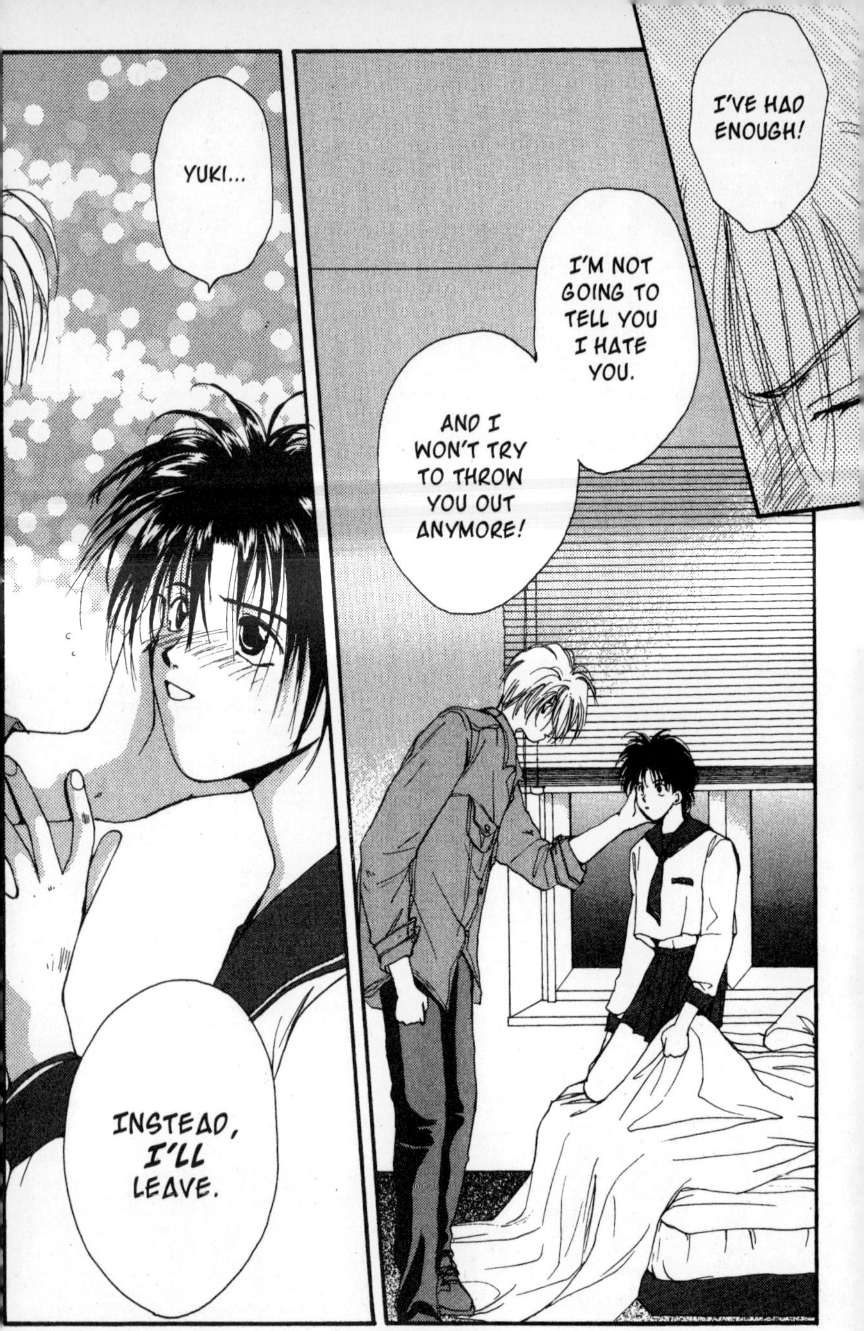
I'VE HAD ENOUGH!
I'M NOT GOING TO TELL YOU I HATE YOU.
AND I WON'T TRY TO THROW YOU OUT ANYMORE!
YUKI...
INSTEAD, I'LL LEAVE.

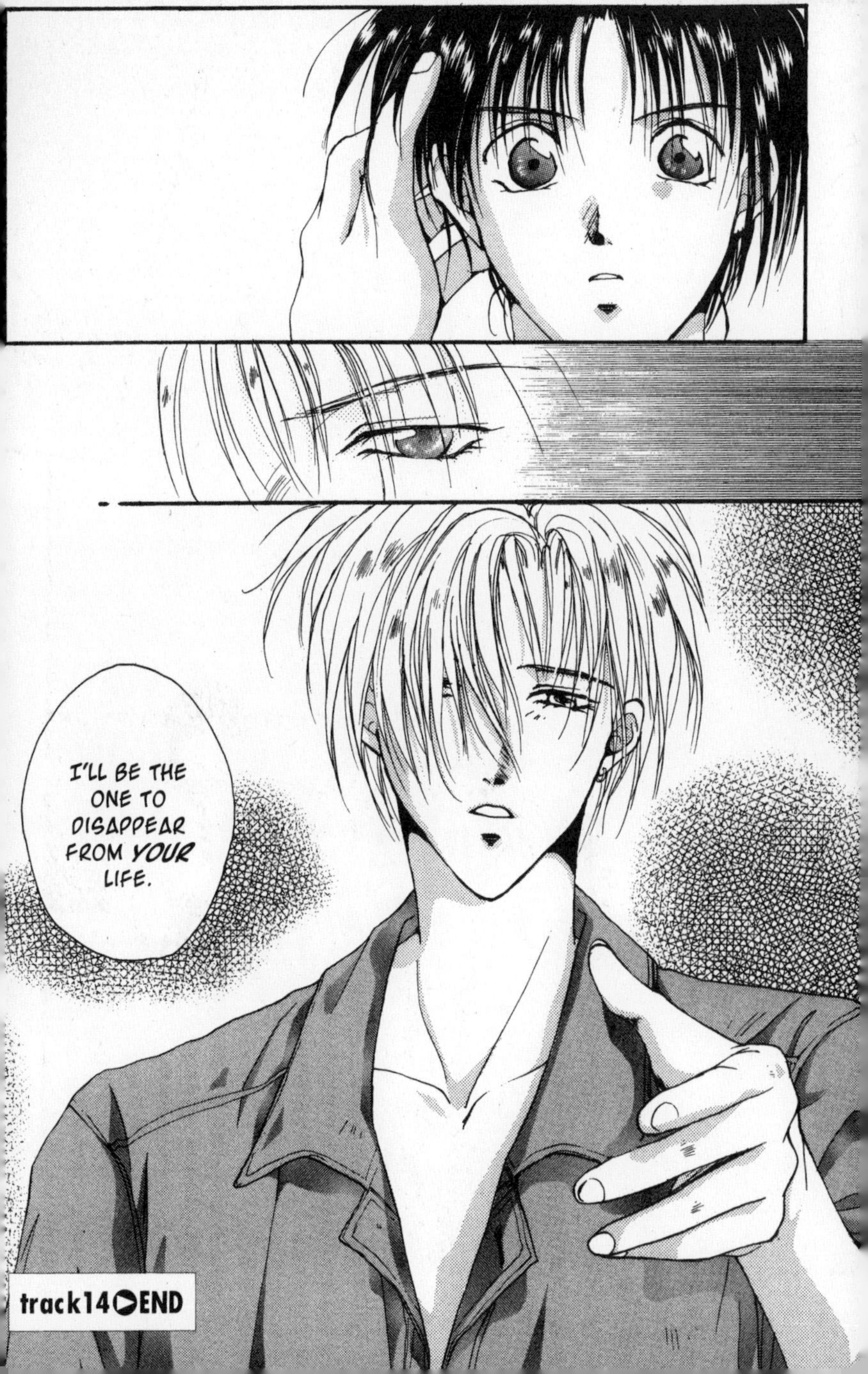
I'LL BE THE ONE TO DISAPPEAR FROM YOUR LIFE.
track14 END

TOHMA
SEGUCHI

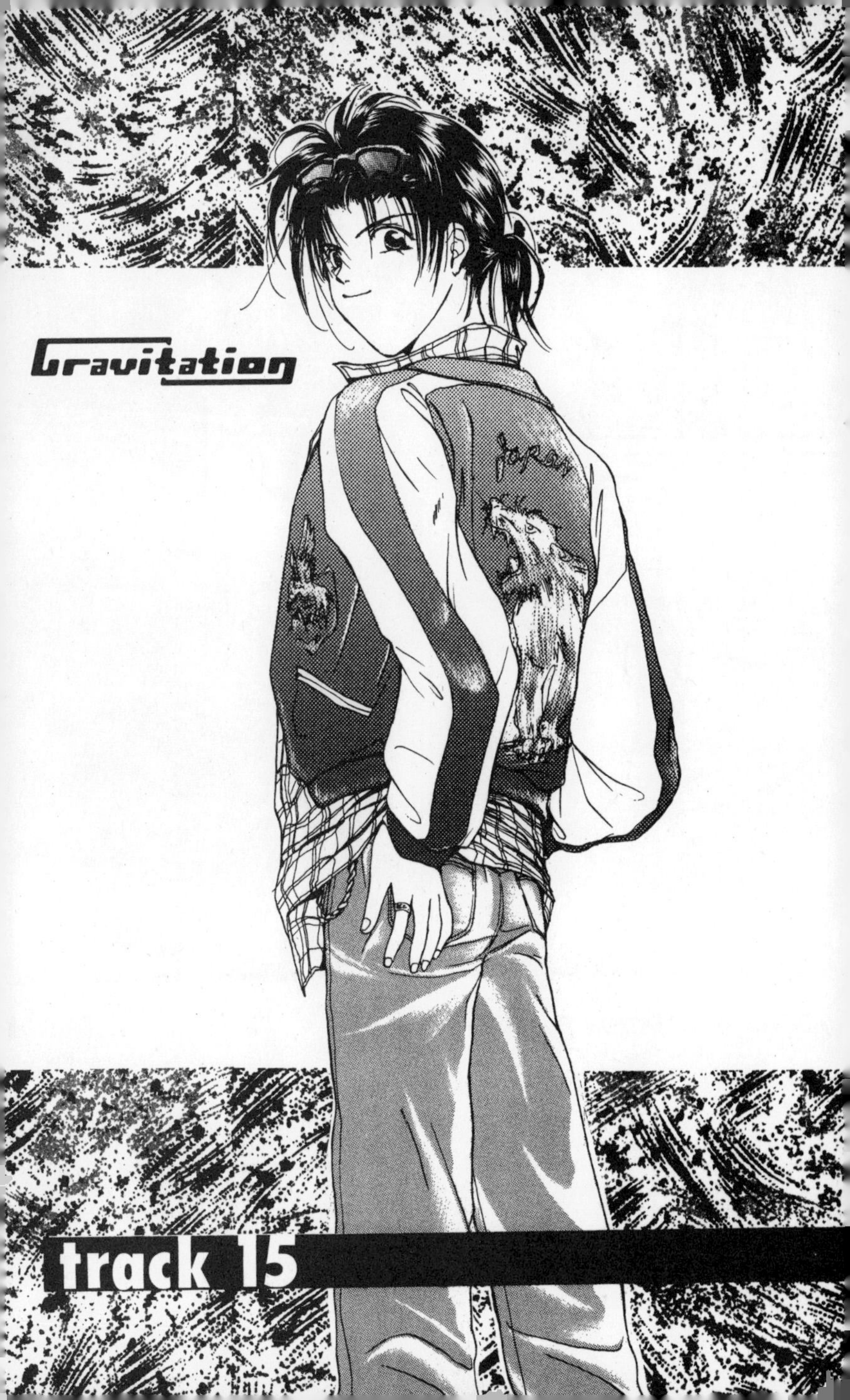

Gravitation
Japan
track 15

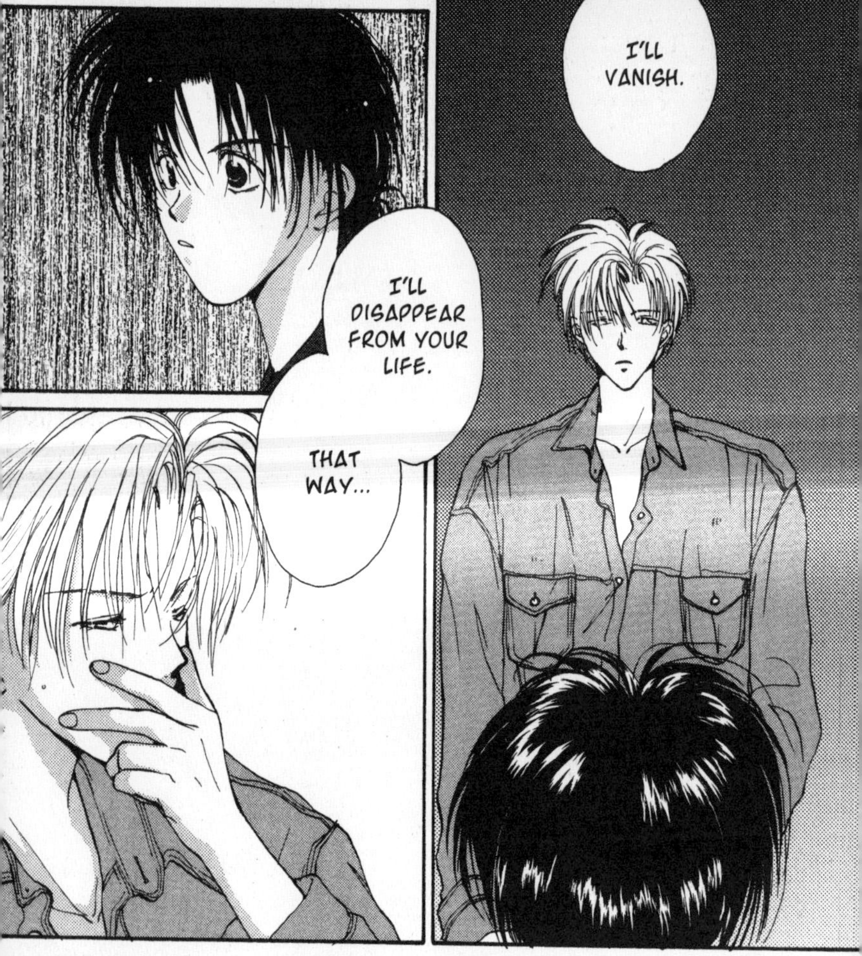
I'LL VANISH.
I'LL DISAPPEAR FROM YOUR LIFE.
THAT WAY...

ABOUT GRAVITATION TRACK 15

I finally did it! Shuichi in a schoolgirl uniform!! It's costumed freak time!!

I'm celebrating! It's like my whole career as a manga artist up until now has been building to this moment! Sorry for digressing into niche territory... Even though the story is treading into darker and darker waters, Shuichi is still keeping his head above water. You're the only guy who could endure this kind of stuff. I'm glad you're such a good boy. He's a real man. He sure is. This is the kind of guy I like to create. I think I raised him well.

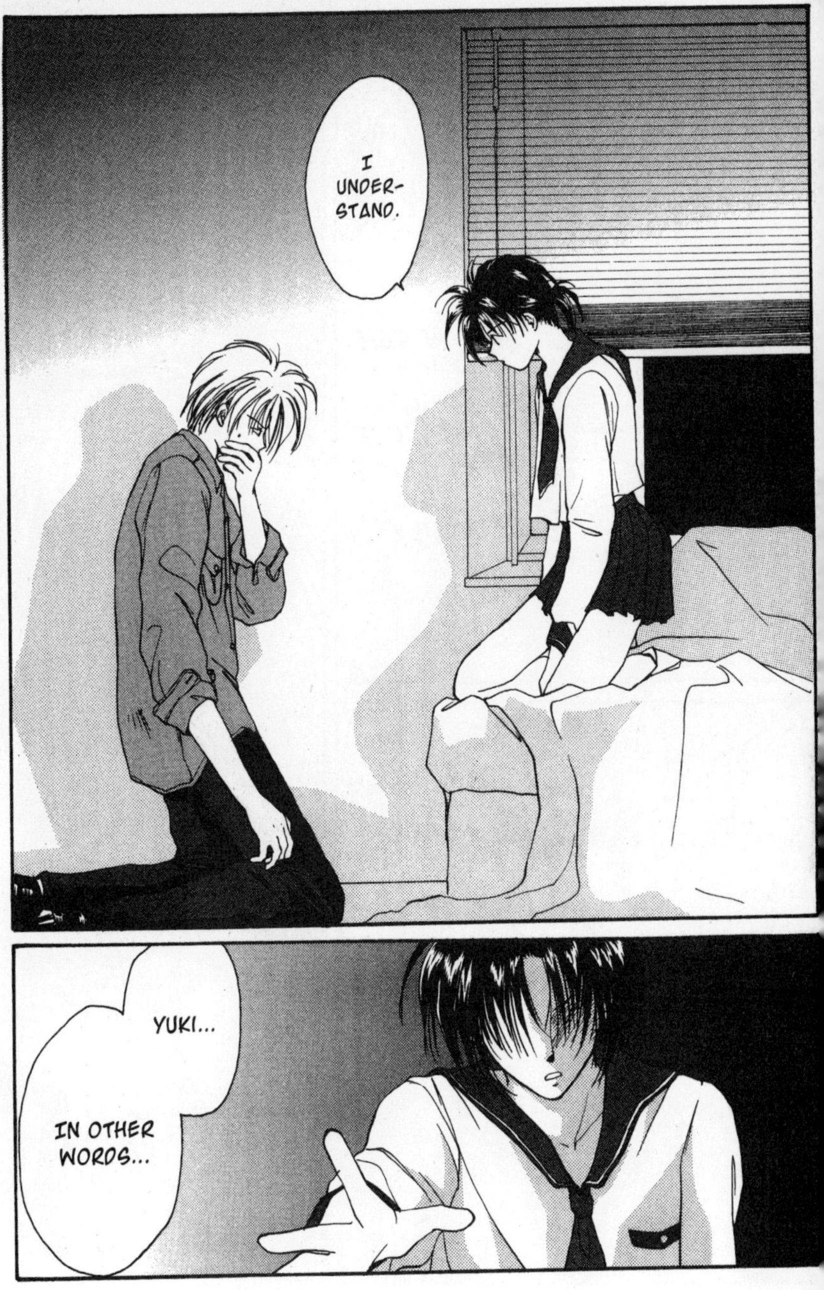
I UNDER-STAND.
YUKI...
IN OTHER WORDS...

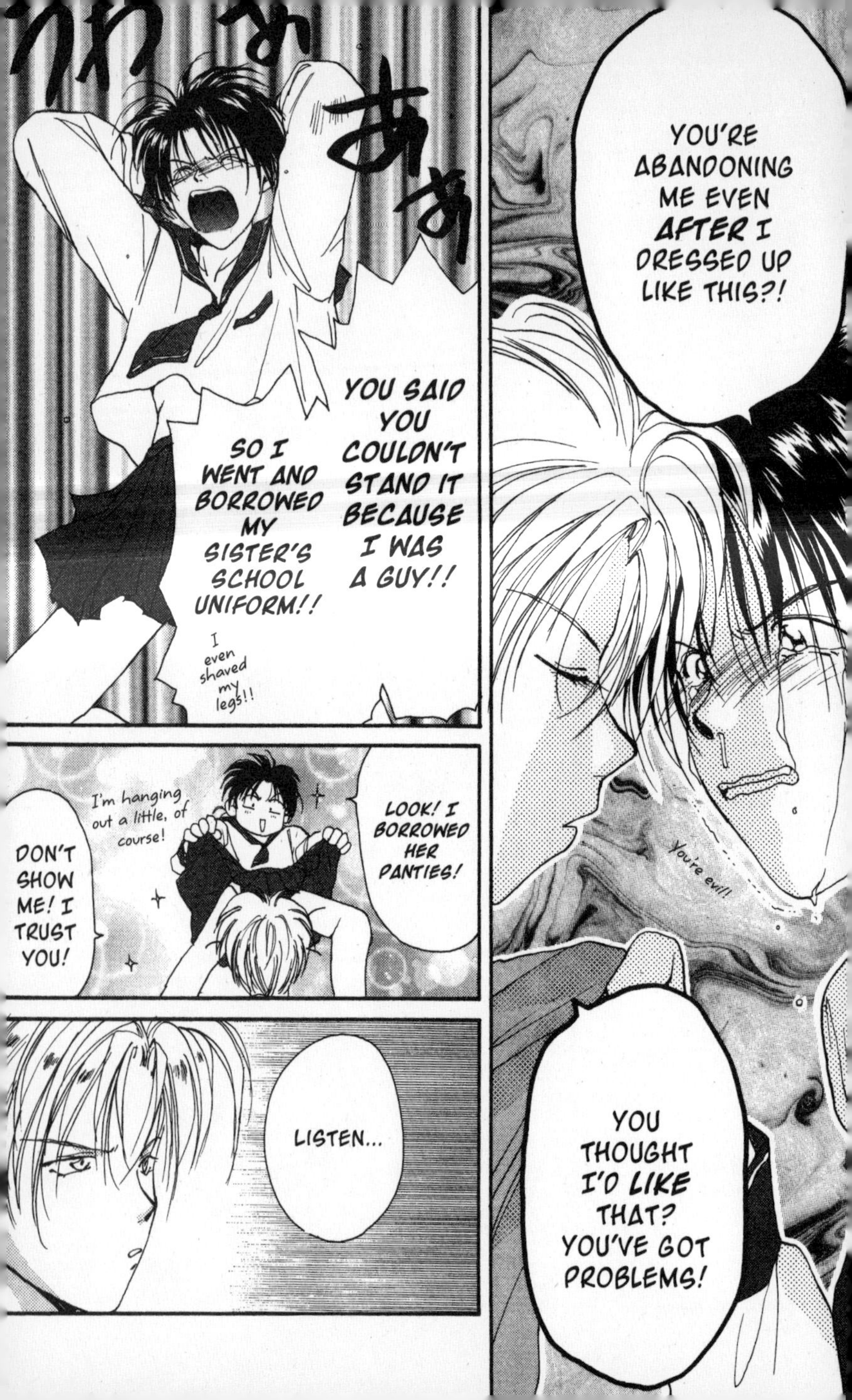
YOU'RE ABANDONING ME EVEN AFTER I DRESSED UP LIKE THIS?!
You're evil!!
YOU THOUGHT I'D LIKE THAT? YOU'VE GOT PROBLEMS!
うわあああ
YOU SAID YOU COULDN'T STAND IT BECAUSE I WAS A GUY!!
SO I WENT AND BORROWED MY SISTER'S SCHOOL UNIFORM!!
I even shaved my legs!!
LOOK! I BORROWED HER PANTIES!
I'm hanging out a little, of course!
DON'T SHOW ME! I TRUST YOU!
LISTEN...

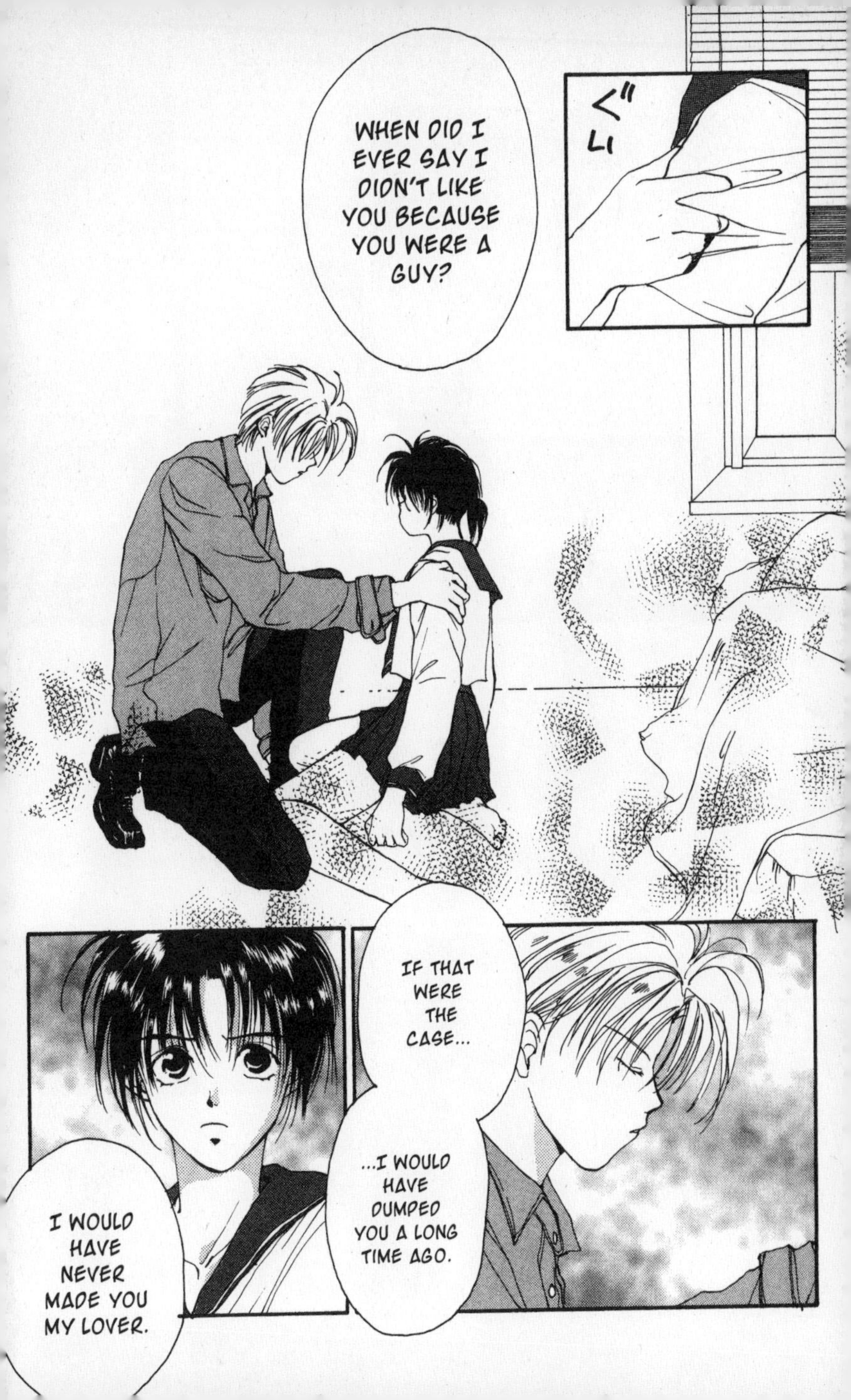
ぐい
WHEN DID I EVER SAY I DIDN'T LIKE YOU BECAUSE YOU WERE A GUY?
IF THAT WERE THE CASE...
...I WOULD HAVE DUMPED YOU A LONG TIME AGO.
I WOULD HAVE NEVER MADE YOU MY LOVER.

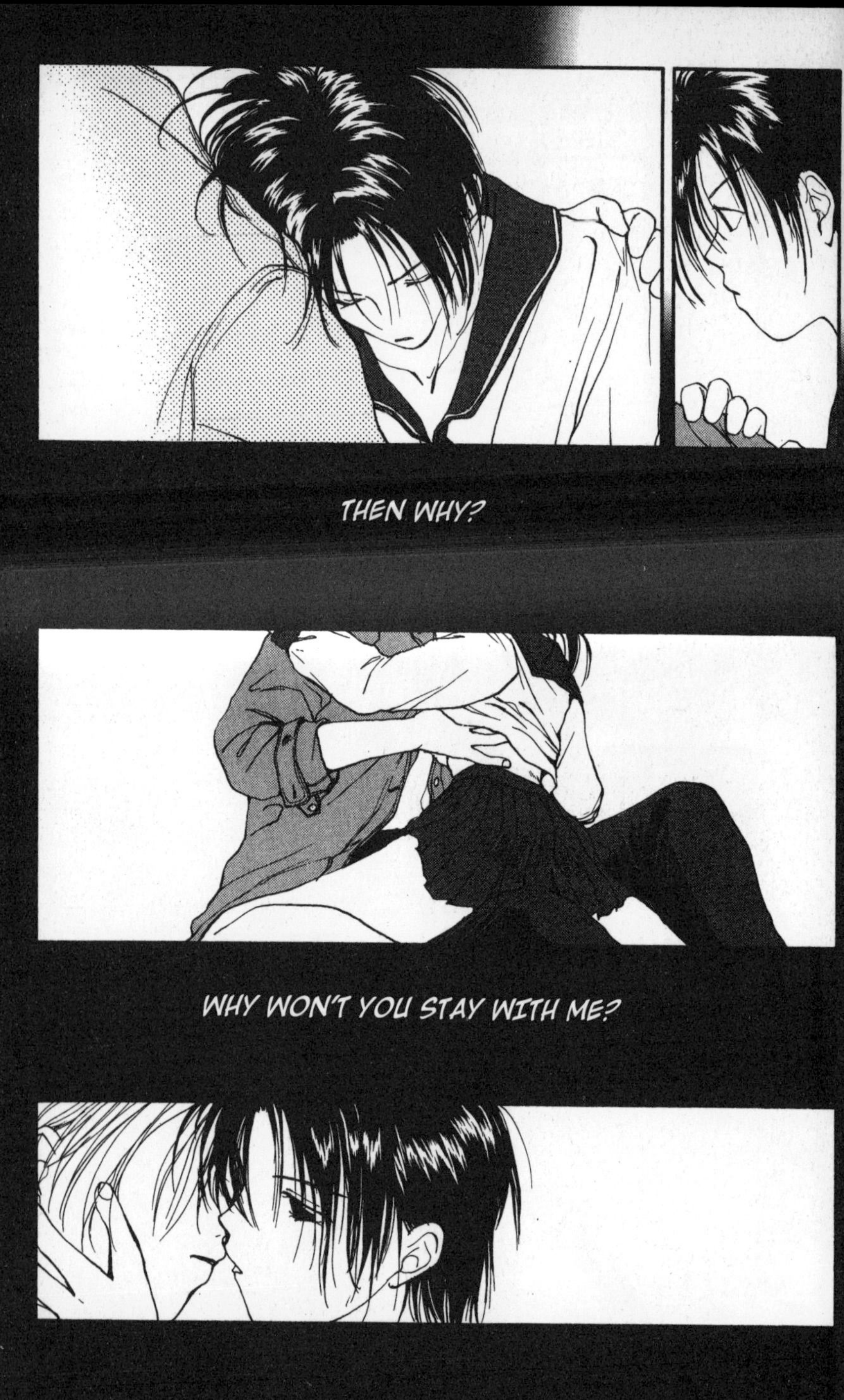
THEN WHY?
WHY WON'T YOU STAY WITH ME?

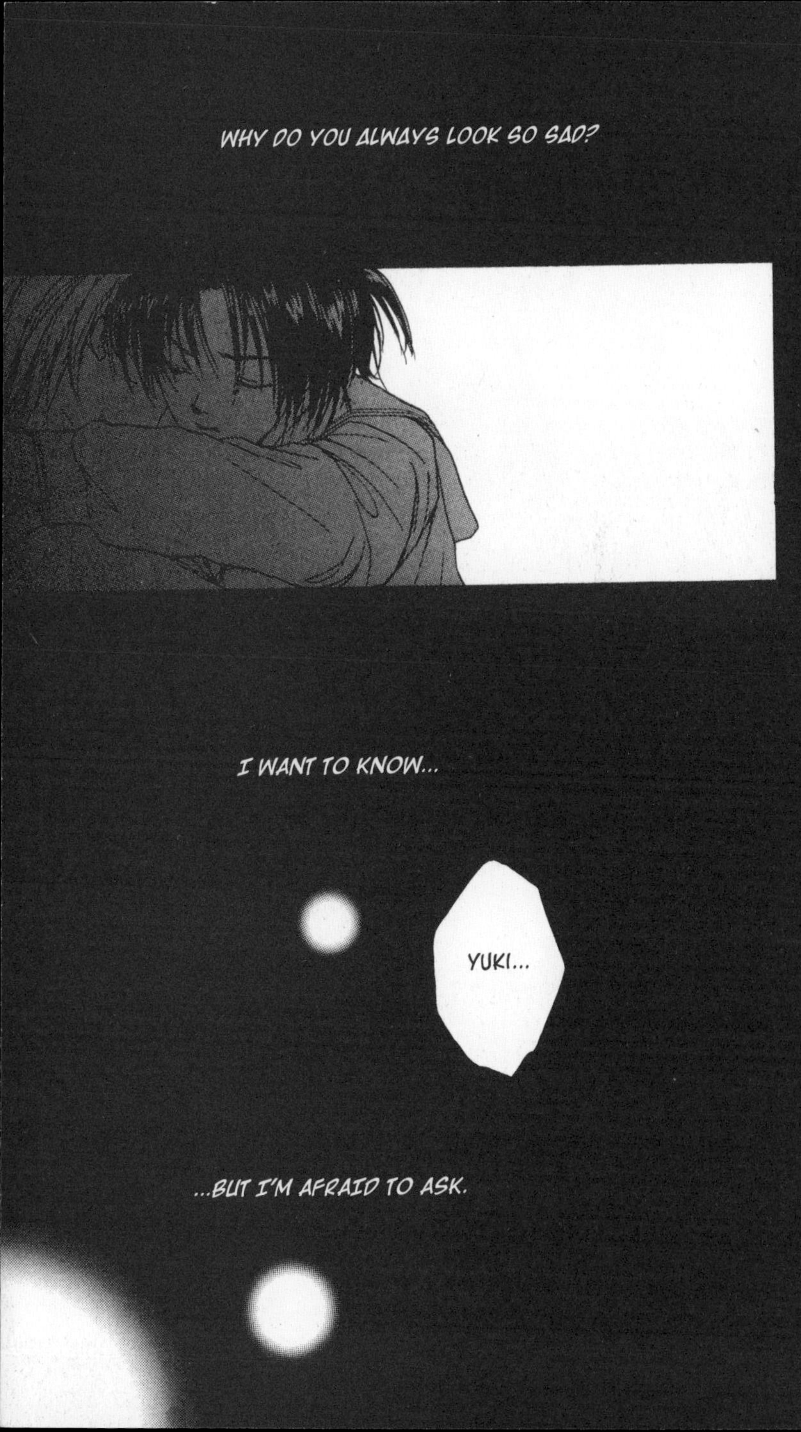
WHY DO YOU ALWAYS LOOK SO SAD?
I WANT TO KNOW...
YUKI...
...BUT I'M AFRAID TO ASK.

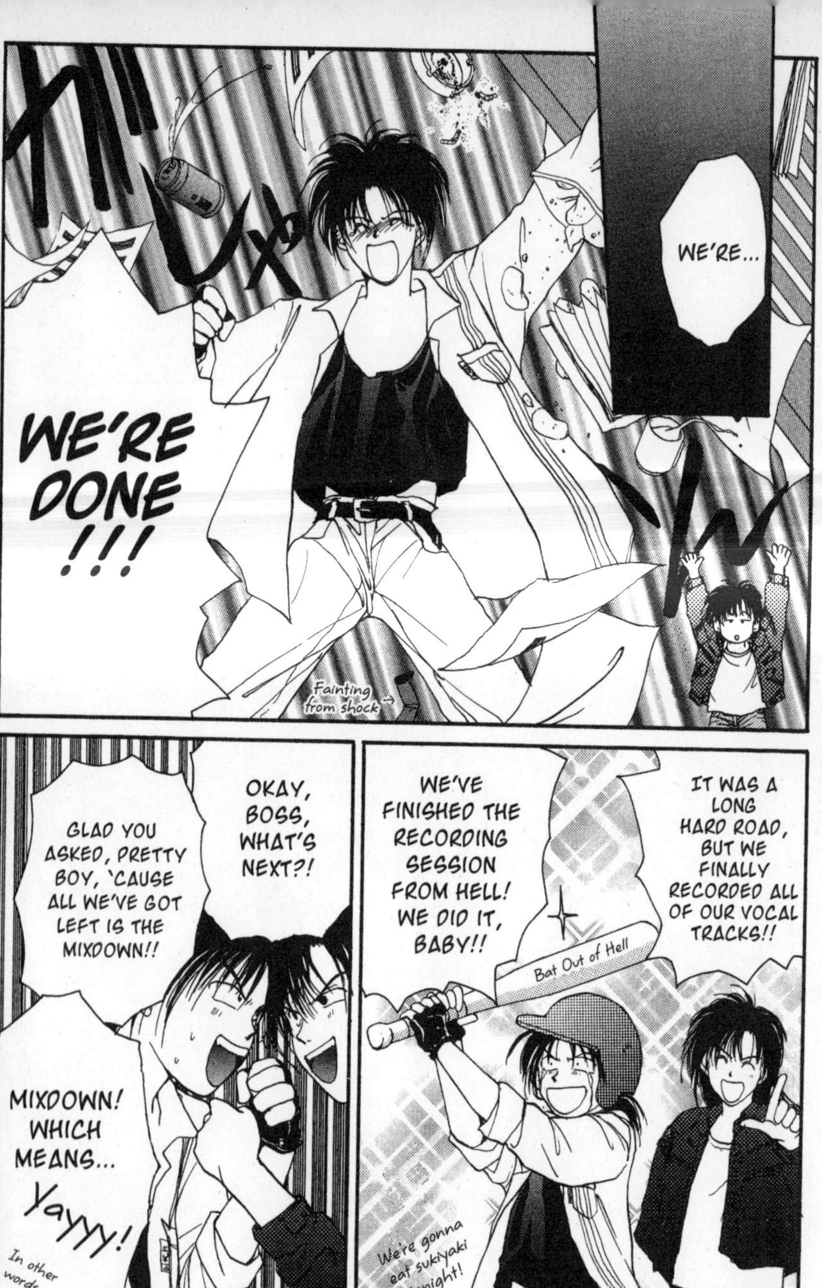
WE'RE...
WE'RE DONE !!!
Fainting from shock
IT WAS A LONG HARD ROAD, BUT WE FINALLY RECORDED ALL OF OUR VOCAL TRACKS!!
WE'VE FINISHED THE RECORDING SESSION FROM HELL! WE DID IT, BABY!!
Bat Out of Hell
We're gonna eat sukiyaki tonight!
OKAY, BOSS, WHAT'S NEXT?!
GLAD YOU ASKED, PRETTY BOY, 'CAUSE ALL WE'VE GOT LEFT IS THE MIXDOWN!!
MIXDOWN! WHICH MEANS...
Yayyy!
In other words...

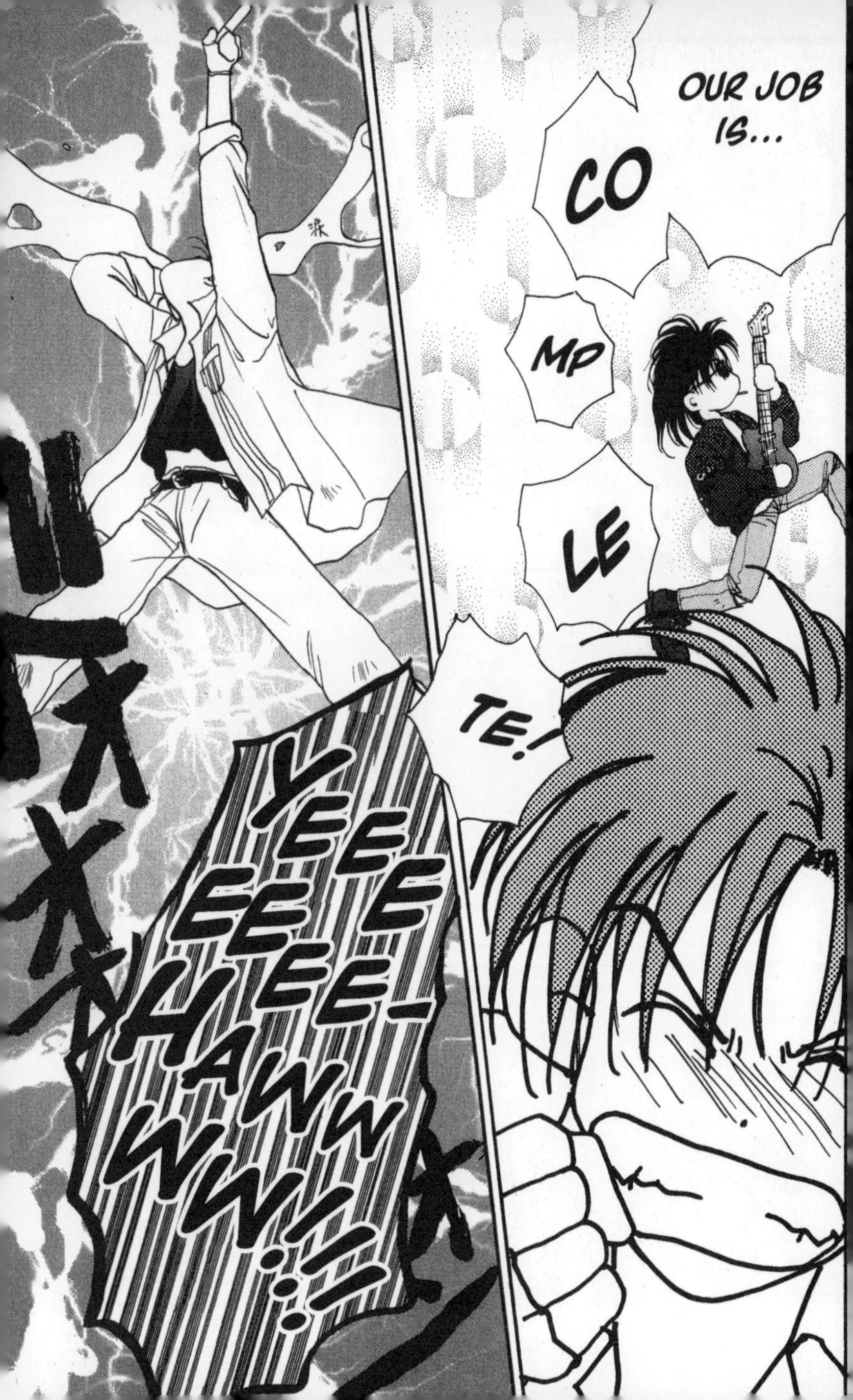
OUR JOB IS...
CO
MP
LE
TE!
YEEEEEEEEEE-HAWWWW!!!

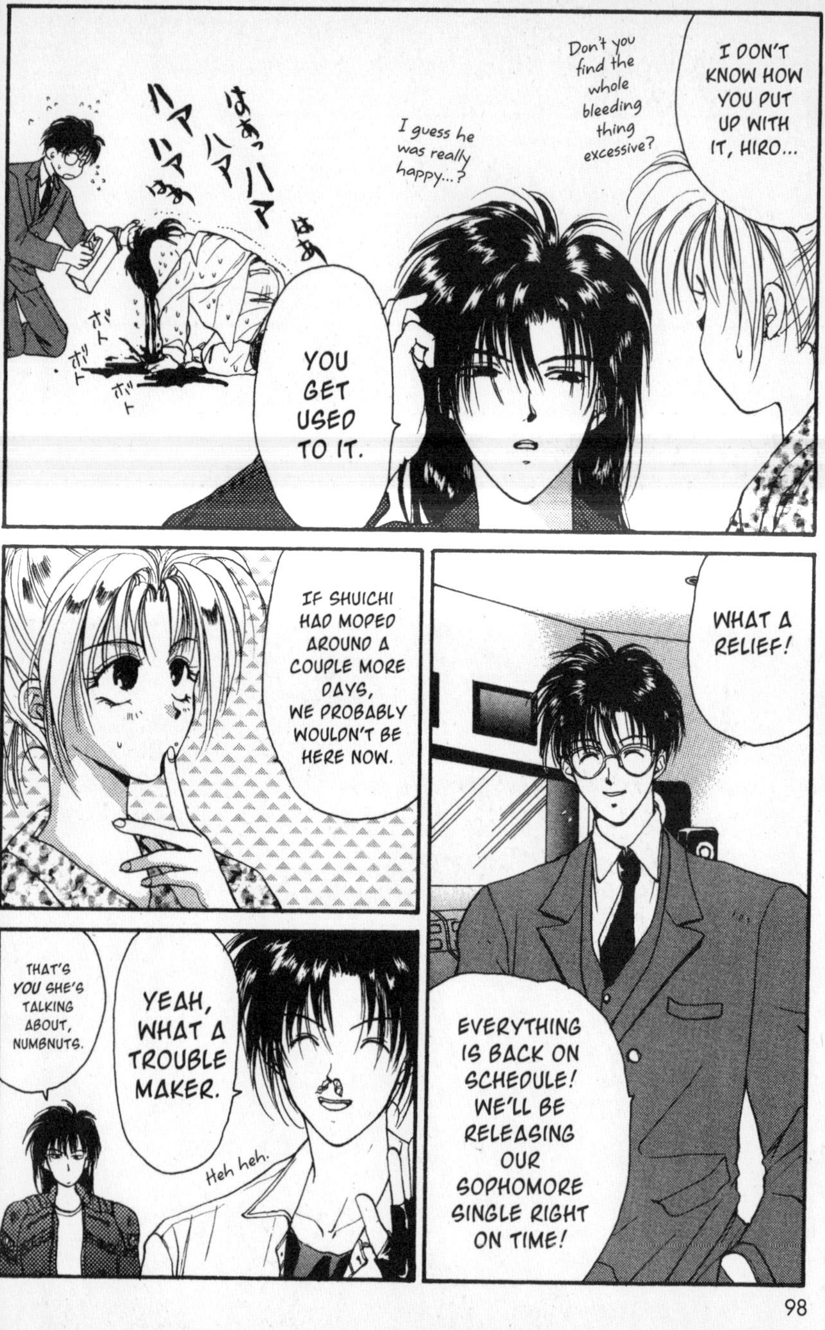
I DON'T KNOW HOW YOU PUT UP WITH IT, HIRO...
Don't you find the whole bleeding thing excessive?
I guess he was really happy...?
はあ
ボト ボト ボト
YOU GET USED TO IT.
WHAT A RELIEF!
EVERYTHING IS BACK ON SCHEDULE! WE'LL BE RELEASING OUR SOPHOMORE SINGLE RIGHT ON TIME!
IF SHUICHI HAD MOPED AROUND A COUPLE MORE DAYS, WE PROBABLY WOULDN'T BE HERE NOW.
YEAH, WHAT A TROUBLE MAKER.
Heh heh.
THAT'S YOU SHE'S TALKING ABOUT, NUMBNUTS.

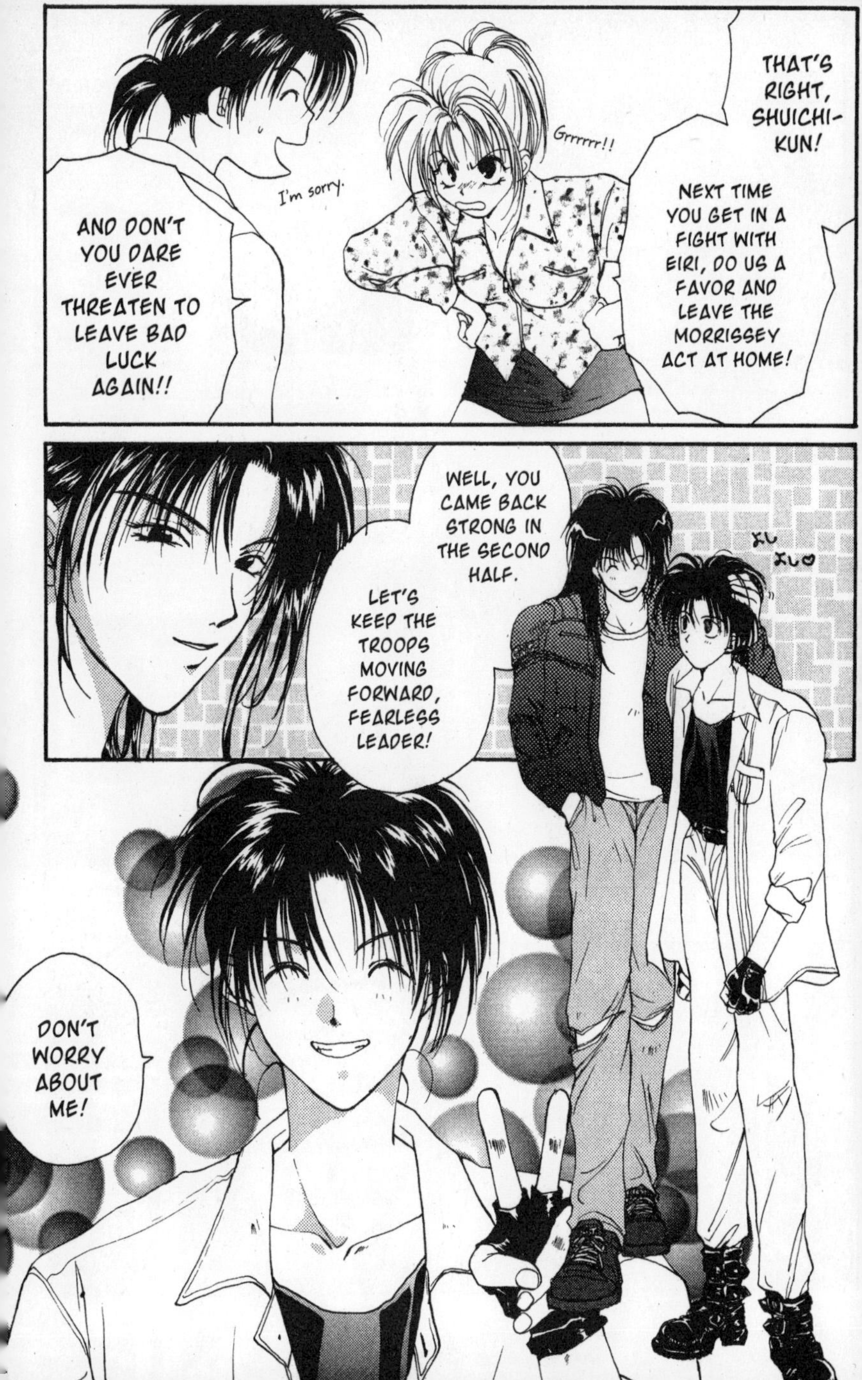
THAT'S RIGHT, SHUICHI-KUN!
NEXT TIME YOU GET IN A FIGHT WITH EIRI, DO US A FAVOR AND LEAVE THE MORRISSEY ACT AT HOME!
Grrrrrr!!
I'm sorry.
AND DON'T YOU DARE EVER THREATEN TO LEAVE BAD LUCK AGAIN!!
よし よし♡
WELL, YOU CAME BACK STRONG IN THE SECOND HALF.
LET'S KEEP THE TROOPS MOVING FORWARD, FEARLESS LEADER!
DON'T WORRY ABOUT ME!

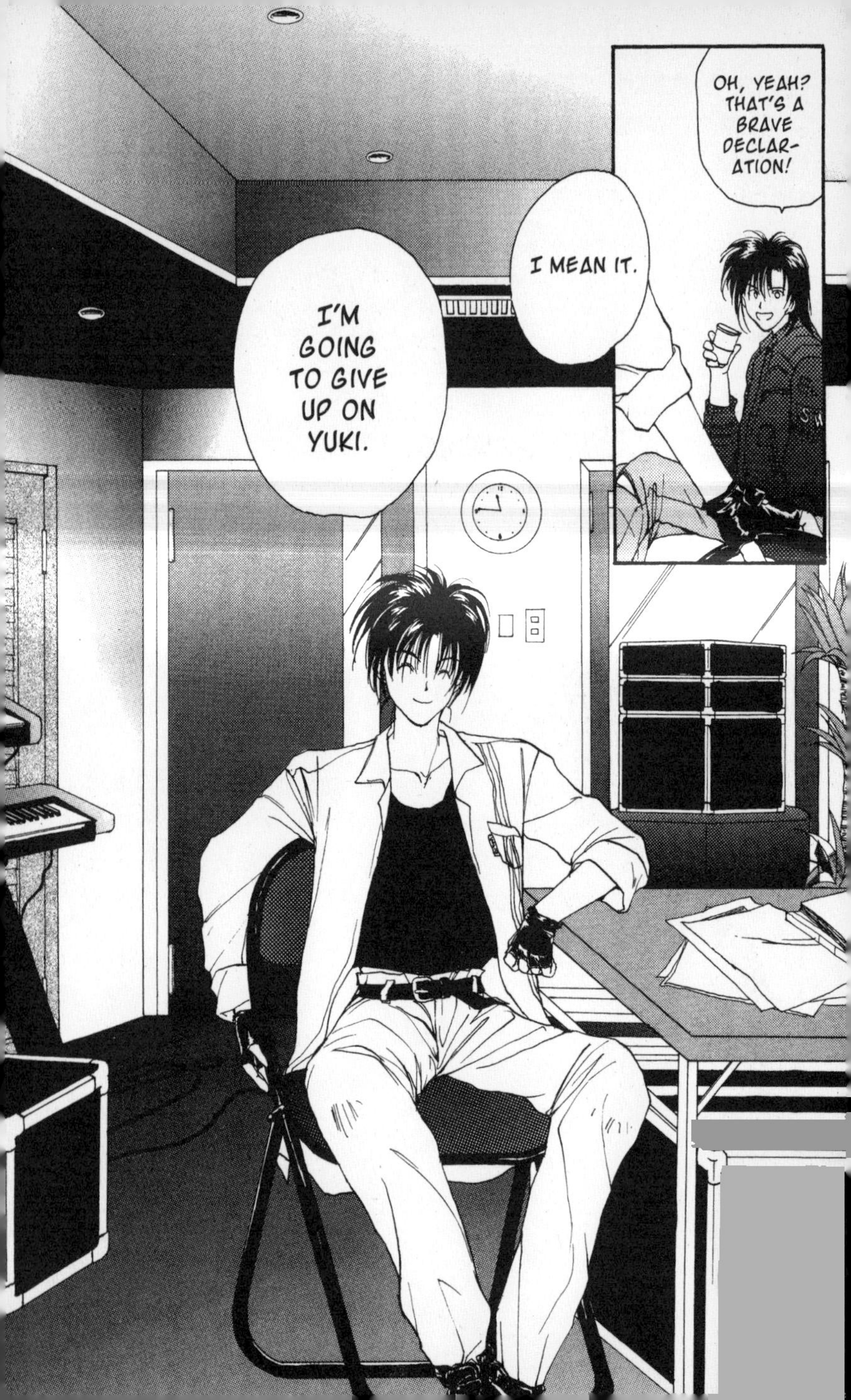
OH, YEAH? THAT'S A BRAVE DECLAR-ATION!
I MEAN IT.
I'M GOING TO GIVE UP ON YUKI.

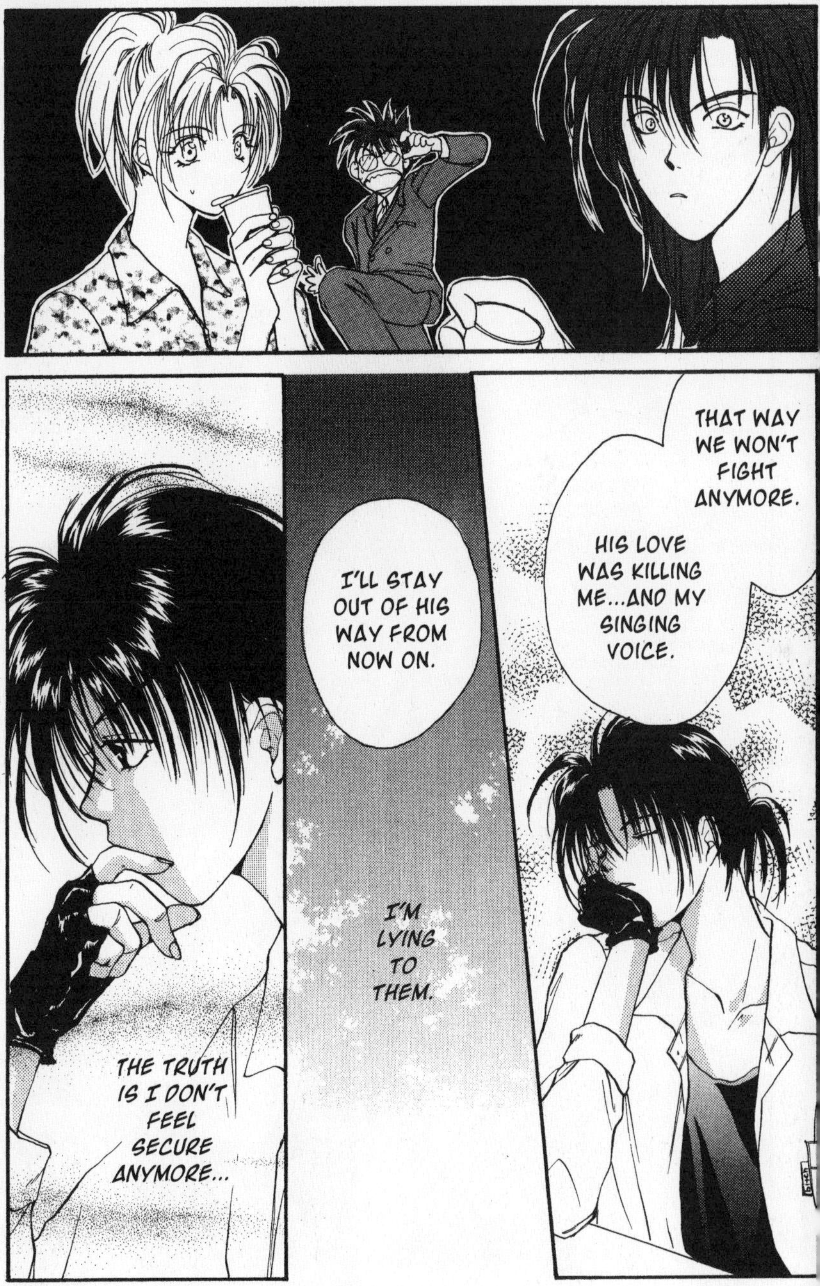
THAT WAY WE WON'T FIGHT ANYMORE.
HIS LOVE WAS KILLING ME...AND MY SINGING VOICE.
I'LL STAY OUT OF HIS WAY FROM NOW ON.
I'M LYING TO THEM.
THE TRUTH IS I DON'T FEEL SECURE ANYMORE...

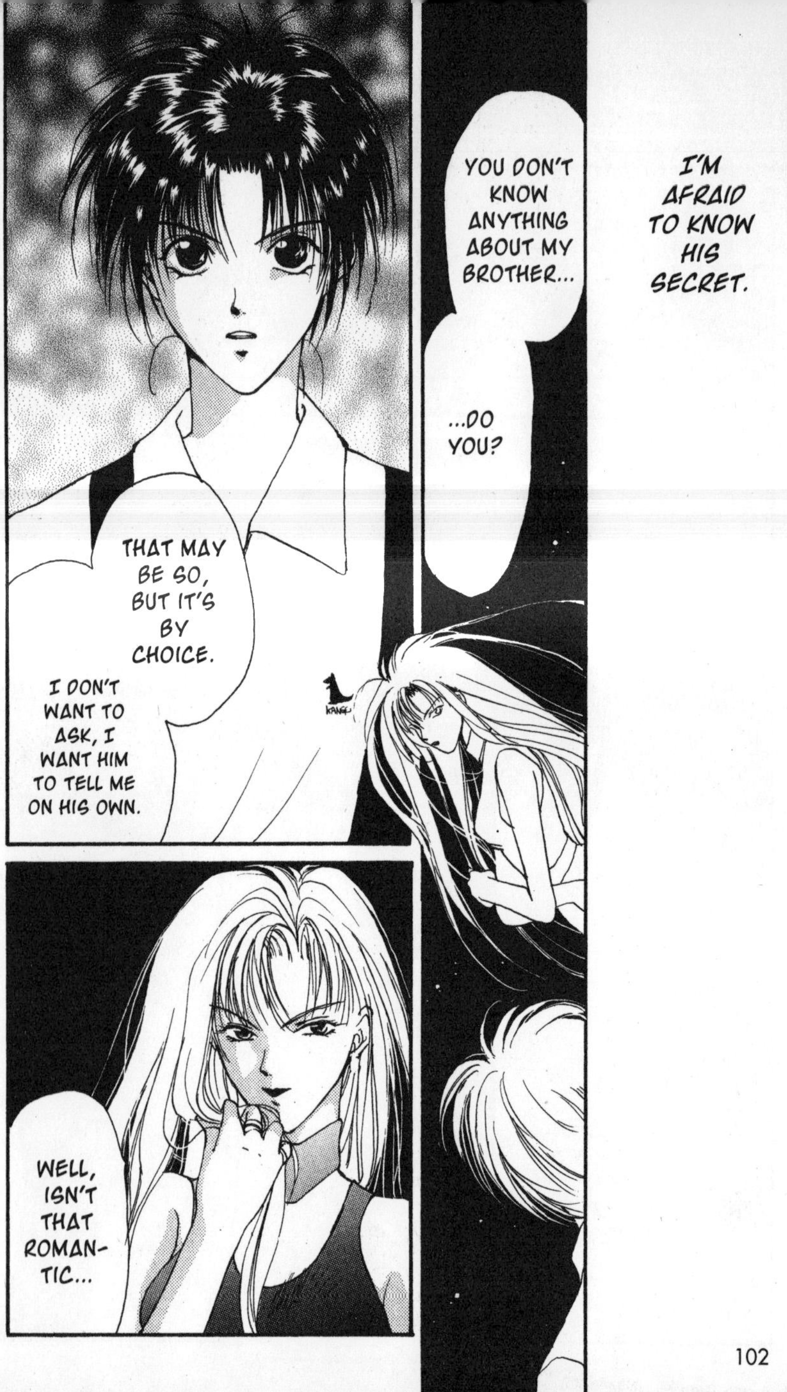
I'M AFRAID TO KNOW HIS SECRET.
YOU DON'T KNOW ANYTHING ABOUT MY BROTHER...
...DO YOU?
THAT MAY BE SO, BUT IT'S BY CHOICE.
I DON'T WANT TO ASK, I WANT HIM TO TELL ME ON HIS OWN.
WELL, ISN'T THAT ROMANTIC...

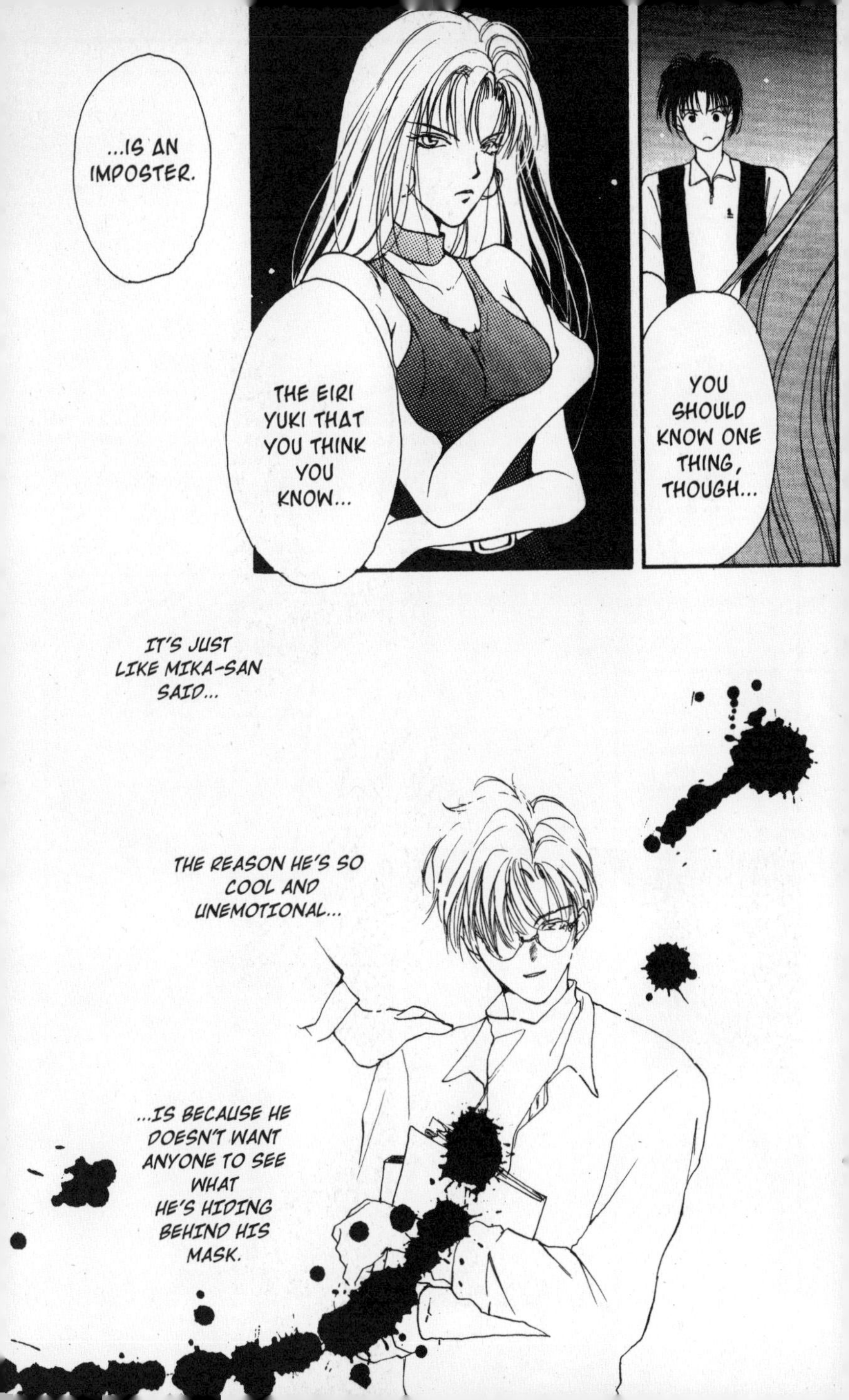
YOU SHOULD KNOW ONE THING, THOUGH...
THE EIRI YUKI THAT YOU THINK YOU KNOW...
...IS AN IMPOSTER.
IT'S JUST LIKE MIKA-SAN SAID...
THE REASON HE'S SO COOL AND UNEMOTIONAL...
...IS BECAUSE HE DOESN'T WANT ANYONE TO SEE WHAT HE'S HIDING BEHIND HIS MASK.

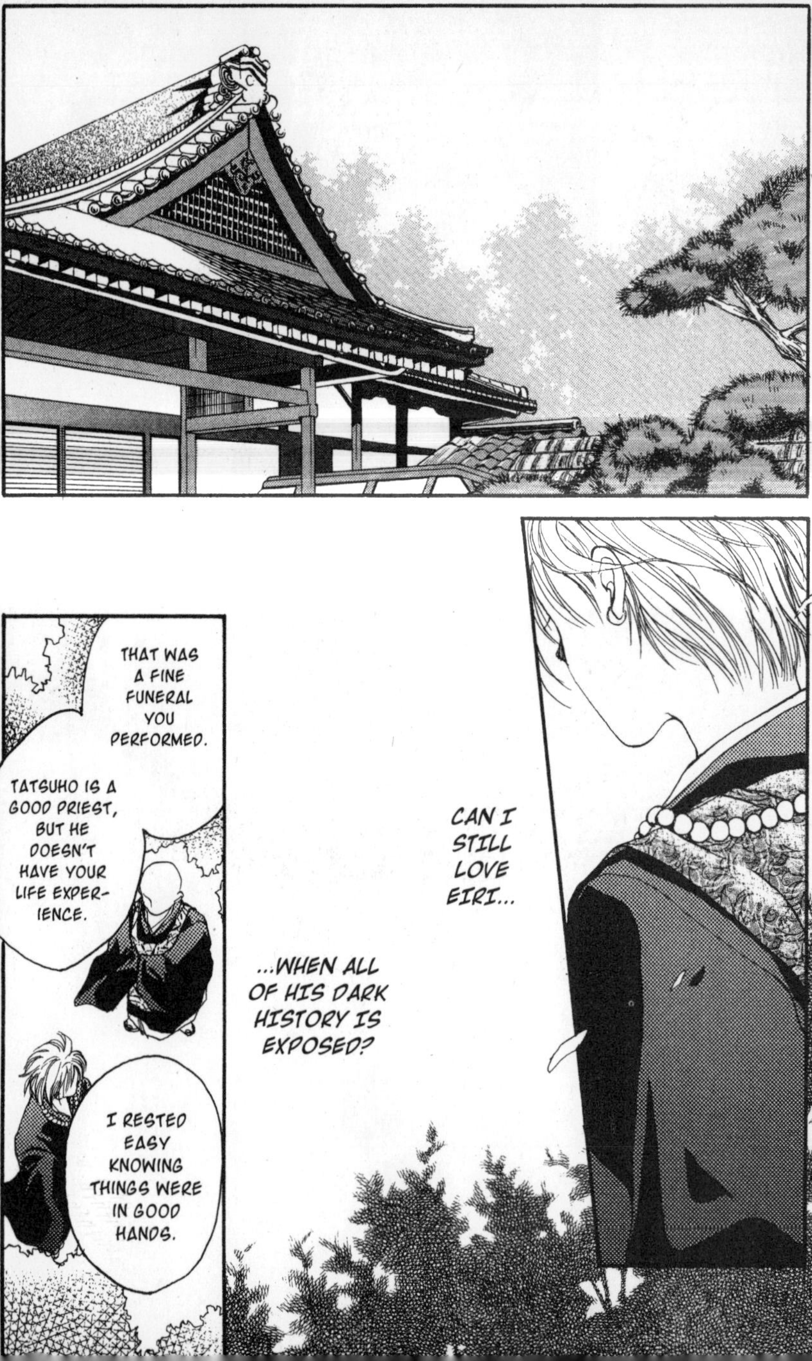
CAN I STILL LOVE EIRI...
...WHEN ALL OF HIS DARK HISTORY IS EXPOSED?
THAT WAS A FINE FUNERAL YOU PERFORMED.
TATSUHO IS A GOOD PRIEST, BUT HE DOESN'T HAVE YOUR LIFE EXPER-IENCE.
I RESTED EASY KNOWING THINGS WERE IN GOOD HANDS.

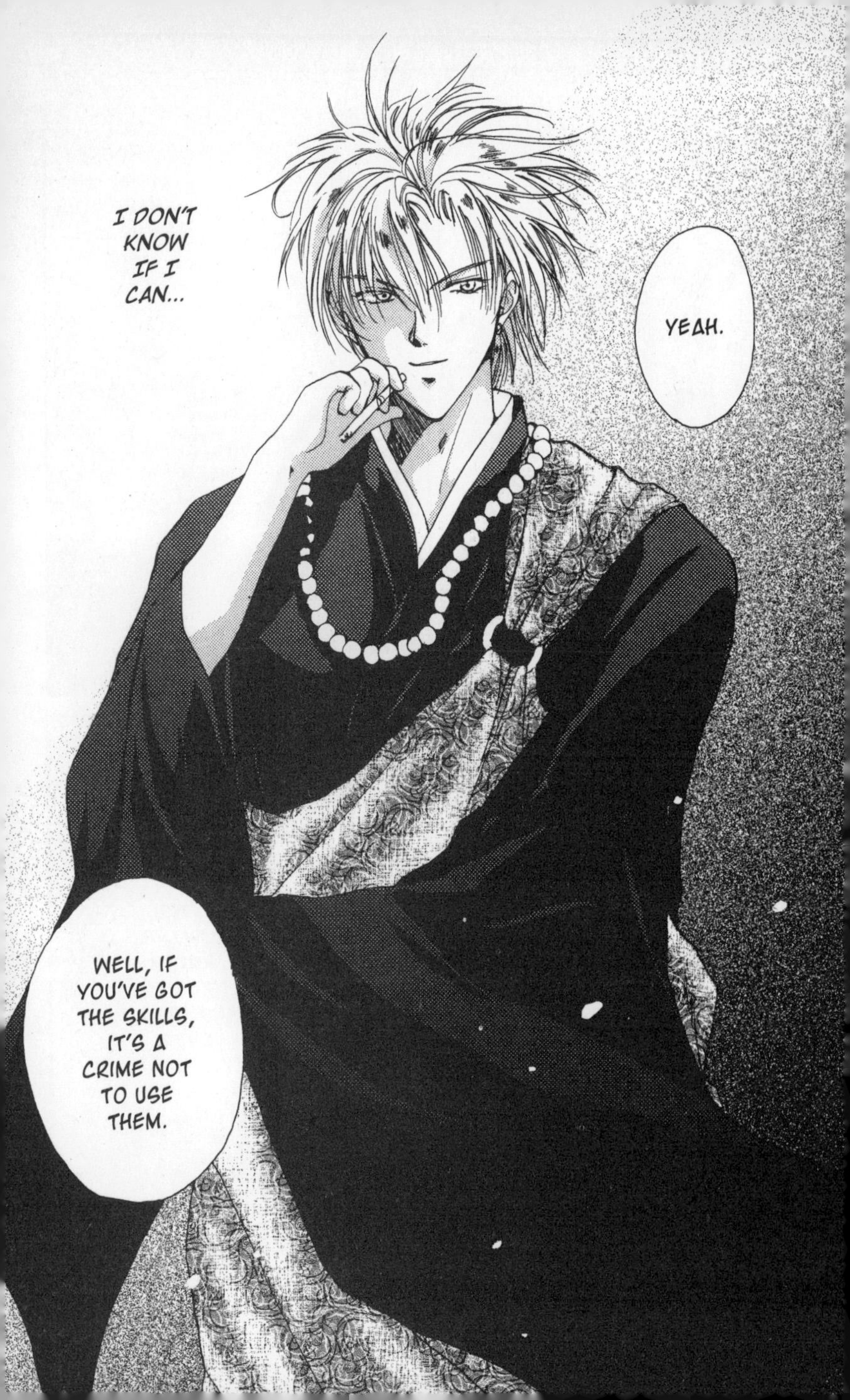
YEAH.
I DON'T KNOW IF I CAN...
WELL, IF YOU'VE GOT THE SKILLS, IT'S A CRIME NOT TO USE THEM.

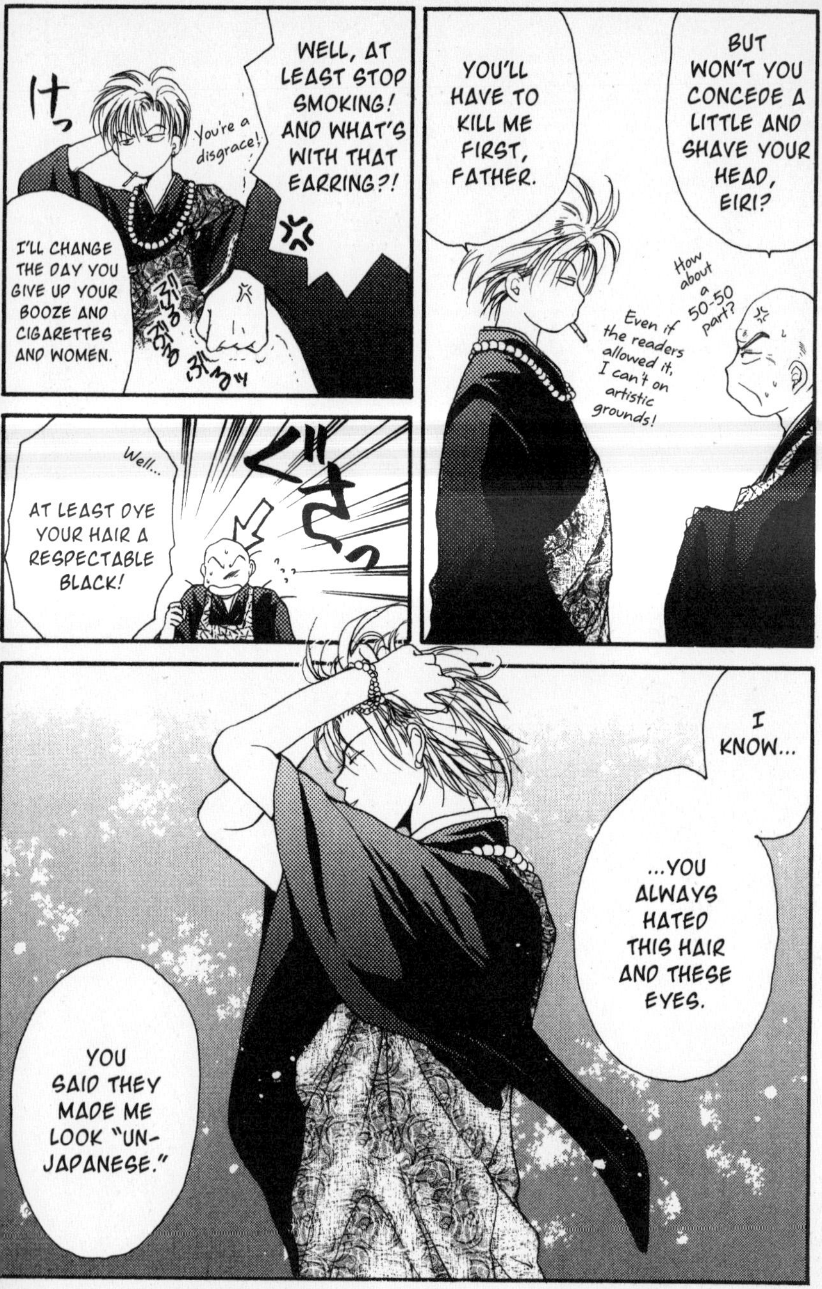
BUT WON'T YOU CONCEDE A LITTLE AND SHAVE YOUR HEAD, EIRI?
YOU'LL HAVE TO KILL ME FIRST, FATHER.
How about a 50-50 part?
Even if the readers allowed it, I can't on artistic grounds!
WELL, AT LEAST STOP SMOKING! AND WHAT'S WITH THAT EARRING?!
You're a disgrace!
けっ
I'LL CHANGE THE DAY YOU GIVE UP YOUR BOOZE AND CIGARETTES AND WOMEN.
Well...
AT LEAST DYE YOUR HAIR A RESPECTABLE BLACK!
ぐさっ
I KNOW...
...YOU ALWAYS HATED THIS HAIR AND THESE EYES.
YOU SAID THEY MADE ME LOOK "UN-JAPANESE."

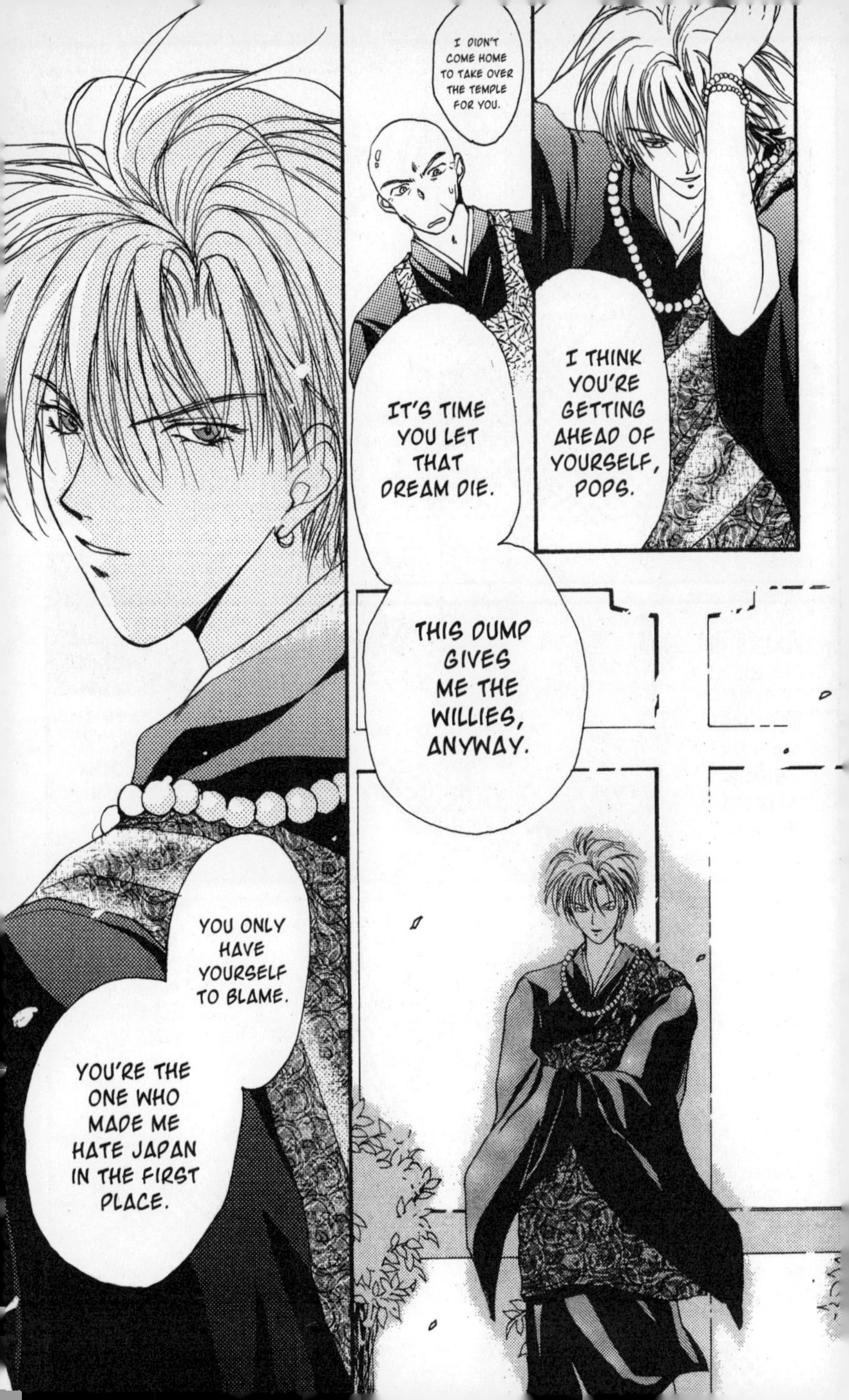
I THINK YOU'RE GETTING AHEAD OF YOURSELF, POPS.
I DIDN'T COME HOME TO TAKE OVER THE TEMPLE FOR YOU.
IT'S TIME YOU LET THAT DREAM DIE.
THIS DUMP GIVES ME THE WILLIES, ANYWAY.
YOU ONLY HAVE YOURSELF TO BLAME.
YOU'RE THE ONE WHO MADE ME HATE JAPAN IN THE FIRST PLACE.

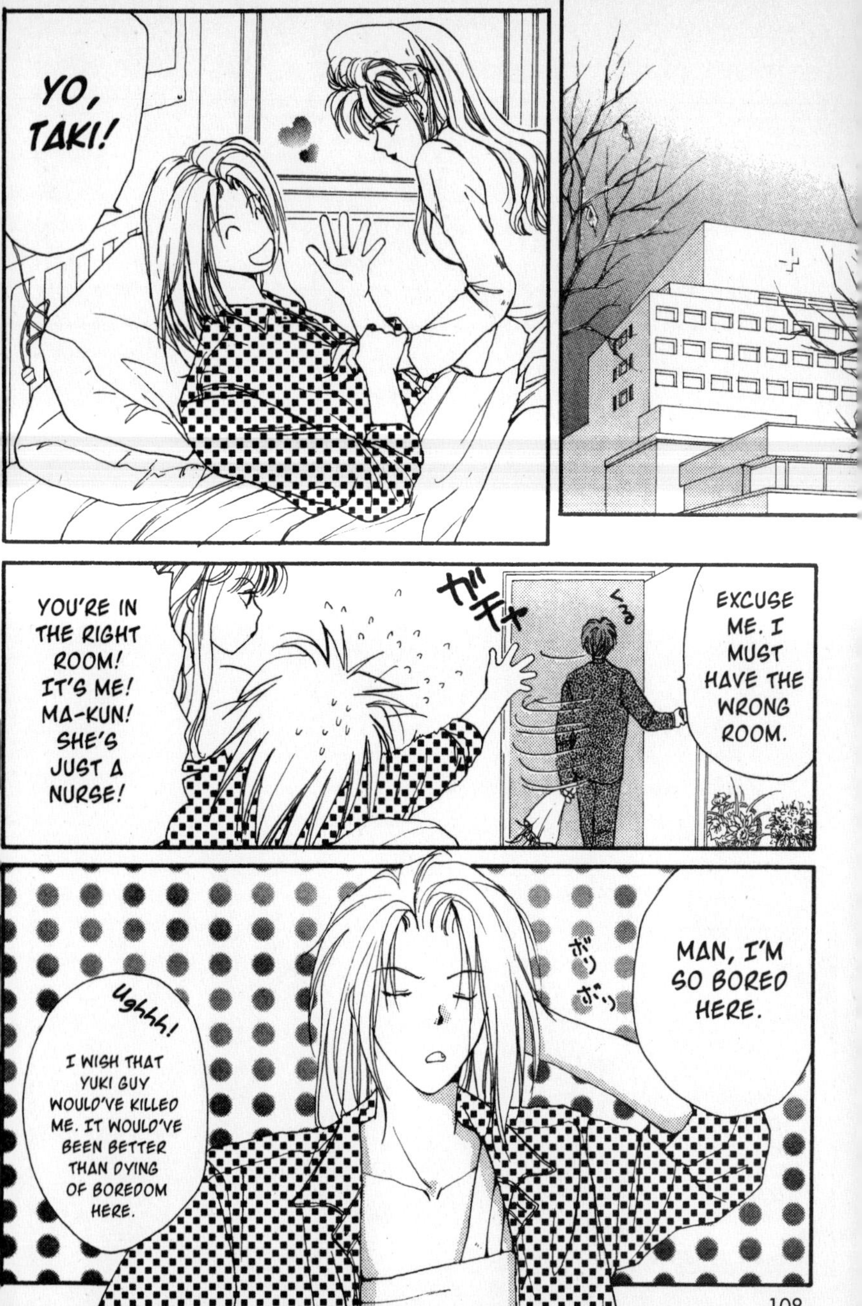
YO, TAKI!
EXCUSE ME. I MUST HAVE THE WRONG ROOM.
ガチャ
くる
YOU'RE IN THE RIGHT ROOM! IT'S ME! MA-KUN! SHE'S JUST A NURSE!
MAN, I'M SO BORED HERE.
ボリ ボリ
Ughhh!
I WISH THAT YUKI GUY WOULD'VE KILLED ME. IT WOULD'VE BEEN BETTER THAN DYING OF BOREDOM HERE.

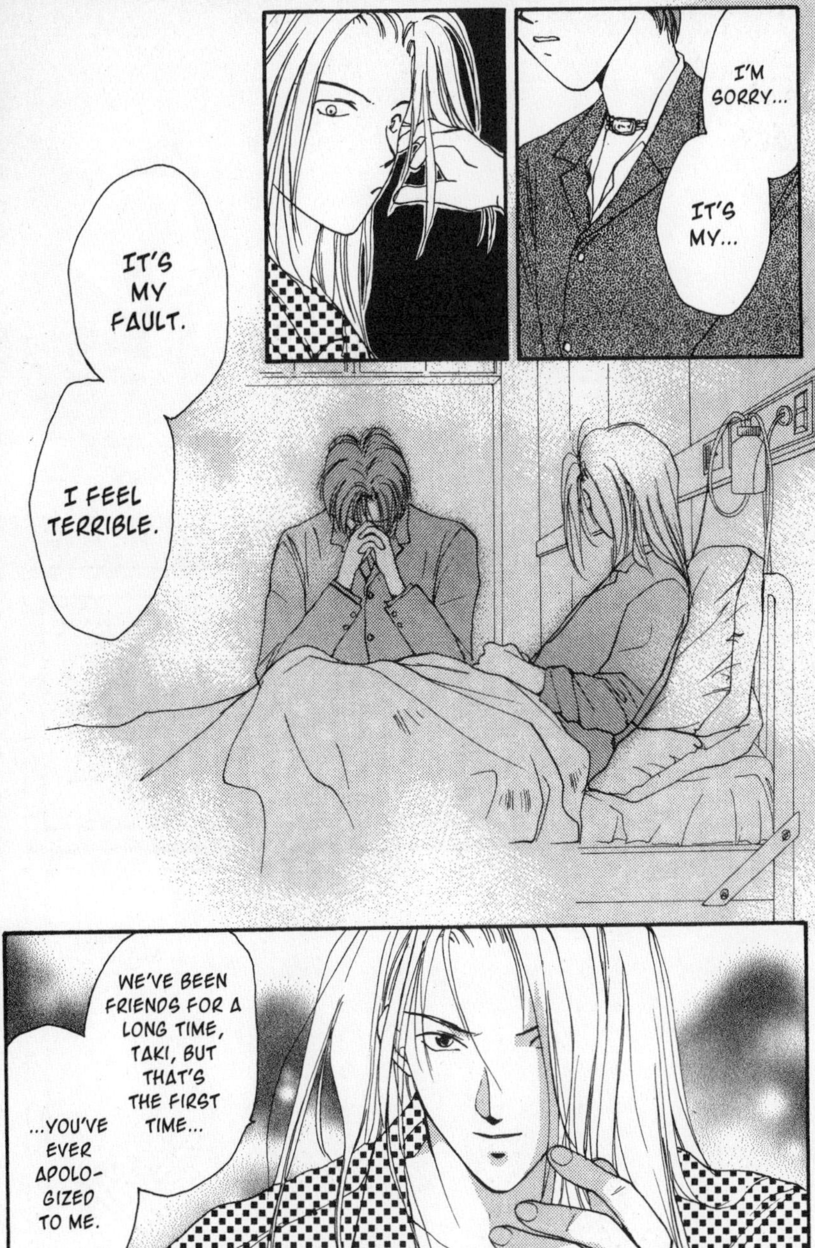
I'M SORRY...
IT'S MY...
IT'S MY FAULT.
I FEEL TERRIBLE.
WE'VE BEEN FRIENDS FOR A LONG TIME, TAKI, BUT THAT'S THE FIRST TIME...
...YOU'VE EVER APOLO-GIZED TO ME.

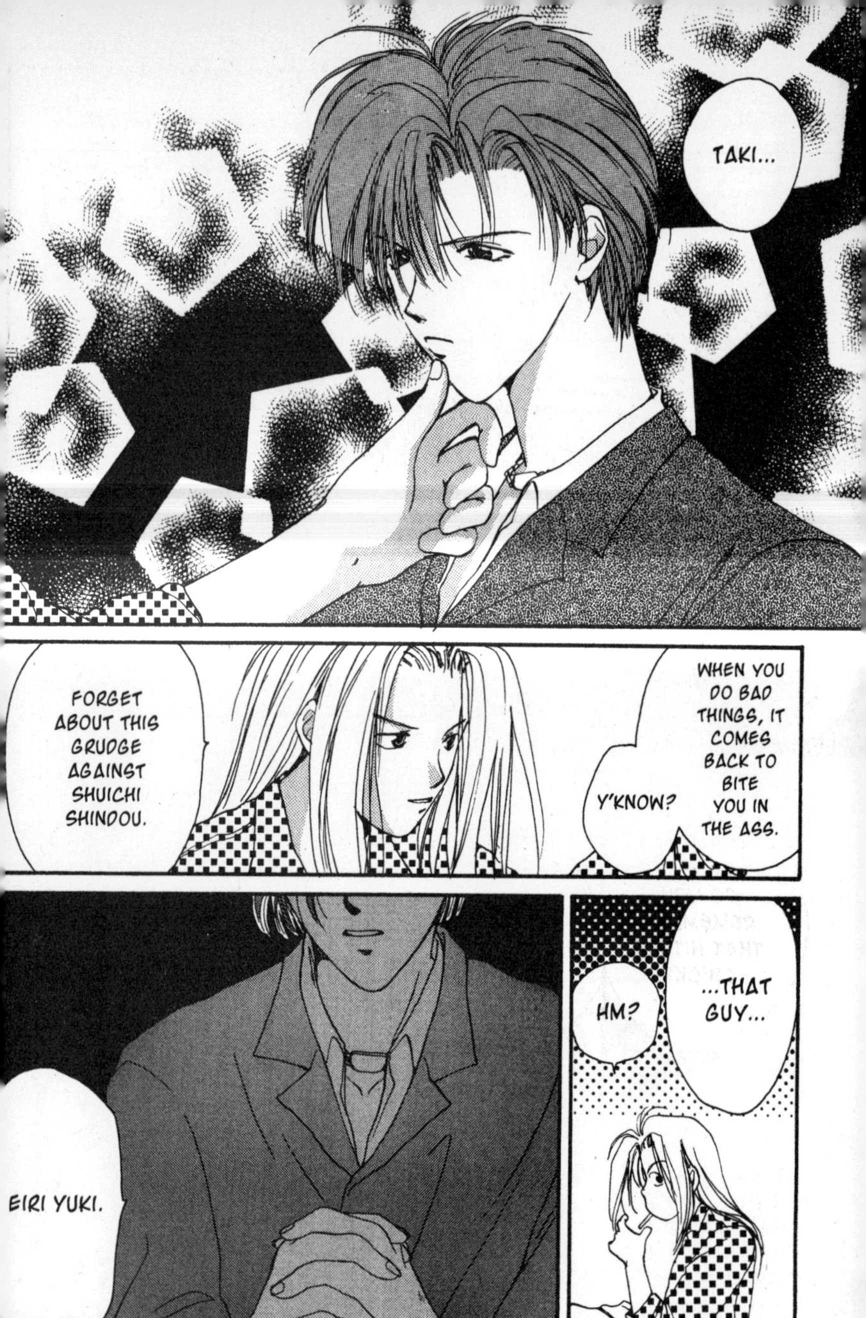
TAKI...
WHEN YOU DO BAD THINGS, IT COMES BACK TO BITE YOU IN THE ASS.
Y'KNOW?
FORGET ABOUT THIS GRUDGE AGAINST SHUICHI SHINDOU.
...THAT GUY...
HM?
EIRI YUKI.

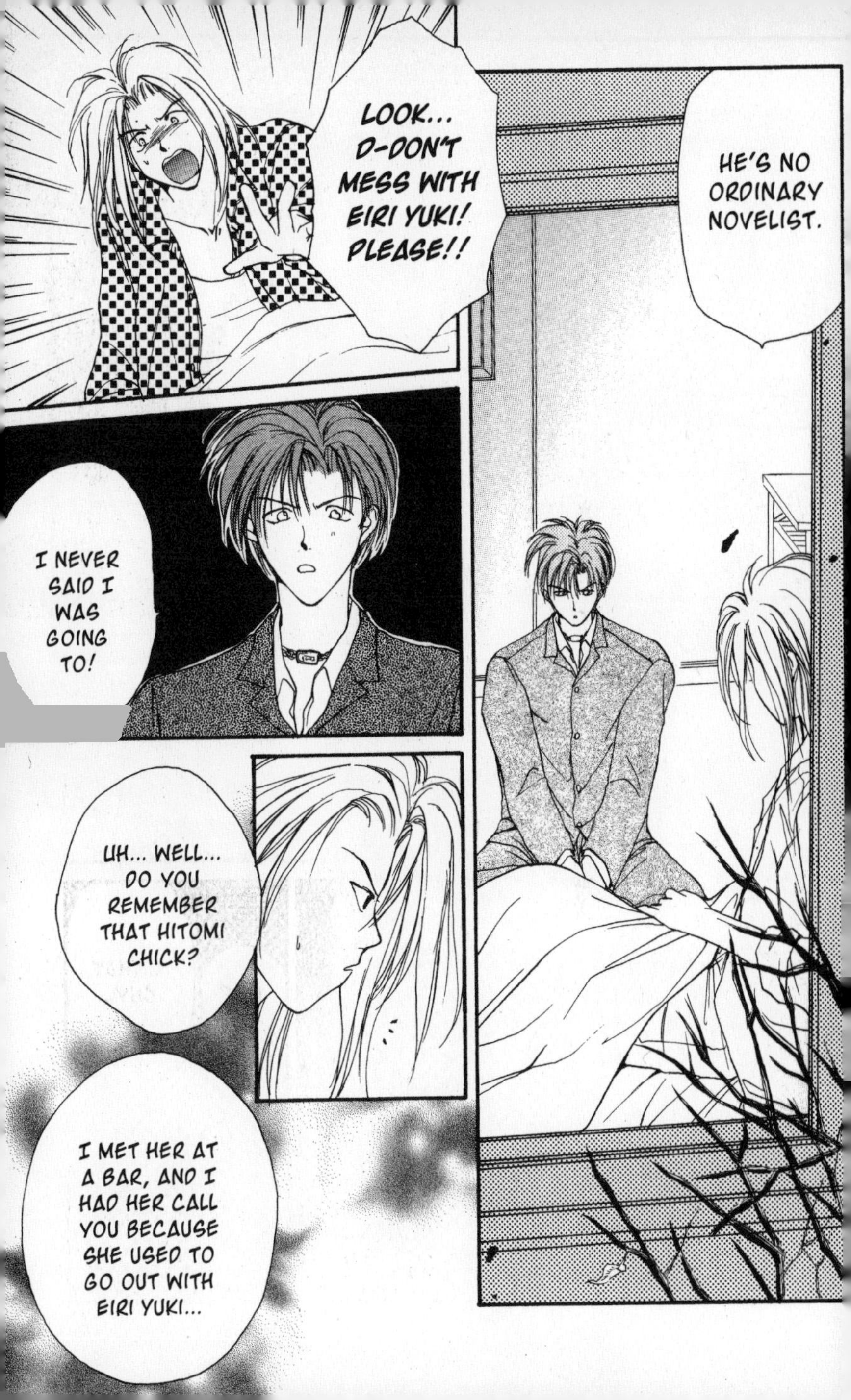
HE'S NO ORDINARY NOVELIST.
LOOK... D-DON'T MESS WITH EIRI YUKI! PLEASE!!
I NEVER SAID I WAS GOING TO!
UH... WELL... DO YOU REMEMBER THAT HITOMI CHICK?
I MET HER AT A BAR, AND I HAD HER CALL YOU BECAUSE SHE USED TO GO OUT WITH EIRI YUKI...

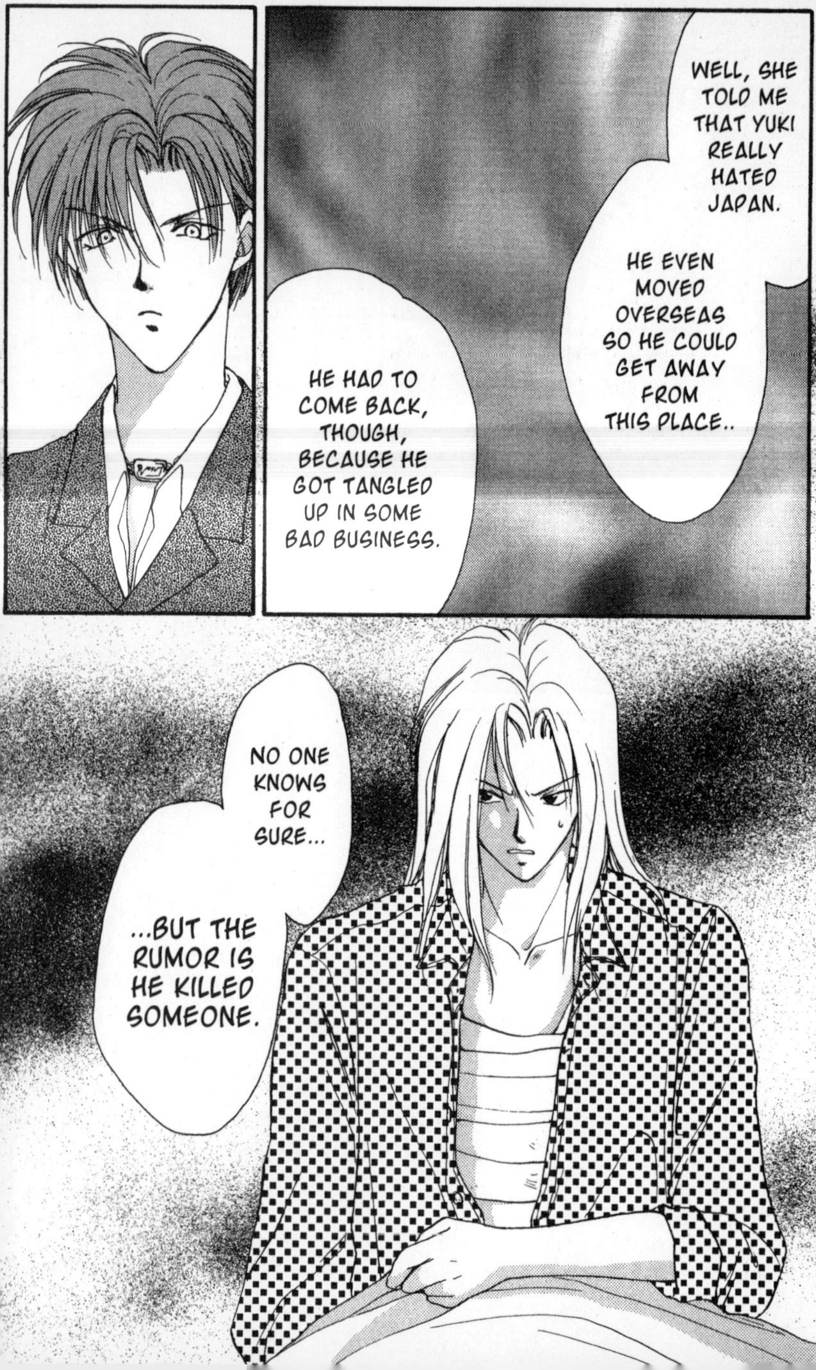
WELL, SHE TOLD ME THAT YUKI REALLY HATED JAPAN.
HE EVEN MOVED OVERSEAS SO HE COULD GET AWAY FROM THIS PLACE..
HE HAD TO COME BACK, THOUGH, BECAUSE HE GOT TANGLED UP IN SOME BAD BUSINESS.
NO ONE KNOWS FOR SURE...
...BUT THE RUMOR IS HE KILLED SOMEONE.

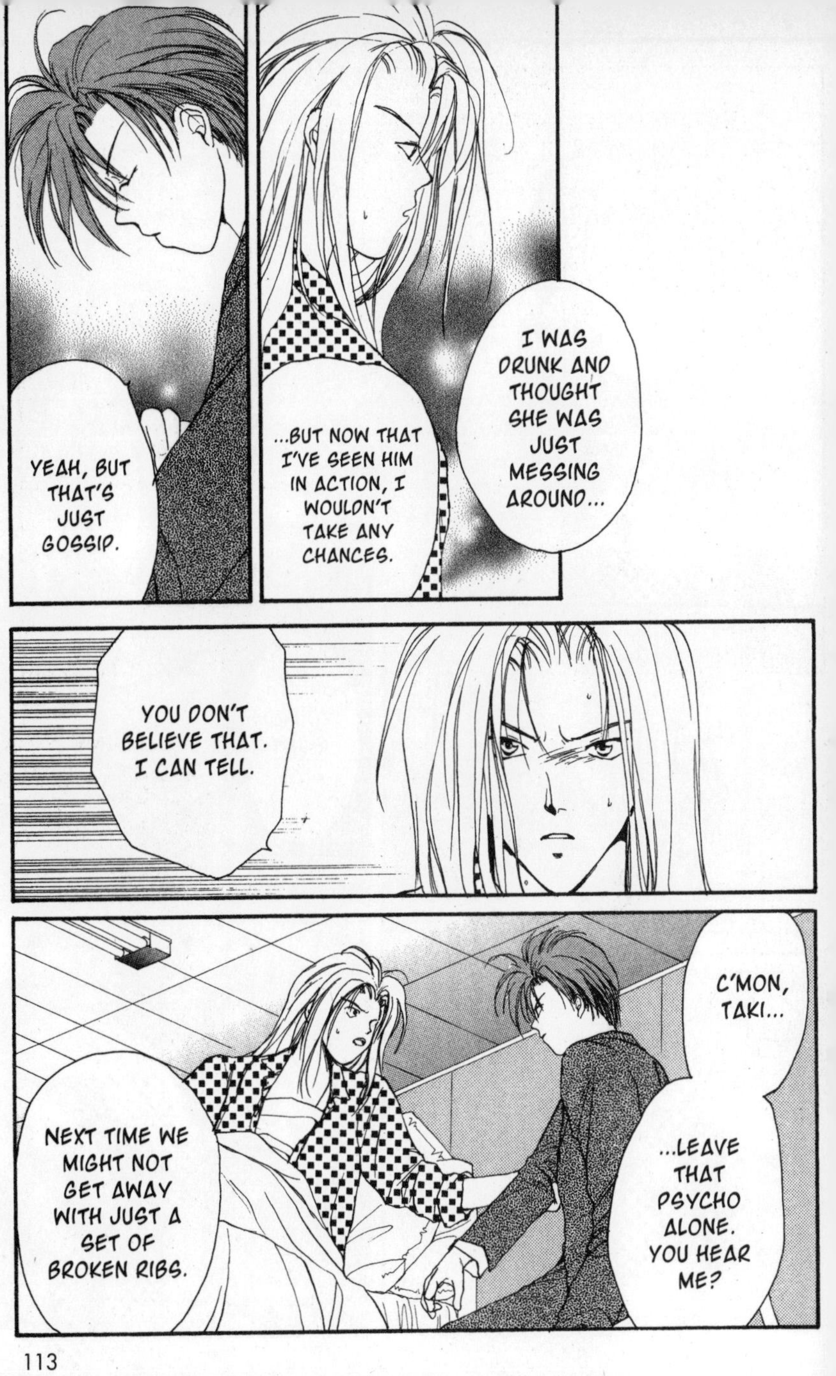
I WAS DRUNK AND THOUGHT SHE WAS JUST MESSING AROUND...
...BUT NOW THAT I'VE SEEN HIM IN ACTION, I WOULDN'T TAKE ANY CHANCES.
YEAH, BUT THAT'S JUST GOSSIP.
YOU DON'T BELIEVE THAT. I CAN TELL.
C'MON, TAKI...
...LEAVE THAT PSYCHO ALONE. YOU HEAR ME?
NEXT TIME WE MIGHT NOT GET AWAY WITH JUST A SET OF BROKEN RIBS.

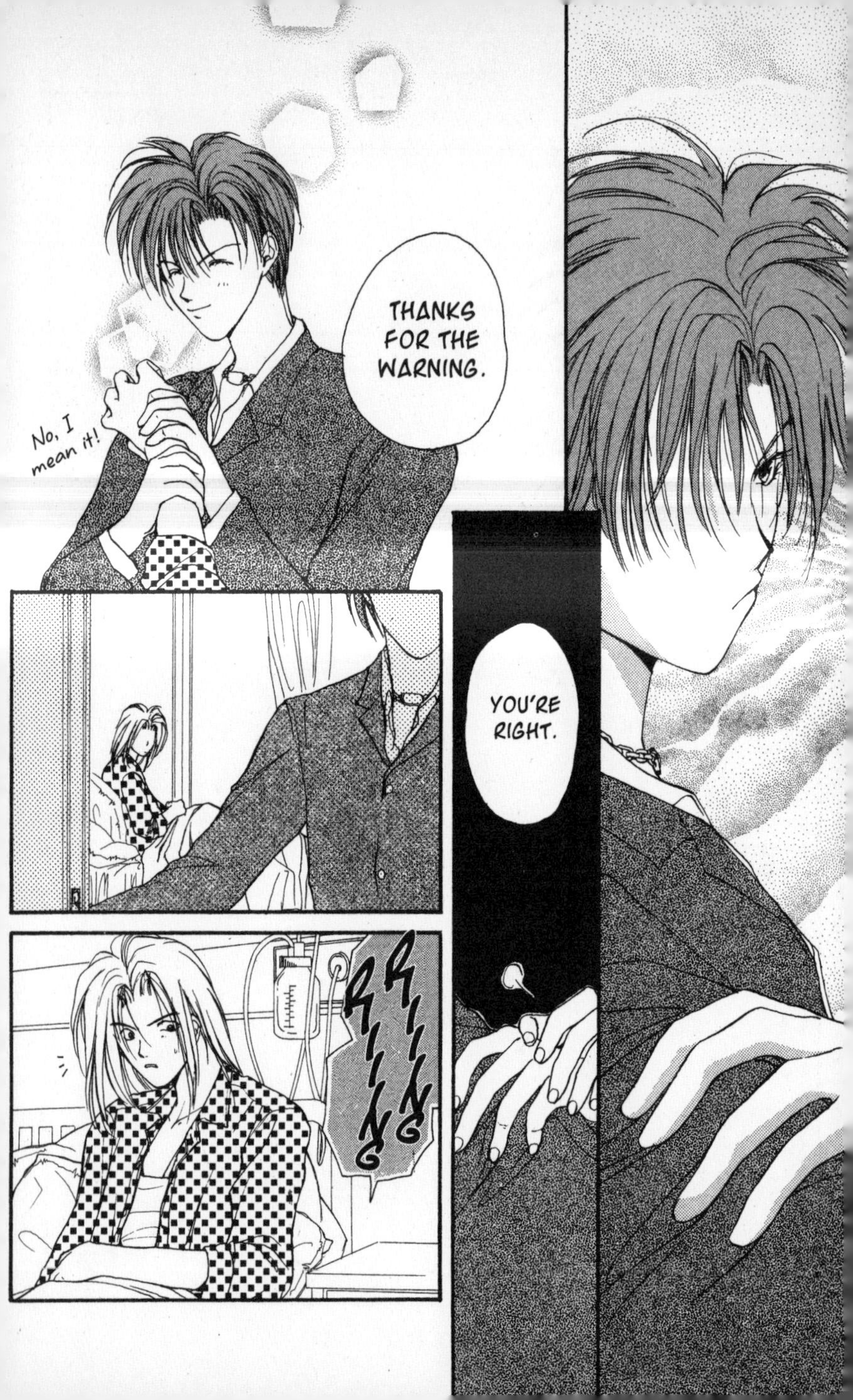
YOU'RE RIGHT.
THANKS FOR THE WARNING.
No, I mean it!
RIIING
RIING

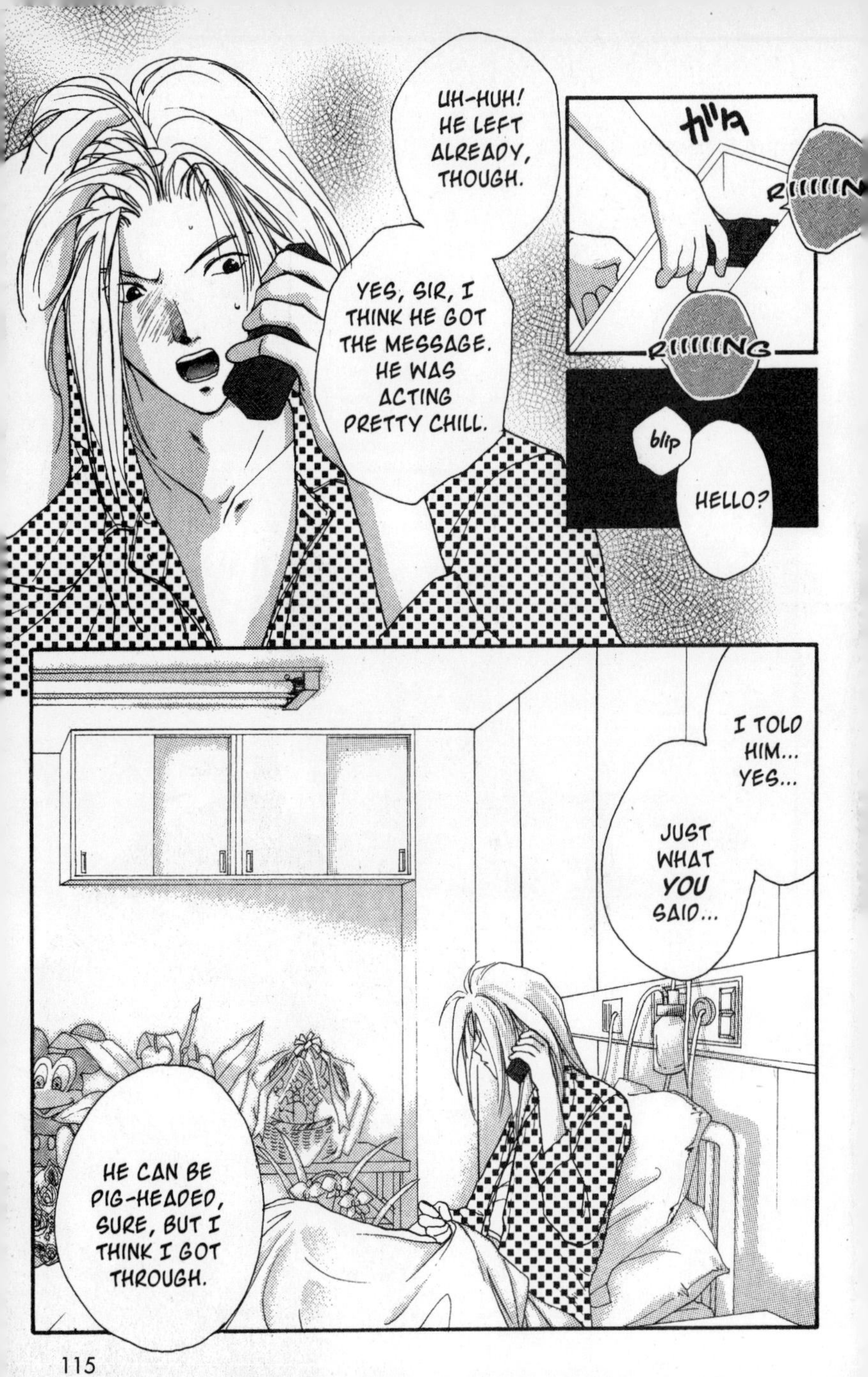
RIIIIIN
RIIIIING
blip
HELLO?
UH-HUH! HE LEFT ALREADY, THOUGH.
YES, SIR, I THINK HE GOT THE MESSAGE. HE WAS ACTING PRETTY CHILL.
I TOLD HIM... YES...
JUST WHAT YOU SAID...
HE CAN BE PIG-HEADED, SURE, BUT I THINK I GOT THROUGH.

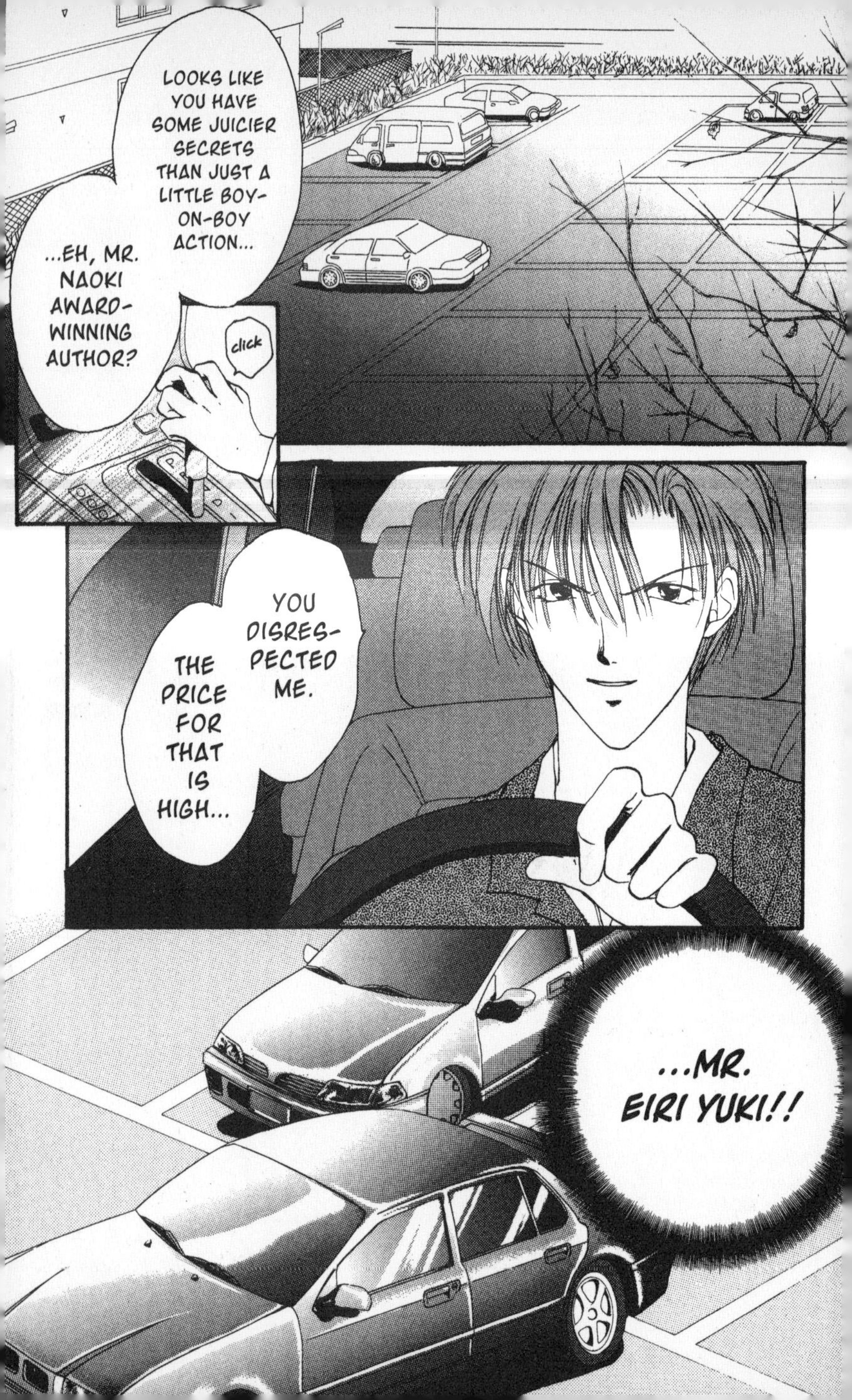
LOOKS LIKE YOU HAVE SOME JUICIER SECRETS THAN JUST A LITTLE BOY-ON-BOY ACTION...
...EH, MR. NAOKI AWARD-WINNING AUTHOR?
click
YOU DISRES-PECTED ME.
THE PRICE FOR THAT IS HIGH...
...MR. EIRI YUKI!!

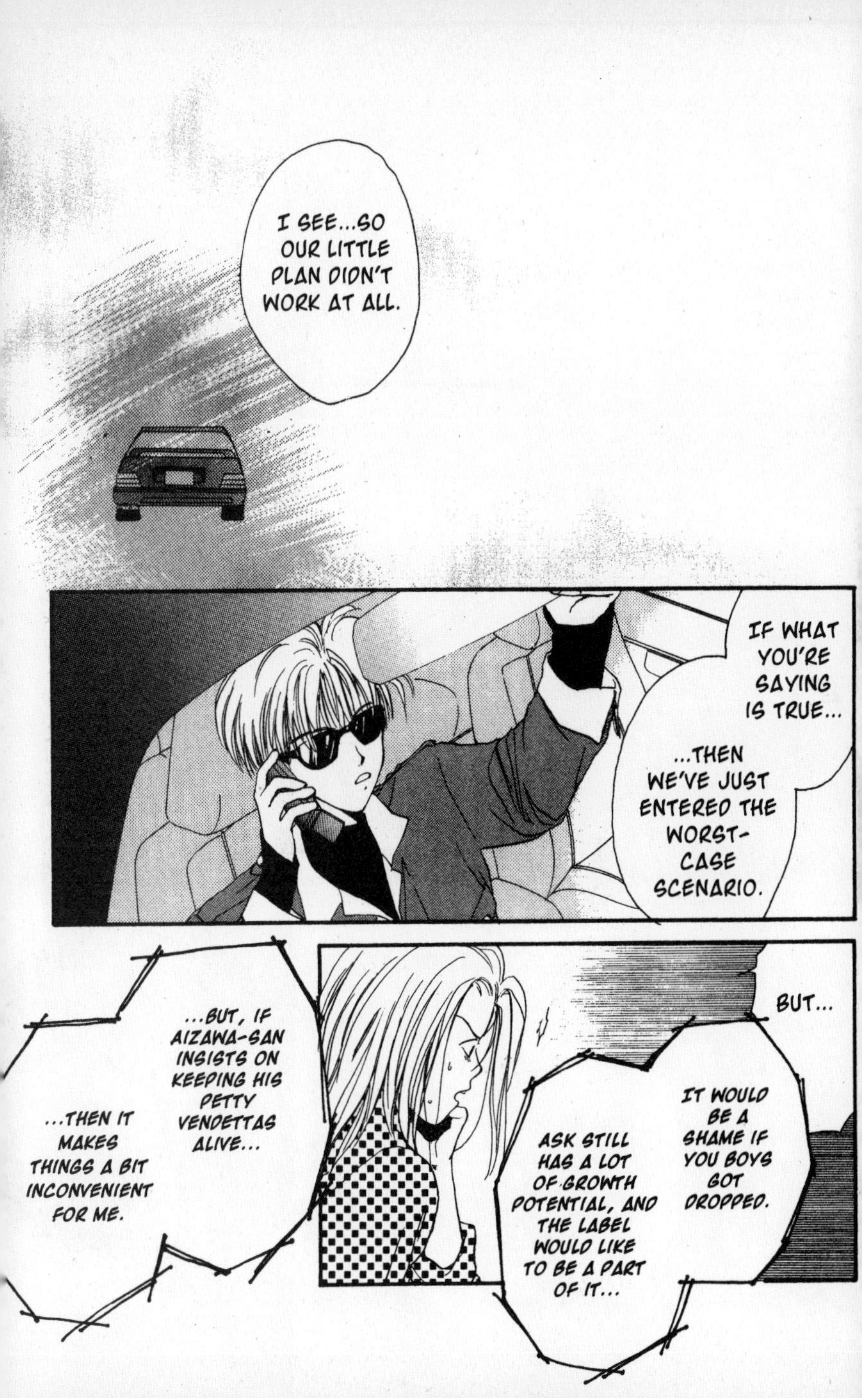
I SEE...SO OUR LITTLE PLAN DIDN'T WORK AT ALL.
IF WHAT YOU'RE SAYING IS TRUE...
...THEN WE'VE JUST ENTERED THE WORST-CASE SCENARIO.
BUT...
IT WOULD BE A SHAME IF YOU BOYS GOT DROPPED.
ASK STILL HAS A LOT OF GROWTH POTENTIAL, AND THE LABEL WOULD LIKE TO BE A PART OF IT...
...BUT, IF AIZAWA-SAN INSISTS ON KEEPING HIS PETTY VENDETTAS ALIVE...
...THEN IT MAKES THINGS A BIT INCONVENIENT FOR ME.

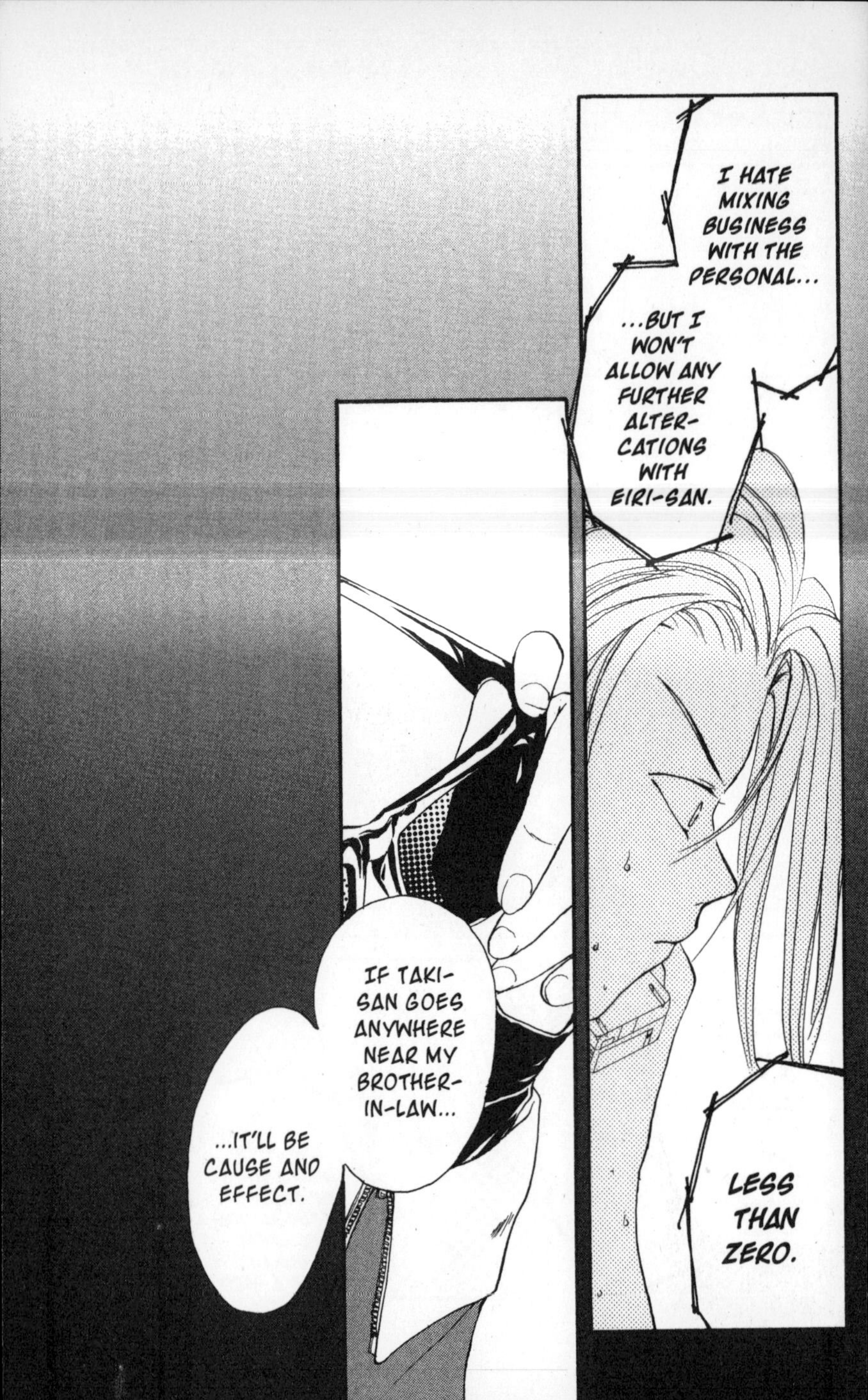
I HATE MIXING BUSINESS WITH THE PERSONAL...
...BUT I WON'T ALLOW ANY FURTHER ALTER-CATIONS WITH EIRI-SAN.
LESS THAN ZERO.
IF TAKI-SAN GOES ANYWHERE NEAR MY BROTHER-IN-LAW...
...IT'LL BE CAUSE AND EFFECT.

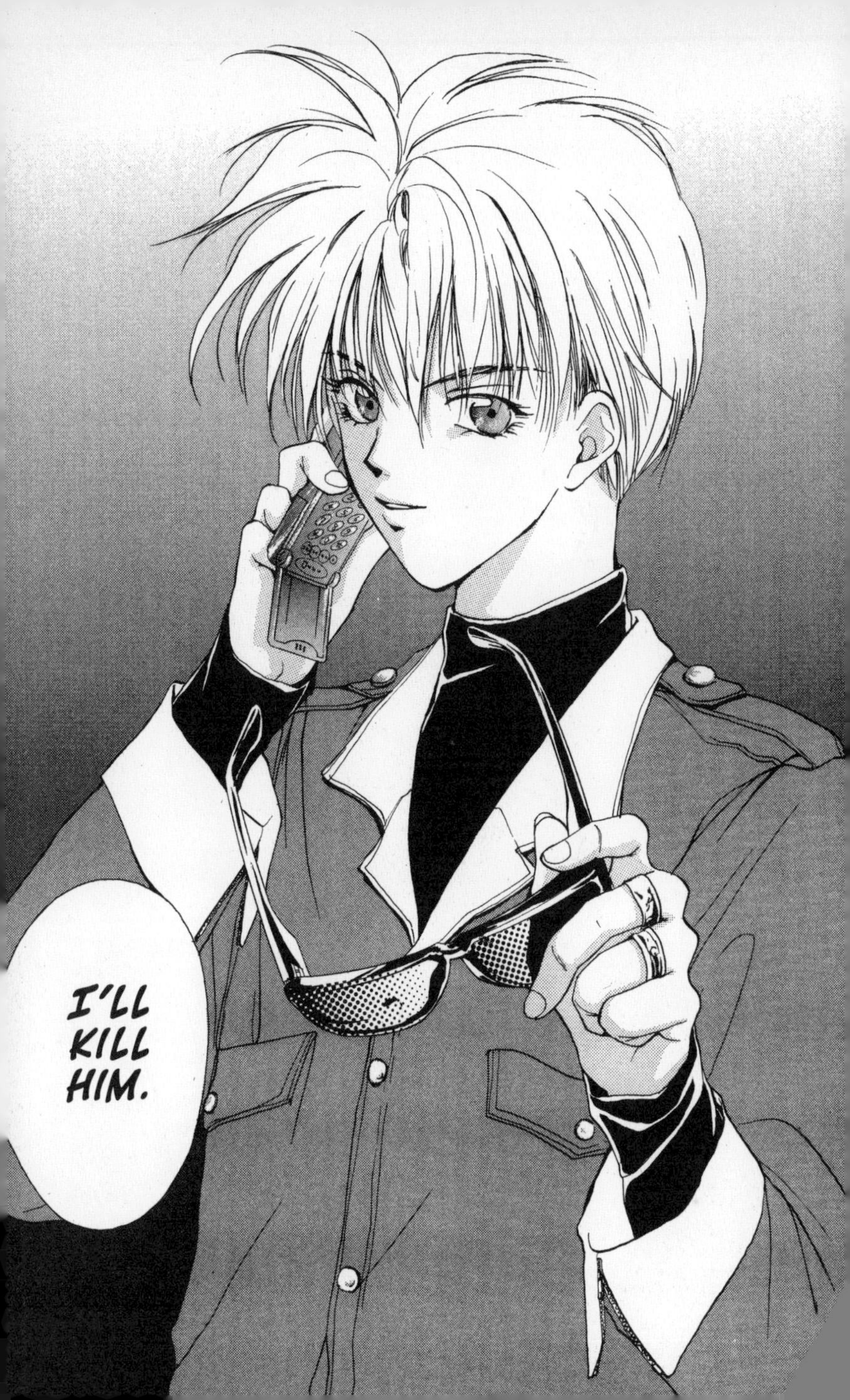
I'LL KILL HIM.

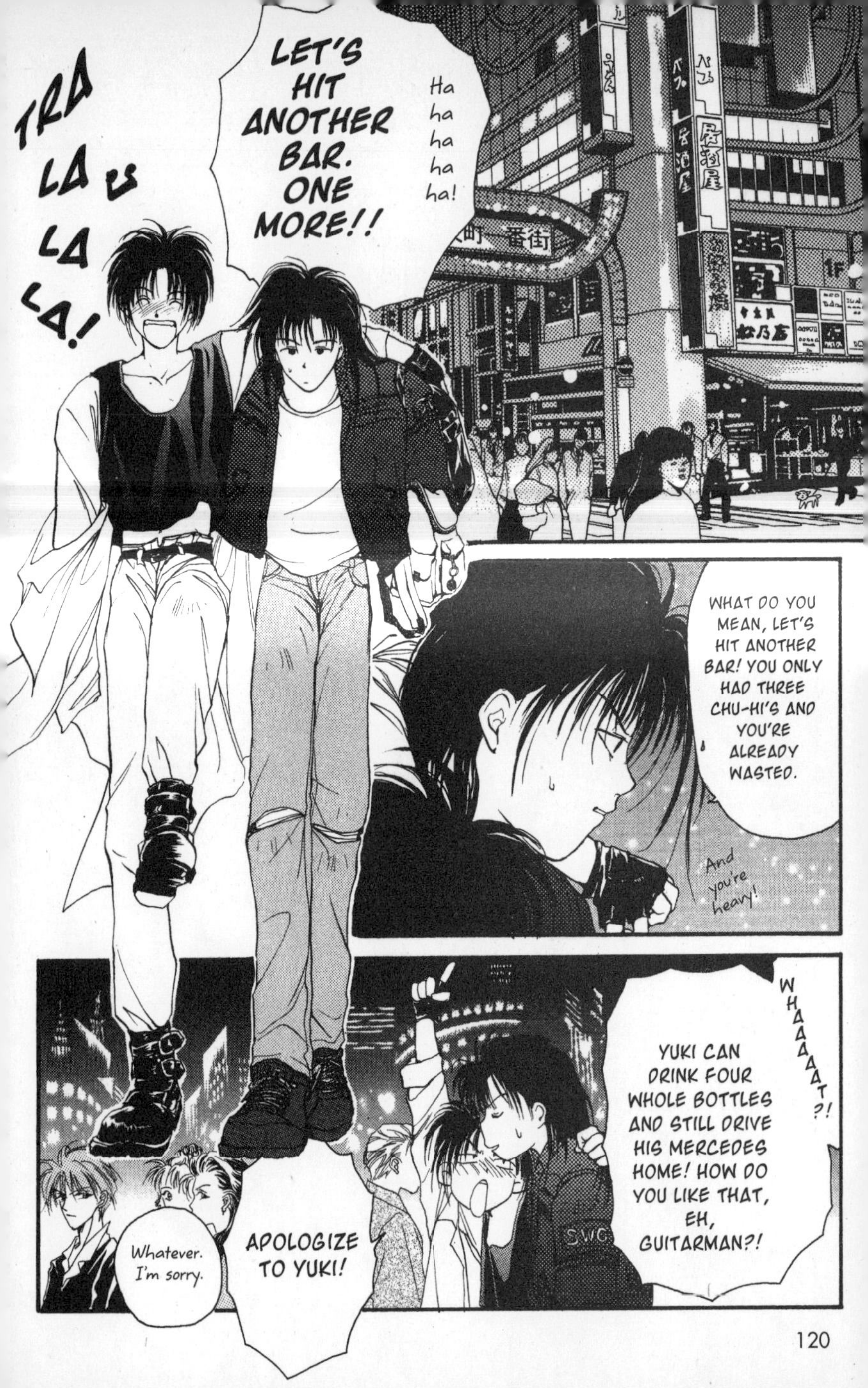
Ha ha ha ha ha!
LET'S HIT ANOTHER BAR. ONE MORE!!
TRA LA LA LA!
WHAT DO YOU MEAN, LET'S HIT ANOTHER BAR! YOU ONLY HAD THREE CHU-HI'S AND YOU'RE ALREADY WASTED.
And you're heavy!
WHAAAAAT?!
YUKI CAN DRINK FOUR WHOLE BOTTLES AND STILL DRIVE HIS MERCEDES HOME! HOW DO YOU LIKE THAT, EH, GUITARMAN?!
APOLOGIZE TO YUKI!
Whatever. I'm sorry.

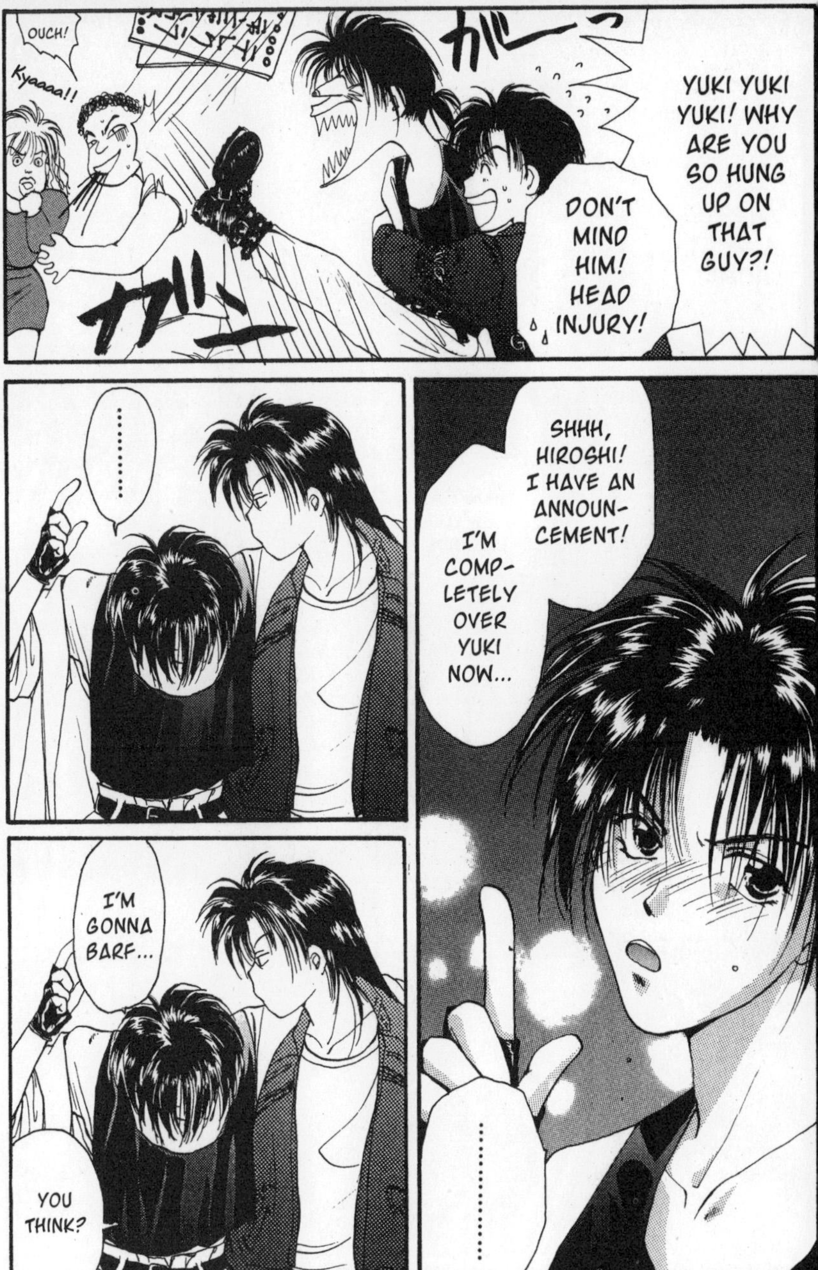
YUKI YUKI YUKI! WHY ARE YOU SO HUNG UP ON THAT GUY?!
DON'T MIND HIM! HEAD INJURY!
OUCH!
Kyaaaa!!
SHHH, HIROSHI! I HAVE AN ANNOUNCEMENT!
I'M COMPLETELY OVER YUKI NOW...
......
......
I'M GONNA BARF...
YOU THINK?

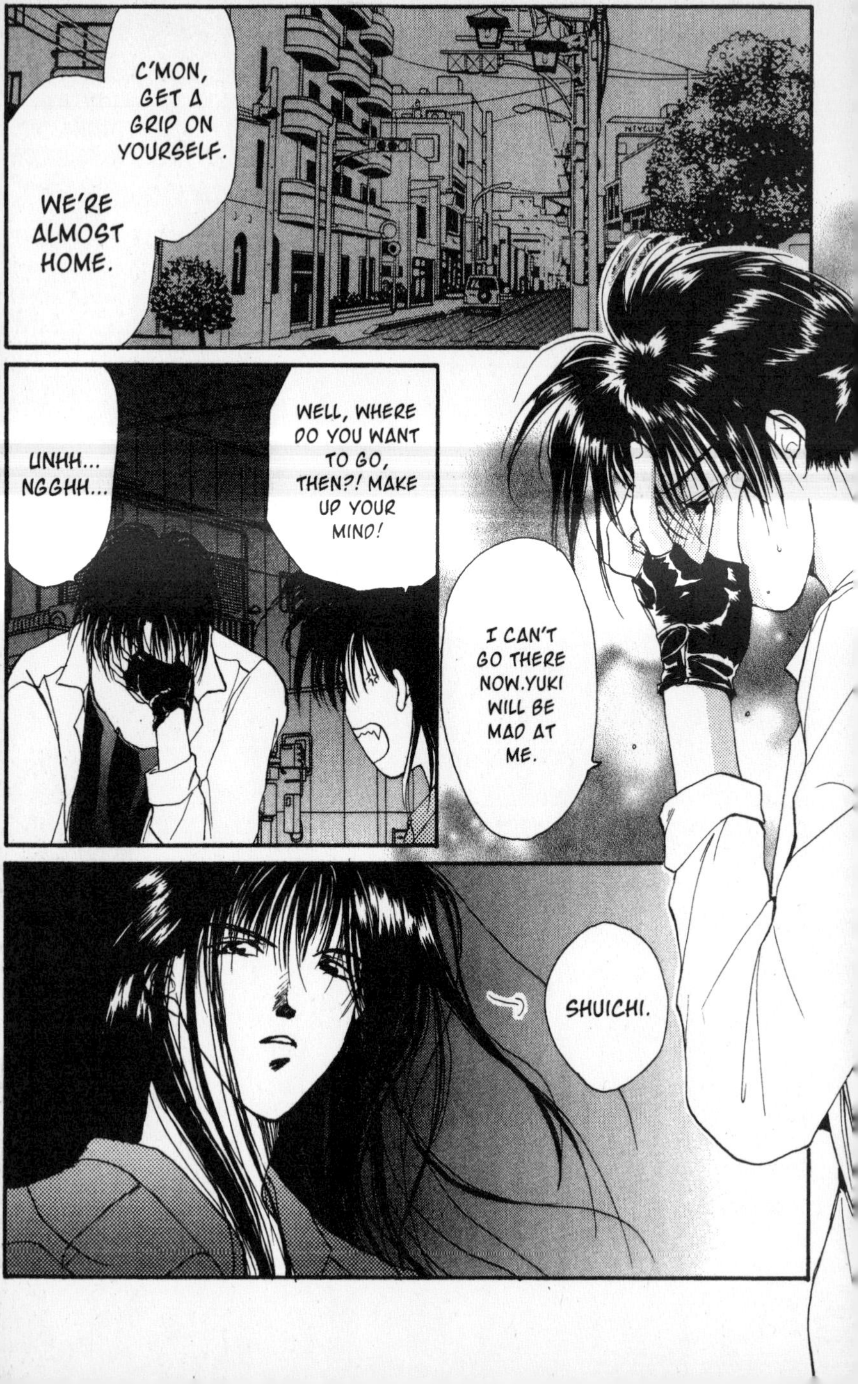
C'MON, GET A GRIP ON YOURSELF.
WE'RE ALMOST HOME.
WELL, WHERE DO YOU WANT TO GO, THEN?! MAKE UP YOUR MIND!
UNHH... NGGHH...
I CAN'T GO THERE NOW. YUKI WILL BE MAD AT ME.
SHUICHI.

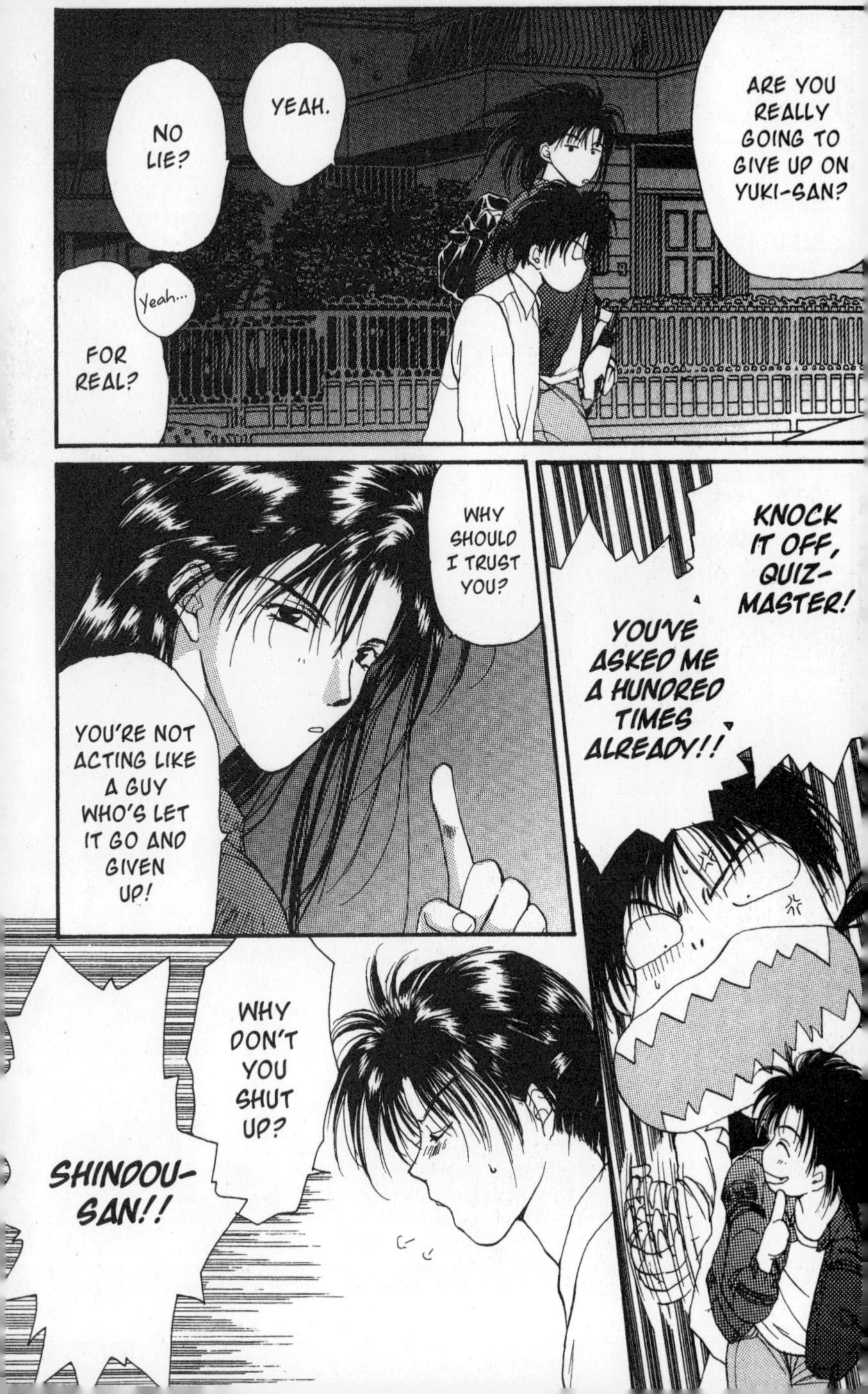
ARE YOU REALLY GOING TO GIVE UP ON YUKI-SAN?
YEAH.
NO LIE?
Yeah...
FOR REAL?
KNOCK IT OFF, QUIZ-MASTER!
YOU'VE ASKED ME A HUNDRED TIMES ALREADY!!
WHY SHOULD I TRUST YOU?
YOU'RE NOT ACTING LIKE A GUY WHO'S LET IT GO AND GIVEN UP!
WHY DON'T YOU SHUT UP?
SHINDOU-SAN!!

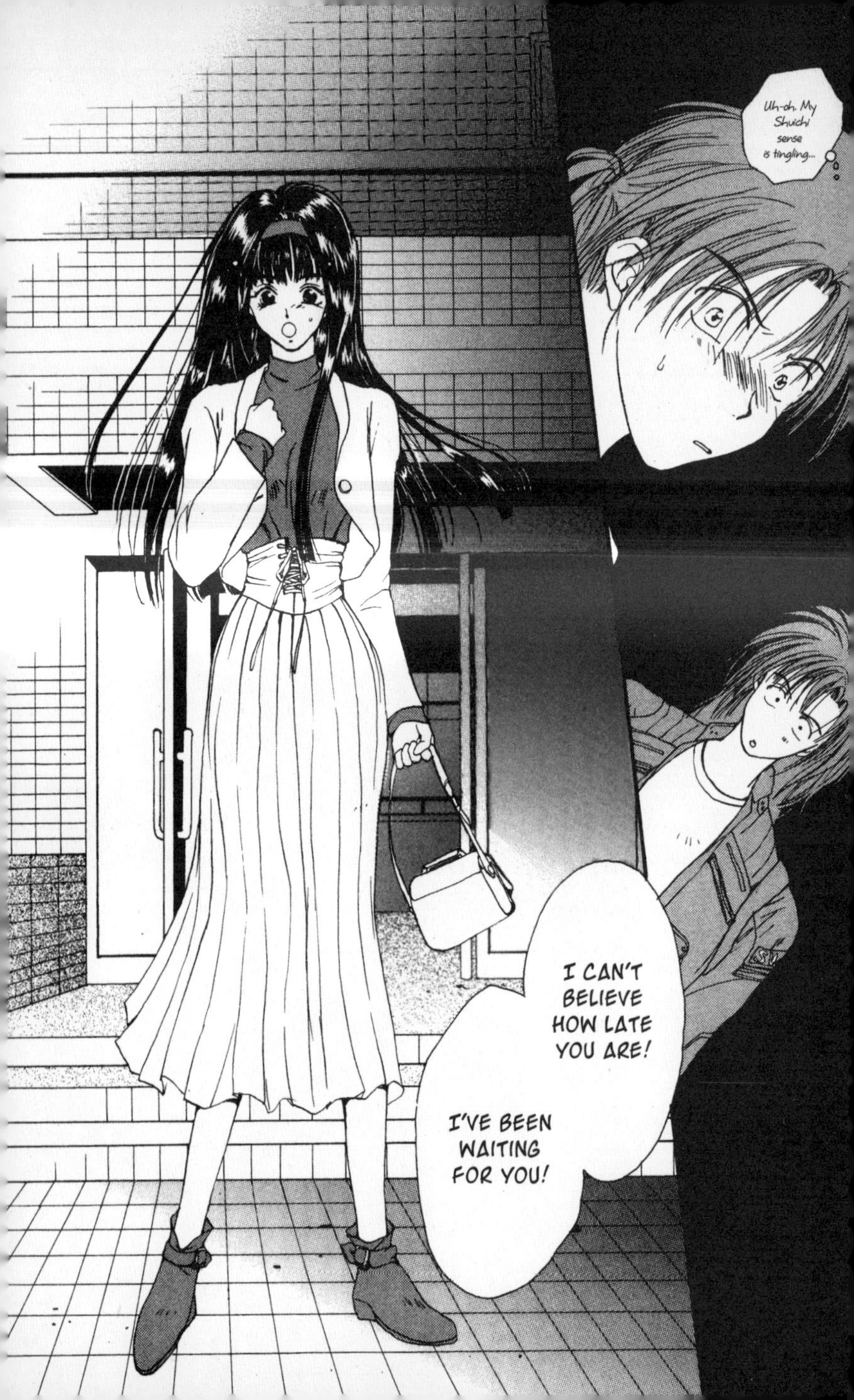
Uh-oh. My Shuichi sense is tingling...
I CAN'T BELIEVE HOW LATE YOU ARE!
I'VE BEEN WAITING FOR YOU!

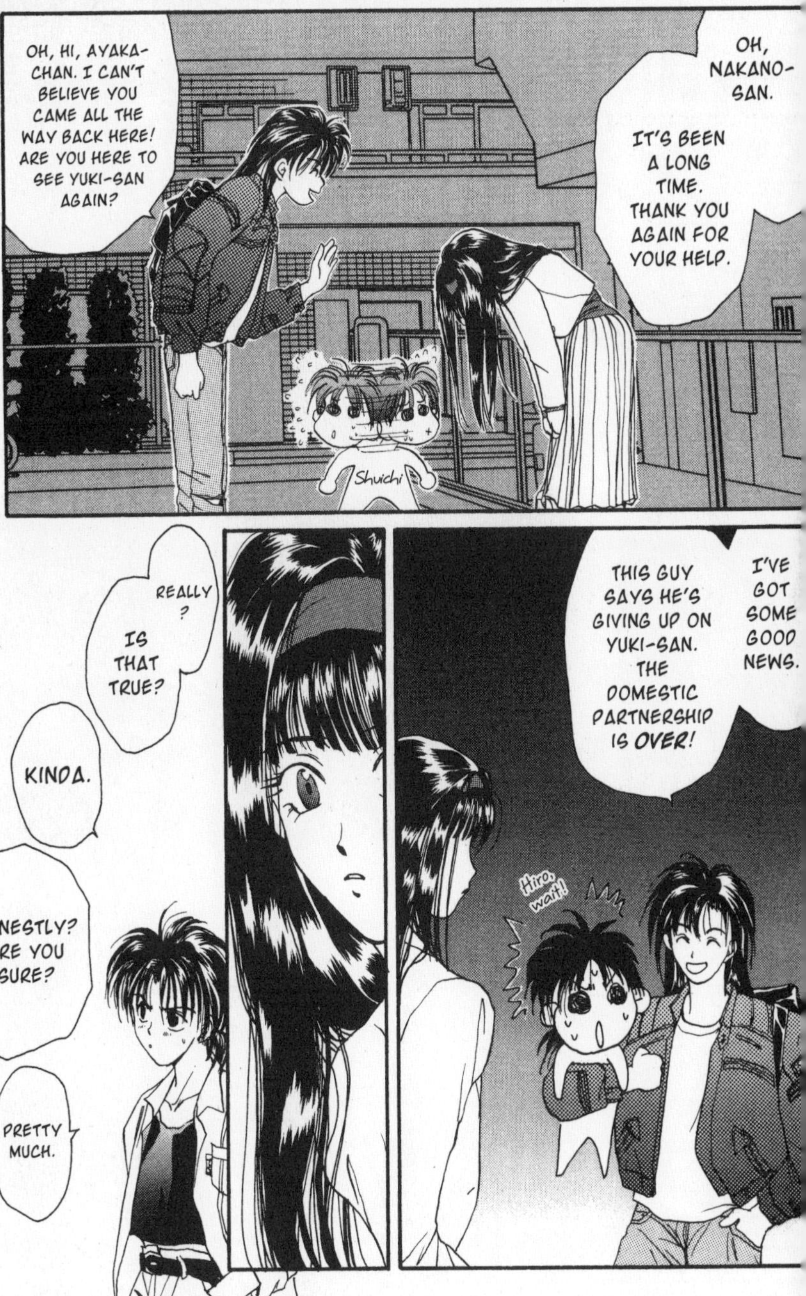
OH, NAKANO-SAN.
IT'S BEEN A LONG TIME. THANK YOU AGAIN FOR YOUR HELP.
OH, HI, AYAKA-CHAN. I CAN'T BELIEVE YOU CAME ALL THE WAY BACK HERE! ARE YOU HERE TO SEE YUKI-SAN AGAIN?
Shuichi
I'VE GOT SOME GOOD NEWS.
THIS GUY SAYS HE'S GIVING UP ON YUKI-SAN. THE DOMESTIC PARTNERSHIP IS OVER!
Hiro, wait!
REALLY? IS THAT TRUE?
KINDA.
HONESTLY? ARE YOU SURE?
PRETTY MUCH.

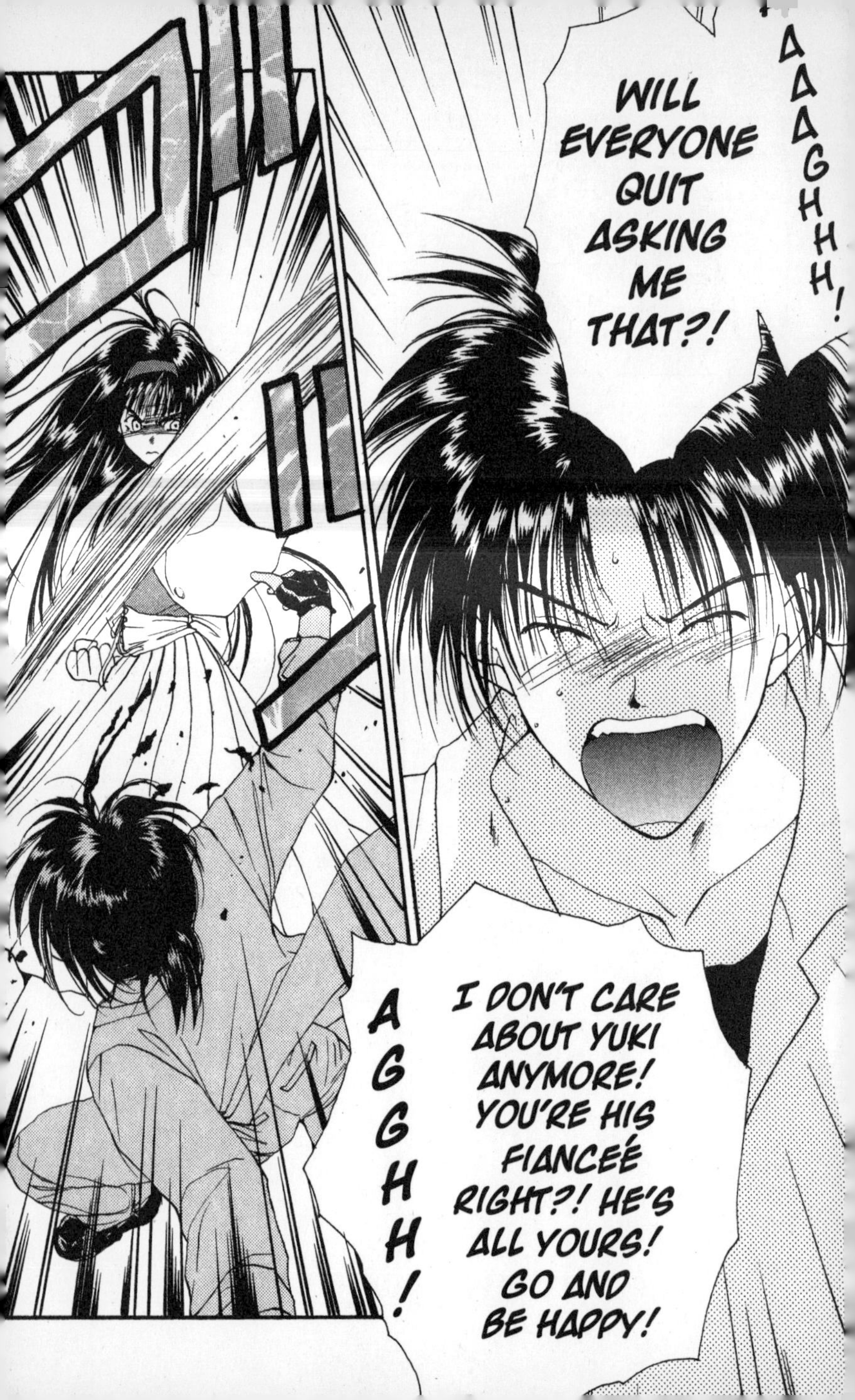
AAAGHHH!
WILL EVERYONE QUIT ASKING ME THAT?!
I DON'T CARE ABOUT YUKI ANYMORE! YOU'RE HIS FIANCEÉ RIGHT?! HE'S ALL YOURS! GO AND BE HAPPY!
AGGHH!

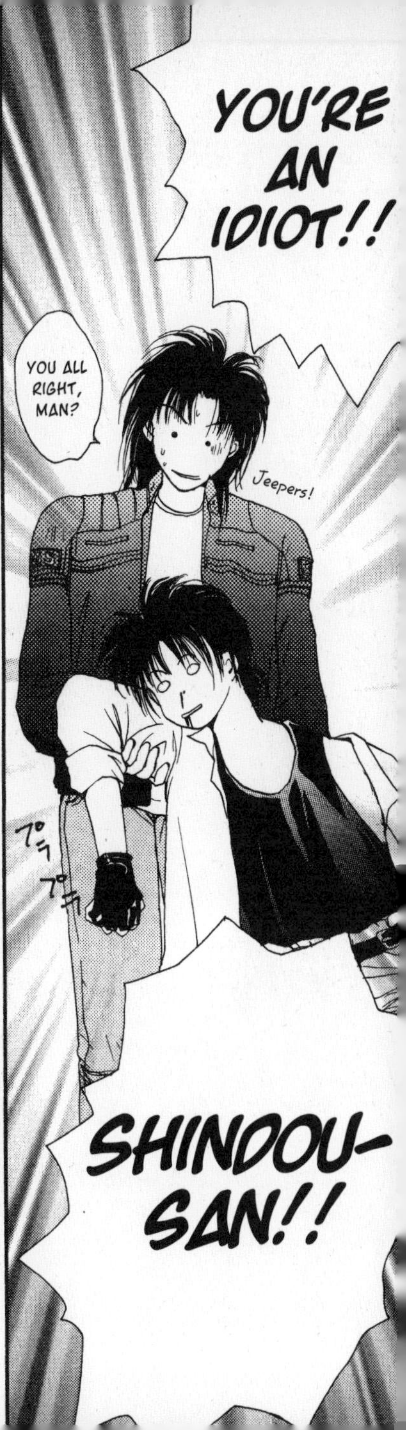
YOU'RE AN IDIOT!!
Jeepers!
YOU ALL RIGHT, MAN?
SHINDOU-SAN!!

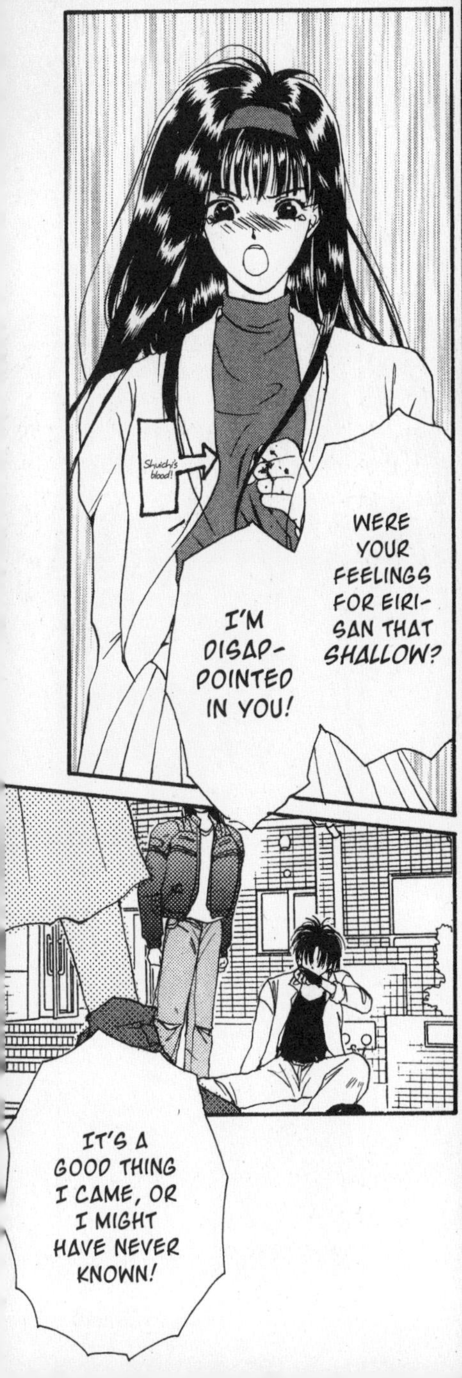
WERE YOUR FEELINGS FOR EIRI-SAN THAT SHALLOW?
I'M DISAP-POINTED IN YOU!
Shuichi's blood!
IT'S A GOOD THING I CAME, OR I MIGHT HAVE NEVER KNOWN!

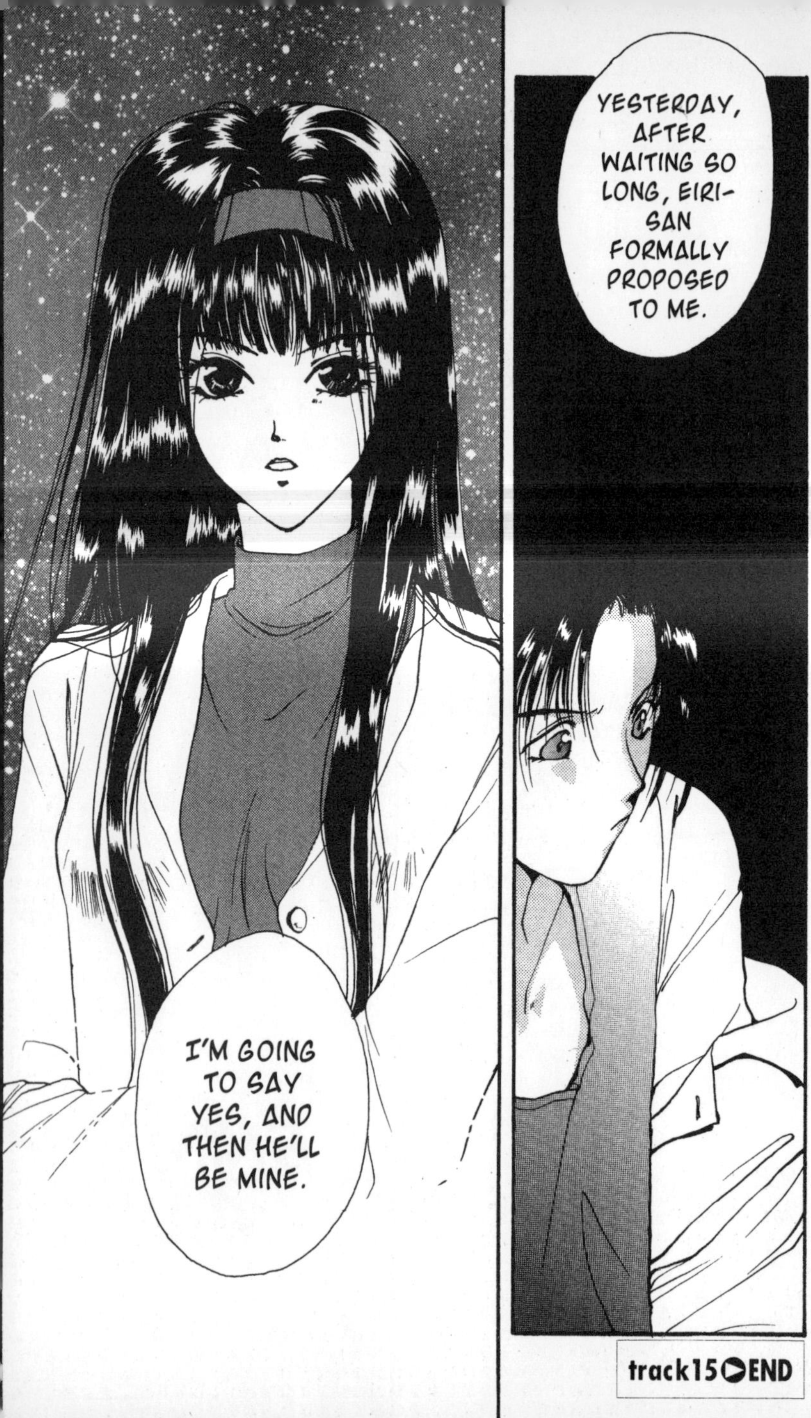
YESTERDAY, AFTER WAITING SO LONG, EIRI-SAN FORMALLY PROPOSED TO ME.
I'M GOING TO SAY YES, AND THEN HE'LL BE MINE.
track15 END

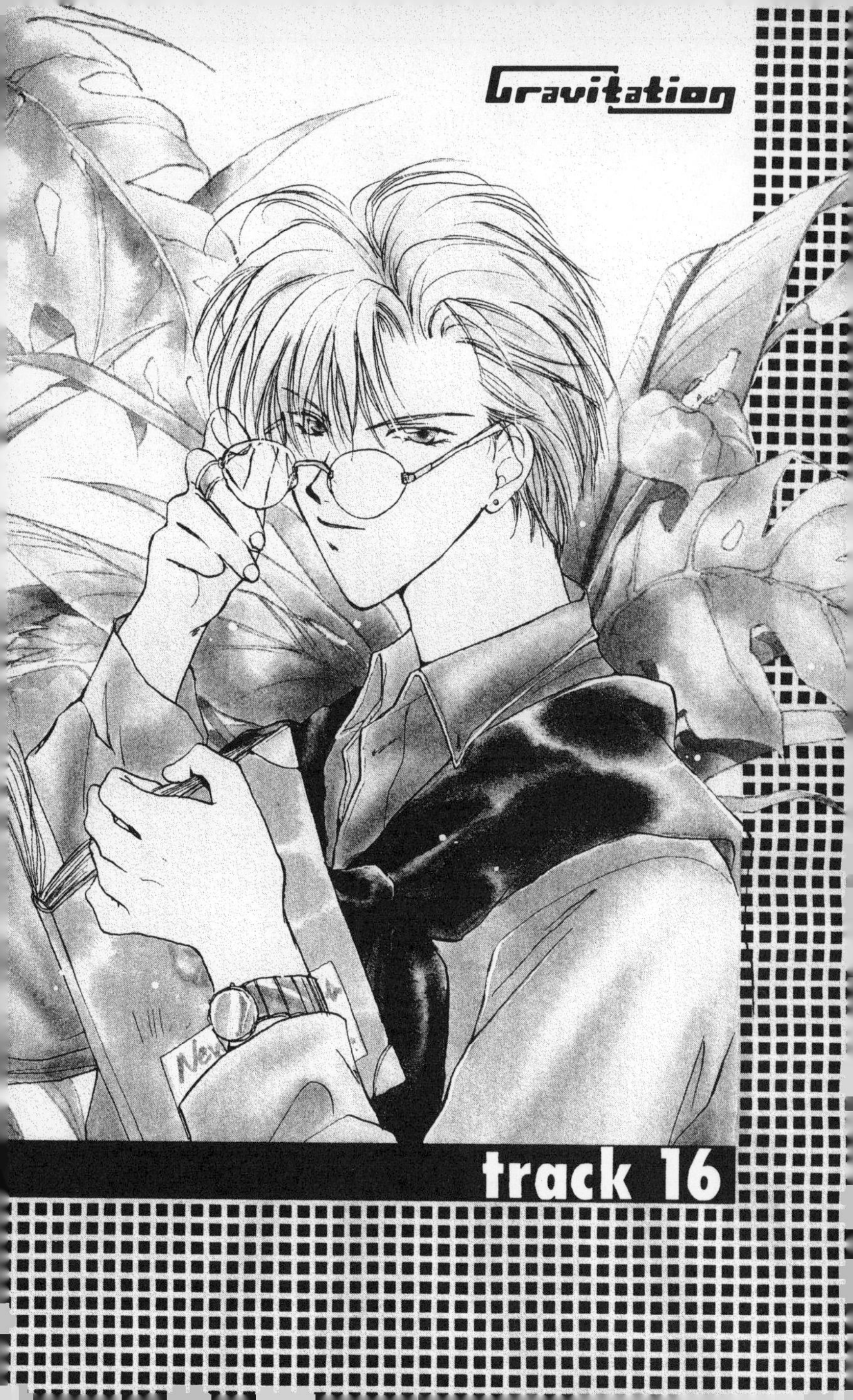
Gravitation
track 16
New

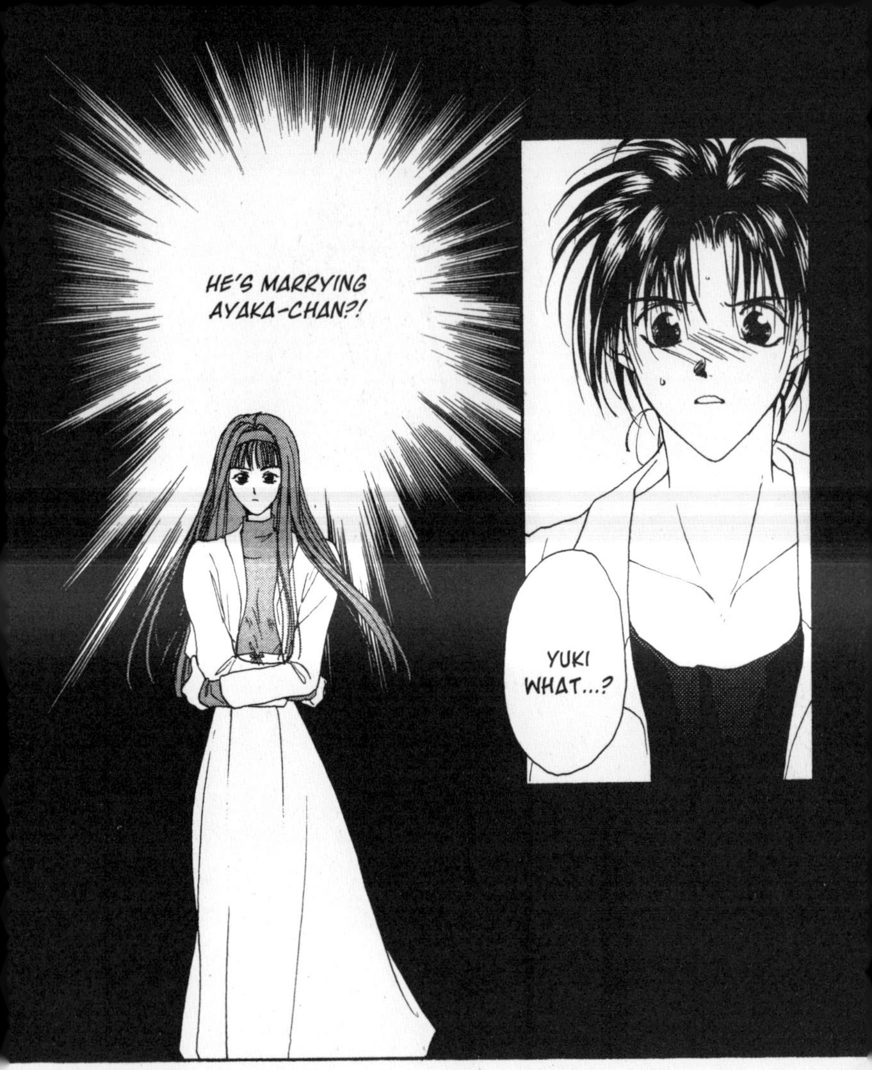
YUKI WHAT...?
HE'S MARRYING AYAKA-CHAN?!

ABOUT GRAVITATION TRACK 16

Ayaka-chan has a long face—literally! My readers ask me, "So what does she eat to get that way?" The queen of long silky hair, Ayaka. Anyway, what's going on with Eiri...oops! It would be no fun if I told you! What do you think all the ruckus will be over this supposed marriage? I'm finally able to fill in the relationship between Eiri and Ayaka properly. Does Ayaka-chan seem like a different person all of a sudden? Don't worry about it. I just changed the way I draw her a bit. (I drew her head a little longer than before!) So sit back, and read on! Things are going to start breaking down from this point forward. So who do you think is going to take the fall? You'll just have to find out in book 5!

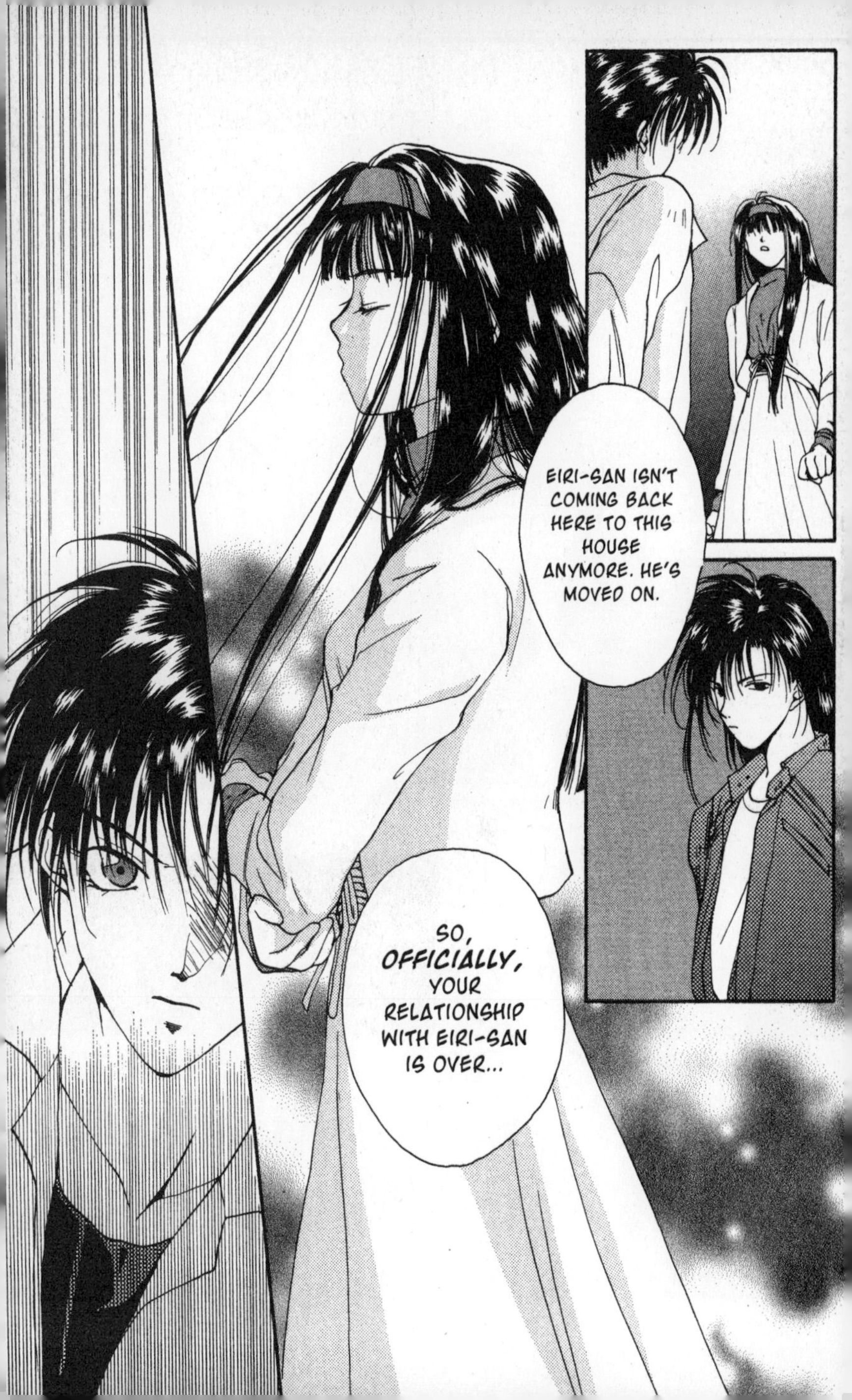
EIRI-SAN ISN'T COMING BACK HERE TO THIS HOUSE ANYMORE. HE'S MOVED ON.
SO, OFFICIALLY, YOUR RELATIONSHIP WITH EIRI-SAN IS OVER...

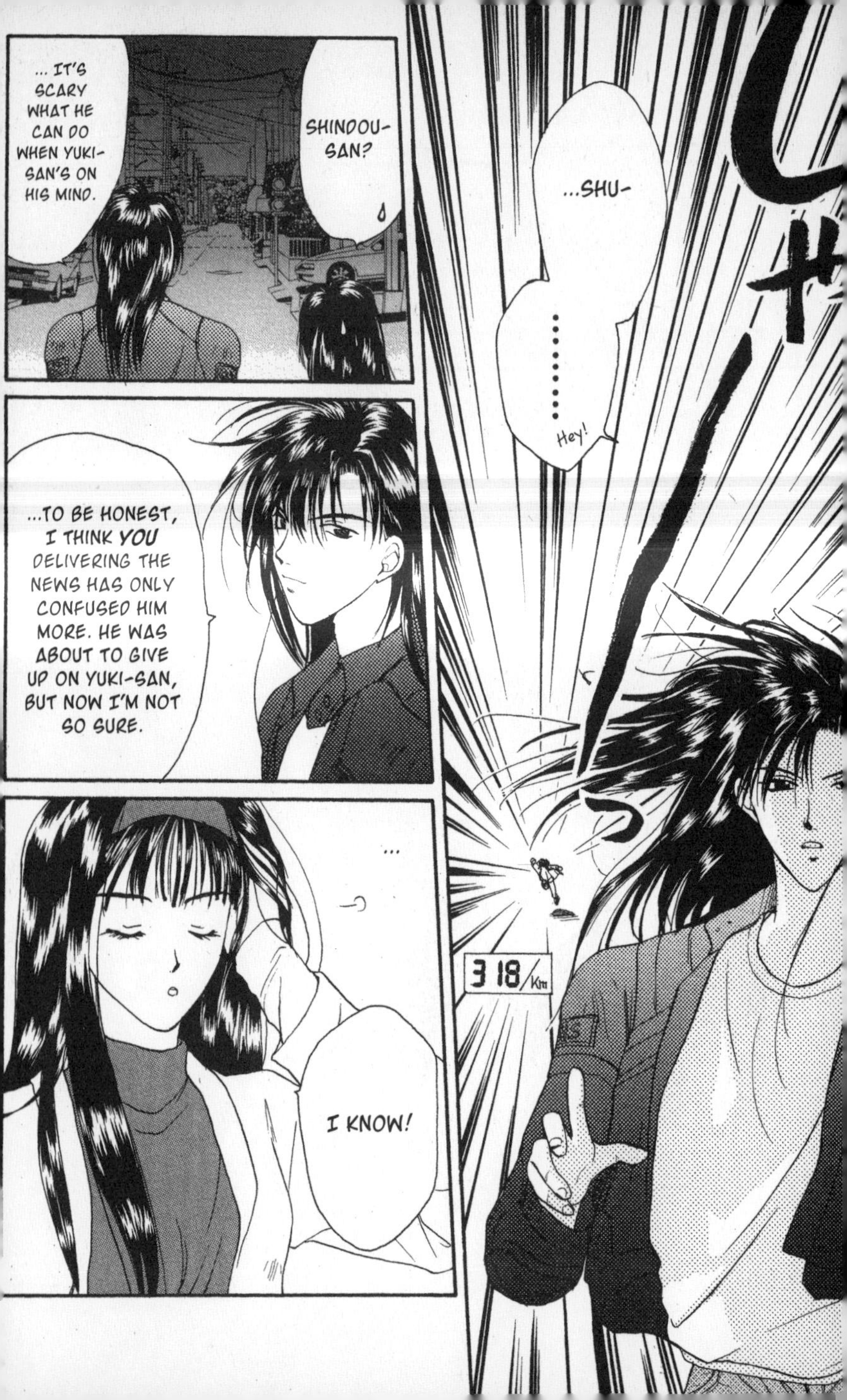
...SHU-
......
Hey!
318/Km
SHINDOU-SAN?
... IT'S SCARY WHAT HE CAN DO WHEN YUKI-SAN'S ON HIS MIND.
...TO BE HONEST, I THINK *YOU* DELIVERING THE NEWS HAS ONLY CONFUSED HIM MORE. HE WAS ABOUT TO GIVE UP ON YUKI-SAN, BUT NOW I'M NOT SO SURE.
...
I KNOW!

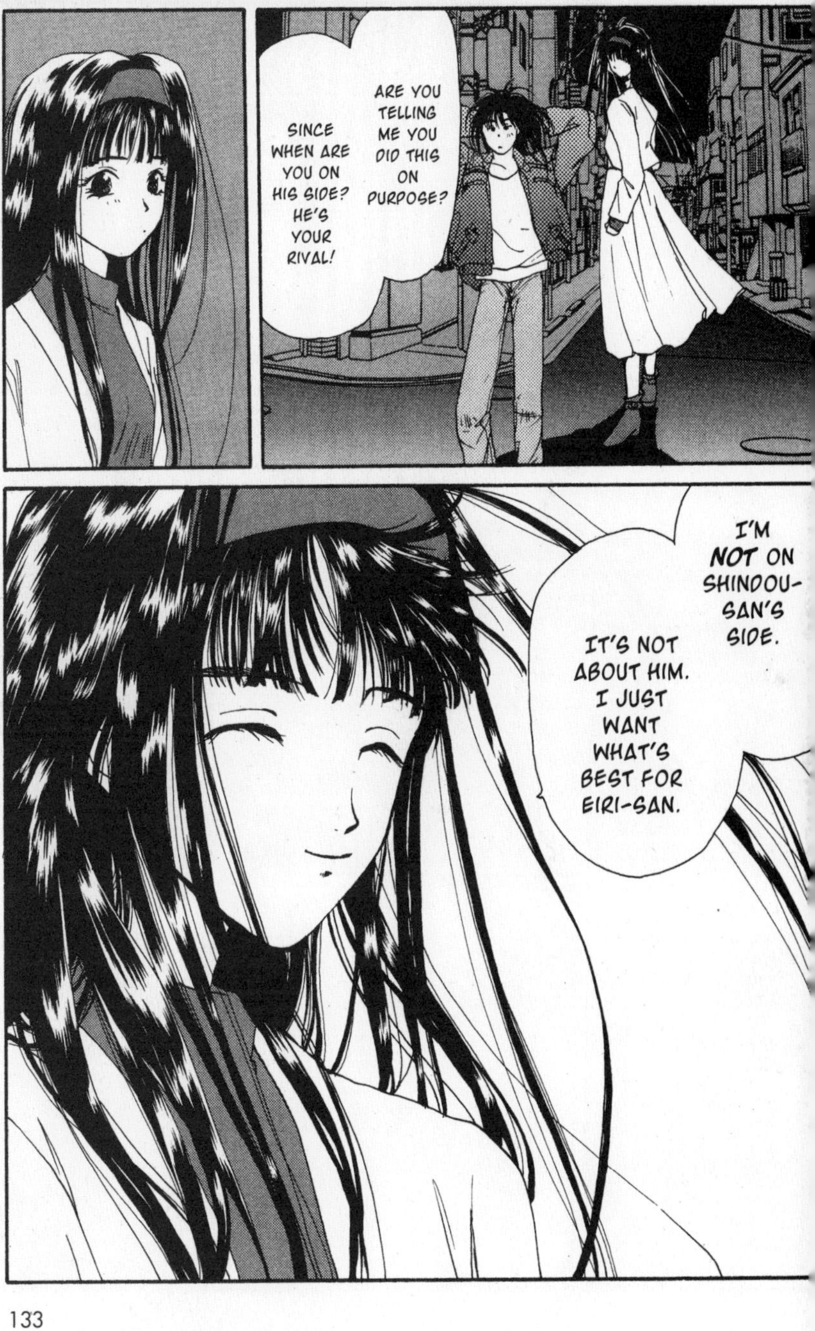
ARE YOU TELLING ME YOU DID THIS ON PURPOSE?
SINCE WHEN ARE YOU ON HIS SIDE? HE'S YOUR RIVAL!
I'M **NOT** ON SHINDOU-SAN'S SIDE.
IT'S NOT ABOUT HIM. I JUST WANT WHAT'S BEST FOR EIRI-SAN.

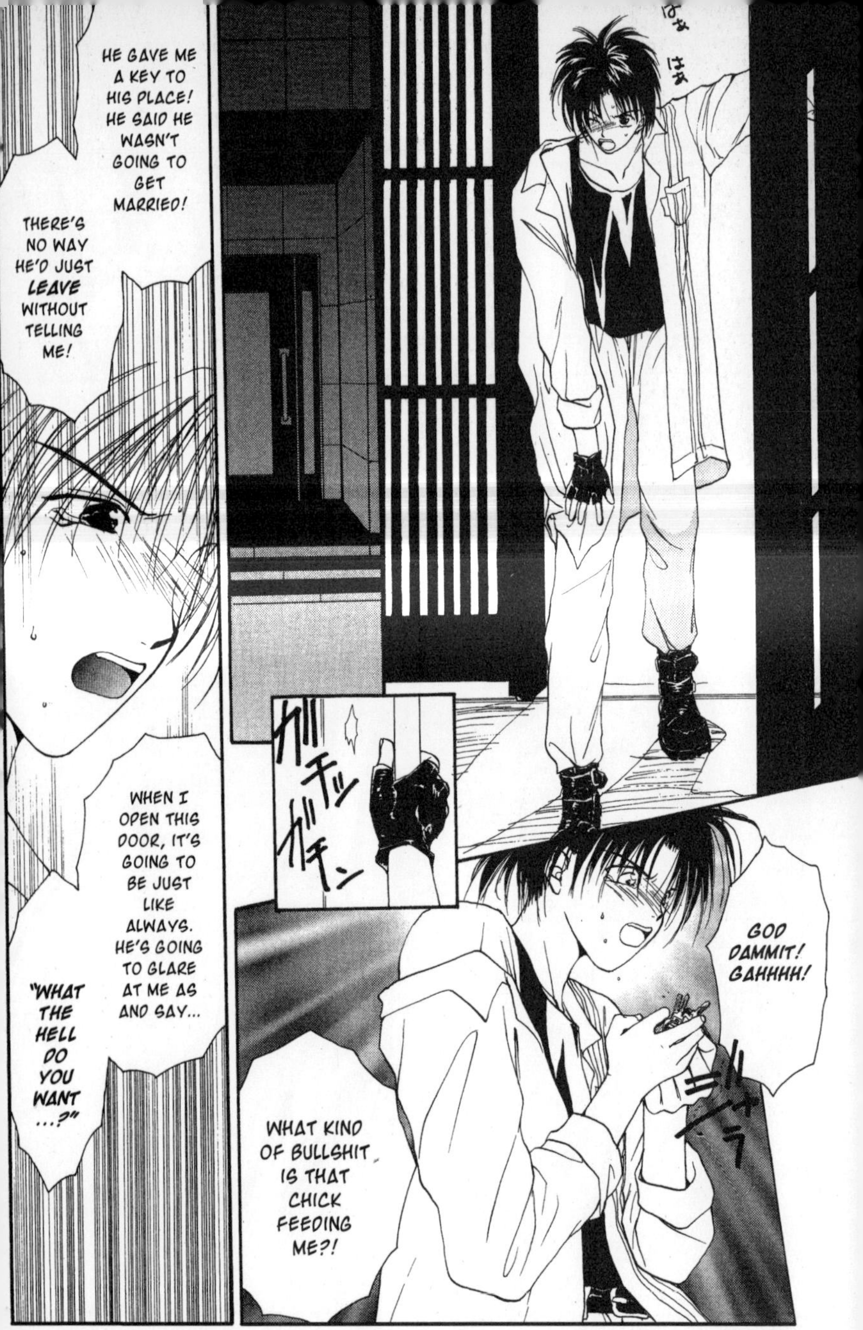
はぁ はぁ
ガチッ ガチン
GOD DAMMIT! GAHHHH!
WHAT KIND OF BULLSHIT IS THAT CHICK FEEDING ME?!
HE GAVE ME A KEY TO HIS PLACE! HE SAID HE WASN'T GOING TO GET MARRIED!
THERE'S NO WAY HE'D JUST LEAVE WITHOUT TELLING ME!
WHEN I OPEN THIS DOOR, IT'S GOING TO BE JUST LIKE ALWAYS. HE'S GOING TO GLARE AT ME AS AND SAY...
"WHAT THE HELL DO YOU WANT...?"

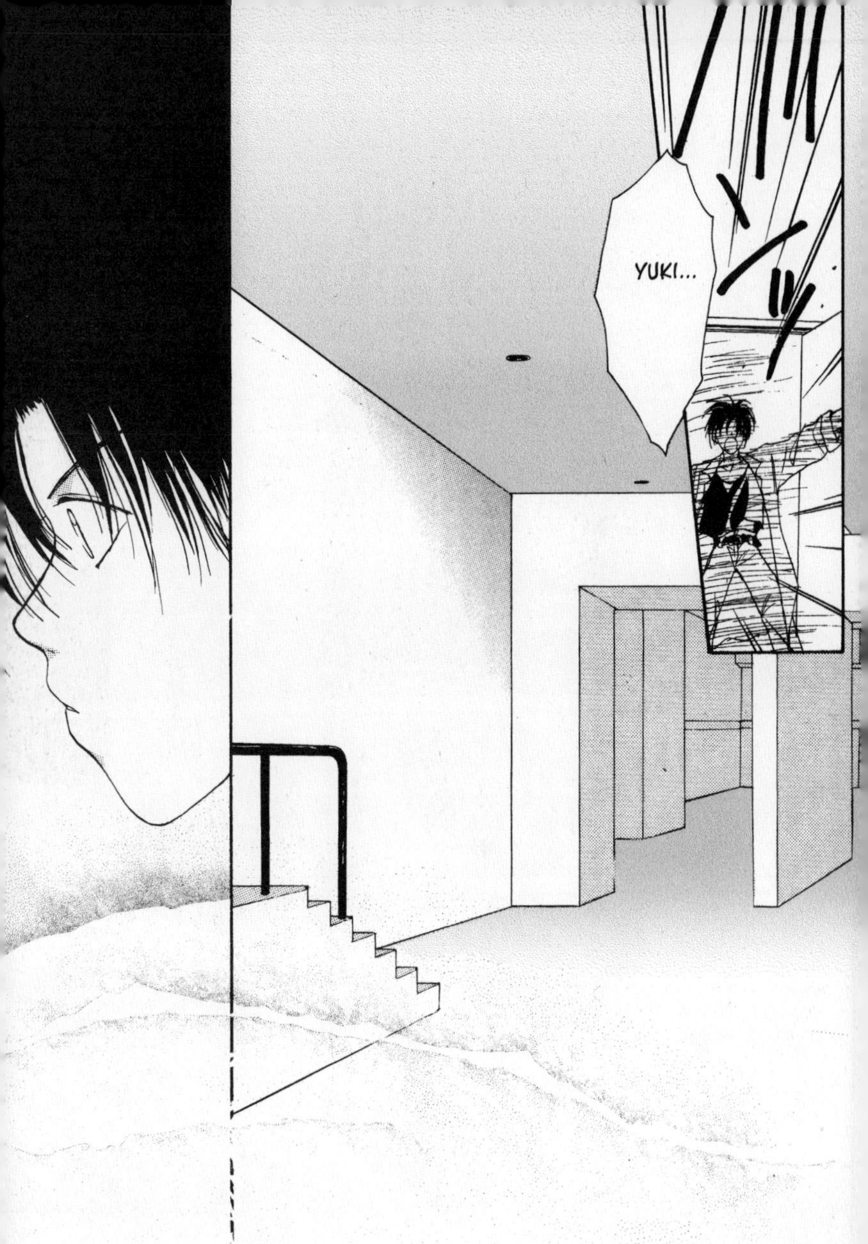
YUKI...

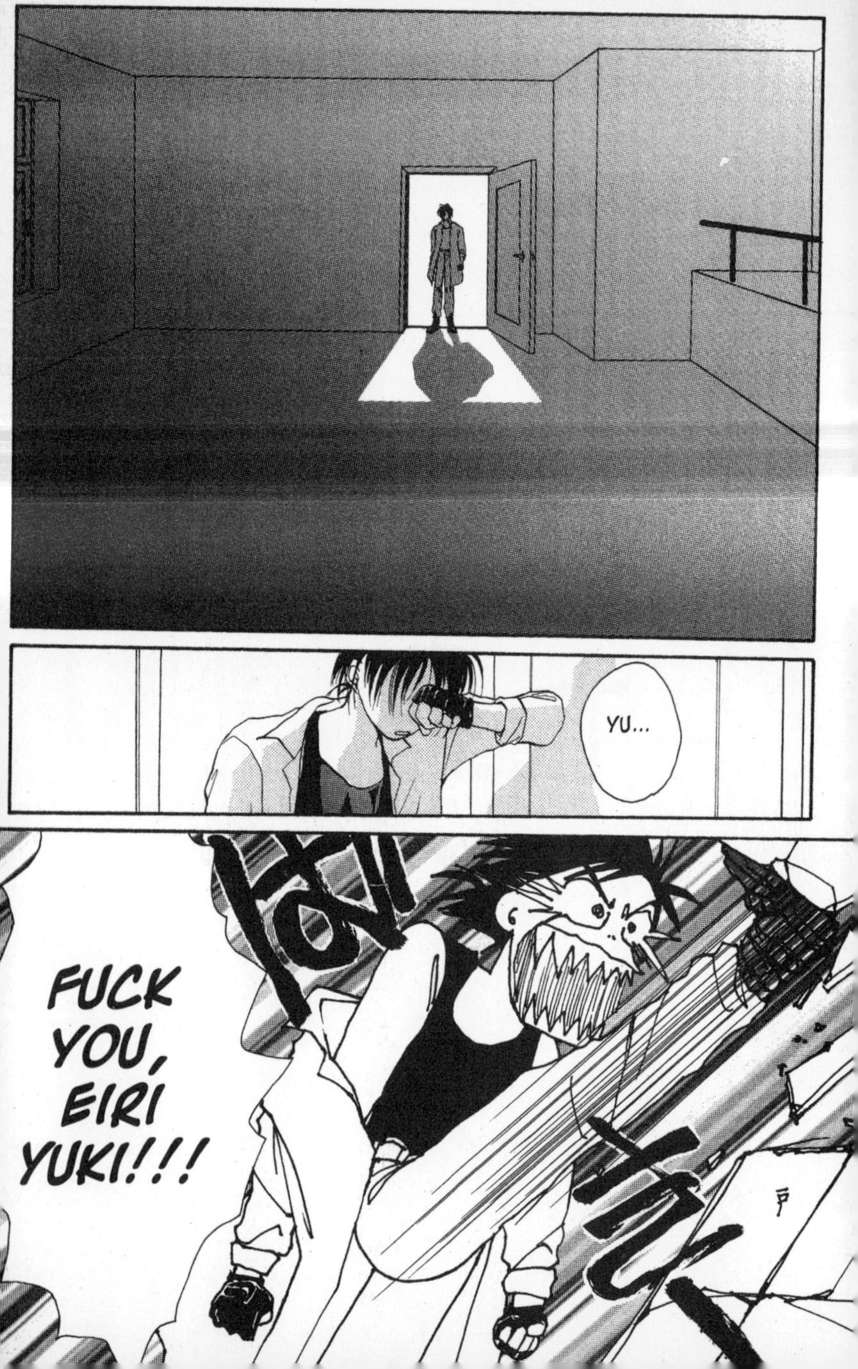
YU...
FUCK YOU, EIRI YUKI!!!

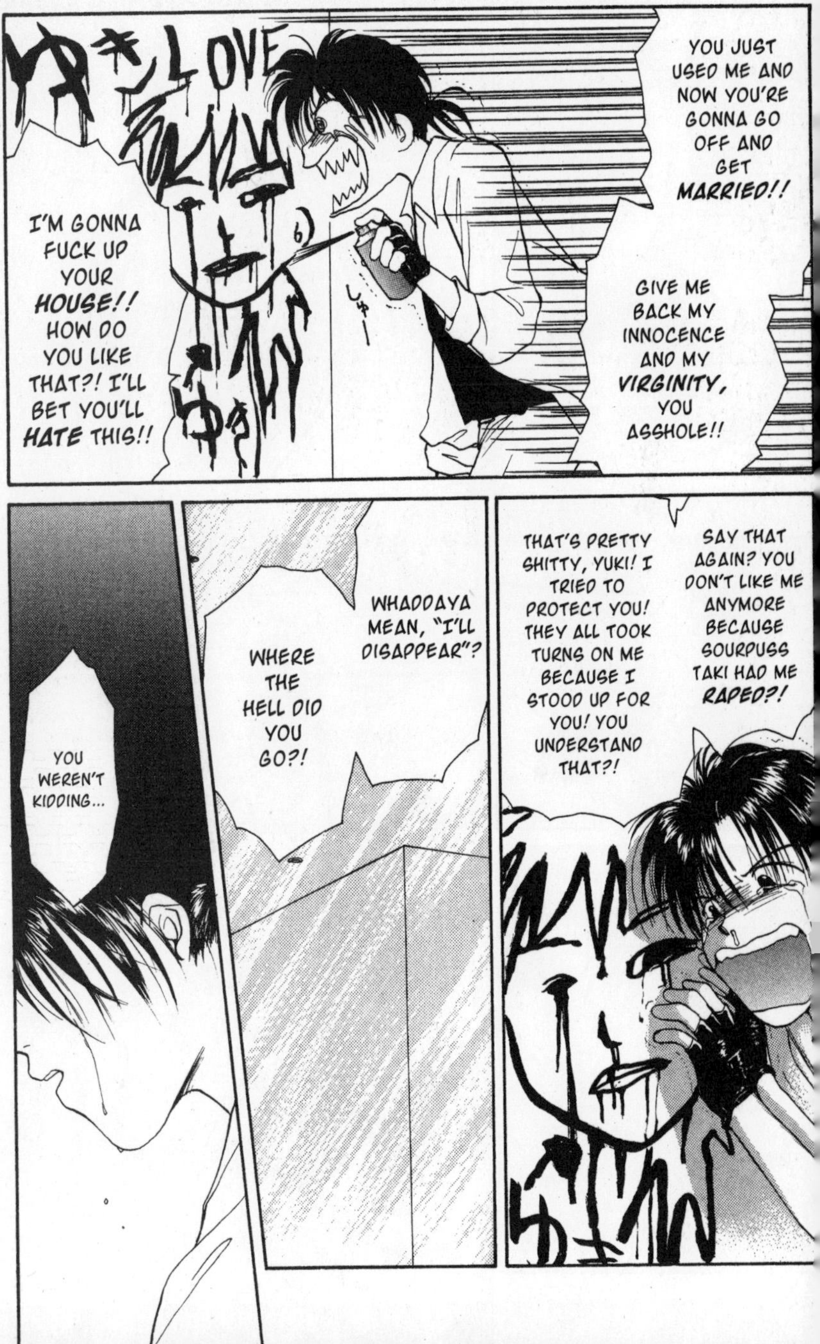
YOU JUST USED ME AND NOW YOU'RE GONNA GO OFF AND GET **MARRIED!!**
GIVE ME BACK MY INNOCENCE AND MY **VIRGINITY,** YOU ASSHOLE!!
I'M GONNA FUCK UP YOUR **HOUSE!!** HOW DO YOU LIKE THAT?! I'LL BET YOU'LL **HATE** THIS!!
LOVE
SAY THAT AGAIN? YOU DON'T LIKE ME ANYMORE BECAUSE SOURPUSS TAKI HAD ME **RAPED?!**
THAT'S PRETTY SHITTY, YUKI! I TRIED TO PROTECT YOU! THEY ALL TOOK TURNS ON ME BECAUSE I STOOD UP FOR YOU! YOU UNDERSTAND THAT?!
WHADDAYA MEAN, "I'LL DISAPPEAR"?
WHERE THE HELL DID YOU GO?!
YOU WEREN'T KIDDING...

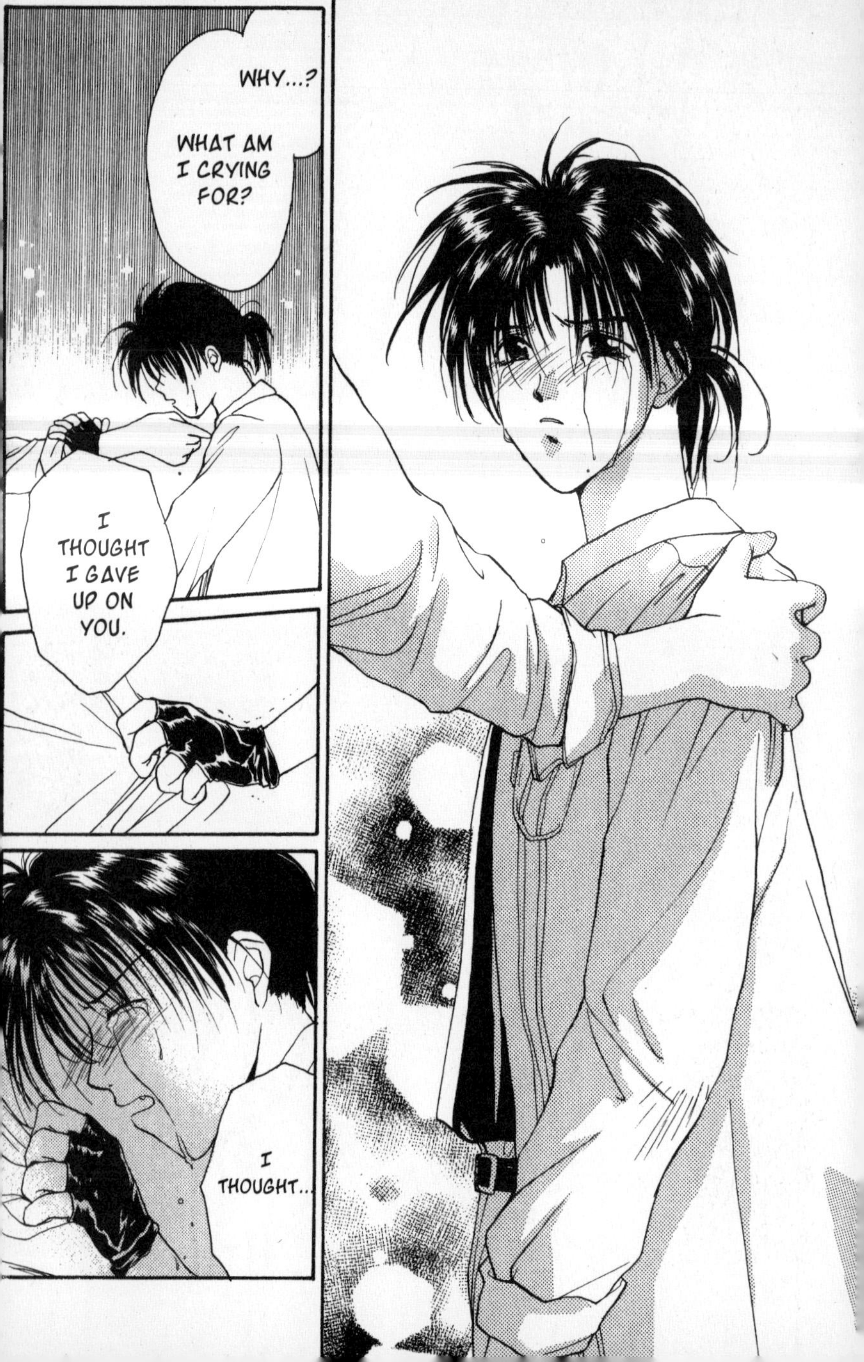
WHY...?
WHAT AM I CRYING FOR?
I THOUGHT I GAVE UP ON YOU.
I THOUGHT...

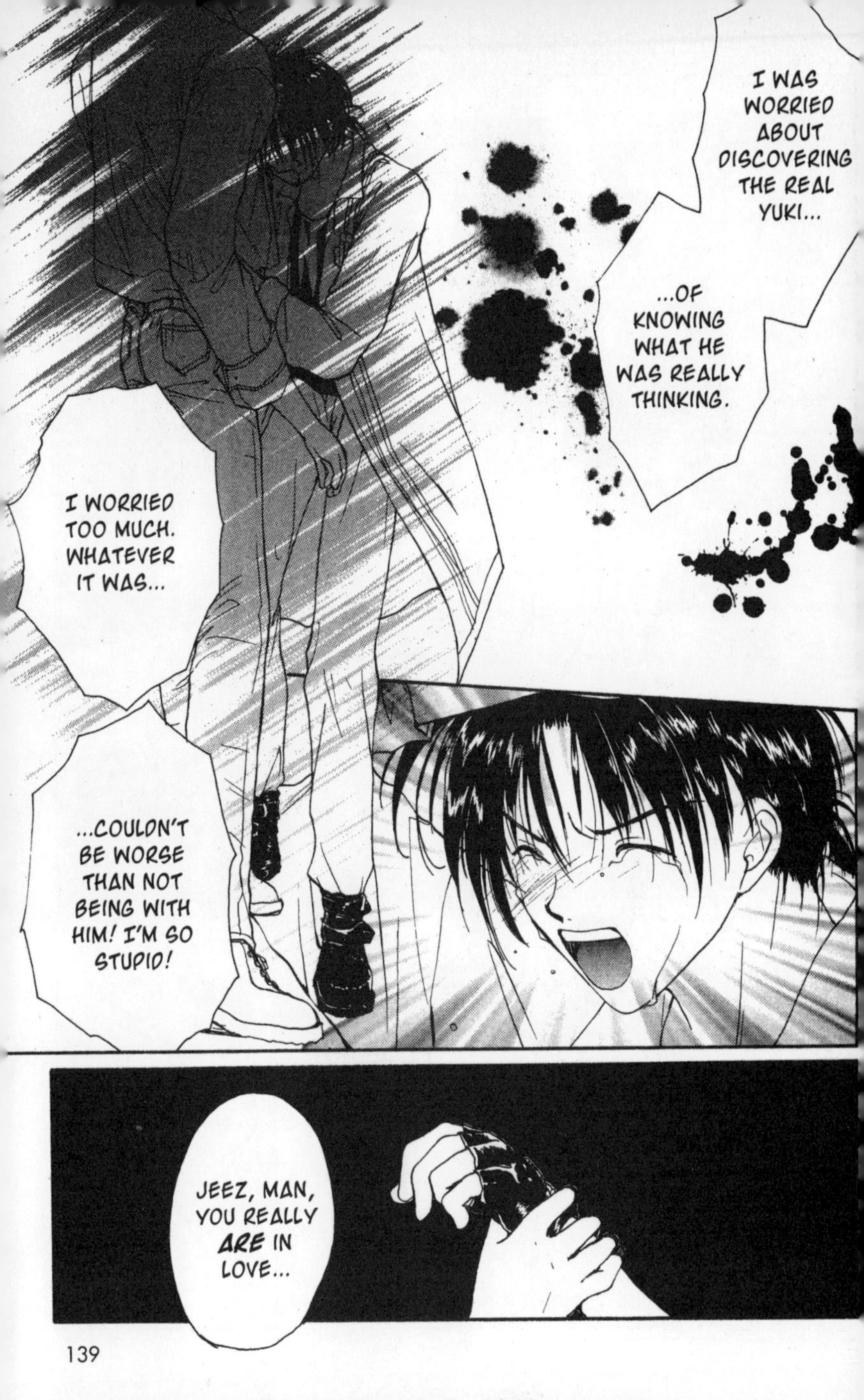
I WAS WORRIED ABOUT DISCOVERING THE REAL YUKI...
...OF KNOWING WHAT HE WAS REALLY THINKING.
I WORRIED TOO MUCH. WHATEVER IT WAS...
...COULDN'T BE WORSE THAN NOT BEING WITH HIM! I'M SO STUPID!
JEEZ, MAN, YOU REALLY **ARE** IN LOVE...

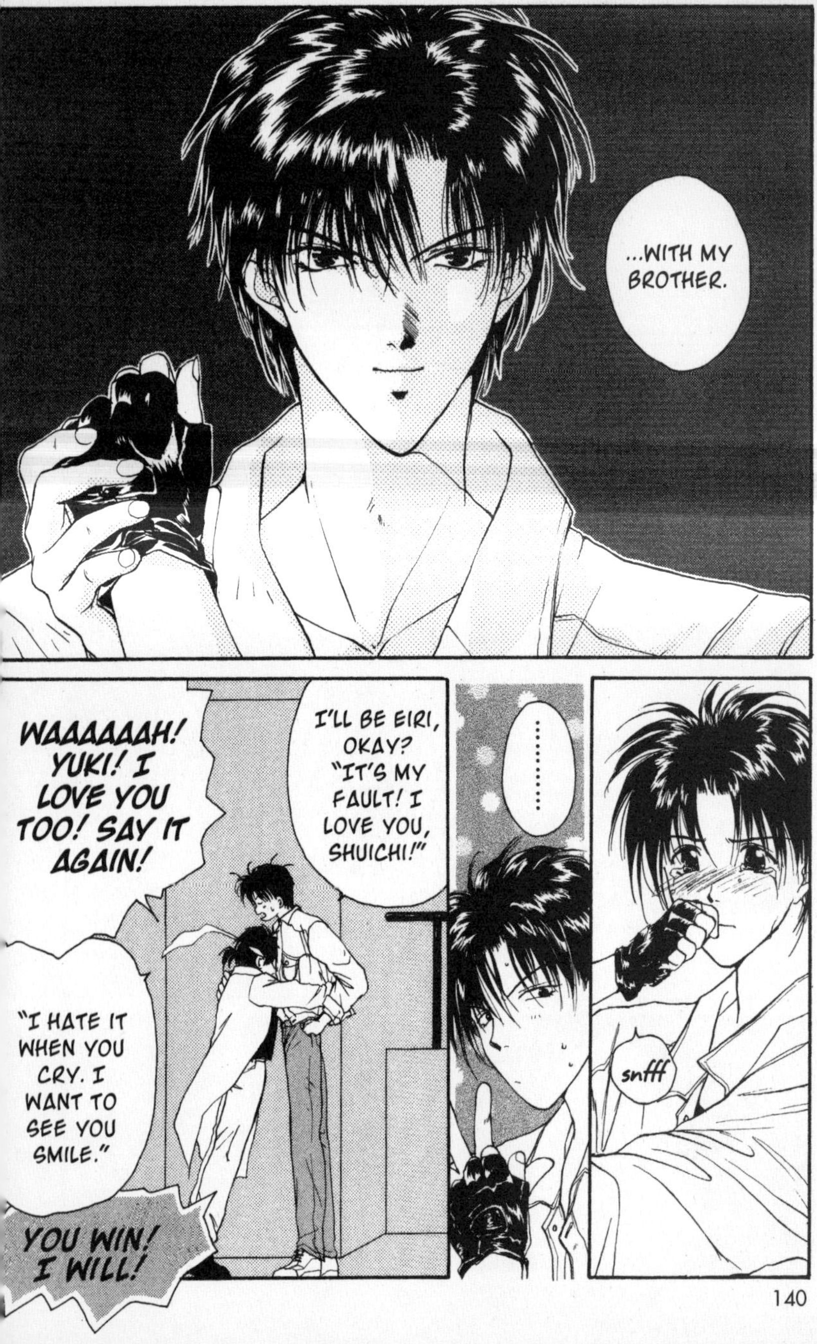
...WITH MY BROTHER.
snfff
......
I'LL BE EIRI, OKAY? "IT'S MY FAULT! I LOVE YOU, SHUICHI!"
WAAAAAAH! YUKI! I LOVE YOU TOO! SAY IT AGAIN!
"I HATE IT WHEN YOU CRY. I WANT TO SEE YOU SMILE."
YOU WIN! I WILL!

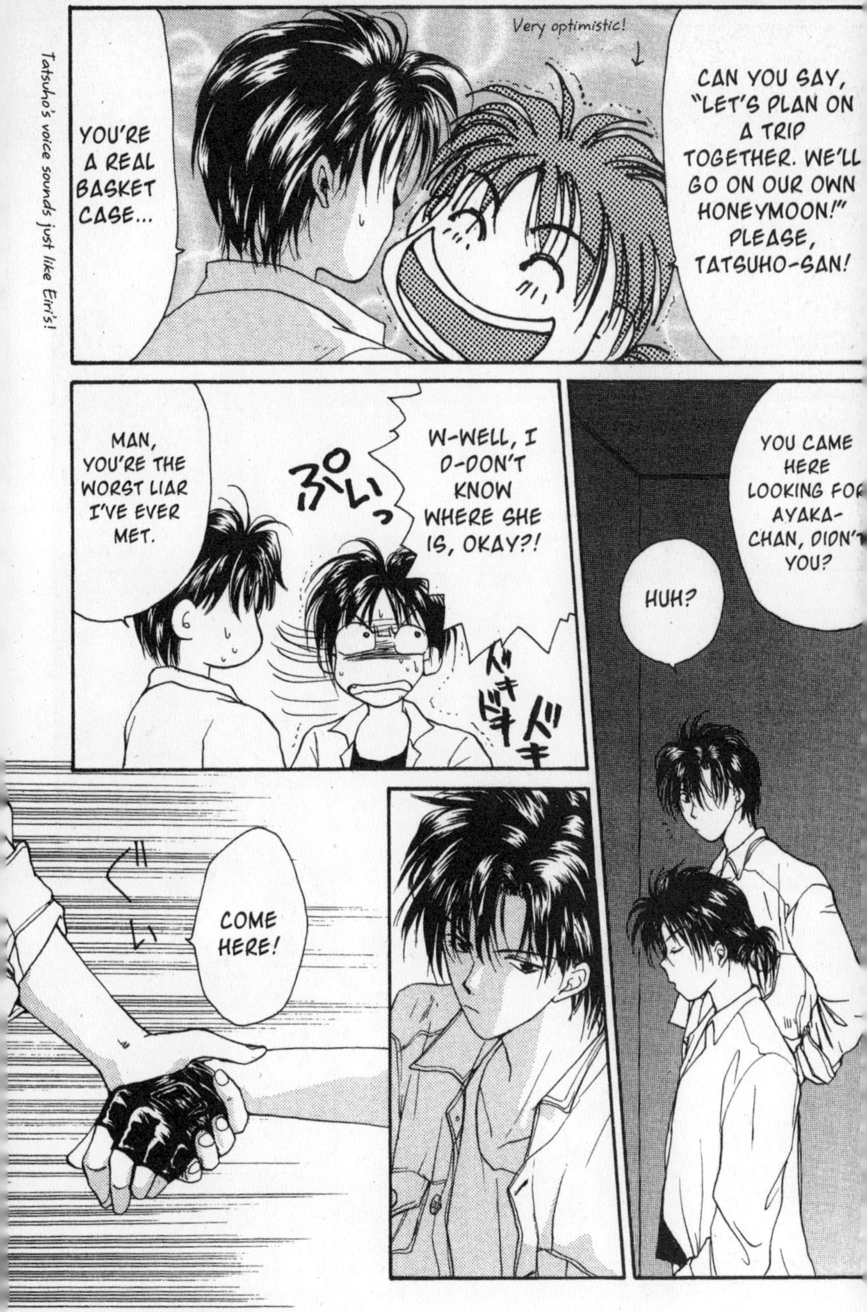
CAN YOU SAY, "LET'S PLAN ON A TRIP TOGETHER. WE'LL GO ON OUR OWN HONEYMOON!" PLEASE, TATSUHO-SAN!
Very optimistic!
YOU'RE A REAL BASKET CASE...
YOU CAME HERE LOOKING FOR AYAKA-CHAN, DIDN'T YOU?
HUH?
W-WELL, I D-DON'T KNOW WHERE SHE IS, OKAY?!
ドキドキ
ぷいっ
MAN, YOU'RE THE WORST LIAR I'VE EVER MET.
COME HERE!
ぐいっ

Tatsuho's voice sounds just like Eiri's!

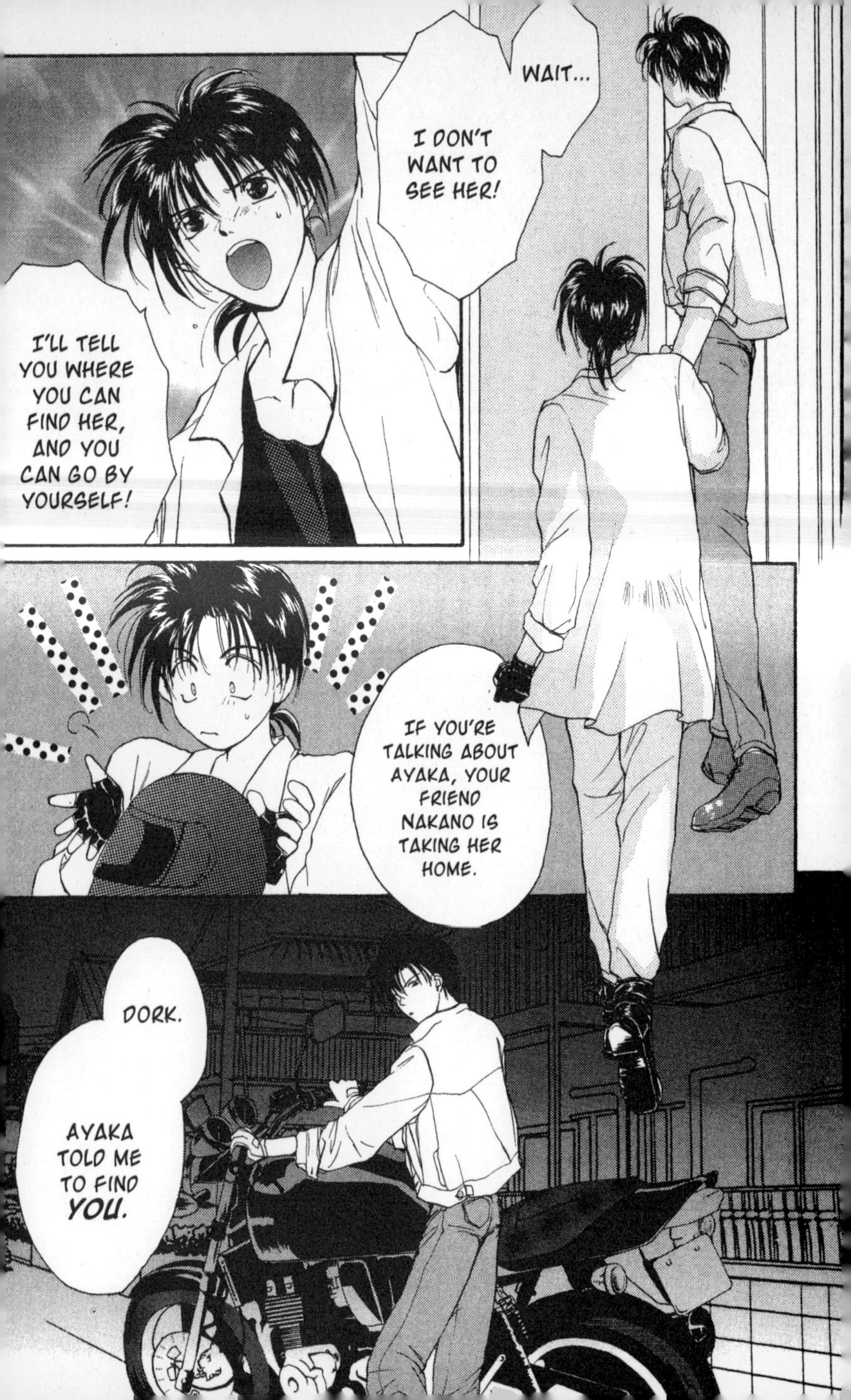
WAIT...
I DON'T WANT TO SEE HER!
I'LL TELL YOU WHERE YOU CAN FIND HER, AND YOU CAN GO BY YOURSELF!
IF YOU'RE TALKING ABOUT AYAKA, YOUR FRIEND NAKANO IS TAKING HER HOME.
DORK.
AYAKA TOLD ME TO FIND *YOU*.

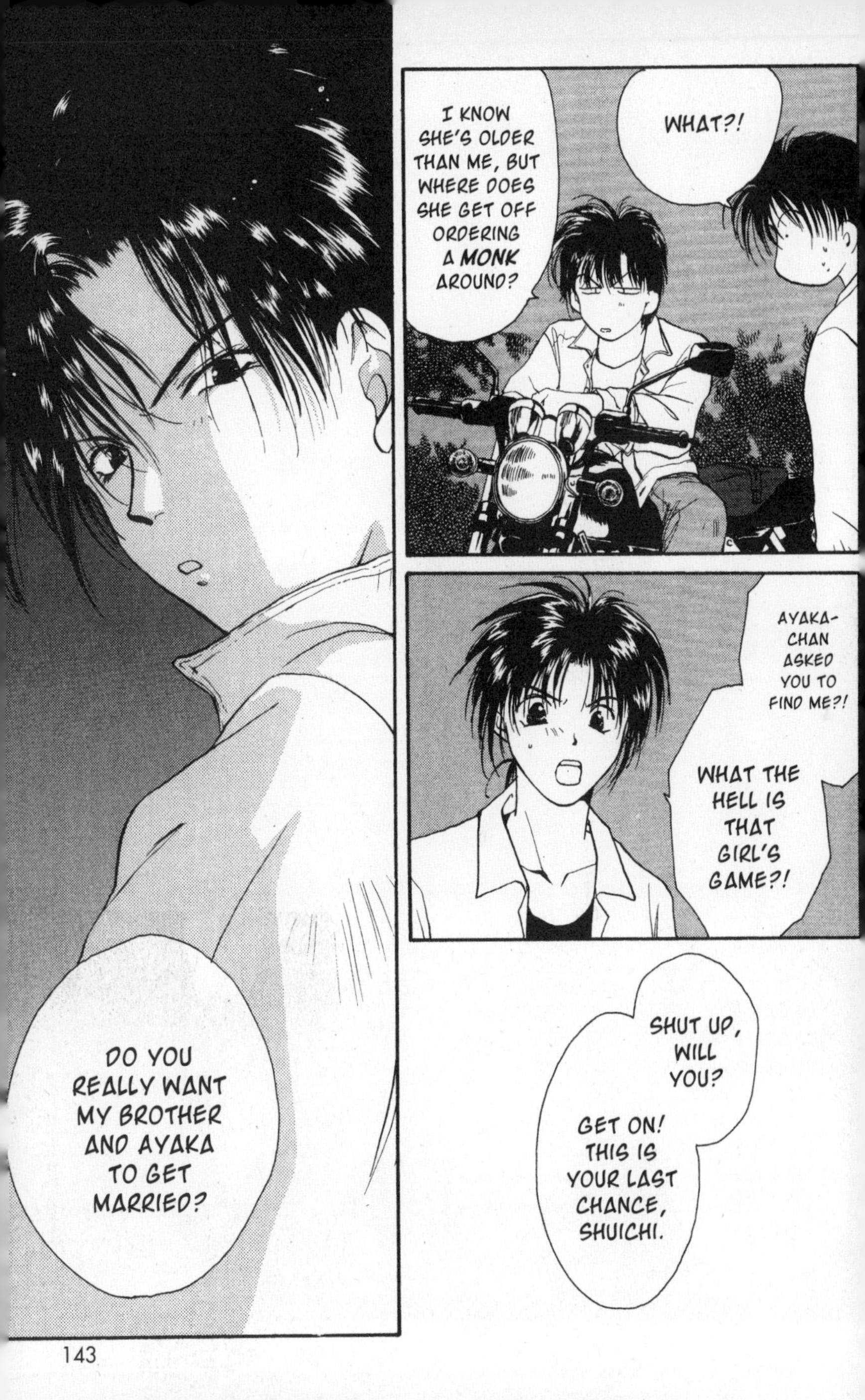
WHAT?!
I KNOW SHE'S OLDER THAN ME, BUT WHERE DOES SHE GET OFF ORDERING A **MONK** AROUND?
AYAKA-CHAN ASKED YOU TO FIND ME?!
WHAT THE HELL IS THAT GIRL'S GAME?!
SHUT UP, WILL YOU?
GET ON! THIS IS YOUR LAST CHANCE, SHUICHI.
DO YOU REALLY WANT MY BROTHER AND AYAKA TO GET MARRIED?

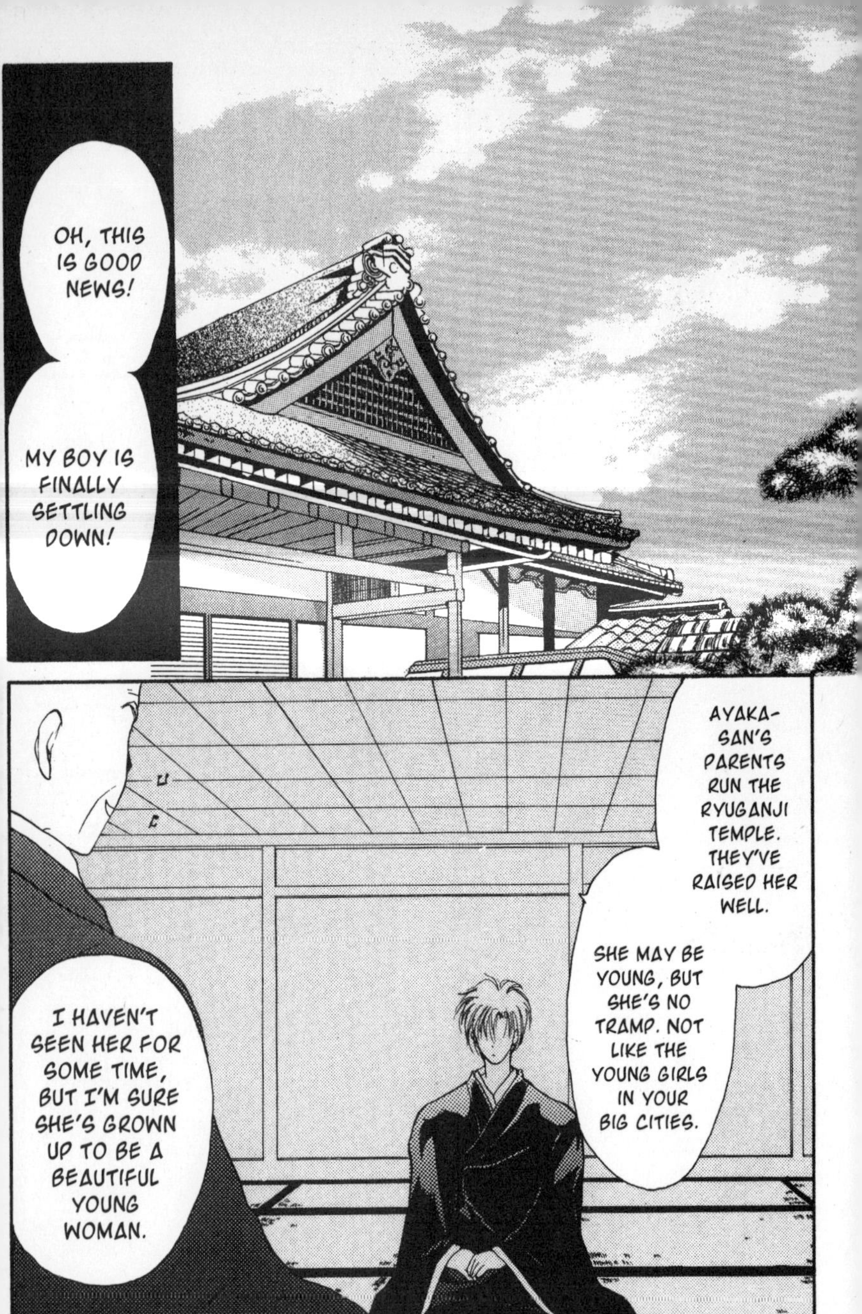
OH, THIS IS GOOD NEWS!
MY BOY IS FINALLY SETTLING DOWN!
AYAKA-SAN'S PARENTS RUN THE RYUGANJI TEMPLE. THEY'VE RAISED HER WELL.
SHE MAY BE YOUNG, BUT SHE'S NO TRAMP. NOT LIKE THE YOUNG GIRLS IN YOUR BIG CITIES.
I HAVEN'T SEEN HER FOR SOME TIME, BUT I'M SURE SHE'S GROWN UP TO BE A BEAUTIFUL YOUNG WOMAN.

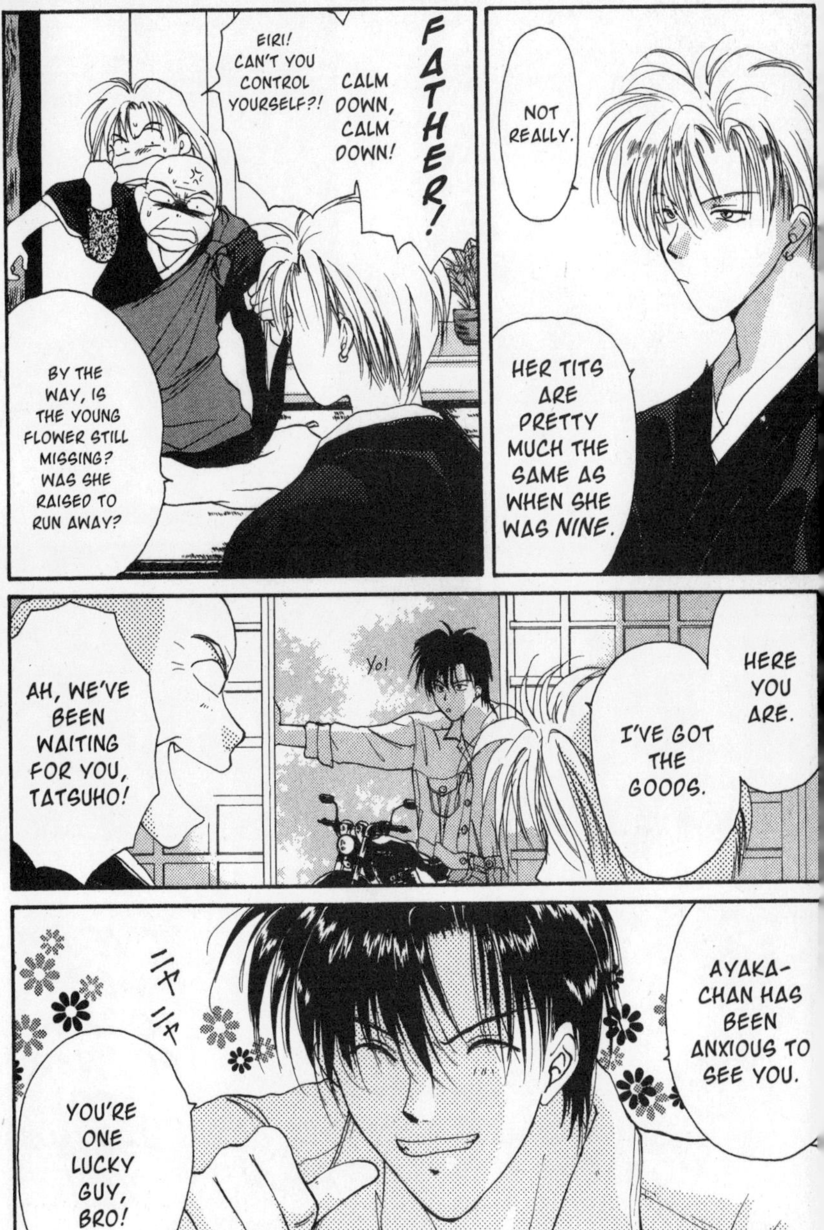
NOT REALLY.
HER TITS ARE PRETTY MUCH THE SAME AS WHEN SHE WAS *NINE*.
FATHER!
CALM DOWN, CALM DOWN!
EIRI! CAN'T YOU CONTROL YOURSELF?!
BY THE WAY, IS THE YOUNG FLOWER STILL MISSING? WAS SHE RAISED TO RUN AWAY?
HERE YOU ARE.
I'VE GOT THE GOODS.
Yo!
AH, WE'VE BEEN WAITING FOR YOU, TATSUHO!
AYAKA-CHAN HAS BEEN ANXIOUS TO SEE YOU.
ニヤ ニヤ
YOU'RE ONE LUCKY GUY, BRO!

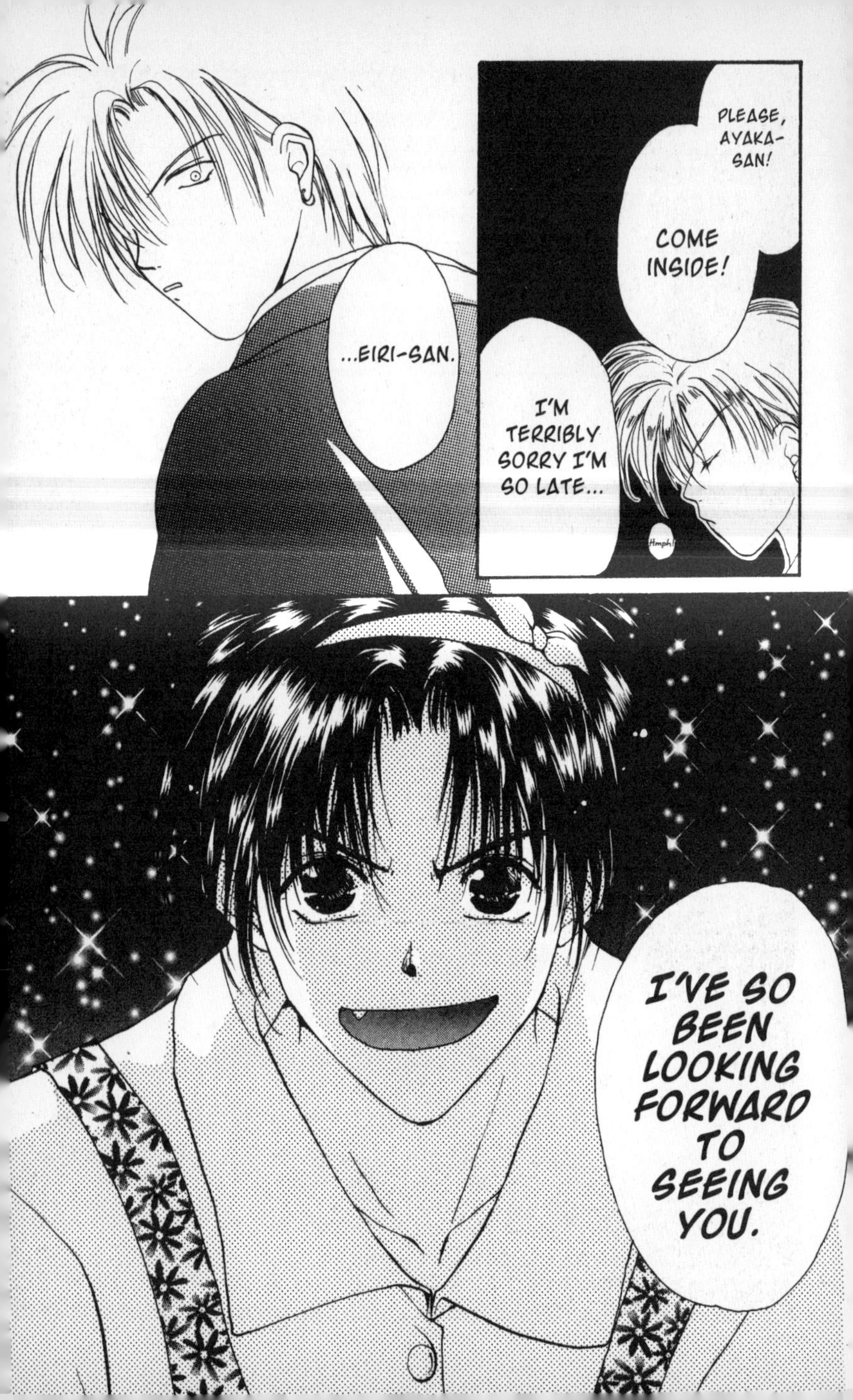
PLEASE, AYAKA-SAN!
COME INSIDE!
I'M TERRIBLY SORRY I'M SO LATE...
Hmph!
...EIRI-SAN.
I'VE SO BEEN LOOKING FORWARD TO SEEING YOU.

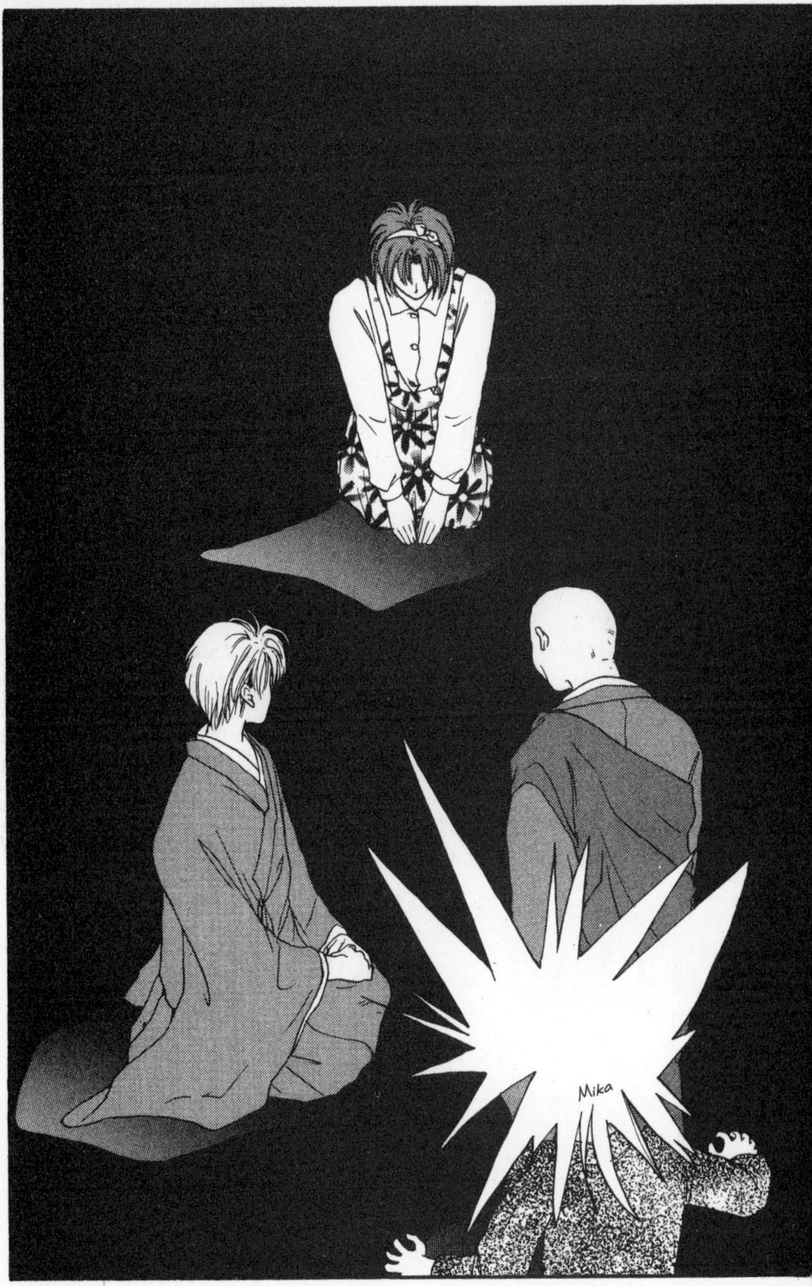
Mika

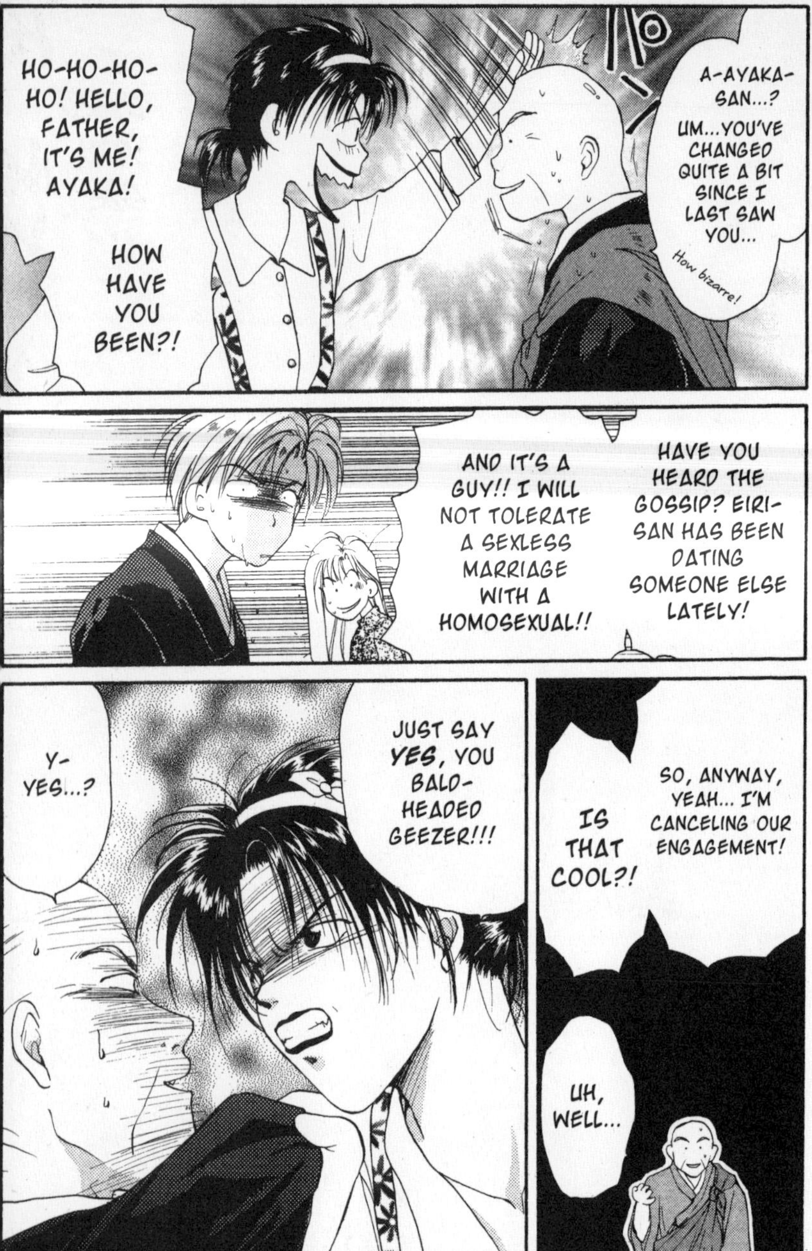
A-AYAKA-SAN...?
UM...YOU'VE CHANGED QUITE A BIT SINCE I LAST SAW YOU...
How bizarre!
HO-HO-HO-HO! HELLO, FATHER, IT'S ME! AYAKA!
HOW HAVE YOU BEEN?!
HAVE YOU HEARD THE GOSSIP? EIRI-SAN HAS BEEN DATING SOMEONE ELSE LATELY!
AND IT'S A GUY!! I WILL NOT TOLERATE A SEXLESS MARRIAGE WITH A HOMOSEXUAL!!
SO, ANYWAY, YEAH... I'M CANCELING OUR ENGAGEMENT!
IS THAT COOL?!
UH, WELL...
JUST SAY YES, YOU BALD-HEADED GEEZER!!!
Y-YES...?

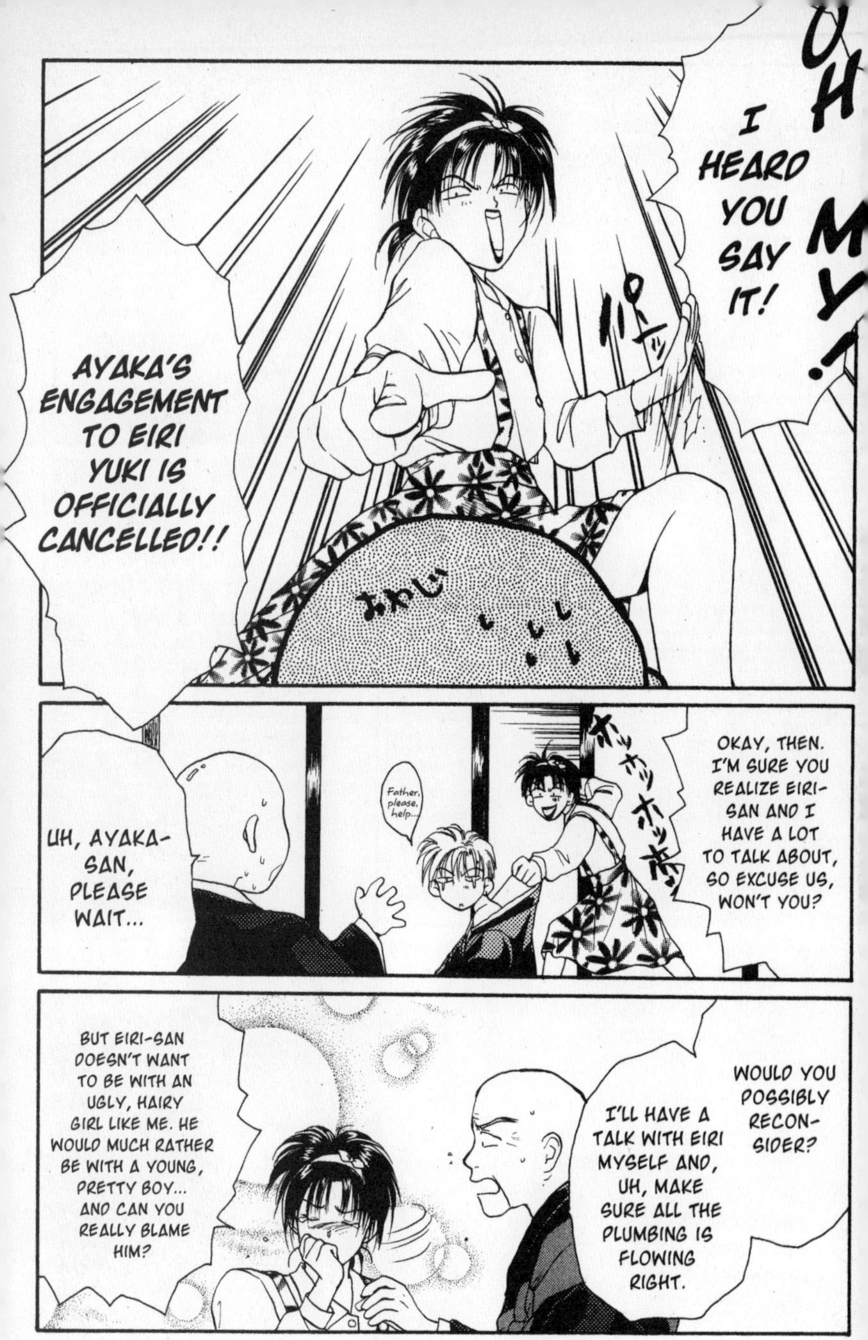
OH MY!
I HEARD YOU SAY IT!
AYAKA'S ENGAGEMENT TO EIRI YUKI IS OFFICIALLY CANCELLED!!
OKAY, THEN. I'M SURE YOU REALIZE EIRI-SAN AND I HAVE A LOT TO TALK ABOUT, SO EXCUSE US, WON'T YOU?
Father, please, help...
UH, AYAKA-SAN, PLEASE WAIT...
WOULD YOU POSSIBLY RECONSIDER?
I'LL HAVE A TALK WITH EIRI MYSELF AND, UH, MAKE SURE ALL THE PLUMBING IS FLOWING RIGHT.
BUT EIRI-SAN DOESN'T WANT TO BE WITH AN UGLY, HAIRY GIRL LIKE ME. HE WOULD MUCH RATHER BE WITH A YOUNG, PRETTY BOY... AND CAN YOU REALLY BLAME HIM?

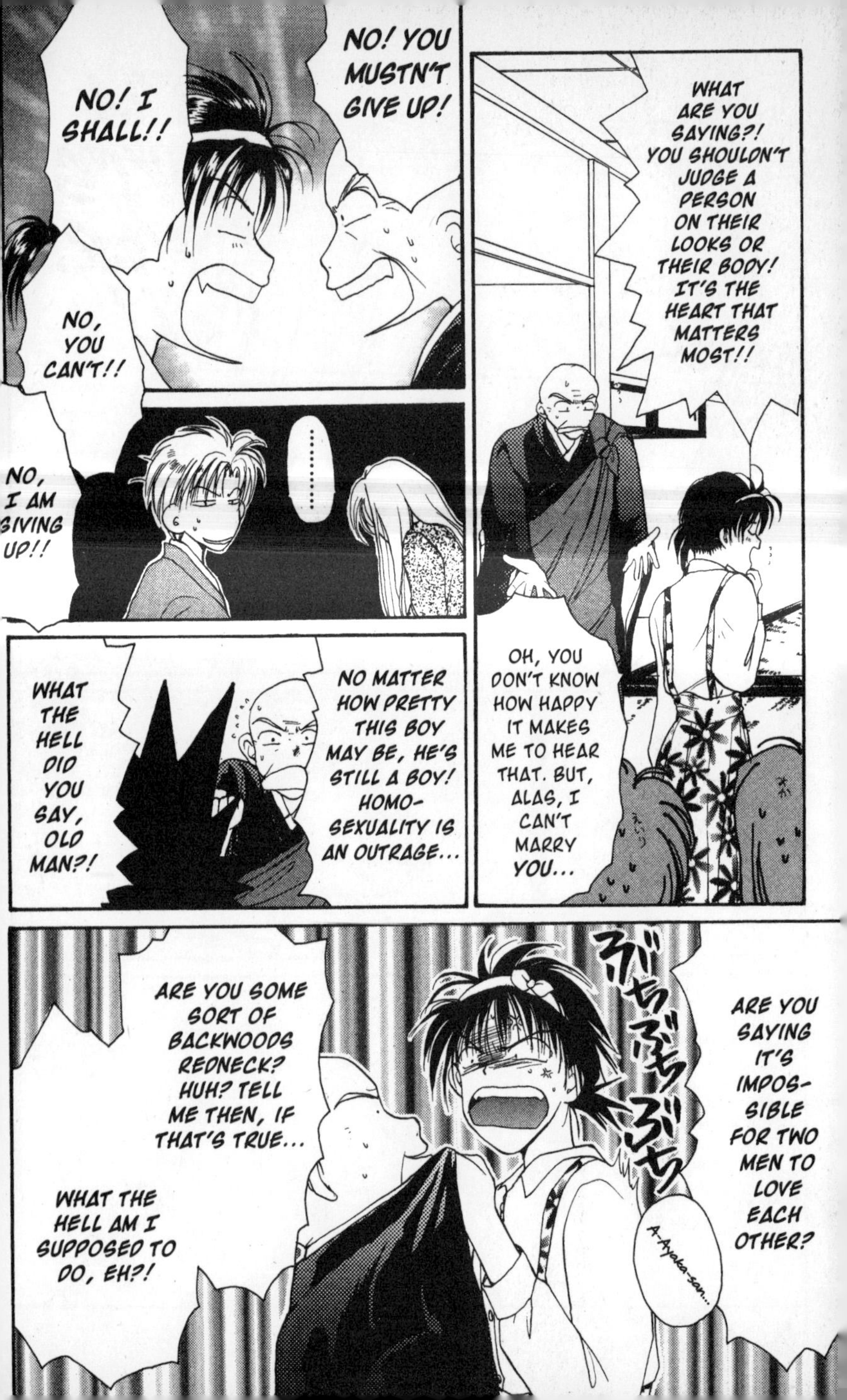
WHAT ARE YOU SAYING?! YOU SHOULDN'T JUDGE A PERSON ON THEIR LOOKS OR THEIR BODY! IT'S THE HEART THAT MATTERS MOST!!
OH, YOU DON'T KNOW HOW HAPPY IT MAKES ME TO HEAR THAT. BUT, ALAS, I CAN'T MARRY YOU...
NO! YOU MUSTN'T GIVE UP!
NO! I SHALL!!
NO, YOU CAN'T!!
NO, I AM GIVING UP!!
......
NO MATTER HOW PRETTY THIS BOY MAY BE, HE'S STILL A BOY! HOMO-SEXUALITY IS AN OUTRAGE...
WHAT THE HELL DID YOU SAY, OLD MAN?!
ARE YOU SAYING IT'S IMPOS-SIBLE FOR TWO MEN TO LOVE EACH OTHER?
ぶちぶちぶち
A-Ayaka-san...
ARE YOU SOME SORT OF BACKWOODS REDNECK? HUH? TELL ME THEN, IF THAT'S TRUE...
WHAT THE HELL AM I SUPPOSED TO DO, EH?!

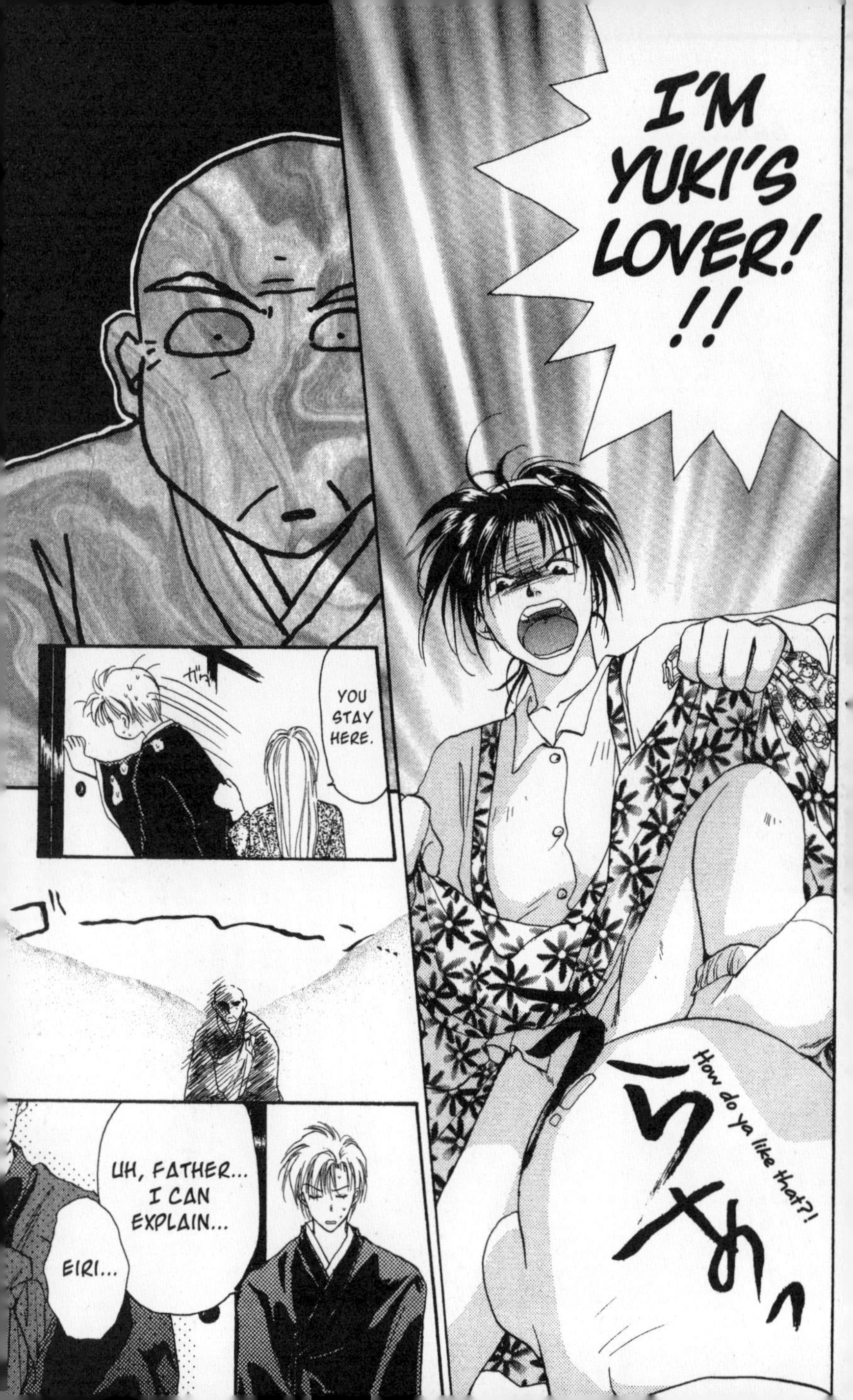
I'M YUKI'S LOVER! !!
How do ya like that?!
YOU STAY HERE.
UH, FATHER... I CAN EXPLAIN...
EIRI...

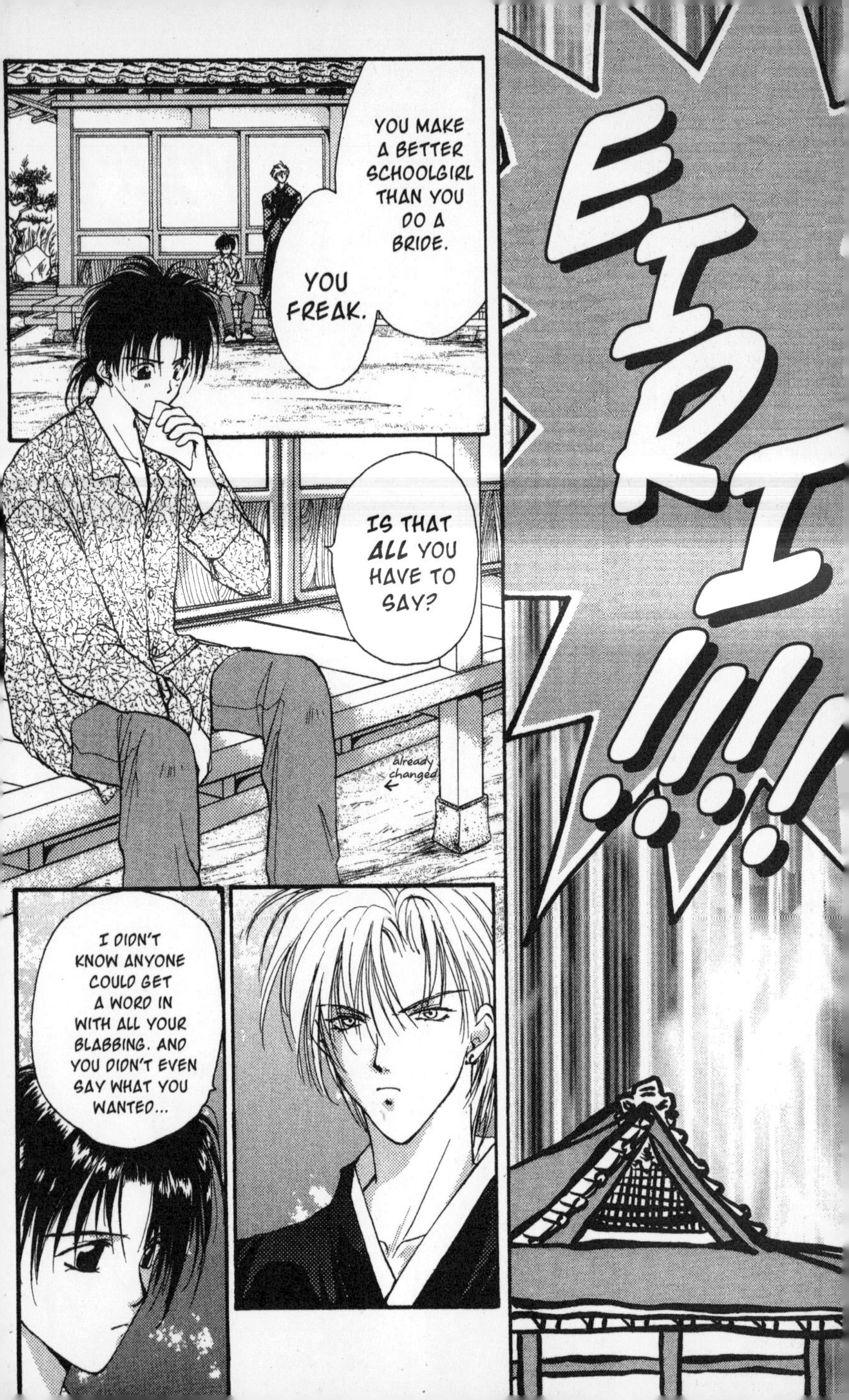
EIRI!!!!
YOU MAKE A BETTER SCHOOLGIRL THAN YOU DO A BRIDE.
YOU FREAK.
IS THAT ALL YOU HAVE TO SAY?
already changed
I DIDN'T KNOW ANYONE COULD GET A WORD IN WITH ALL YOUR BLABBING. AND YOU DIDN'T EVEN SAY WHAT YOU WANTED...

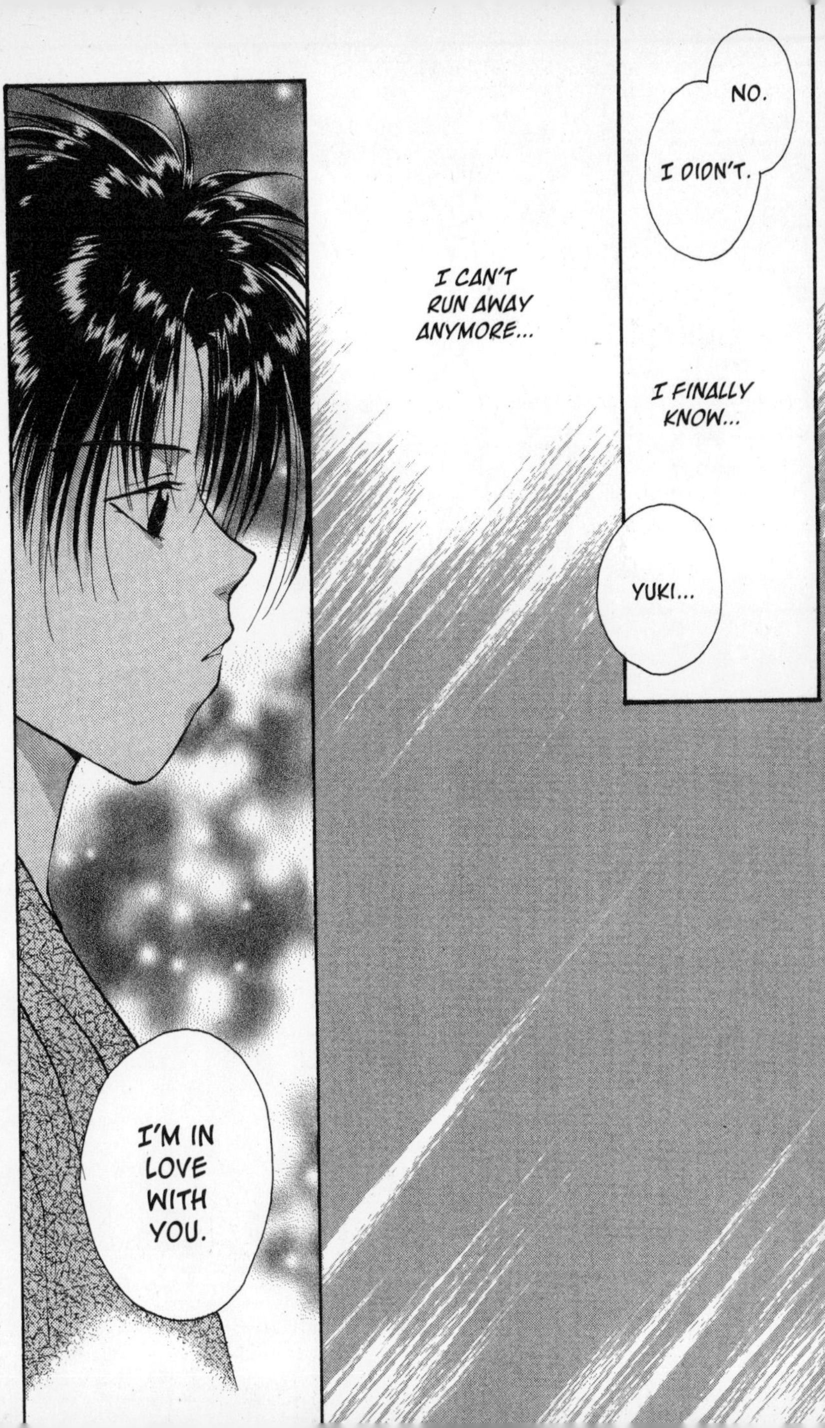
NO.
I DIDN'T.
I FINALLY KNOW...
YUKI...
I CAN'T RUN AWAY ANYMORE...
I'M IN LOVE WITH YOU.

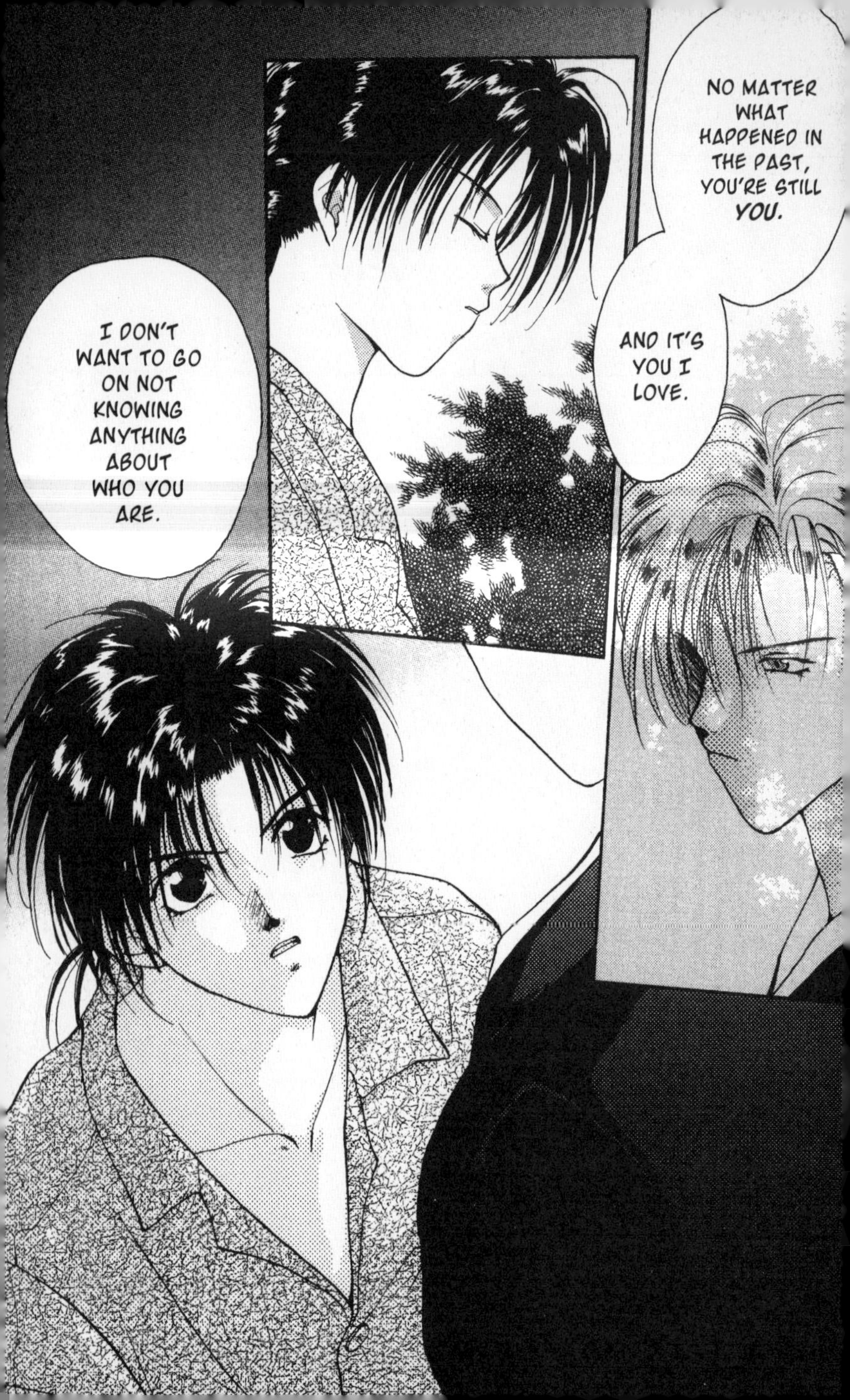
NO MATTER WHAT HAPPENED IN THE PAST, YOU'RE STILL *YOU.*
AND IT'S YOU I LOVE.
I DON'T WANT TO GO ON NOT KNOWING ANYTHING ABOUT WHO YOU ARE.

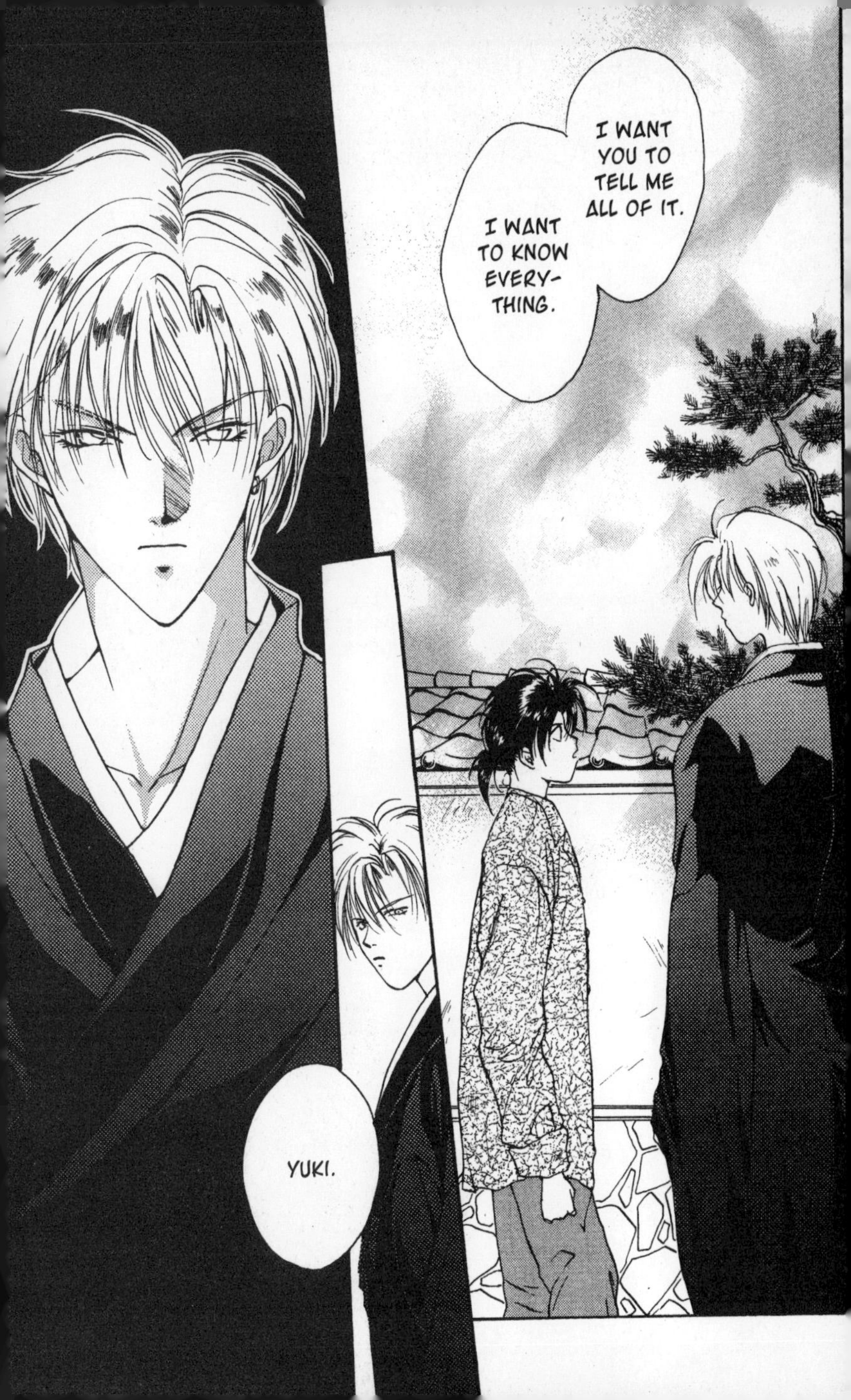
I WANT YOU TO TELL ME ALL OF IT.
I WANT TO KNOW EVERY-THING.
YUKI.

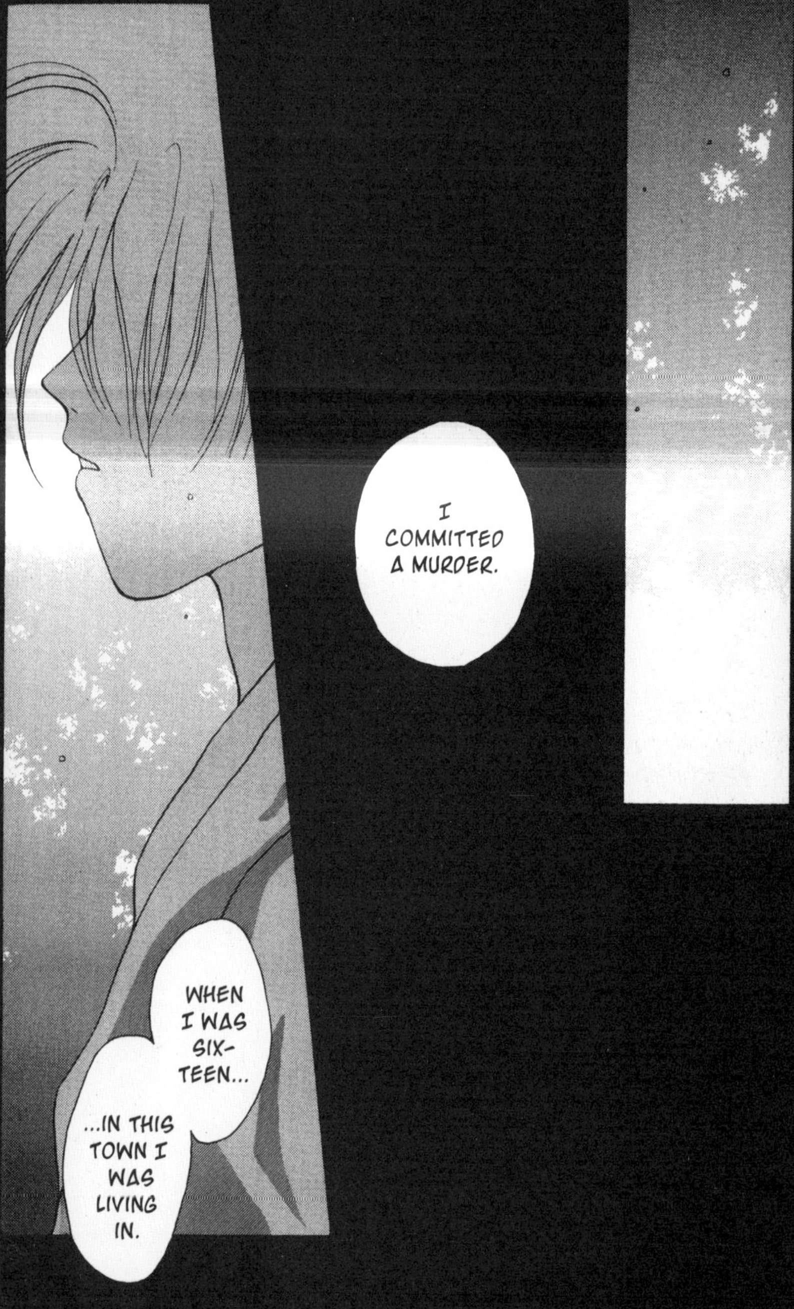
I COMMITTED A MURDER.
WHEN I WAS SIX-TEEN...
...IN THIS TOWN I WAS LIVING IN.

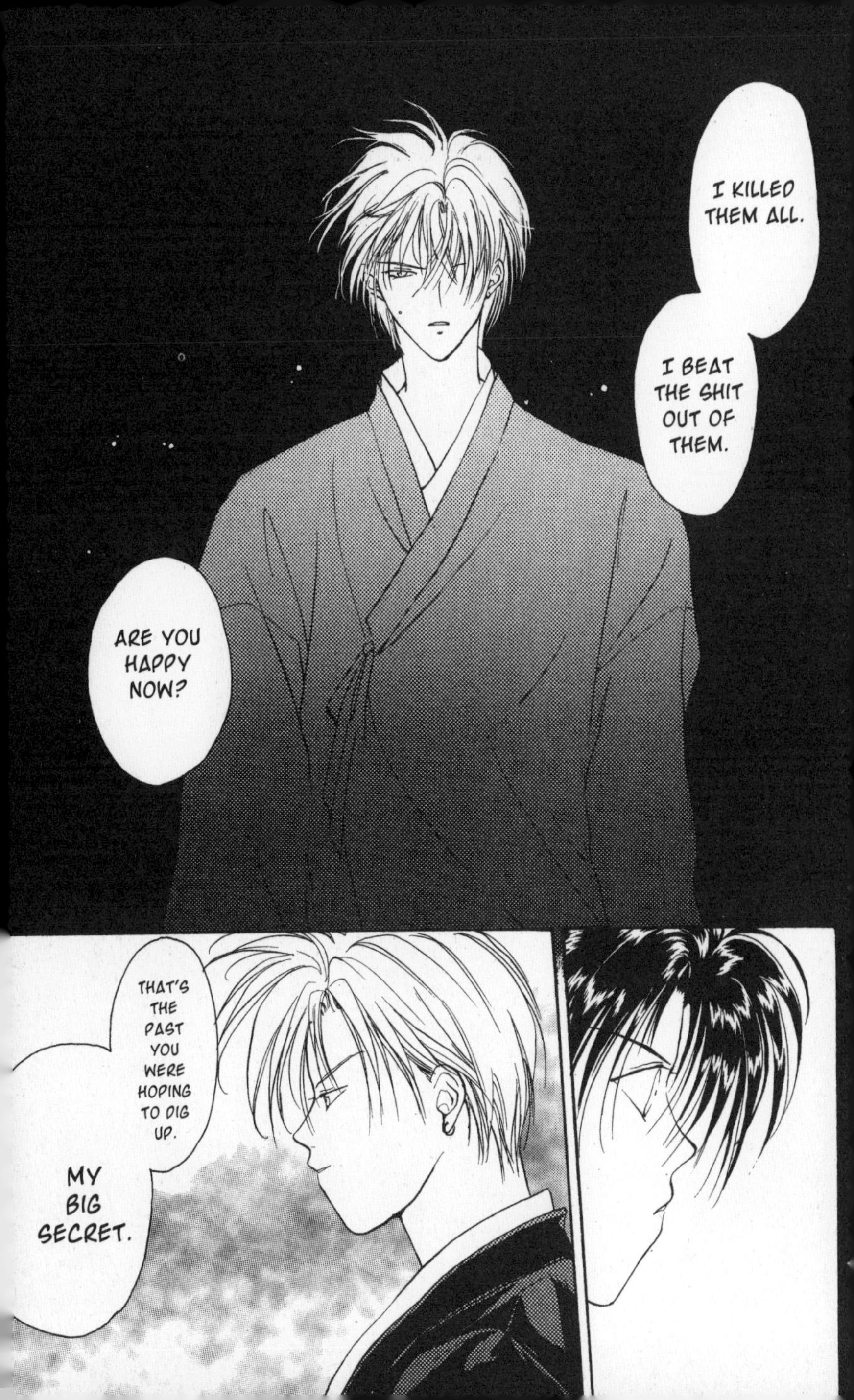
I KILLED THEM ALL.
I BEAT THE SHIT OUT OF THEM.
ARE YOU HAPPY NOW?
THAT'S THE PAST YOU WERE HOPING TO DIG UP.
MY BIG SECRET.

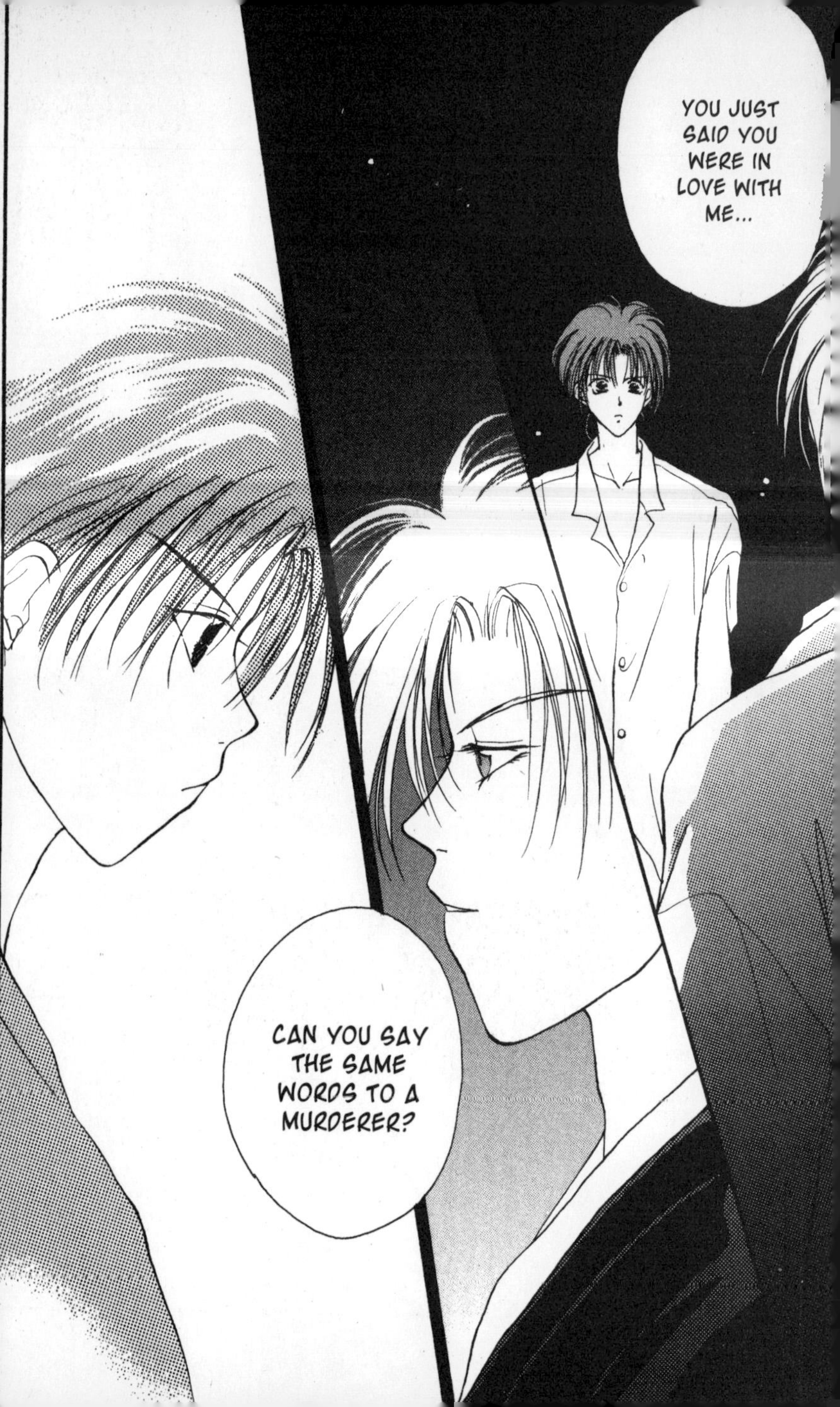
YOU JUST SAID YOU WERE IN LOVE WITH ME...
CAN YOU SAY THE SAME WORDS TO A MURDERER?

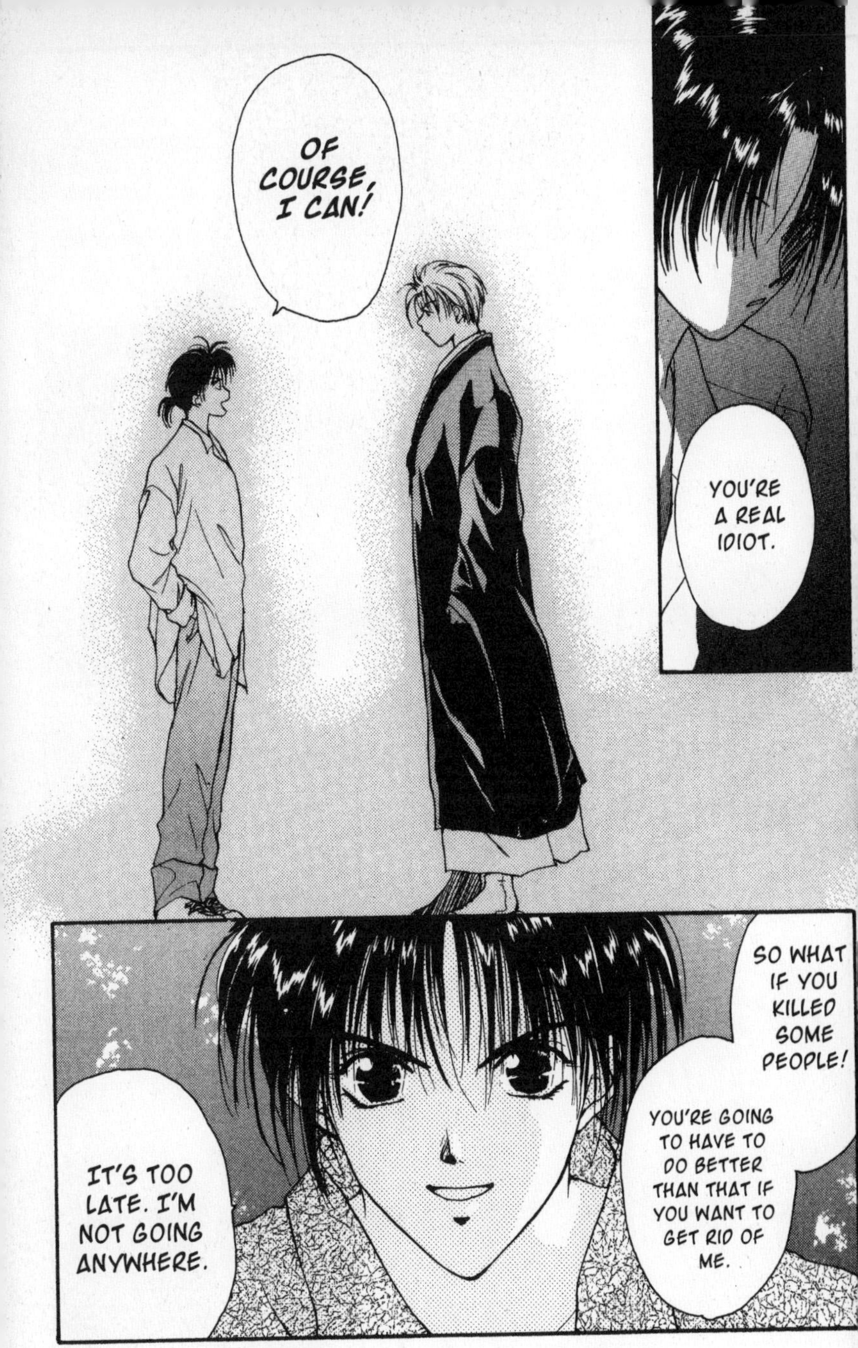
YOU'RE A REAL IDIOT.
OF COURSE, I CAN!
SO WHAT IF YOU KILLED SOME PEOPLE!
YOU'RE GOING TO HAVE TO DO BETTER THAN THAT IF YOU WANT TO GET RID OF ME.
IT'S TOO LATE. I'M NOT GOING ANYWHERE.

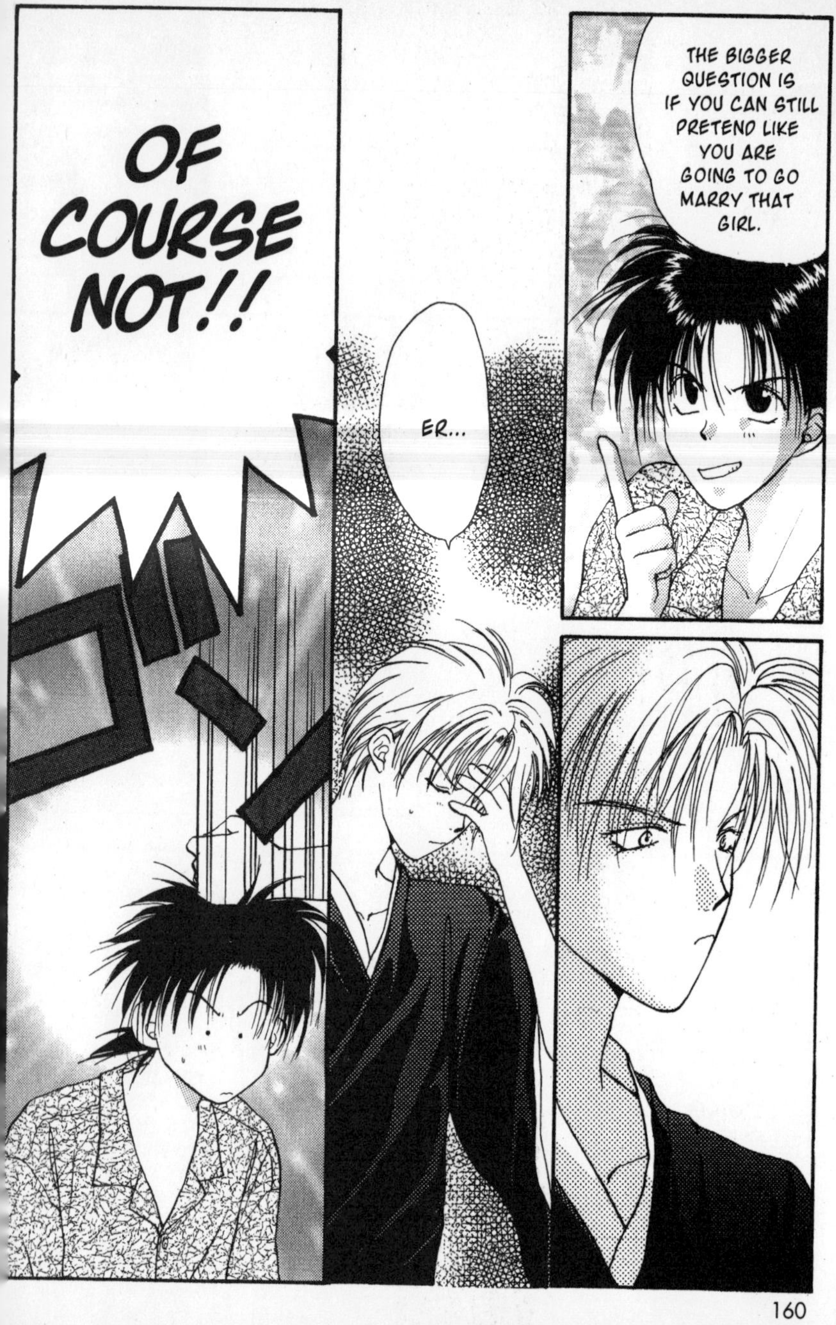
THE BIGGER QUESTION IS IF YOU CAN STILL PRETEND LIKE YOU ARE GOING TO GO MARRY THAT GIRL.
ER...
OF COURSE NOT!!

OWWWWW!
WHAT WAS THAT FOR?!
SHUT UP AND GO HOME!
STUPID SHUICHI!!
WHA--?
"SHUICHI..."?
HE CALLED ME BY MY NAME!
じーーん‥
YUKI! SAY IT AGAIN!!
だあー
STOP SNIVELING!! YOU'RE DROOLING EVERYWHERE, AND YOUR NOSE IS RUNNING!
WHILE YOU'RE WEARING MY CLOTHES!!
You're disgusting!

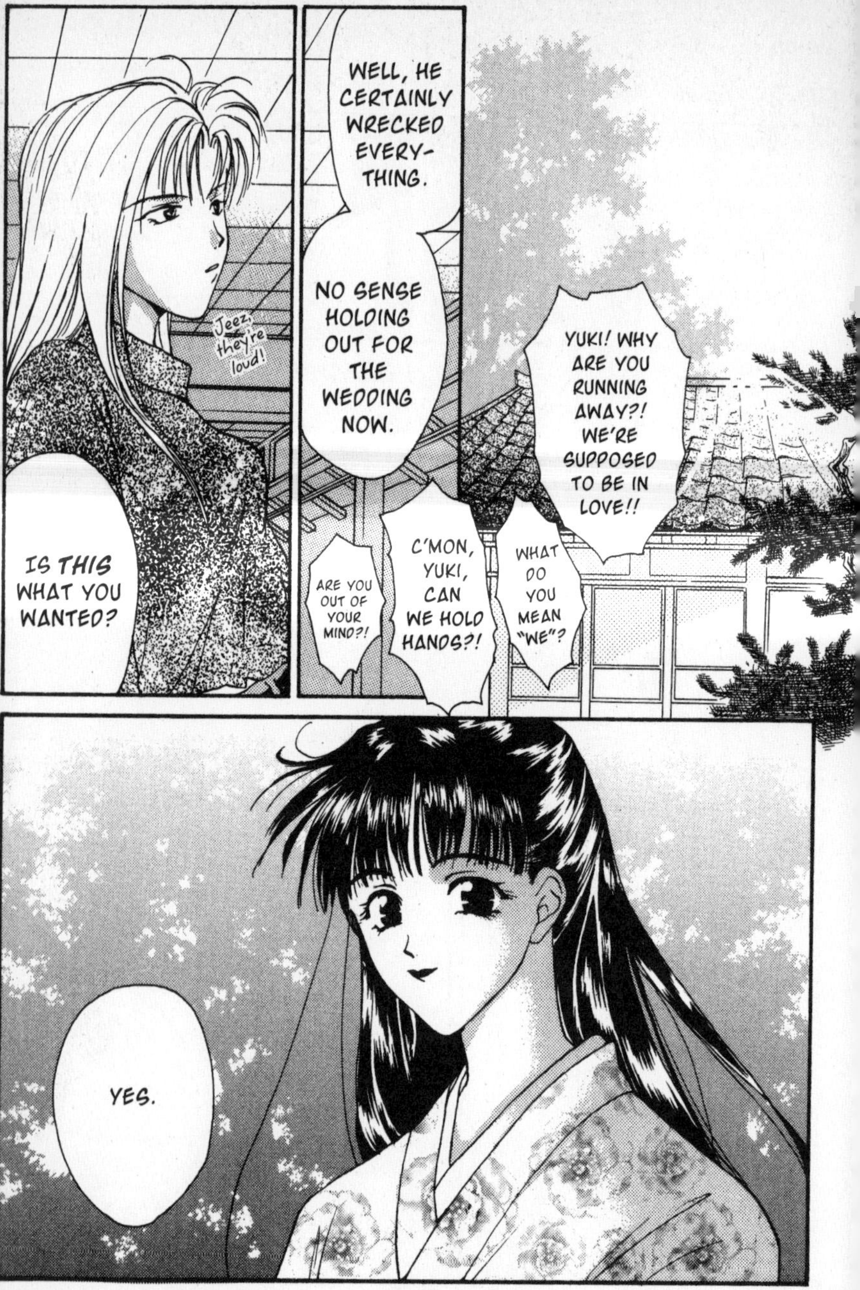
YUKI! WHY ARE YOU RUNNING AWAY?! WE'RE SUPPOSED TO BE IN LOVE!!
WHAT DO YOU MEAN "WE"?
C'MON, YUKI, CAN WE HOLD HANDS?!
ARE YOU OUT OF YOUR MIND?!
WELL, HE CERTAINLY WRECKED EVERYTHING.
NO SENSE HOLDING OUT FOR THE WEDDING NOW.
Jeez, they're loud!
IS THIS WHAT YOU WANTED?
YES.

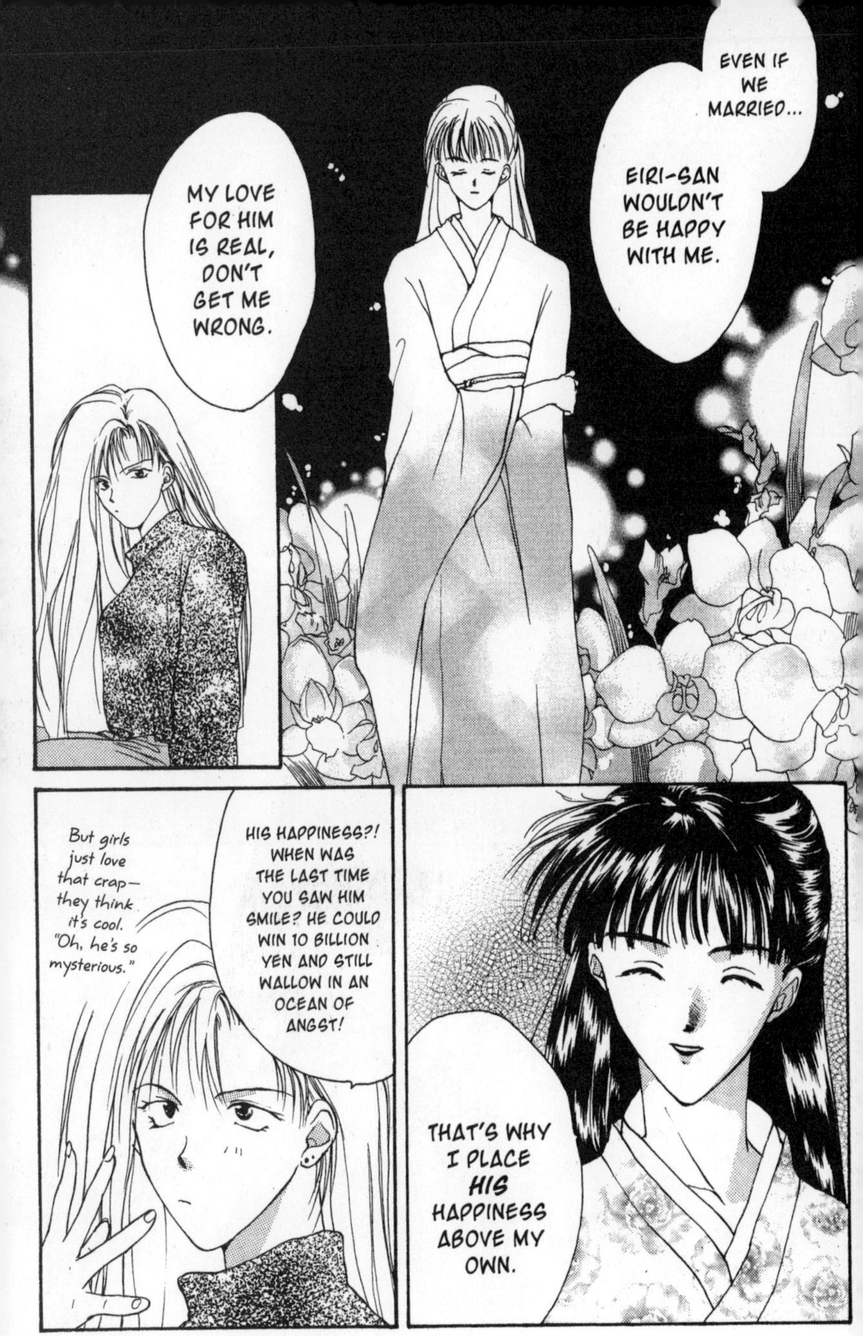
EVEN IF WE MARRIED...
EIRI-SAN WOULDN'T BE HAPPY WITH ME.
MY LOVE FOR HIM IS REAL, DON'T GET ME WRONG.
THAT'S WHY I PLACE *HIS* HAPPINESS ABOVE MY OWN.
HIS HAPPINESS?! WHEN WAS THE LAST TIME YOU SAW HIM SMILE? HE COULD WIN 10 BILLION YEN AND STILL WALLOW IN AN OCEAN OF ANGST!
But girls just love that crap—they think it's cool. "Oh, he's so mysterious."

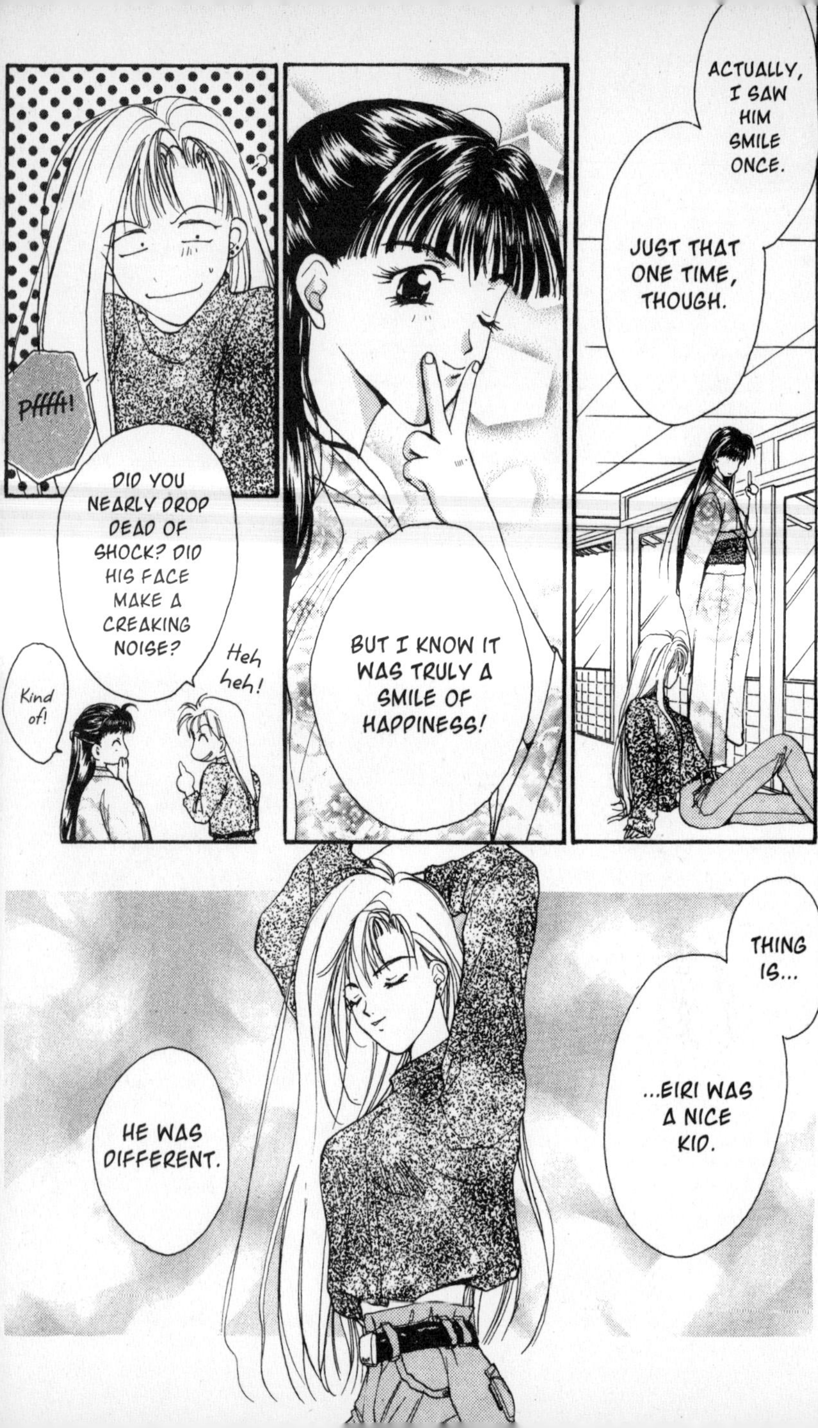
ACTUALLY, I SAW HIM SMILE ONCE.
JUST THAT ONE TIME, THOUGH.
BUT I KNOW IT WAS TRULY A SMILE OF HAPPINESS!
Pfffft!
DID YOU NEARLY DROP DEAD OF SHOCK? DID HIS FACE MAKE A CREAKING NOISE?
Heh heh!
Kind of!
THING IS...
...EIRI WAS A NICE KID.
HE WAS DIFFERENT.

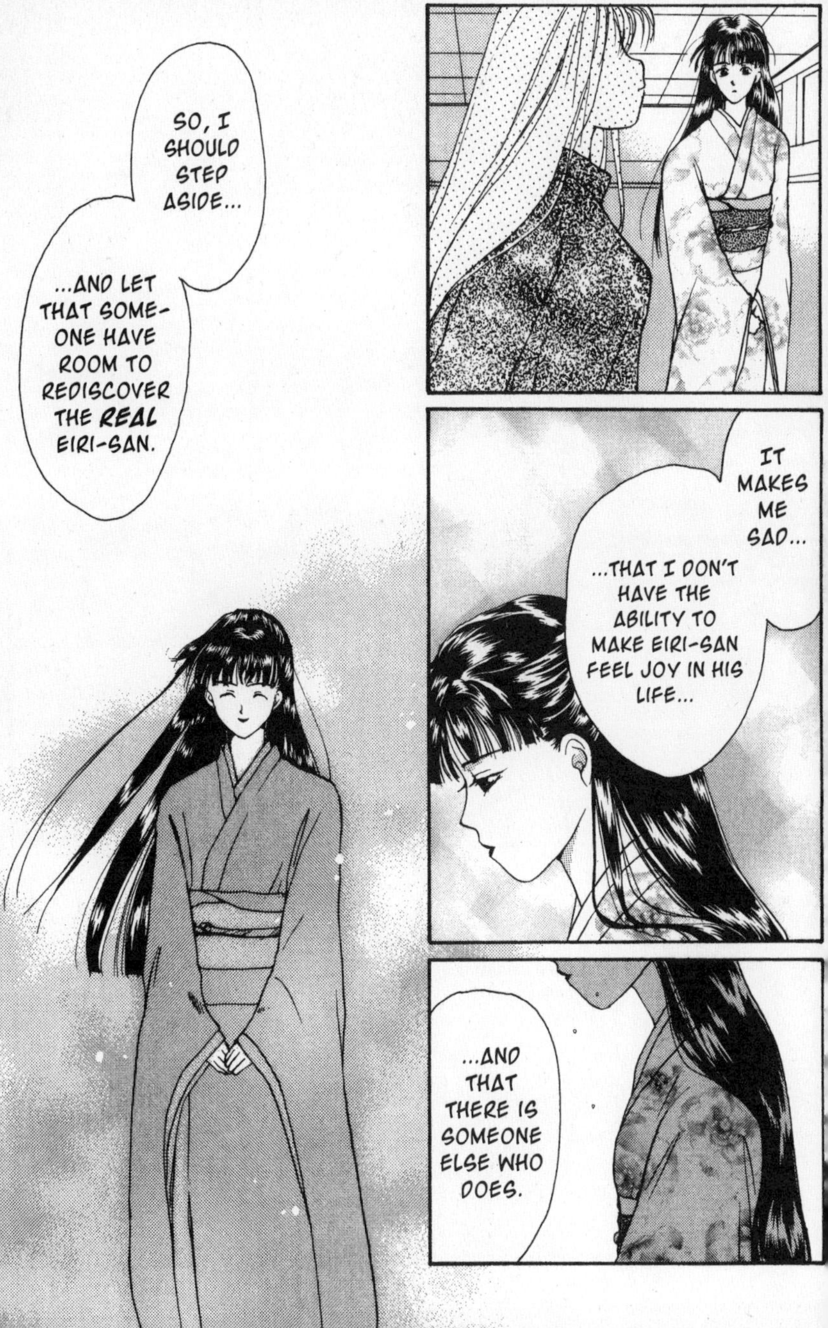
IT MAKES ME SAD...
...THAT I DON'T HAVE THE ABILITY TO MAKE EIRI-SAN FEEL JOY IN HIS LIFE...
...AND THAT THERE IS SOMEONE ELSE WHO DOES.
SO, I SHOULD STEP ASIDE...
...AND LET THAT SOME-ONE HAVE ROOM TO REDISCOVER THE REAL EIRI-SAN.

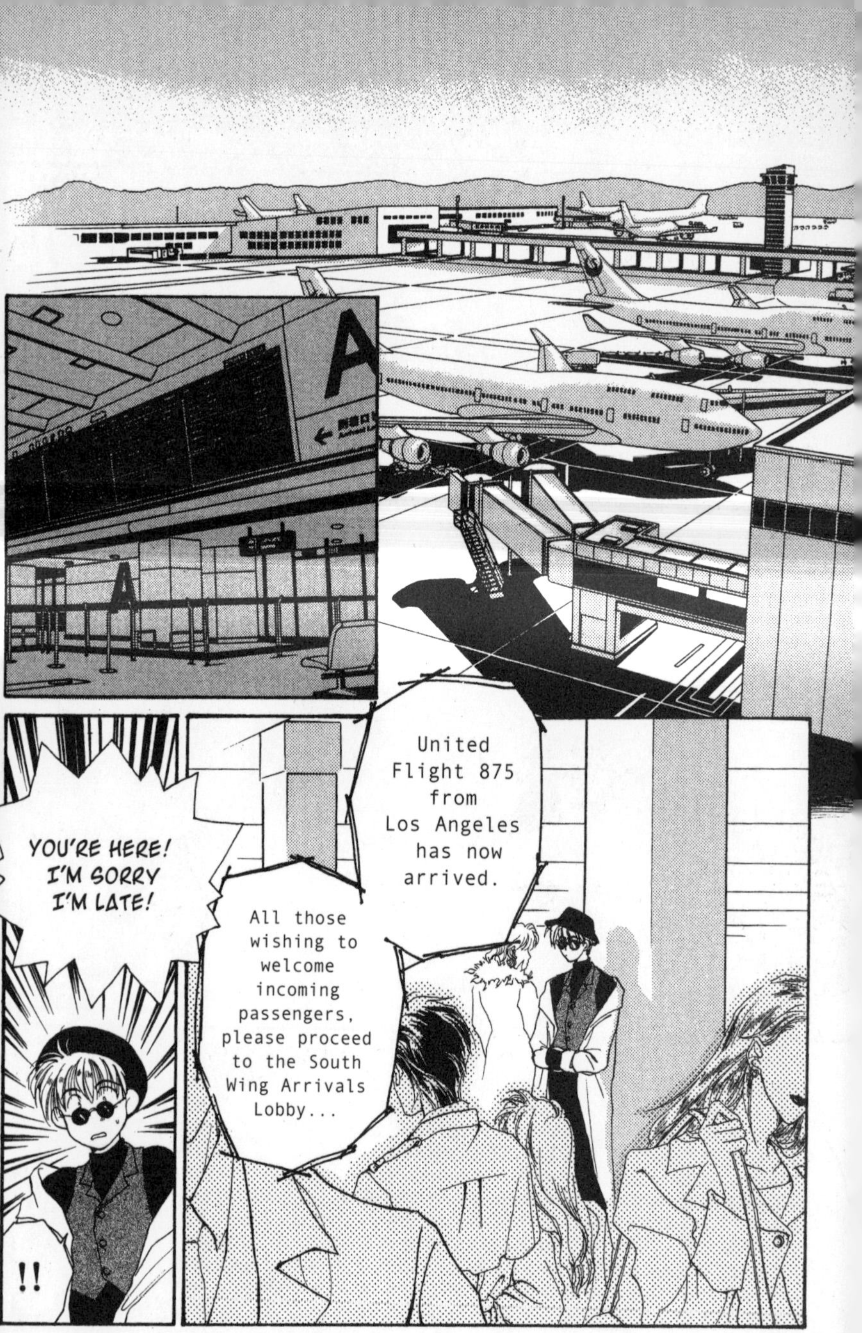
United Flight 875 from Los Angeles has now arrived.
All those wishing to welcome incoming passengers, please proceed to the South Wing Arrivals Lobby...
YOU'RE HERE! I'M SORRY I'M LATE!
!!

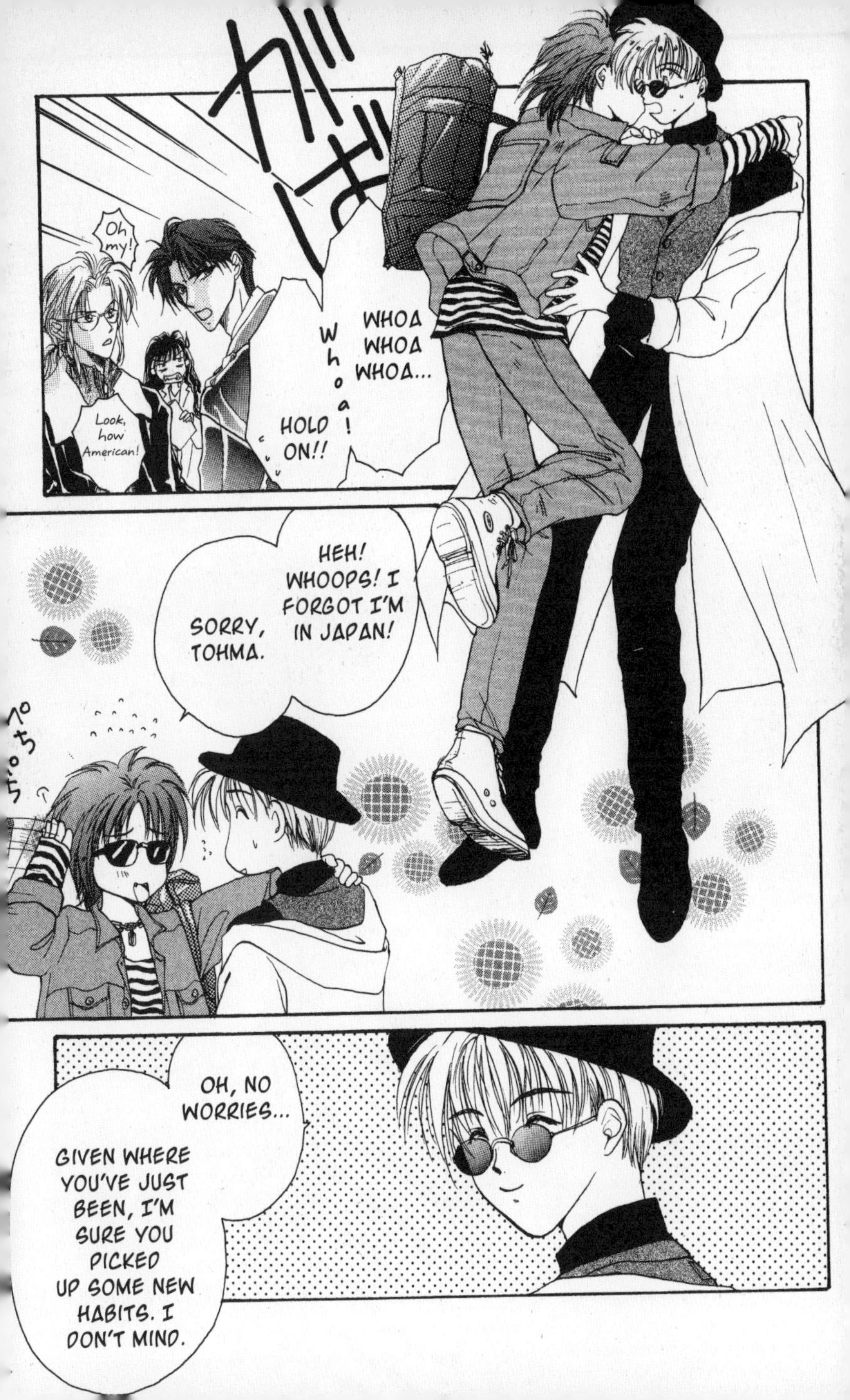
WHOA WHOA WHOA...
Whoa!
HOLD ON!!
Oh my!
Look, how American!
HEH! WHOOPS! I FORGOT I'M IN JAPAN!
SORRY, TOHMA.
OH, NO WORRIES...
GIVEN WHERE YOU'VE JUST BEEN, I'M SURE YOU PICKED UP SOME NEW HABITS. I DON'T MIND.

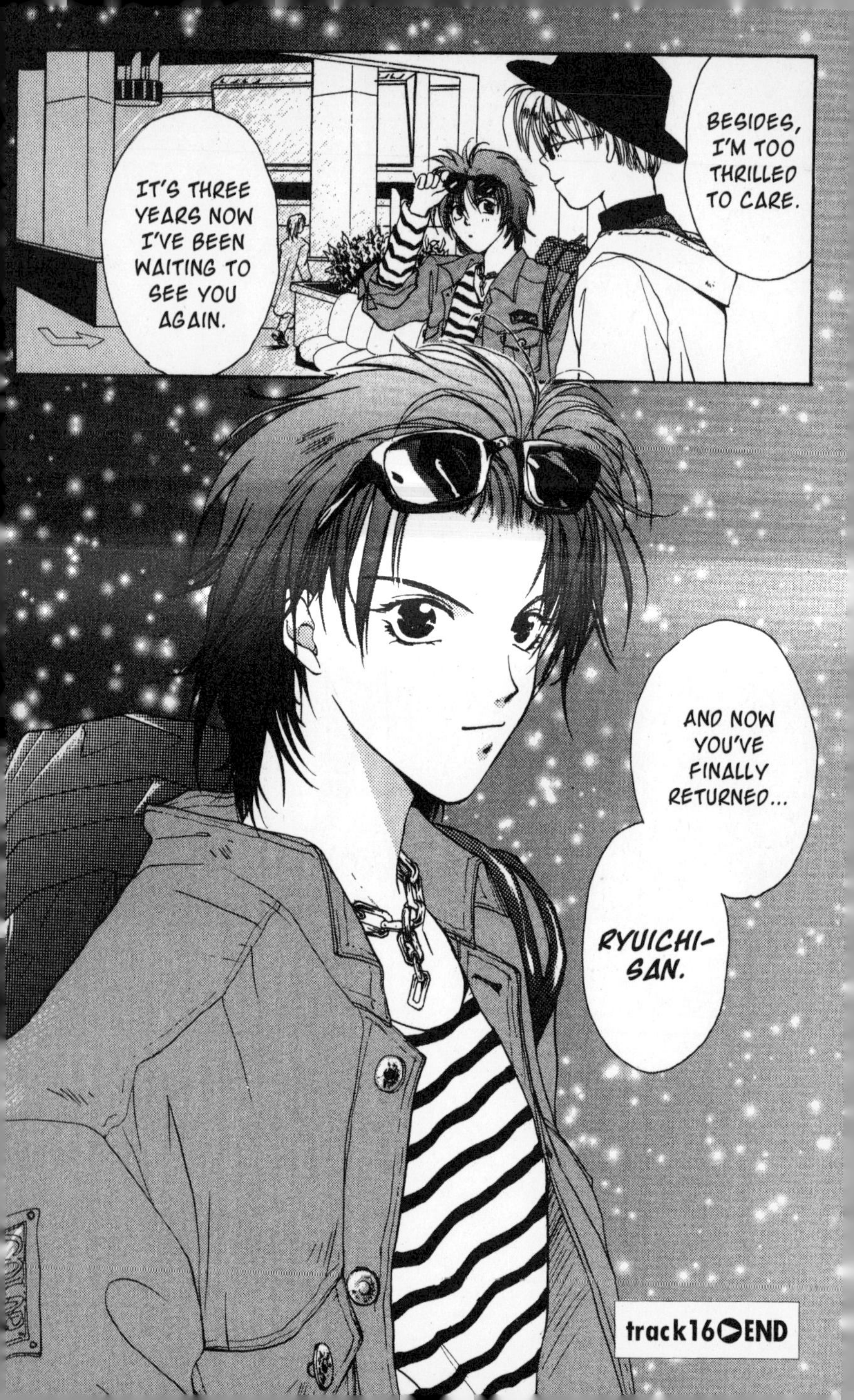
BESIDES, I'M TOO THRILLED TO CARE.
IT'S THREE YEARS NOW I'VE BEEN WAITING TO SEE YOU AGAIN.
AND NOW YOU'VE FINALLY RETURNED...
RYUICHI-SAN.
track16 END

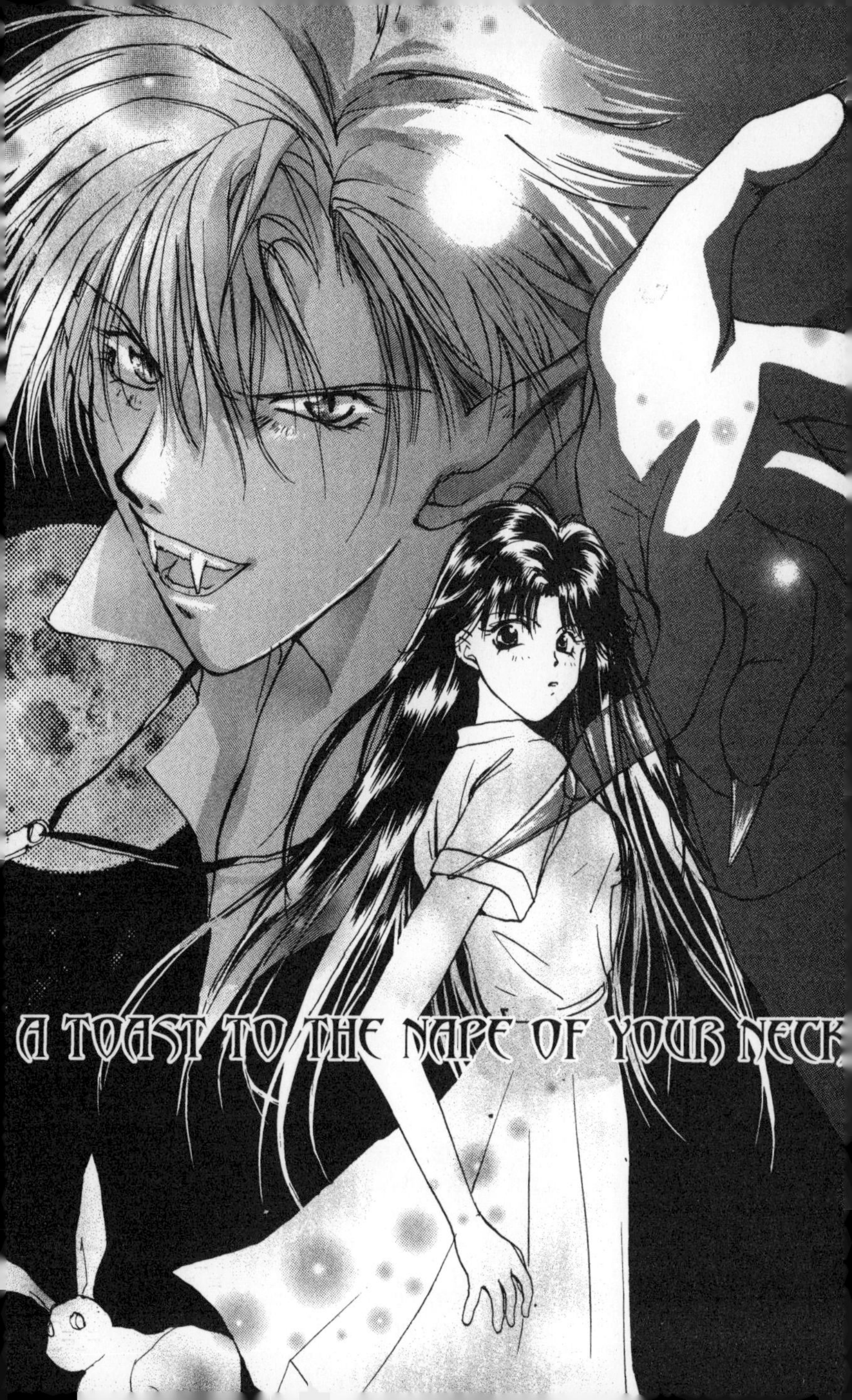
A TOAST TO THE NAPE OF YOUR NECK

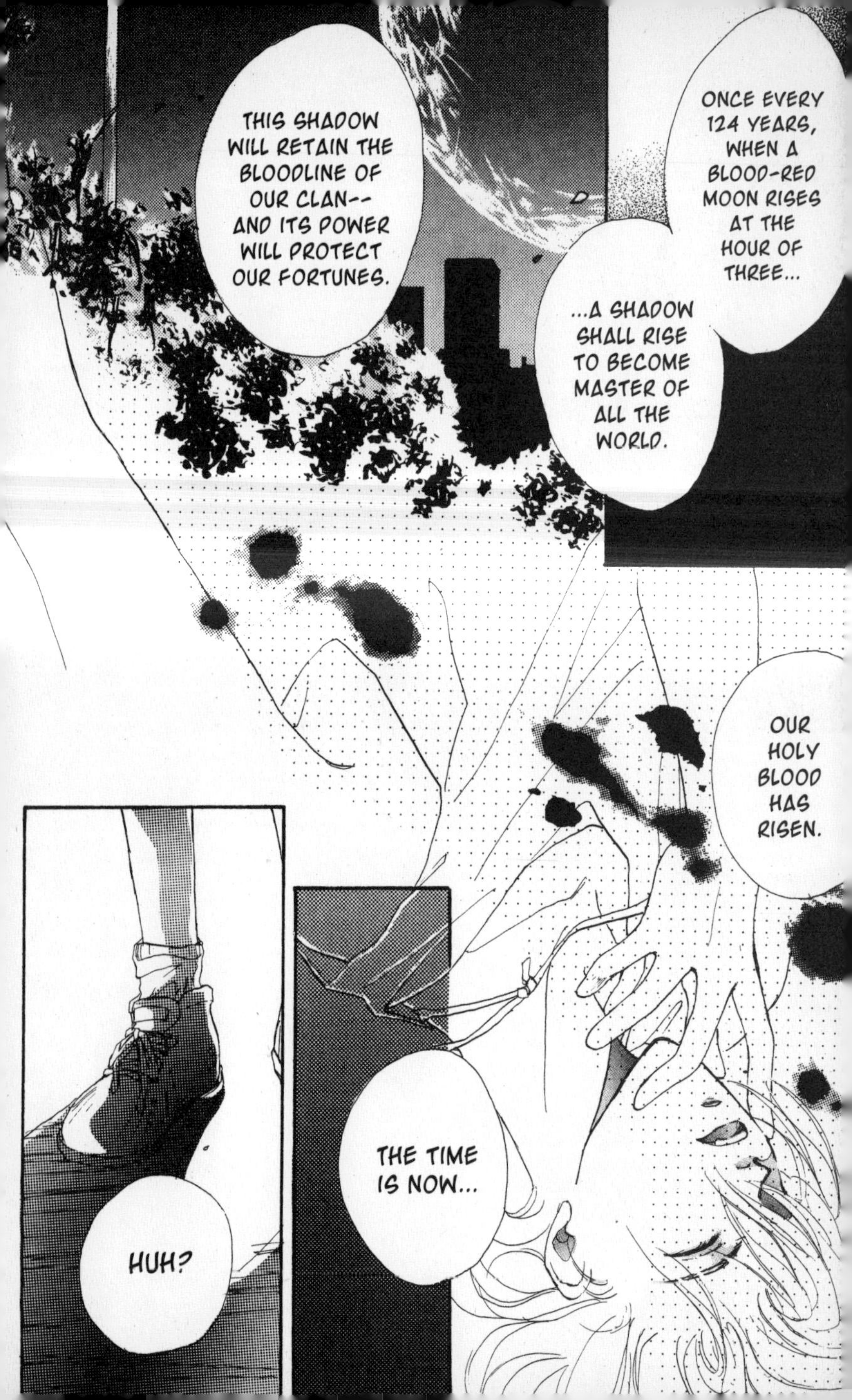
ONCE EVERY 124 YEARS, WHEN A BLOOD-RED MOON RISES AT THE HOUR OF THREE...
...A SHADOW SHALL RISE TO BECOME MASTER OF ALL THE WORLD.
THIS SHADOW WILL RETAIN THE BLOODLINE OF OUR CLAN-- AND ITS POWER WILL PROTECT OUR FORTUNES.
OUR HOLY BLOOD HAS RISEN.
THE TIME IS NOW...
HUH?

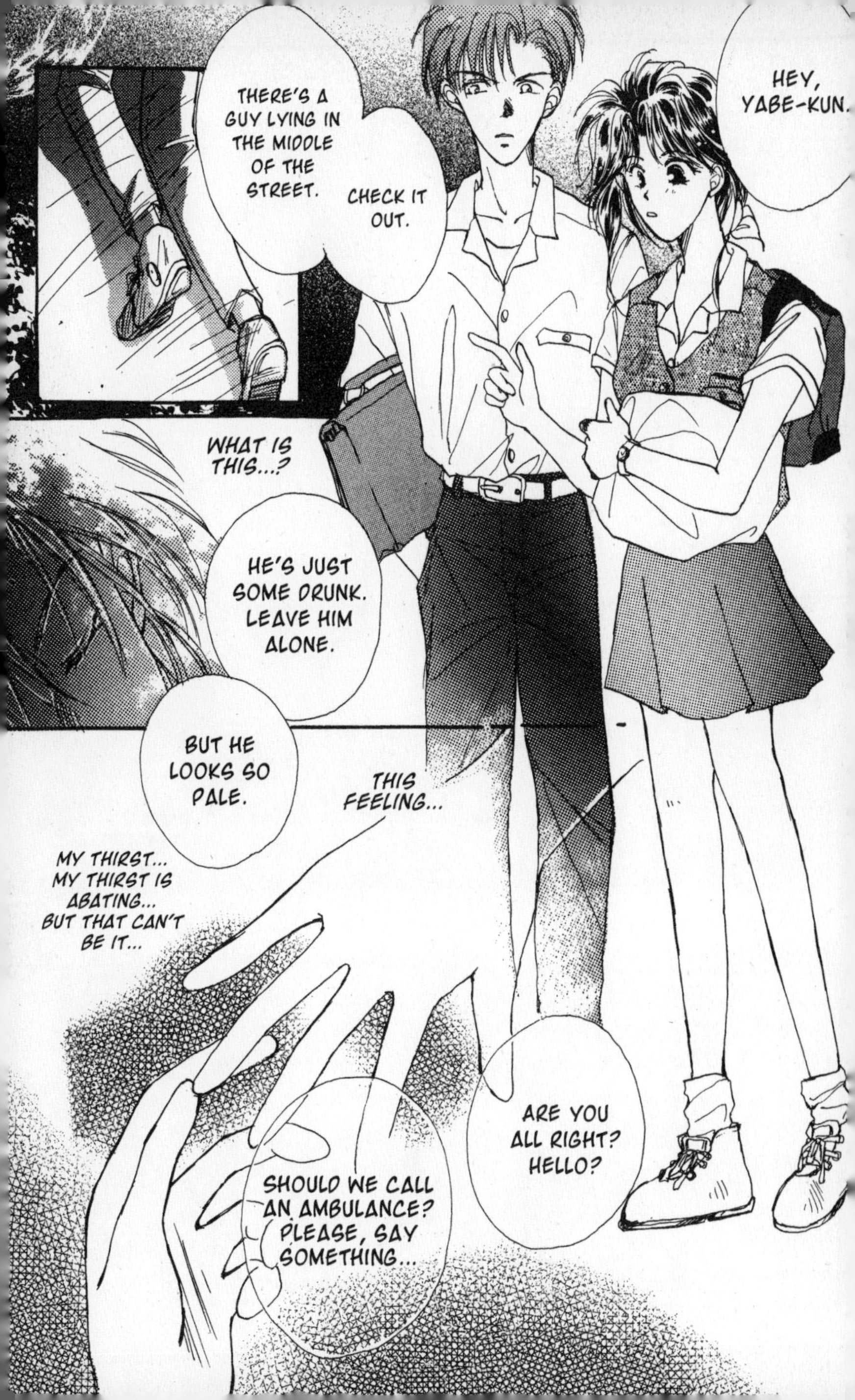
HEY, YABE-KUN.
THERE'S A GUY LYING IN THE MIDDLE OF THE STREET.
CHECK IT OUT.
WHAT IS THIS...?
HE'S JUST SOME DRUNK. LEAVE HIM ALONE.
BUT HE LOOKS SO PALE.
THIS FEELING...
MY THIRST... MY THIRST IS ABATING... BUT THAT CAN'T BE IT...
ARE YOU ALL RIGHT? HELLO?
SHOULD WE CALL AN AMBULANCE? PLEASE, SAY SOMETHING...

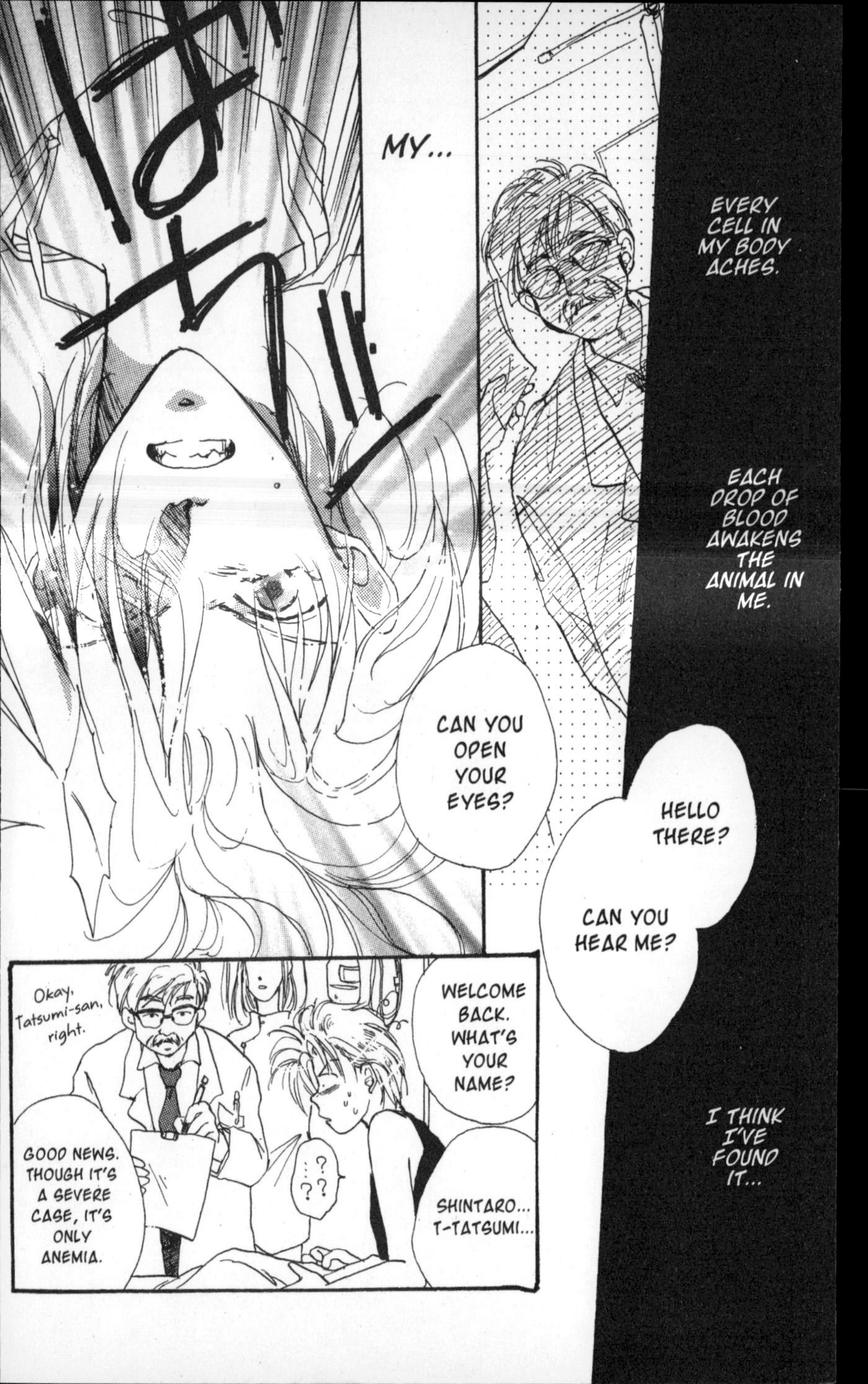
EVERY CELL IN MY BODY ACHES.
EACH DROP OF BLOOD AWAKENS THE ANIMAL IN ME.
MY...
はっ!!
HELLO THERE? CAN YOU HEAR ME?
CAN YOU OPEN YOUR EYES?
I THINK I'VE FOUND IT...
WELCOME BACK. WHAT'S YOUR NAME?
SHINTARO... T-TATSUMI...
...? ??
Okay, Tatsumi-san, right.
GOOD NEWS. THOUGH IT'S A SEVERE CASE, IT'S ONLY ANEMIA.

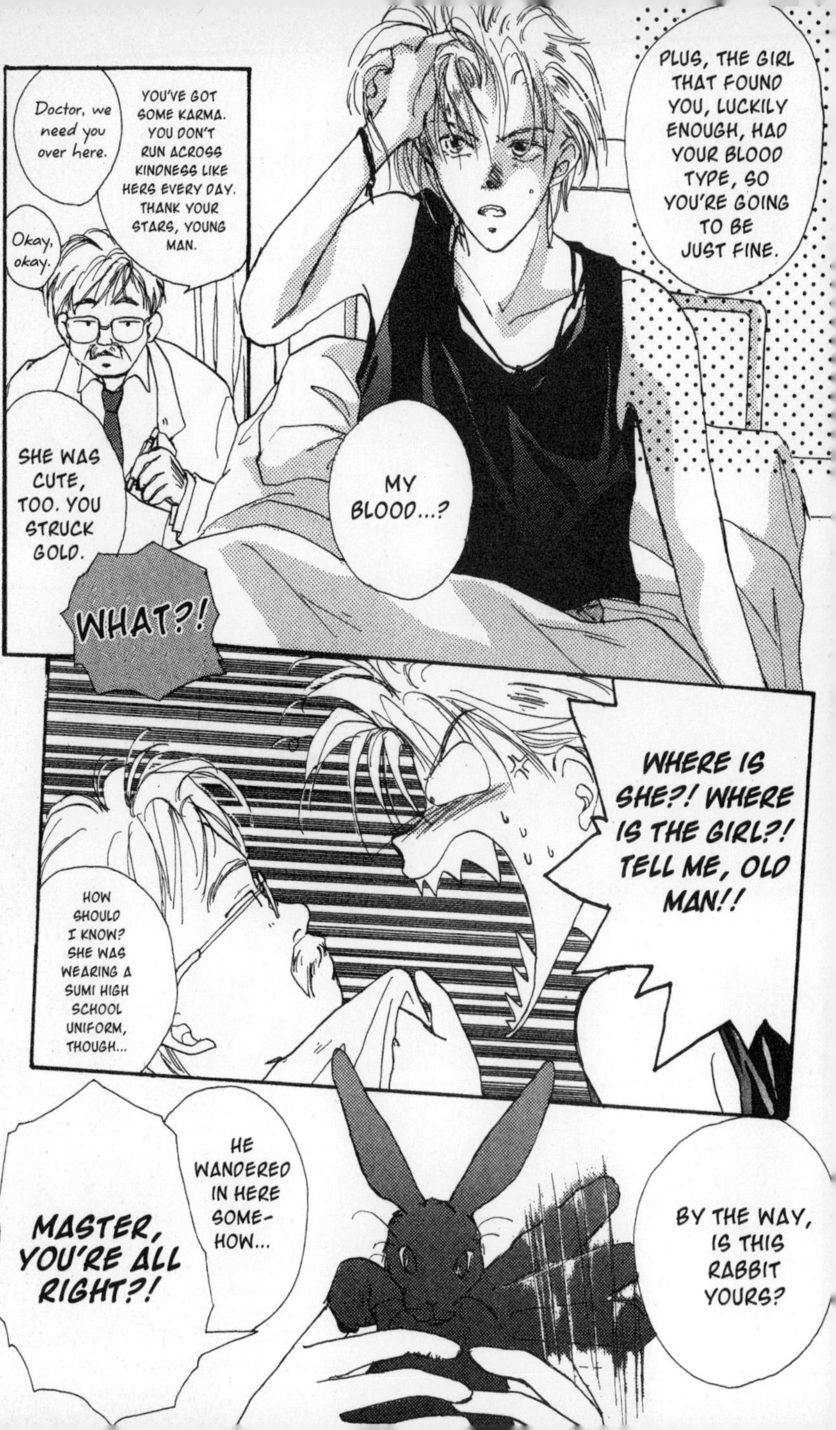
PLUS, THE GIRL THAT FOUND YOU, LUCKILY ENOUGH, HAD YOUR BLOOD TYPE, SO YOU'RE GOING TO BE JUST FINE.
MY BLOOD...?
YOU'VE GOT SOME KARMA. YOU DON'T RUN ACROSS KINDNESS LIKE HERS EVERY DAY. THANK YOUR STARS, YOUNG MAN.
Doctor, we need you over here.
Okay, okay.
SHE WAS CUTE, TOO. YOU STRUCK GOLD.
WHAT?!
WHERE IS SHE?! WHERE IS THE GIRL?! TELL ME, OLD MAN!!
HOW SHOULD I KNOW? SHE WAS WEARING A SUMI HIGH SCHOOL UNIFORM, THOUGH...
BY THE WAY, IS THIS RABBIT YOURS?
HE WANDERED IN HERE SOMEHOW...
MASTER, YOU'RE ALL RIGHT?!

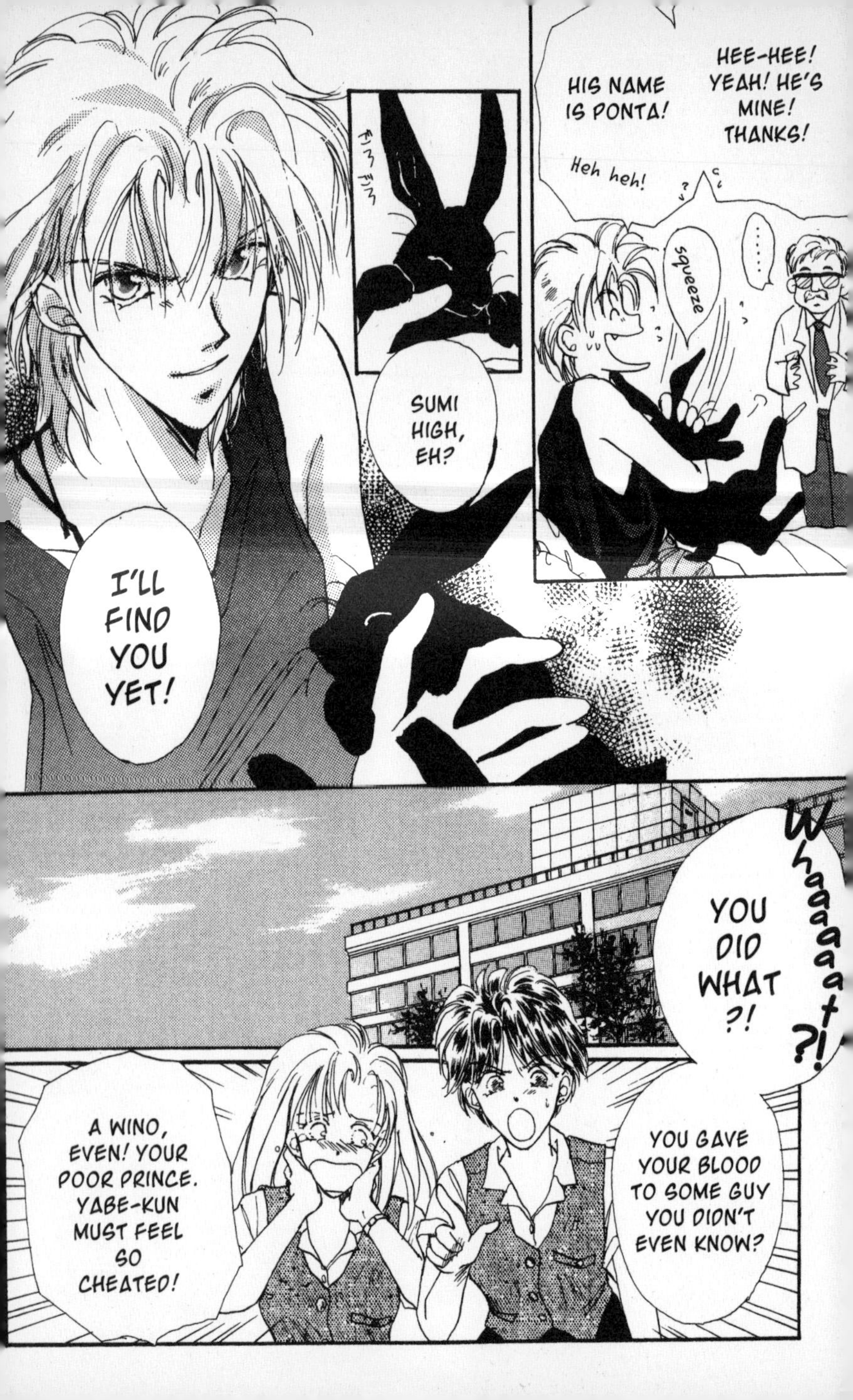
HEE-HEE! YEAH! HE'S MINE! THANKS!
HIS NAME IS PONTA!
Heh heh!
......
squeeze
fim fim
SUMI HIGH, EH?
I'LL FIND YOU YET!
Whaaaaat?!
YOU DID WHAT?!
YOU GAVE YOUR BLOOD TO SOME GUY YOU DIDN'T EVEN KNOW?
A WINO, EVEN! YOUR POOR PRINCE. YABE-KUN MUST FEEL SO CHEATED!

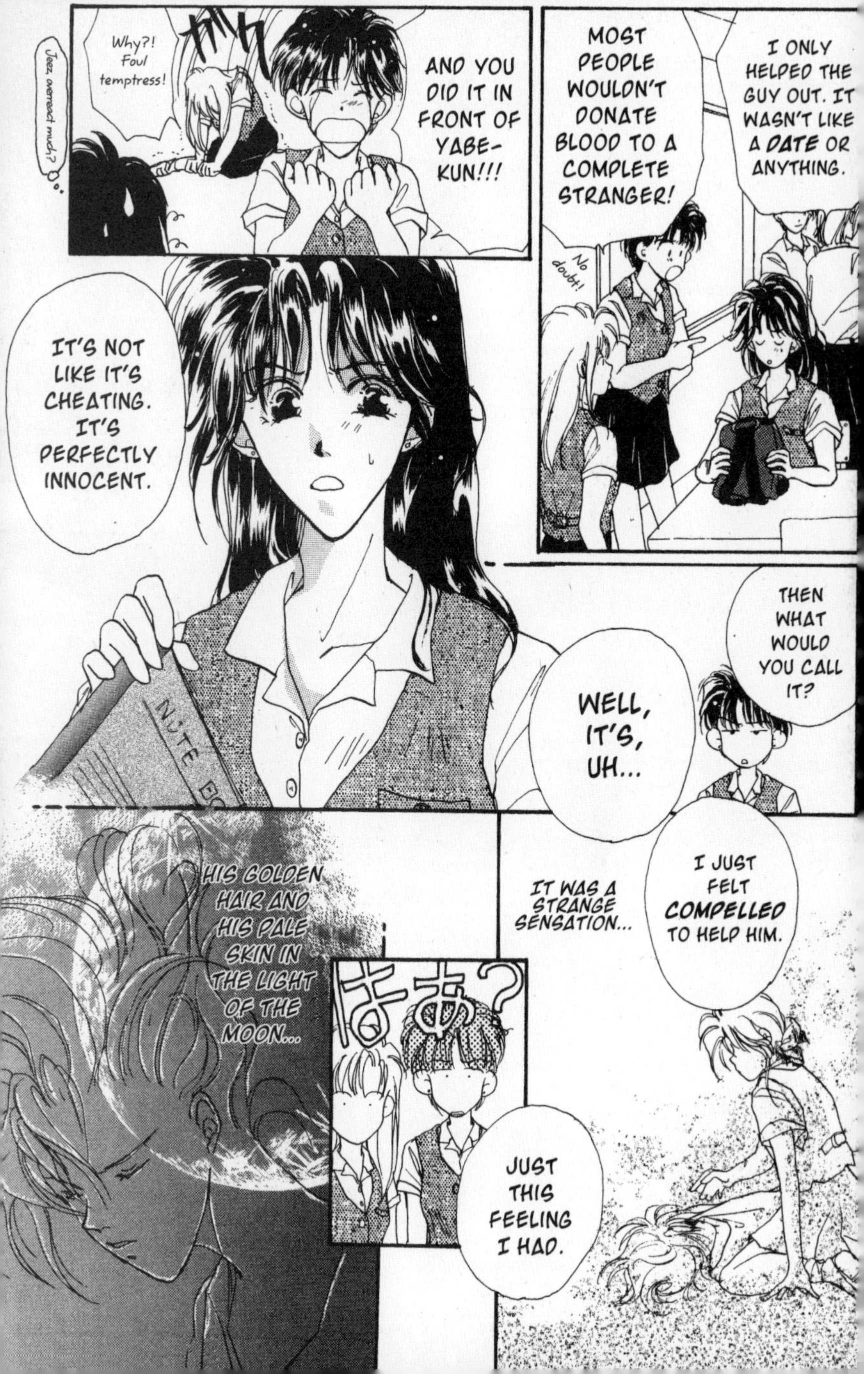

I ONLY HELPED THE GUY OUT. IT WASN'T LIKE A ***DATE*** OR ANYTHING.
MOST PEOPLE WOULDN'T DONATE BLOOD TO A COMPLETE STRANGER!
No doubt!
AND YOU DID IT IN FRONT OF YABE-KUN!!!
Why?! Foul temptress!
Jeez, overreact much?
IT'S NOT LIKE IT'S CHEATING. IT'S PERFECTLY INNOCENT.
NOTE
THEN WHAT WOULD YOU CALL IT?
WELL, IT'S, UH...
I JUST FELT **COMPELLED** TO HELP HIM.
IT WAS A STRANGE SENSATION...
JUST THIS FEELING I HAD.
はぁ?
HIS GOLDEN HAIR AND HIS PALE SKIN IN THE LIGHT OF THE MOON...

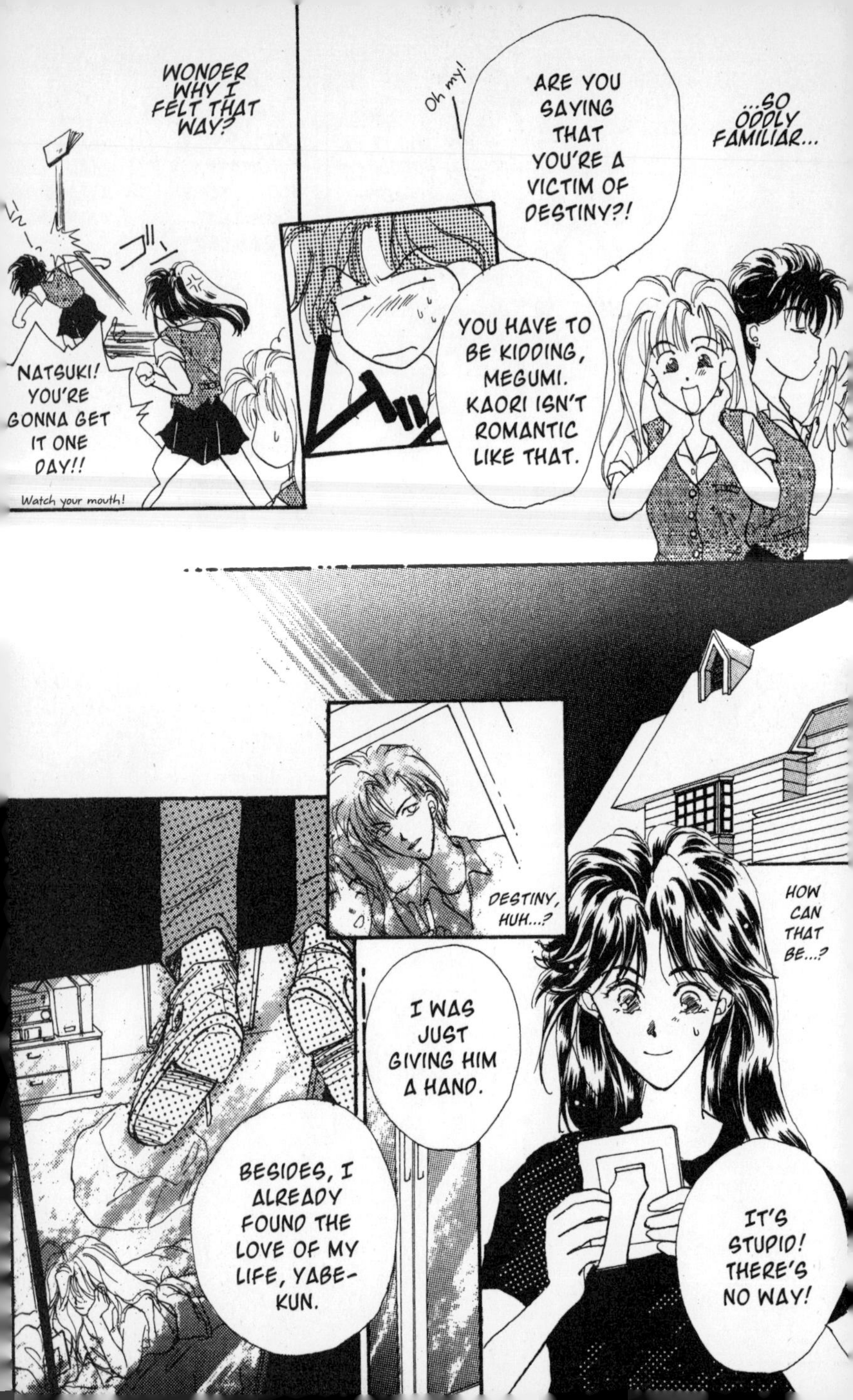
...SO ODDLY FAMILIAR...
ARE YOU SAYING THAT YOU'RE A VICTIM OF DESTINY?!
Oh my!
YOU HAVE TO BE KIDDING, MEGUMI. KAORI ISN'T ROMANTIC LIKE THAT.
WONDER WHY I FELT THAT WAY?
NATSUKI! YOU'RE GONNA GET IT ONE DAY!!
Watch your mouth!
DESTINY, HUH...?
HOW CAN THAT BE...?
IT'S STUPID! THERE'S NO WAY!
I WAS JUST GIVING HIM A HAND.
BESIDES, I ALREADY FOUND THE LOVE OF MY LIFE, YABE-KUN.

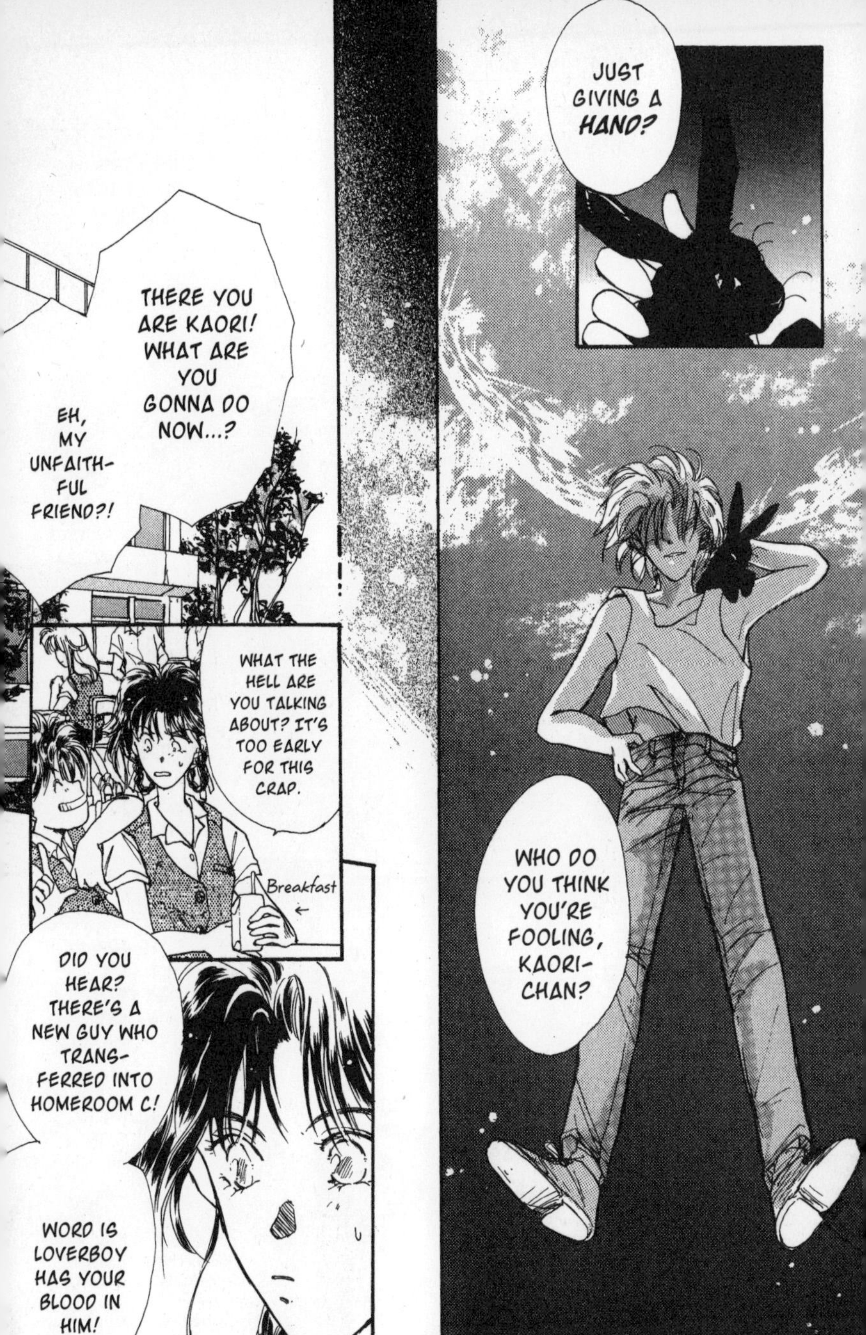
JUST GIVING A HAND?
WHO DO YOU THINK YOU'RE FOOLING, KAORI-CHAN?
THERE YOU ARE KAORI! WHAT ARE YOU GONNA DO NOW...?
EH, MY UNFAITH-FUL FRIEND?!
WHAT THE HELL ARE YOU TALKING ABOUT? IT'S TOO EARLY FOR THIS CRAP.
Breakfast
DID YOU HEAR? THERE'S A NEW GUY WHO TRANS-FERRED INTO HOMEROOM C!
WORD IS LOVERBOY HAS YOUR BLOOD IN HIM!

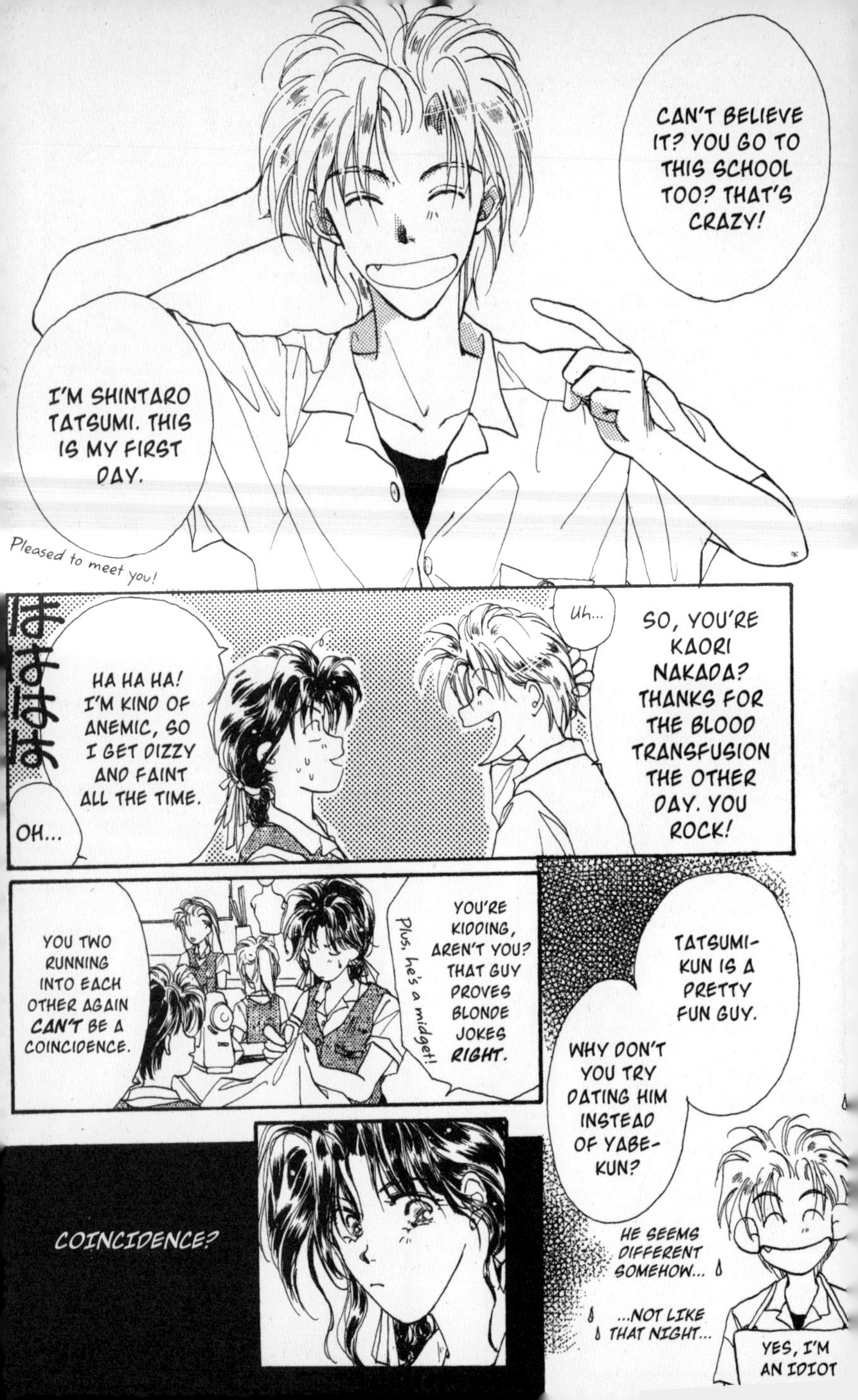
CAN'T BELIEVE IT? YOU GO TO THIS SCHOOL TOO? THAT'S CRAZY!
I'M SHINTARO TATSUMI. THIS IS MY FIRST DAY.
Pleased to meet you!
Uh...
SO, YOU'RE KAORI NAKADA? THANKS FOR THE BLOOD TRANSFUSION THE OTHER DAY. YOU ROCK!
HA HA HA! I'M KIND OF ANEMIC, SO I GET DIZZY AND FAINT ALL THE TIME.
OH...
TATSUMI-KUN IS A PRETTY FUN GUY.
WHY DON'T YOU TRY DATING HIM INSTEAD OF YABE-KUN?
YOU'RE KIDDING, AREN'T YOU? THAT GUY PROVES BLONDE JOKES **RIGHT**.
Plus, he's a midget!
YOU TWO RUNNING INTO EACH OTHER AGAIN **CAN'T** BE A COINCIDENCE.
YES, I'M AN IDIOT
HE SEEMS DIFFERENT SOMEHOW...
...NOT LIKE THAT NIGHT...
COINCIDENCE?

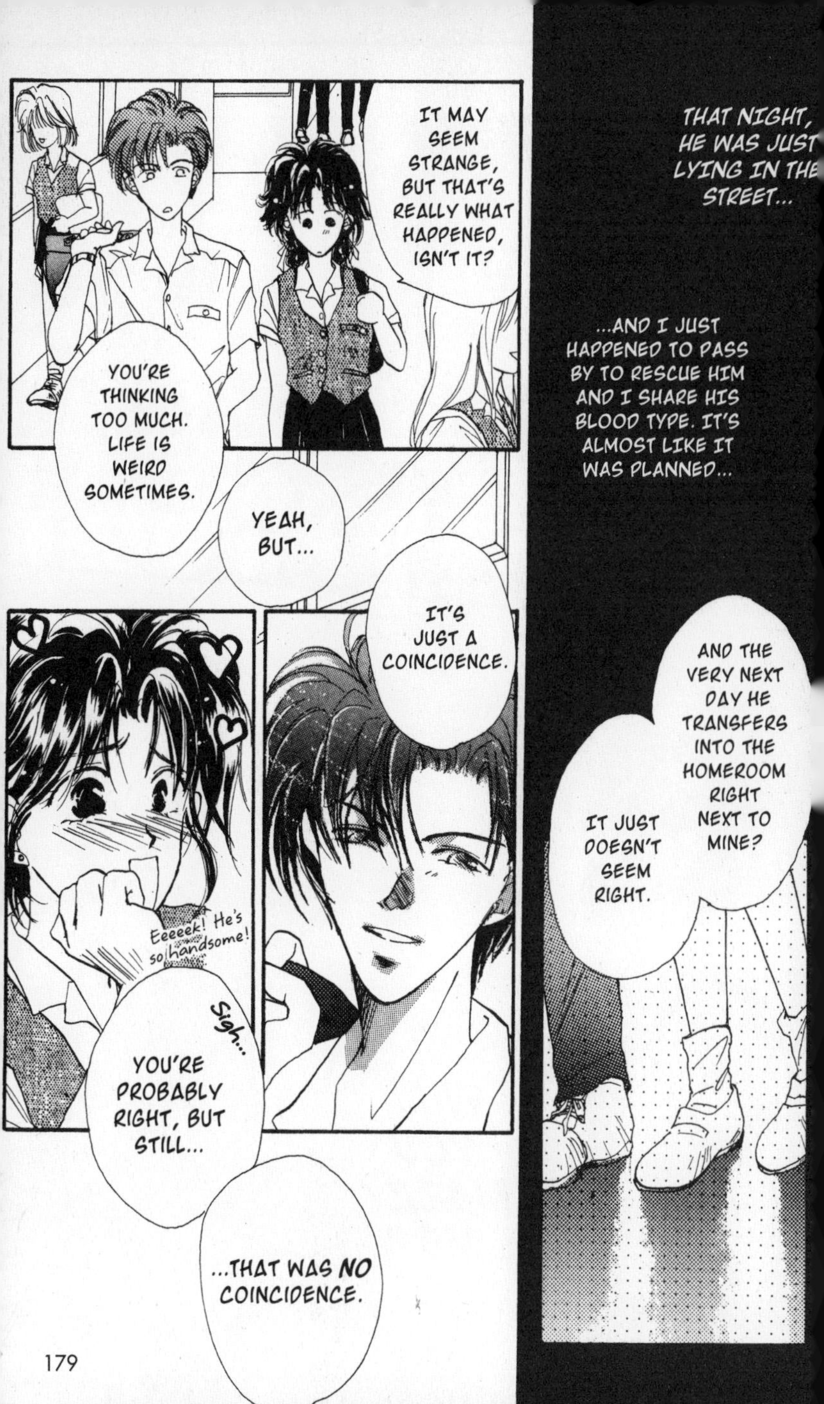
THAT NIGHT, HE WAS JUST LYING IN THE STREET...
...AND I JUST HAPPENED TO PASS BY TO RESCUE HIM AND I SHARE HIS BLOOD TYPE. IT'S ALMOST LIKE IT WAS PLANNED...
AND THE VERY NEXT DAY HE TRANSFERS INTO THE HOMEROOM RIGHT NEXT TO MINE?
IT JUST DOESN'T SEEM RIGHT.
IT MAY SEEM STRANGE, BUT THAT'S REALLY WHAT HAPPENED, ISN'T IT?
YOU'RE THINKING TOO MUCH. LIFE IS WEIRD SOMETIMES.
YEAH, BUT...
IT'S JUST A COINCIDENCE.
Eeeeek! He's so handsome!
Sigh...
YOU'RE PROBABLY RIGHT, BUT STILL...
...THAT WAS NO COINCIDENCE.

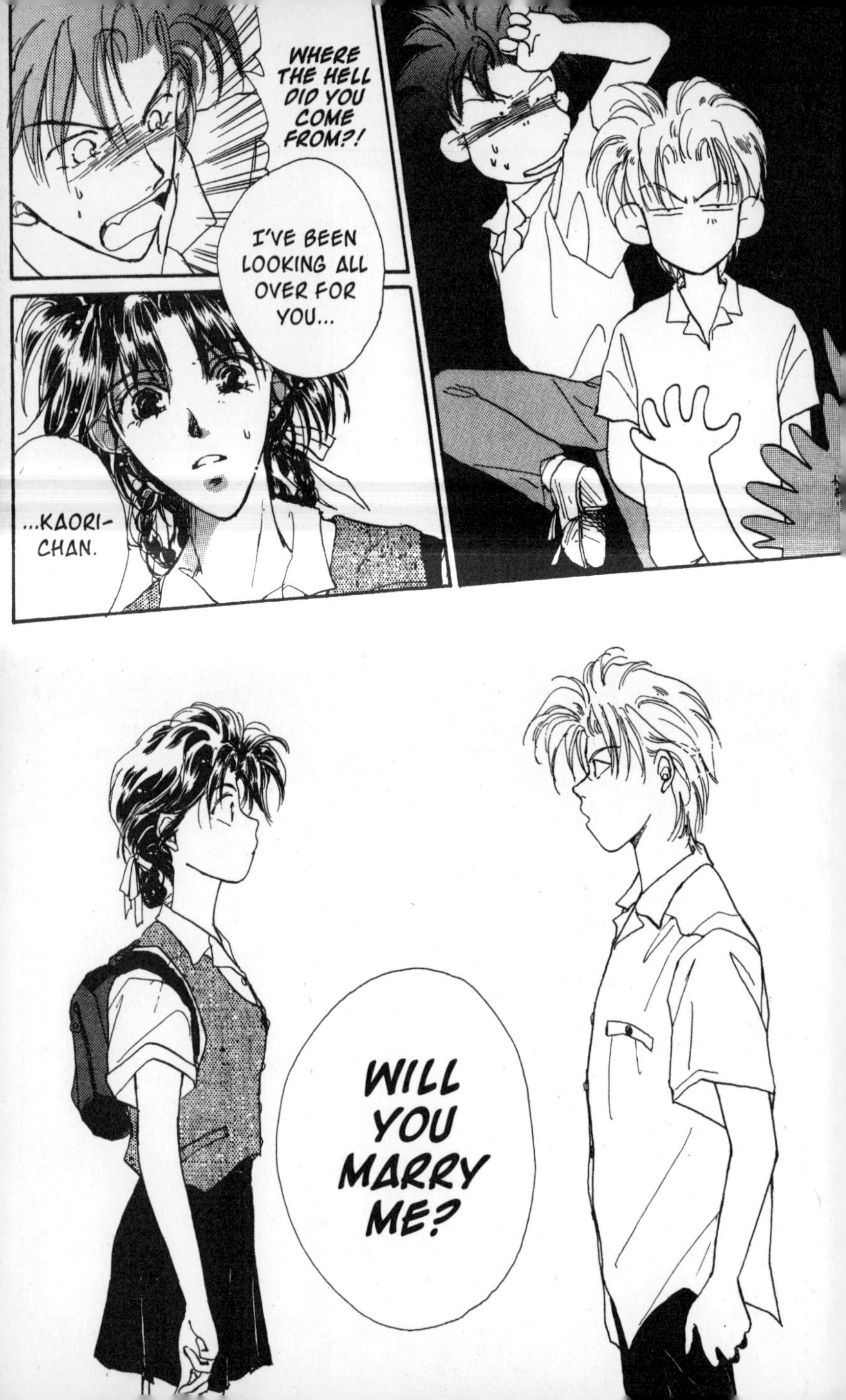
WHERE THE HELL DID YOU COME FROM?!
I'VE BEEN LOOKING ALL OVER FOR YOU...
...KAORI-CHAN.
WILL YOU MARRY ME?

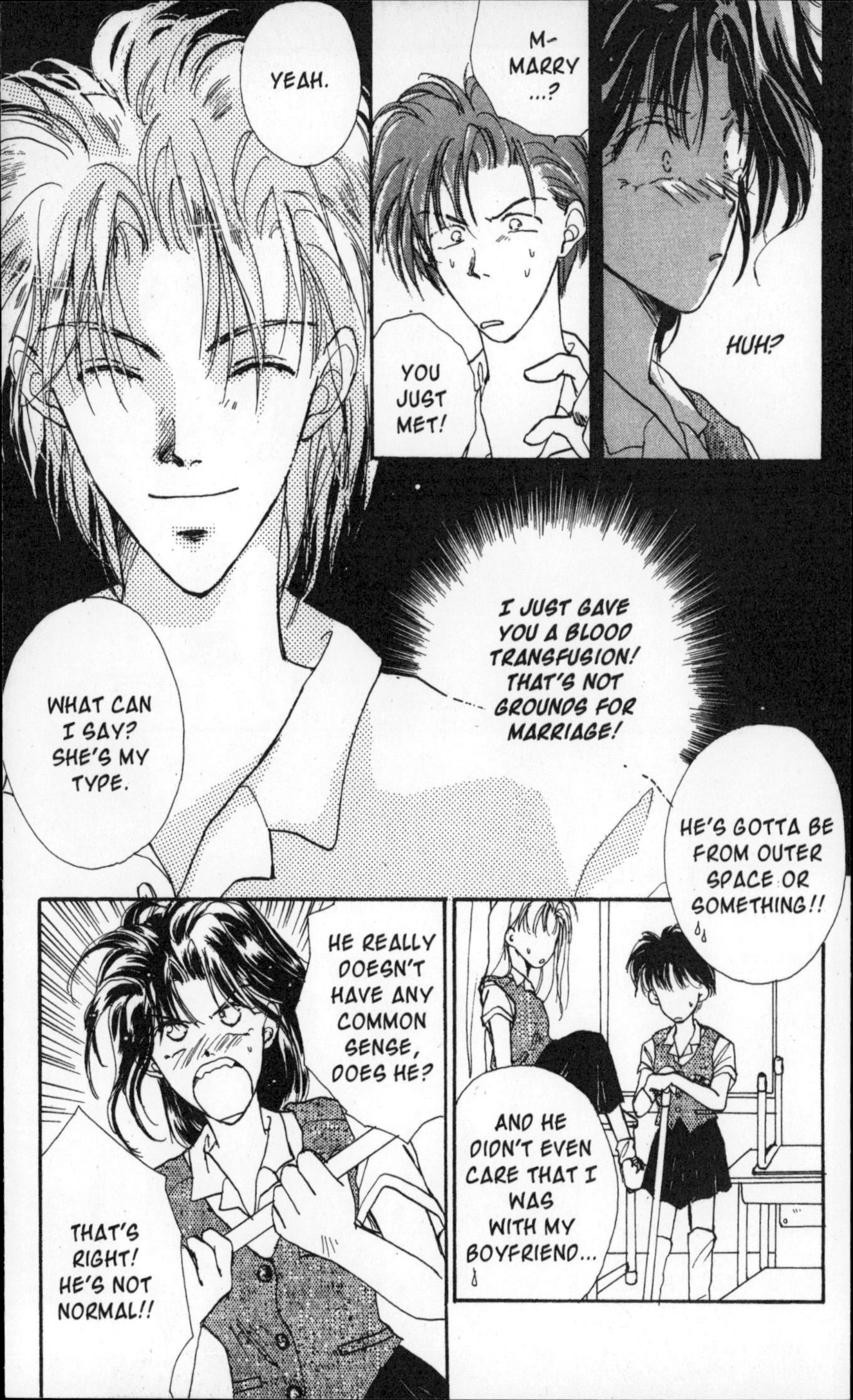
HUH?
M-MARRY ...?
YOU JUST MET!
YEAH.
WHAT CAN I SAY? SHE'S MY TYPE.
I JUST GAVE YOU A BLOOD TRANSFUSION! THAT'S NOT GROUNDS FOR MARRIAGE!
HE'S GOTTA BE FROM OUTER SPACE OR SOMETHING!!
AND HE DIDN'T EVEN CARE THAT I WAS WITH MY BOYFRIEND...
HE REALLY DOESN'T HAVE ANY COMMON SENSE, DOES HE?
THAT'S RIGHT! HE'S NOT NORMAL!!

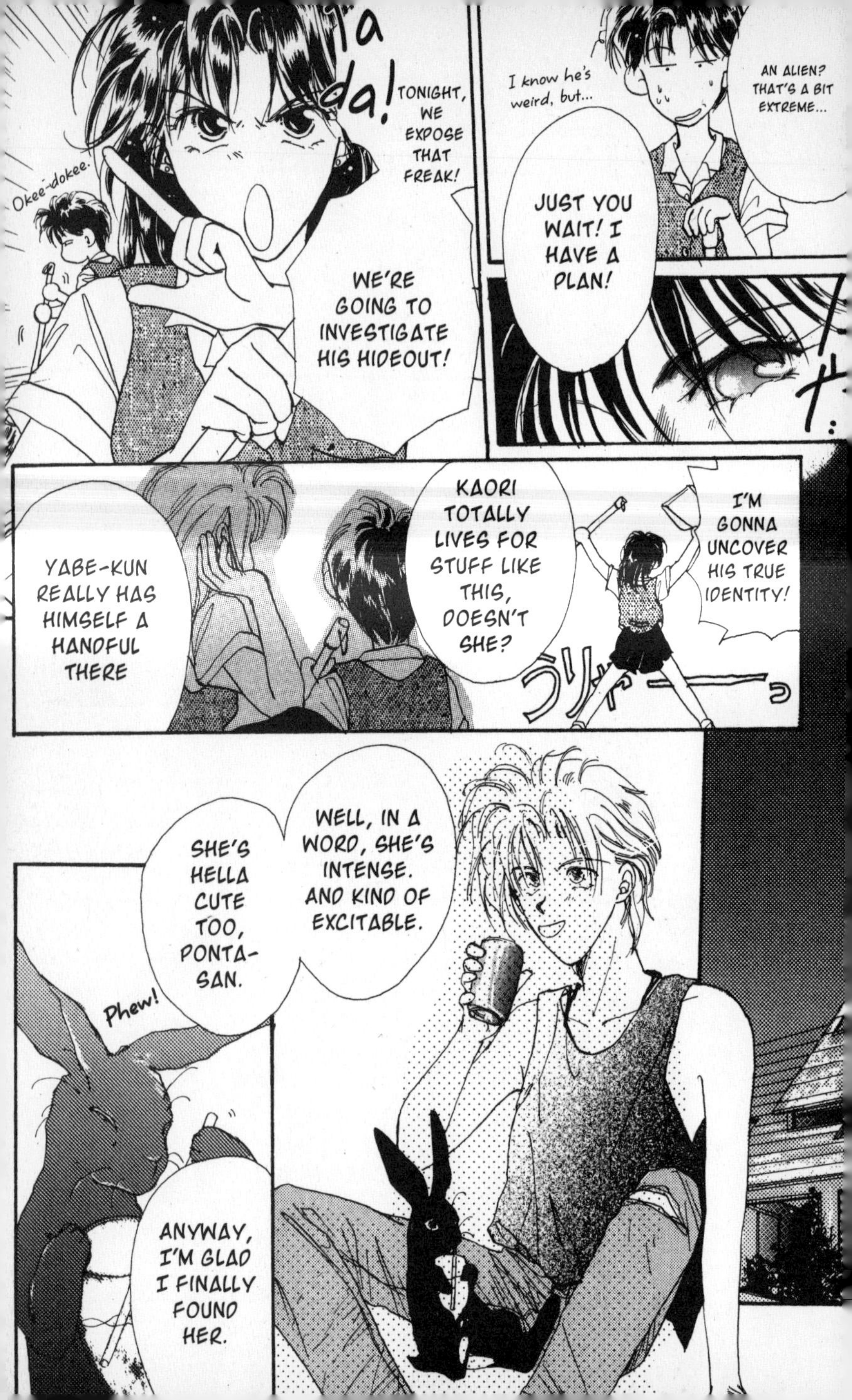
AN ALIEN? THAT'S A BIT EXTREME...
I know he's weird, but...
JUST YOU WAIT! I HAVE A PLAN!
Ta da!
TONIGHT, WE EXPOSE THAT FREAK!
WE'RE GOING TO INVESTIGATE HIS HIDEOUT!
Okee-dokee.
I'M GONNA UNCOVER HIS TRUE IDENTITY!
KAORI TOTALLY LIVES FOR STUFF LIKE THIS, DOESN'T SHE?
YABE-KUN REALLY HAS HIMSELF A HANDFUL THERE
WELL, IN A WORD, SHE'S INTENSE. AND KIND OF EXCITABLE.
SHE'S HELLA CUTE TOO, PONTA-SAN.
Phew!
ANYWAY, I'M GLAD I FINALLY FOUND HER.

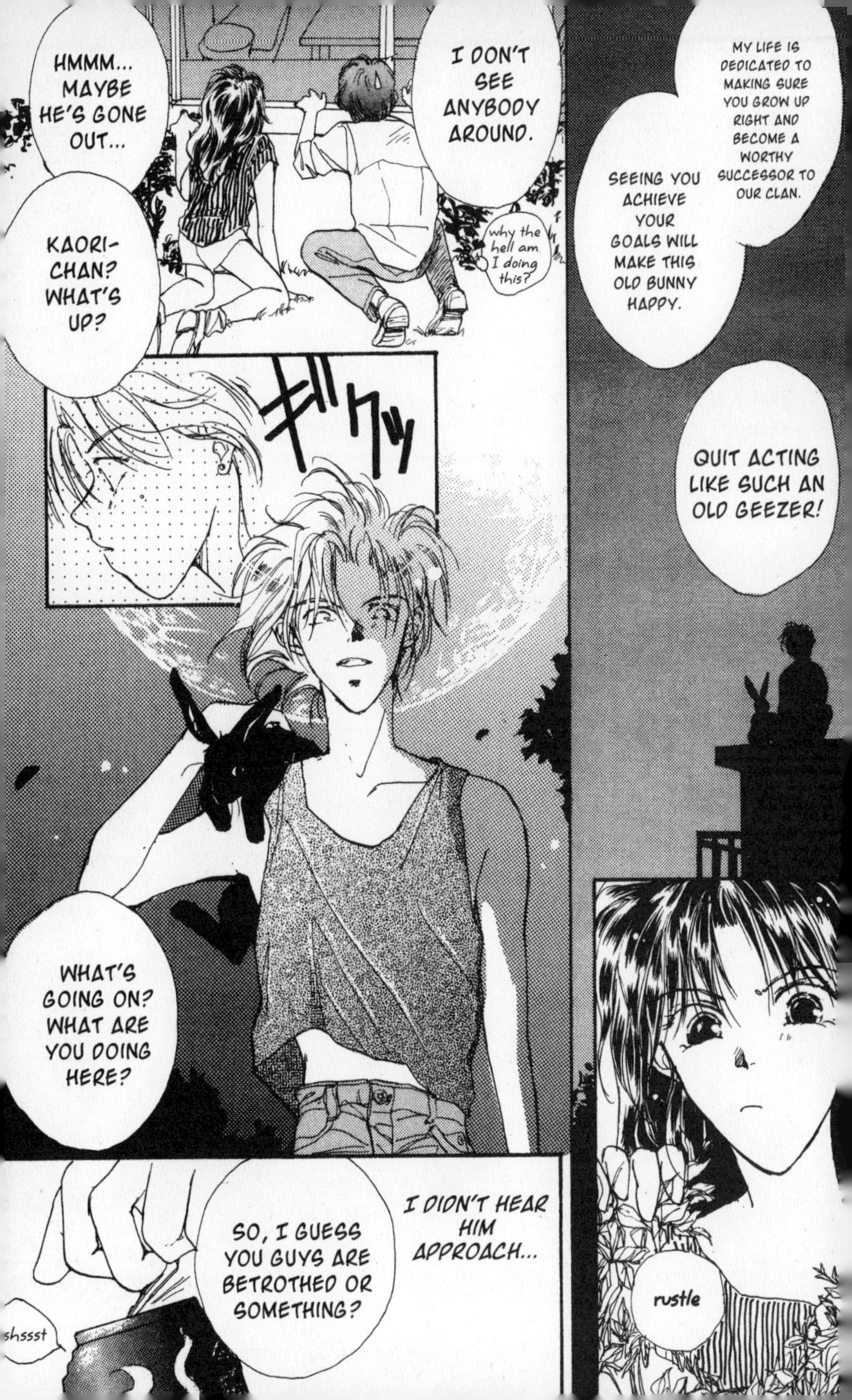
MY LIFE IS DEDICATED TO MAKING SURE YOU GROW UP RIGHT AND BECOME A WORTHY SUCCESSOR TO OUR CLAN.
SEEING YOU ACHIEVE YOUR GOALS WILL MAKE THIS OLD BUNNY HAPPY.
QUIT ACTING LIKE SUCH AN OLD GEEZER!
rustle
I DON'T SEE ANYBODY AROUND.
why the hell am I doing this?
HMMM... MAYBE HE'S GONE OUT...
KAORI-CHAN? WHAT'S UP?
ギクッ
WHAT'S GOING ON? WHAT ARE YOU DOING HERE?
I DIDN'T HEAR HIM APPROACH...
SO, I GUESS YOU GUYS ARE BETROTHED OR SOMETHING?
shssst

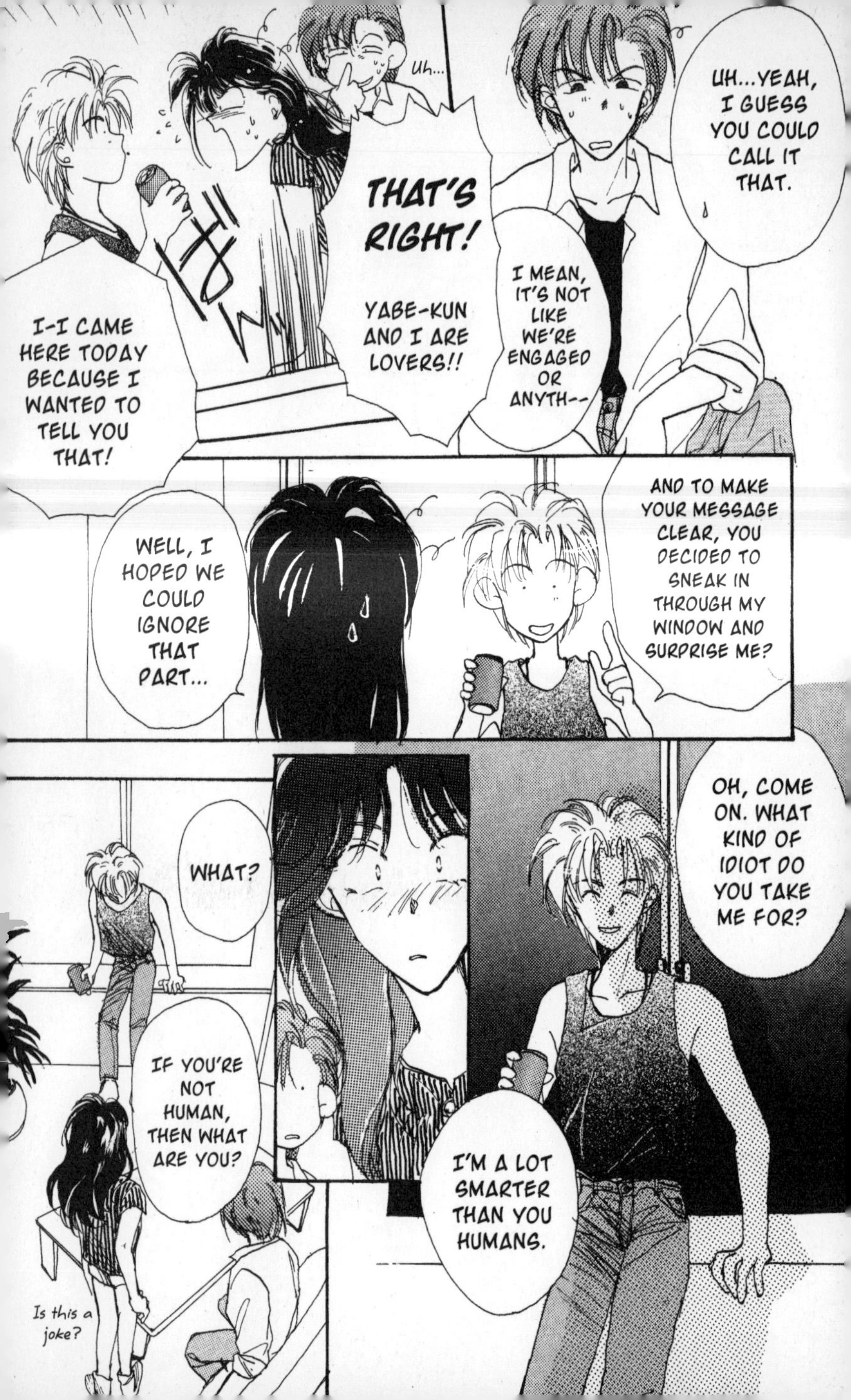
UH...YEAH, I GUESS YOU COULD CALL IT THAT.
I MEAN, IT'S NOT LIKE WE'RE ENGAGED OR ANYTH--
Uh...
THAT'S RIGHT!
YABE-KUN AND I ARE LOVERS!!
I-I CAME HERE TODAY BECAUSE I WANTED TO TELL YOU THAT!
AND TO MAKE YOUR MESSAGE CLEAR, YOU DECIDED TO SNEAK IN THROUGH MY WINDOW AND SURPRISE ME?
WELL, I HOPED WE COULD IGNORE THAT PART...
OH, COME ON. WHAT KIND OF IDIOT DO YOU TAKE ME FOR?
I'M A LOT SMARTER THAN YOU HUMANS.
WHAT?
IF YOU'RE NOT HUMAN, THEN WHAT ARE YOU?
Is this a joke?

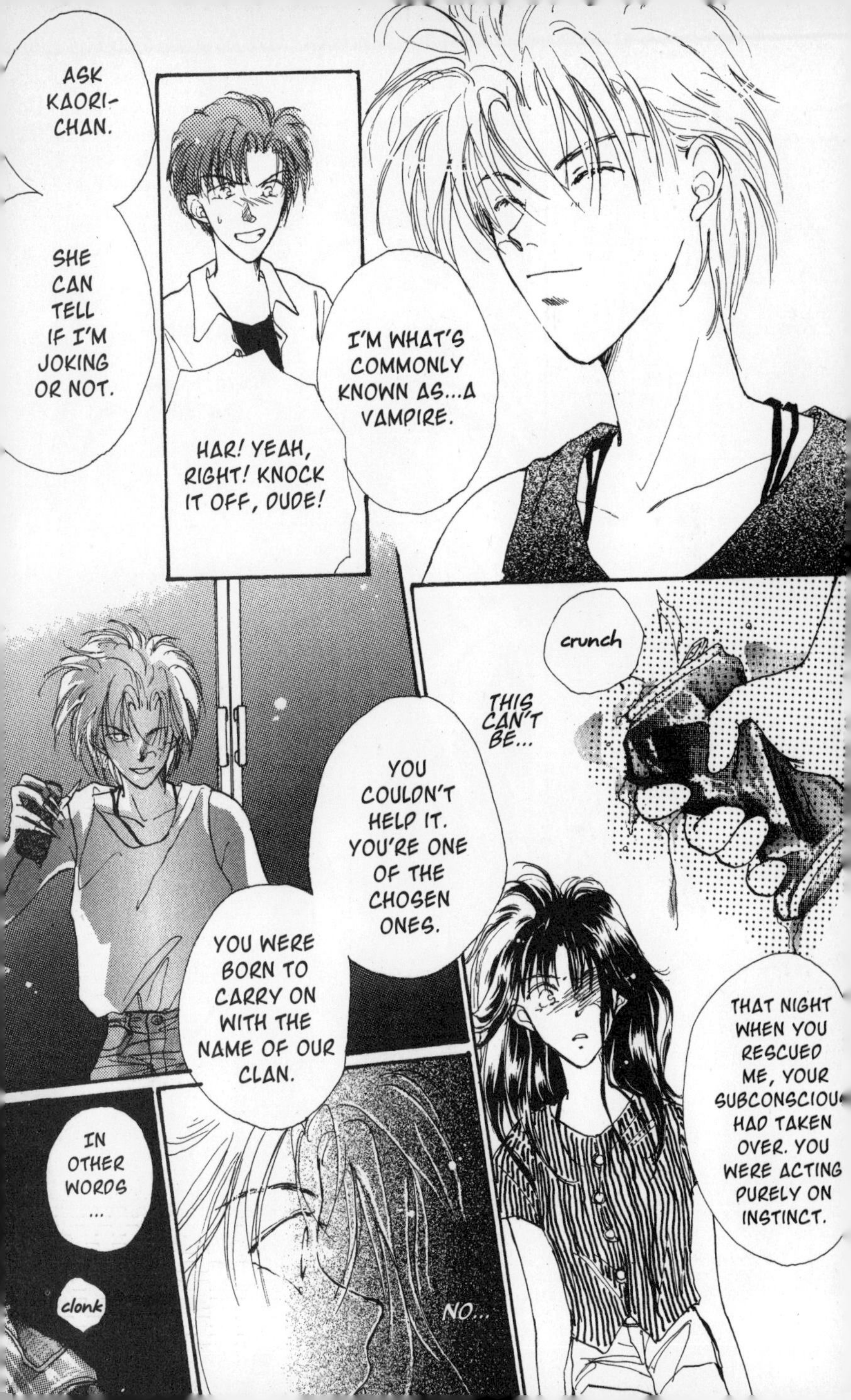

I'M WHAT'S COMMONLY KNOWN AS...A VAMPIRE.
HAR! YEAH, RIGHT! KNOCK IT OFF, DUDE!
ASK KAORI-CHAN.
SHE CAN TELL IF I'M JOKING OR NOT.
crunch
THIS CAN'T BE...
THAT NIGHT WHEN YOU RESCUED ME, YOUR SUBCONSCIOU[S] HAD TAKEN OVER. YOU WERE ACTING PURELY ON INSTINCT.
YOU COULDN'T HELP IT. YOU'RE ONE OF THE CHOSEN ONES.
YOU WERE BORN TO CARRY ON WITH THE NAME OF OUR CLAN.
IN OTHER WORDS...
clonk
NO...

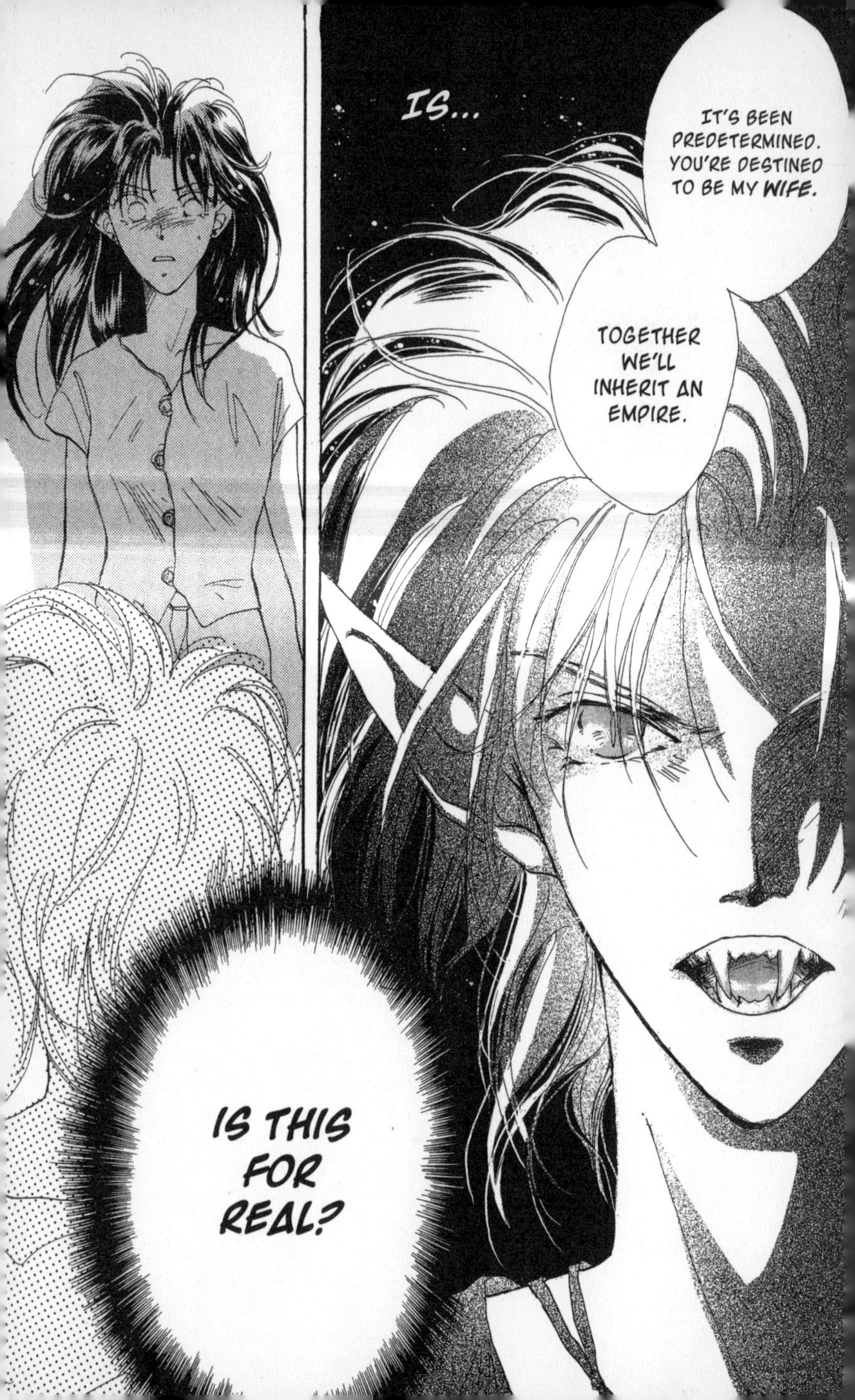
IT'S BEEN PREDETERMINED. YOU'RE DESTINED TO BE MY WIFE.
TOGETHER WE'LL INHERIT AN EMPIRE.
IS...
IS THIS FOR REAL?

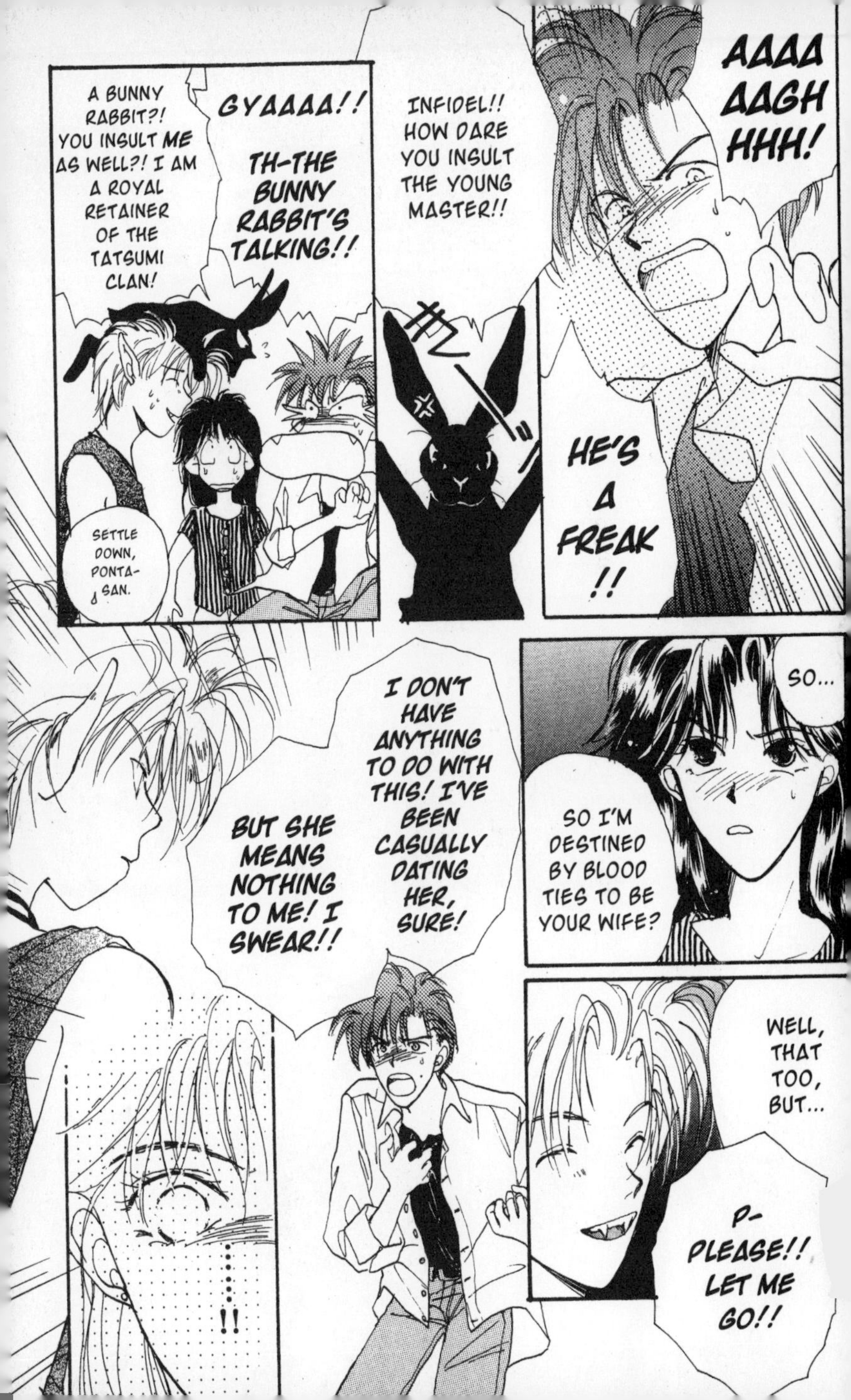
AAAA AAGH HHH!
HE'S A FREAK!!
INFIDEL!! HOW DARE YOU INSULT THE YOUNG MASTER!!
GYAAAA!!
TH-THE BUNNY RABBIT'S TALKING!!
A BUNNY RABBIT?! YOU INSULT ME AS WELL?! I AM A ROYAL RETAINER OF THE TATSUMI CLAN!
SETTLE DOWN, PONTA-SAN. ♪
SO...
SO I'M DESTINED BY BLOOD TIES TO BE YOUR WIFE?
WELL, THAT TOO, BUT...
P-PLEASE!! LET ME GO!!
I DON'T HAVE ANYTHING TO DO WITH THIS! I'VE BEEN CASUALLY DATING HER, SURE!
BUT SHE MEANS NOTHING TO ME! I SWEAR!!
......!!

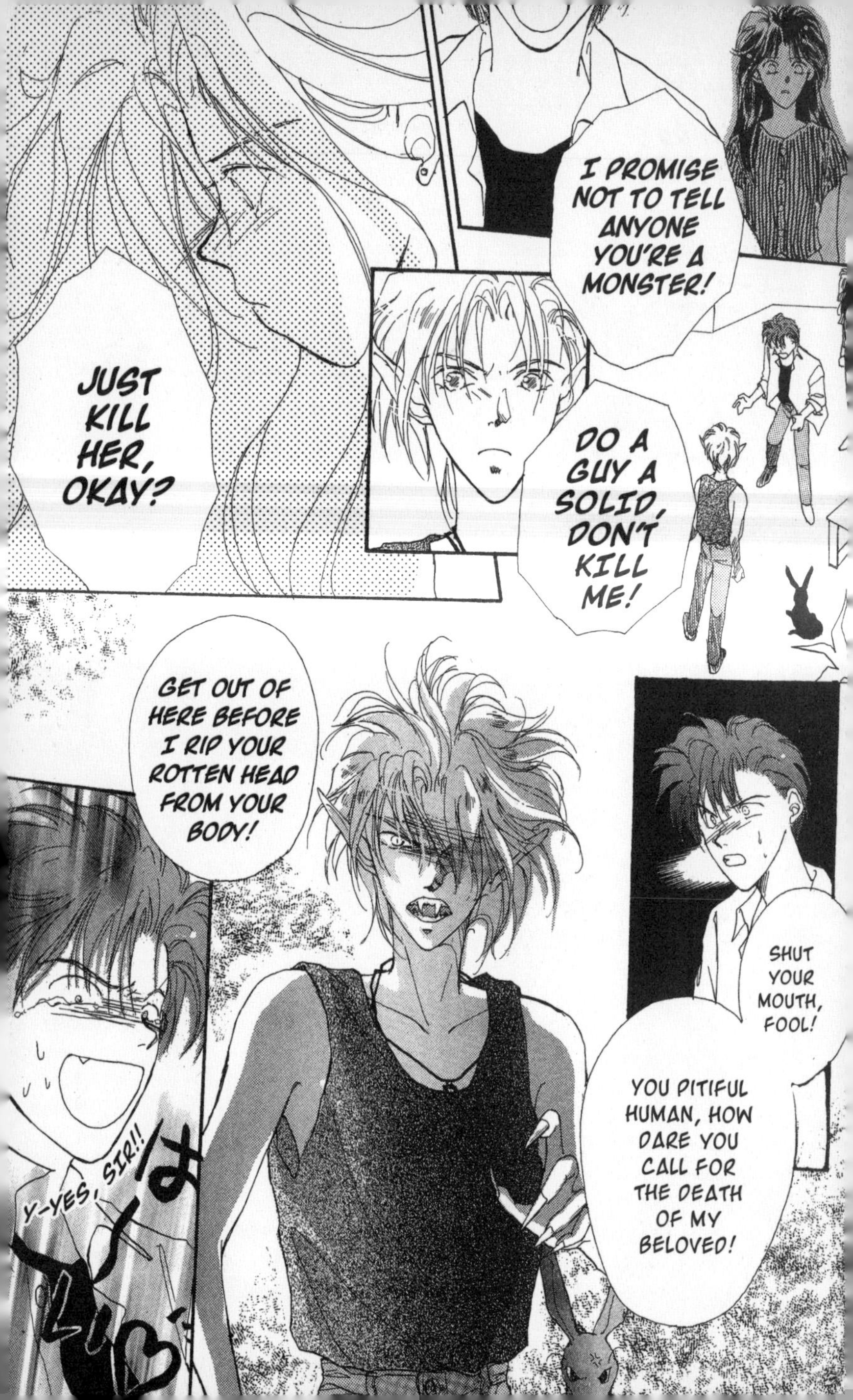
I PROMISE NOT TO TELL ANYONE YOU'RE A MONSTER!
DO A GUY A SOLID, DON'T KILL ME!
JUST KILL HER, OKAY?
SHUT YOUR MOUTH, FOOL!
YOU PITIFUL HUMAN, HOW DARE YOU CALL FOR THE DEATH OF MY BELOVED!
GET OUT OF HERE BEFORE I RIP YOUR ROTTEN HEAD FROM YOUR BODY!
Y-YES, SIR!!

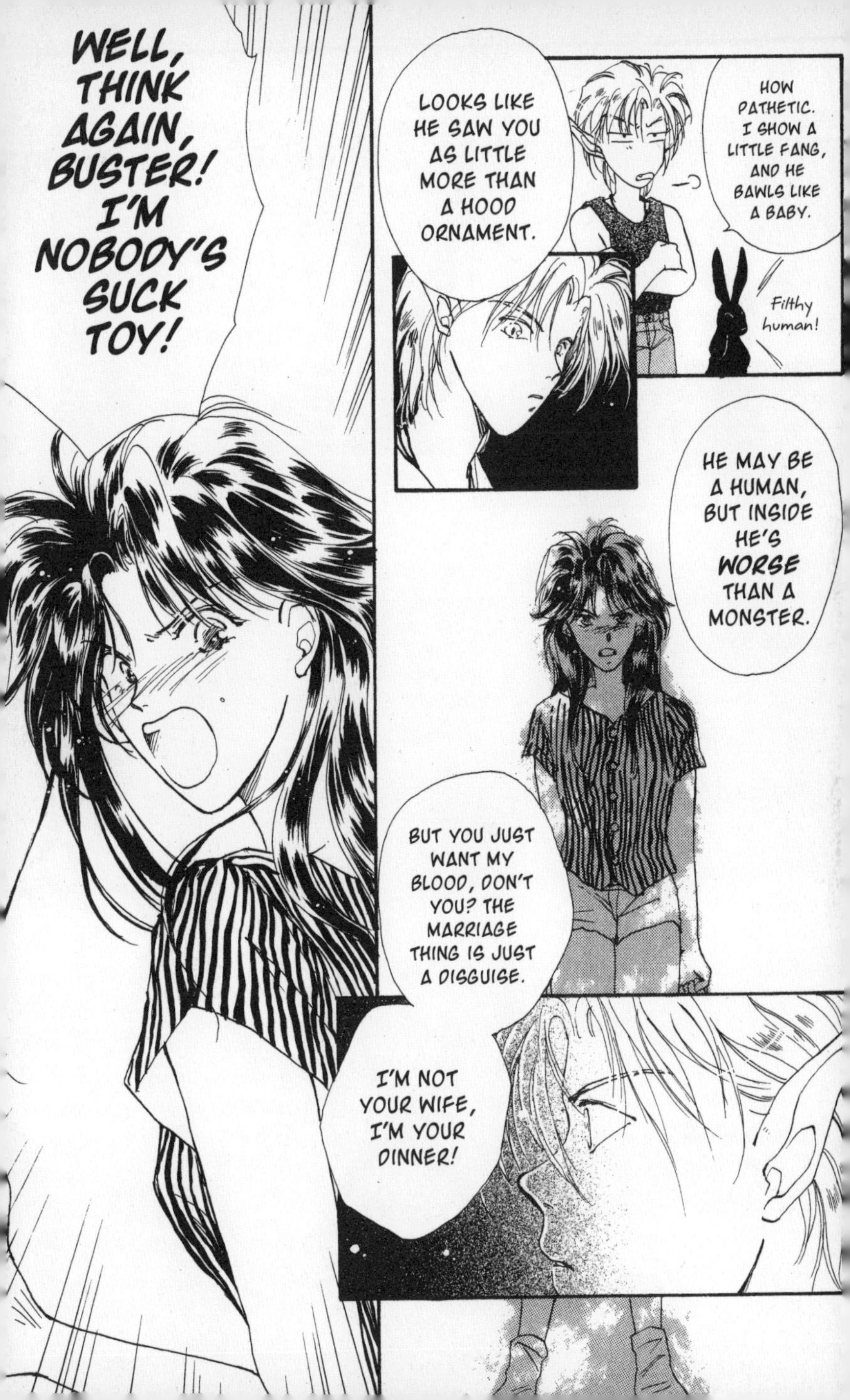
HOW PATHETIC. I SHOW A LITTLE FANG, AND HE BAWLS LIKE A BABY.
Filthy human!
LOOKS LIKE HE SAW YOU AS LITTLE MORE THAN A HOOD ORNAMENT.
HE MAY BE A HUMAN, BUT INSIDE HE'S WORSE THAN A MONSTER.
BUT YOU JUST WANT MY BLOOD, DON'T YOU? THE MARRIAGE THING IS JUST A DISGUISE.
I'M NOT YOUR WIFE, I'M YOUR DINNER!
WELL, THINK AGAIN, BUSTER! I'M NOBODY'S SUCK TOY!

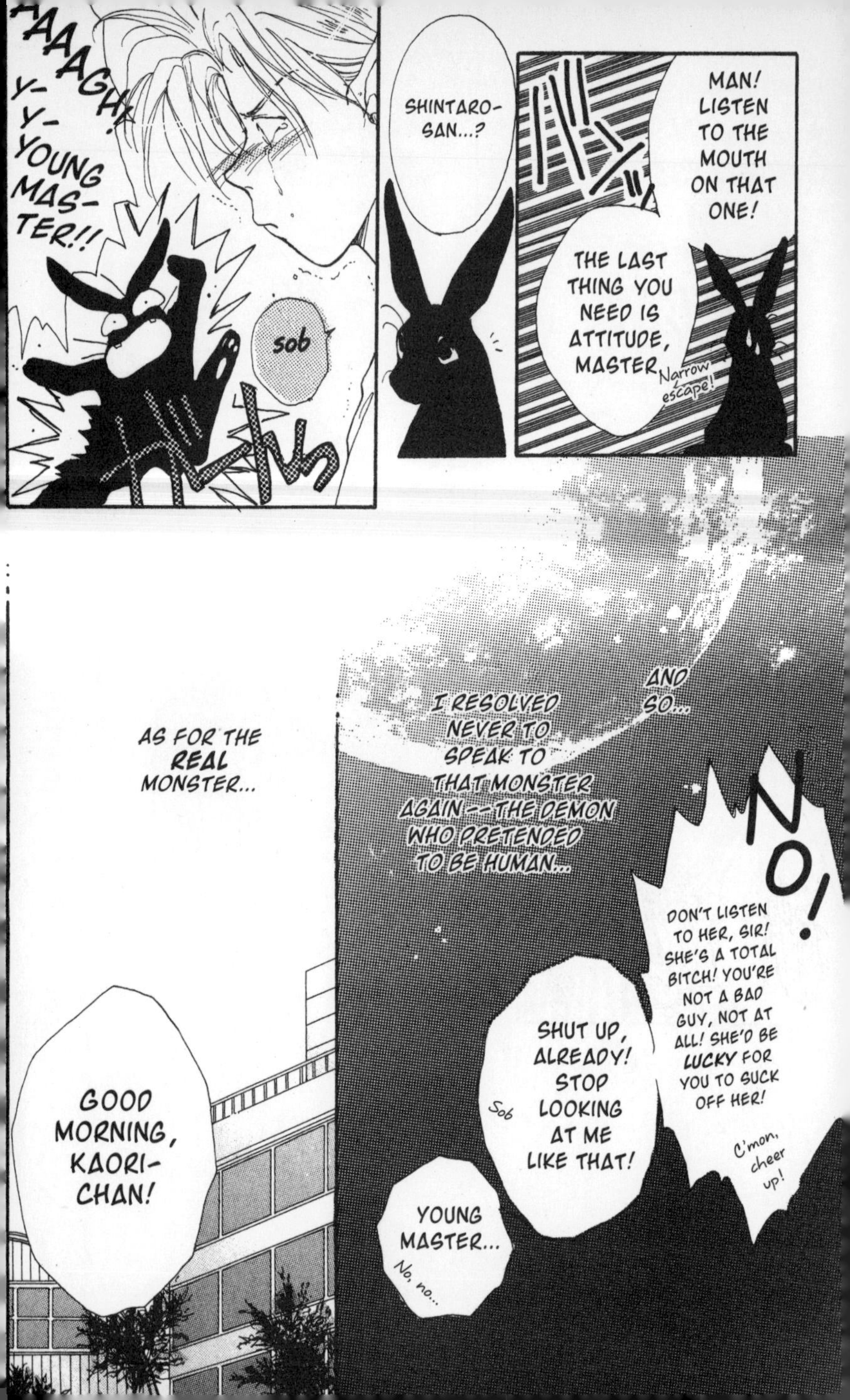
MAN! LISTEN TO THE MOUTH ON THAT ONE!
THE LAST THING YOU NEED IS ATTITUDE, MASTER.
Narrow escape!
SHINTARO-SAN...?
AAAGH! Y-Y-YOUNG MASTER!!
sob
AND SO...
I RESOLVED NEVER TO SPEAK TO THAT MONSTER AGAIN -- THE DEMON WHO PRETENDED TO BE HUMAN...
NO!
DON'T LISTEN TO HER, SIR! SHE'S A TOTAL BITCH! YOU'RE NOT A BAD GUY, NOT AT ALL! SHE'D BE LUCKY FOR YOU TO SUCK OFF HER!
C'mon, cheer up!
SHUT UP, ALREADY! STOP LOOKING AT ME LIKE THAT!
Sob
YOUNG MASTER...
No, no...
AS FOR THE REAL MONSTER...
GOOD MORNING, KAORI-CHAN!

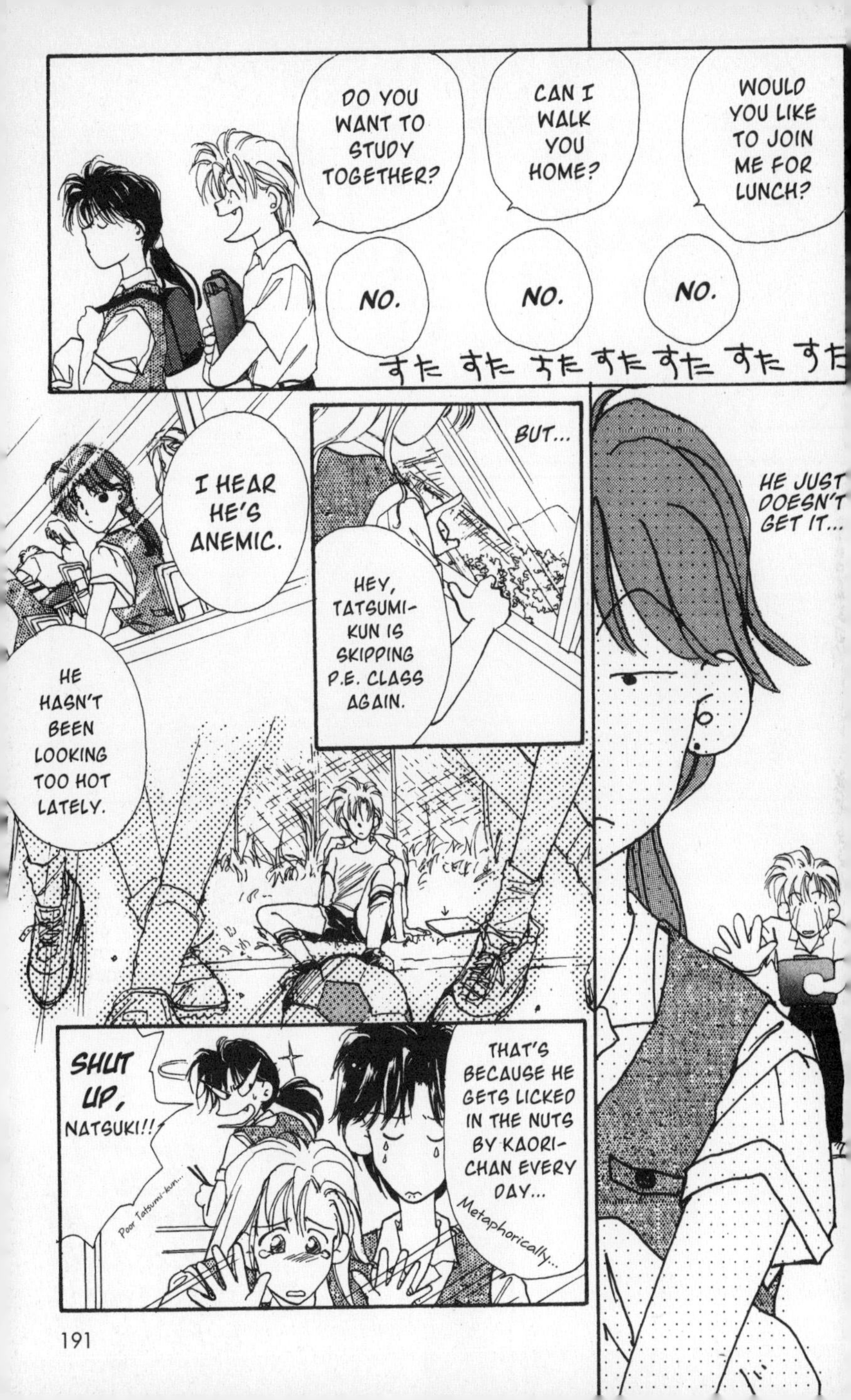
WOULD YOU LIKE TO JOIN ME FOR LUNCH?
NO.
CAN I WALK YOU HOME?
NO.
DO YOU WANT TO STUDY TOGETHER?
NO.
すた すた すた すた すた すた すた
HE JUST DOESN'T GET IT...
BUT...
HEY, TATSUMI-KUN IS SKIPPING P.E. CLASS AGAIN.
I HEAR HE'S ANEMIC.
HE HASN'T BEEN LOOKING TOO HOT LATELY.
THAT'S BECAUSE HE GETS LICKED IN THE NUTS BY KAORI-CHAN EVERY DAY...
Metaphorically...
SHUT UP, NATSUKI!!
Poor Tatsumi-kun...

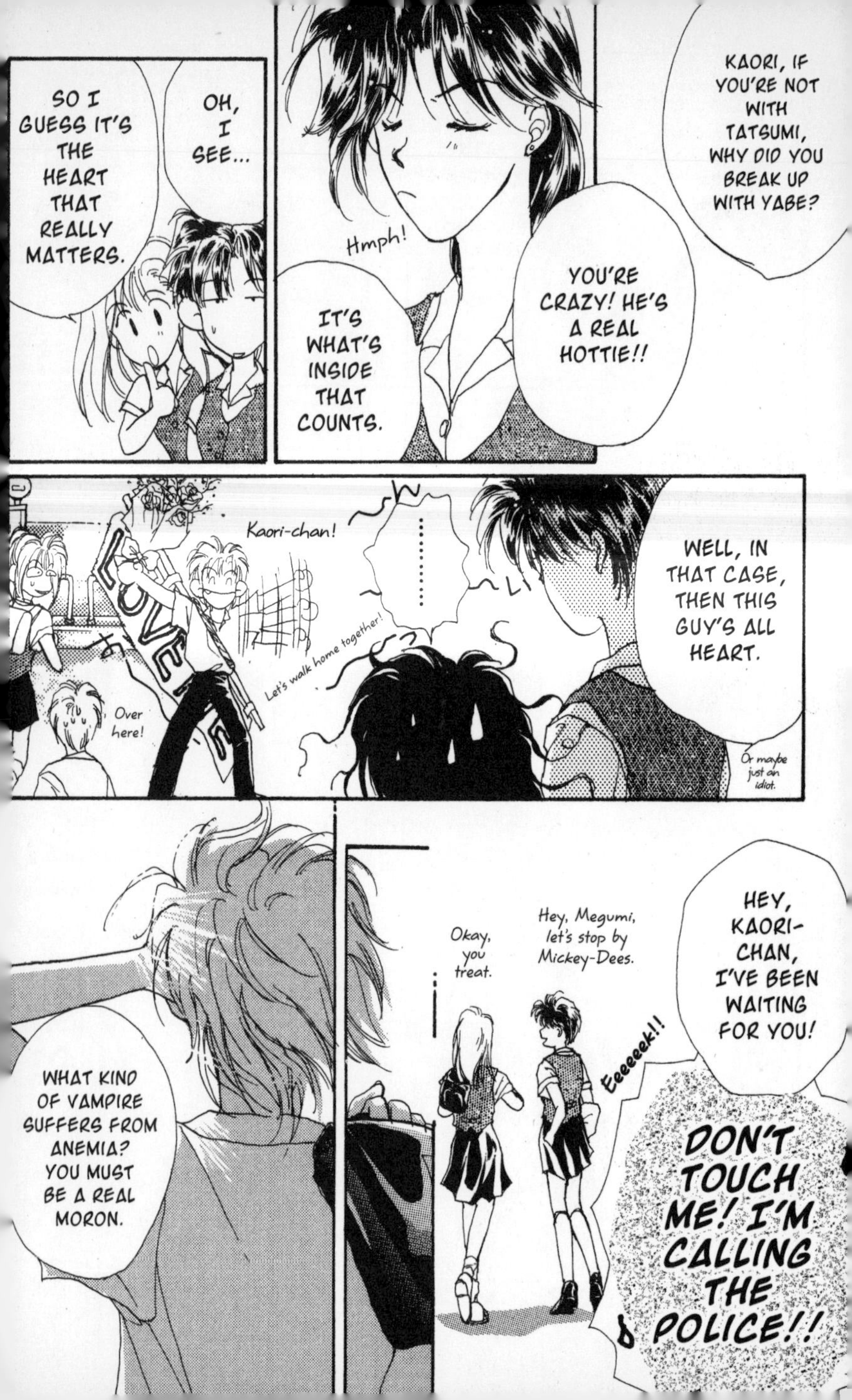
KAORI, IF YOU'RE NOT WITH TATSUMI, WHY DID YOU BREAK UP WITH YABE?
YOU'RE CRAZY! HE'S A REAL HOTTIE!!
Hmph!
IT'S WHAT'S INSIDE THAT COUNTS.
OH, I SEE...
SO I GUESS IT'S THE HEART THAT REALLY MATTERS.
WELL, IN THAT CASE, THEN THIS GUY'S ALL HEART.
Or maybe just an idiot.
Kaori-chan!
Let's walk home together!
Over here!
HEY, KAORI-CHAN, I'VE BEEN WAITING FOR YOU!
DON'T TOUCH ME! I'M CALLING THE POLICE!!
Eeeeeek!!
Hey, Megumi, let's stop by Mickey-Dees.
Okay, you treat.
WHAT KIND OF VAMPIRE SUFFERS FROM ANEMIA? YOU MUST BE A REAL MORON.

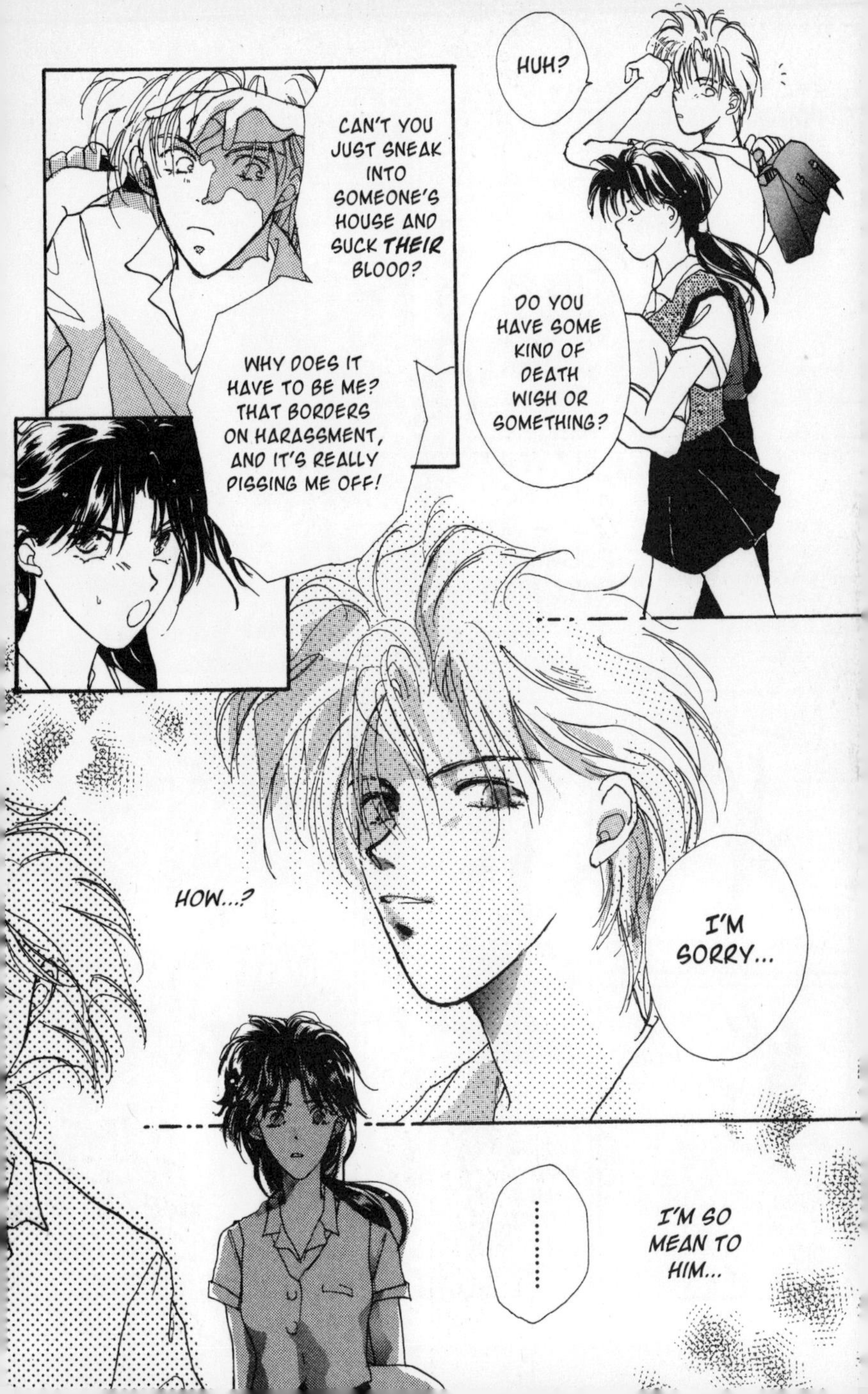
HUH?
DO YOU HAVE SOME KIND OF DEATH WISH OR SOMETHING?
CAN'T YOU JUST SNEAK INTO SOMEONE'S HOUSE AND SUCK **THEIR** BLOOD?
WHY DOES IT HAVE TO BE ME? THAT BORDERS ON HARASSMENT, AND IT'S REALLY PISSING ME OFF!
I'M SORRY...
HOW...?
......
I'M SO MEAN TO HIM...

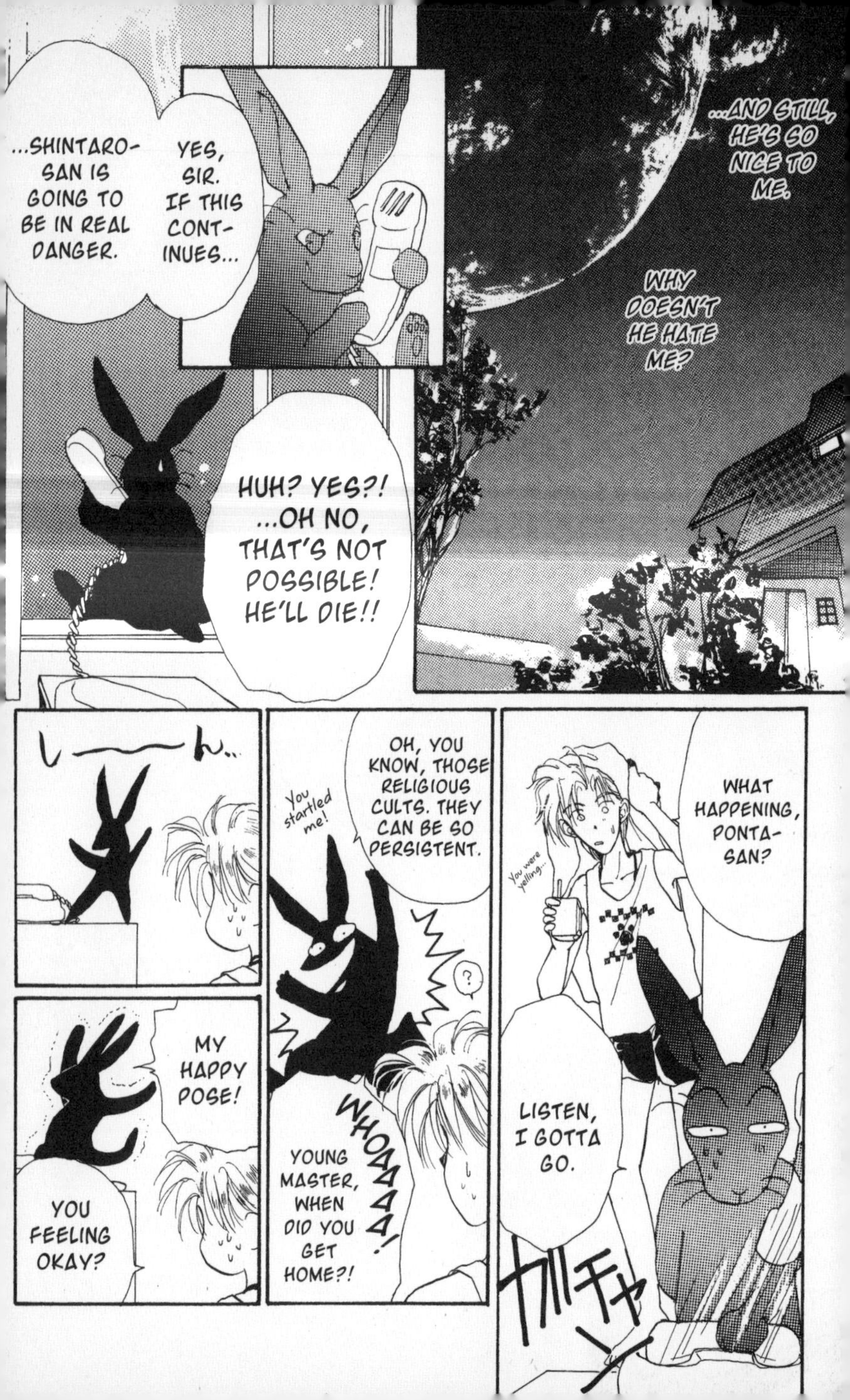
...AND STILL, HE'S SO NICE TO ME.
WHY DOESN'T HE HATE ME?
YES, SIR. IF THIS CONTINUES...
...SHINTARO-SAN IS GOING TO BE IN REAL DANGER.
HUH? YES?! ...OH NO, THAT'S NOT POSSIBLE! HE'LL DIE!!
WHAT HAPPENING, PONTA-SAN?
You were yelling...
LISTEN, I GOTTA GO.
ガチャ
OH, YOU KNOW, THOSE RELIGIOUS CULTS. THEY CAN BE SO PERSISTENT.
You startled me!
?
WHOAAAAA!
YOUNG MASTER, WHEN DID YOU GET HOME?!
しーーん..
MY HAPPY POSE!
YOU FEELING OKAY?

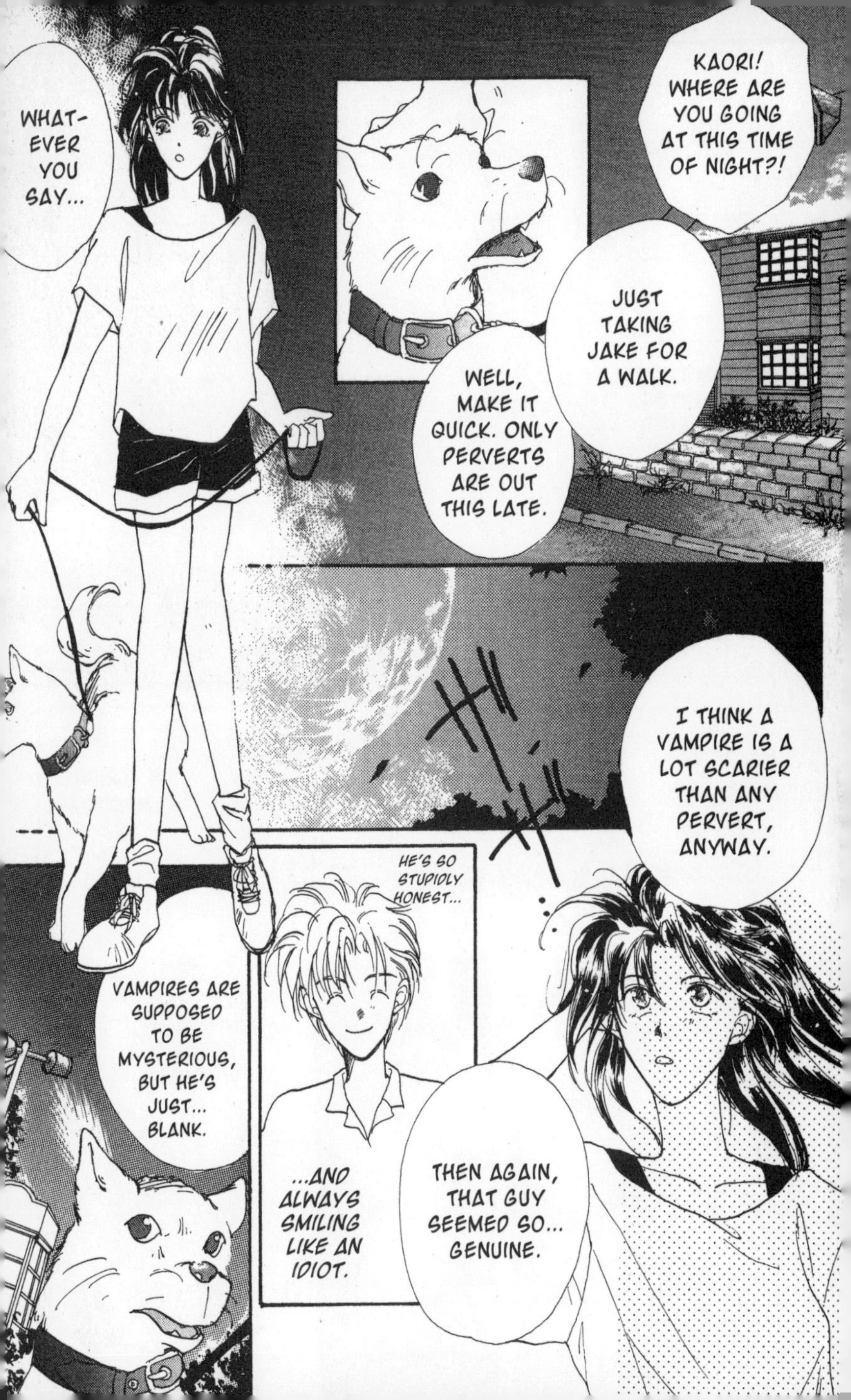
KAORI! WHERE ARE YOU GOING AT THIS TIME OF NIGHT?!
JUST TAKING JAKE FOR A WALK.
WELL, MAKE IT QUICK. ONLY PERVERTS ARE OUT THIS LATE.
WHAT-EVER YOU SAY...
I THINK A VAMPIRE IS A LOT SCARIER THAN ANY PERVERT, ANYWAY.
THEN AGAIN, THAT GUY SEEMED SO... GENUINE.
HE'S SO STUPIDLY HONEST...
...AND ALWAYS SMILING LIKE AN IDIOT.
VAMPIRES ARE SUPPOSED TO BE MYSTERIOUS, BUT HE'S JUST... BLANK.

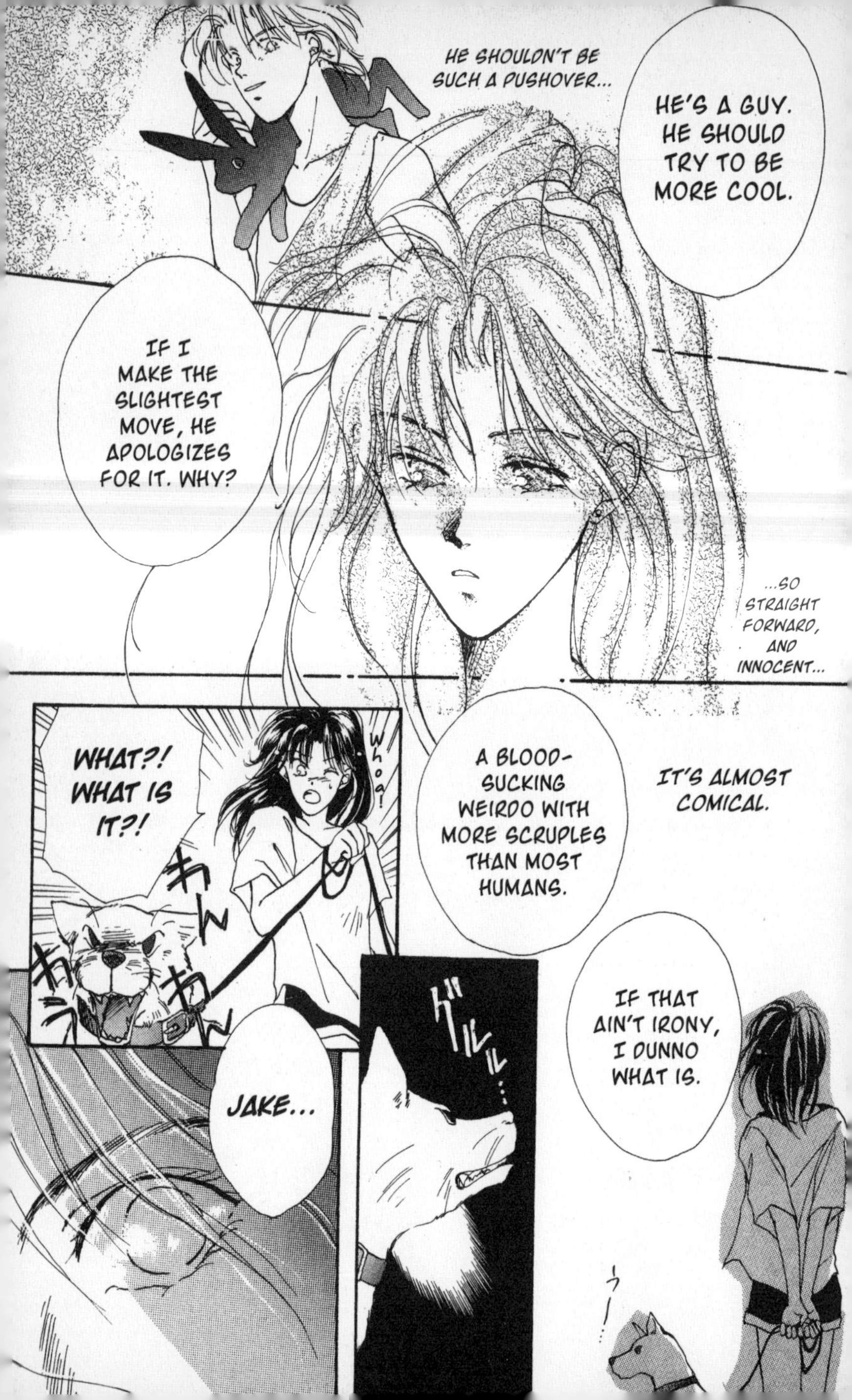

HE'S A GUY. HE SHOULD TRY TO BE MORE COOL.
HE SHOULDN'T BE SUCH A PUSHOVER...
IF I MAKE THE SLIGHTEST MOVE, HE APOLOGIZES FOR IT. WHY?
...SO STRAIGHT FORWARD, AND INNOCENT...
IT'S ALMOST COMICAL.
A BLOOD-SUCKING WEIRDO WITH MORE SCRUPLES THAN MOST HUMANS.
IF THAT AIN'T IRONY, I DUNNO WHAT IS.
JAKE...
WHAT?! WHAT IS IT?!
Whoa!

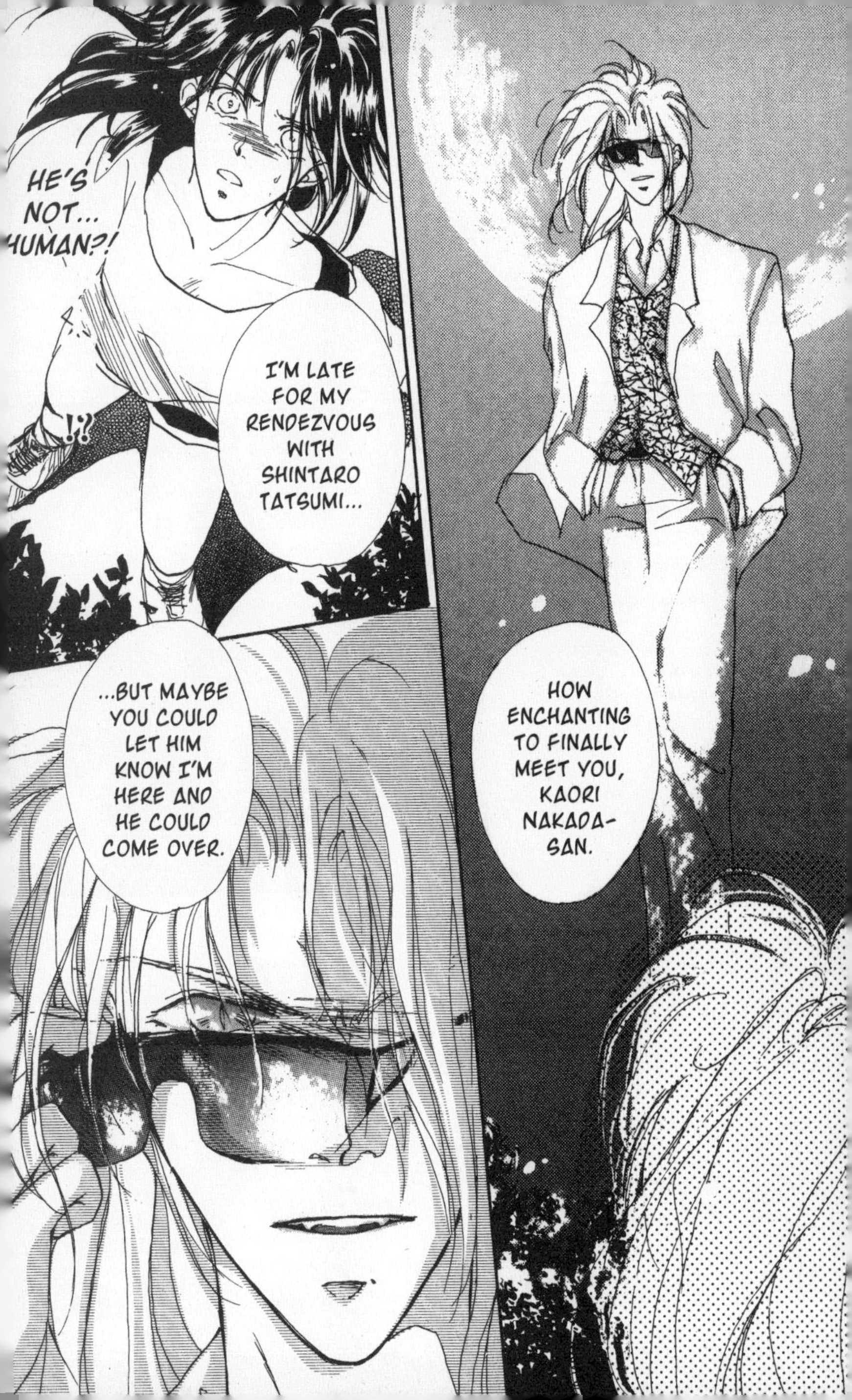
HOW ENCHANTING TO FINALLY MEET YOU, KAORI NAKADA-SAN.
HE'S NOT... HUMAN?!
!?
I'M LATE FOR MY RENDEZVOUS WITH SHINTARO TATSUMI...
...BUT MAYBE YOU COULD LET HIM KNOW I'M HERE AND HE COULD COME OVER.

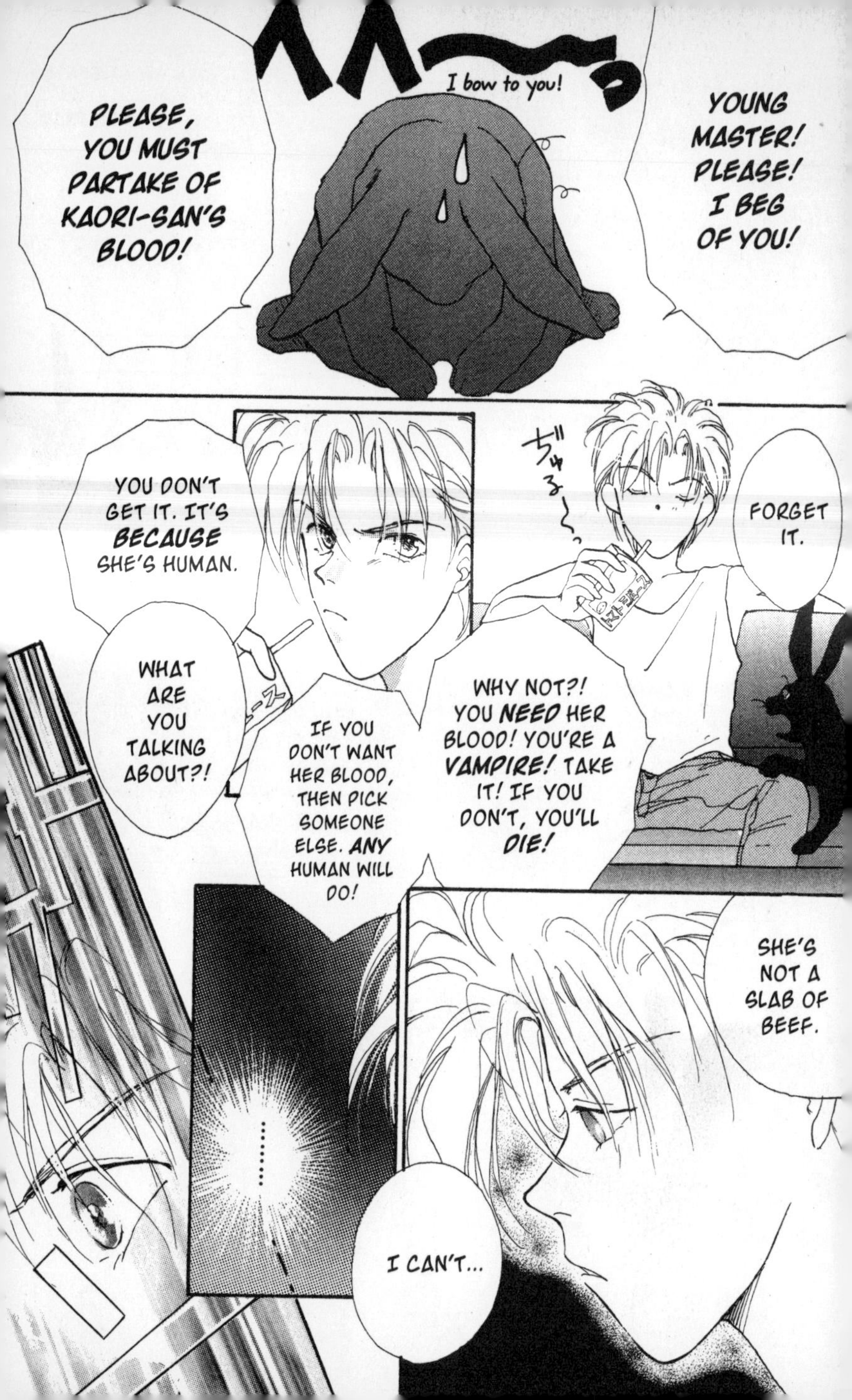
YOUNG MASTER! PLEASE! I BEG OF YOU!
I bow to you!
PLEASE, YOU MUST PARTAKE OF KAORI-SAN'S BLOOD!
FORGET IT.
WHY NOT?! YOU NEED HER BLOOD! YOU'RE A VAMPIRE! TAKE IT! IF YOU DON'T, YOU'LL DIE!
YOU DON'T GET IT. IT'S BECAUSE SHE'S HUMAN.
WHAT ARE YOU TALKING ABOUT?!
IF YOU DON'T WANT HER BLOOD, THEN PICK SOMEONE ELSE. ANY HUMAN WILL DO!
SHE'S NOT A SLAB OF BEEF.
I CAN'T...

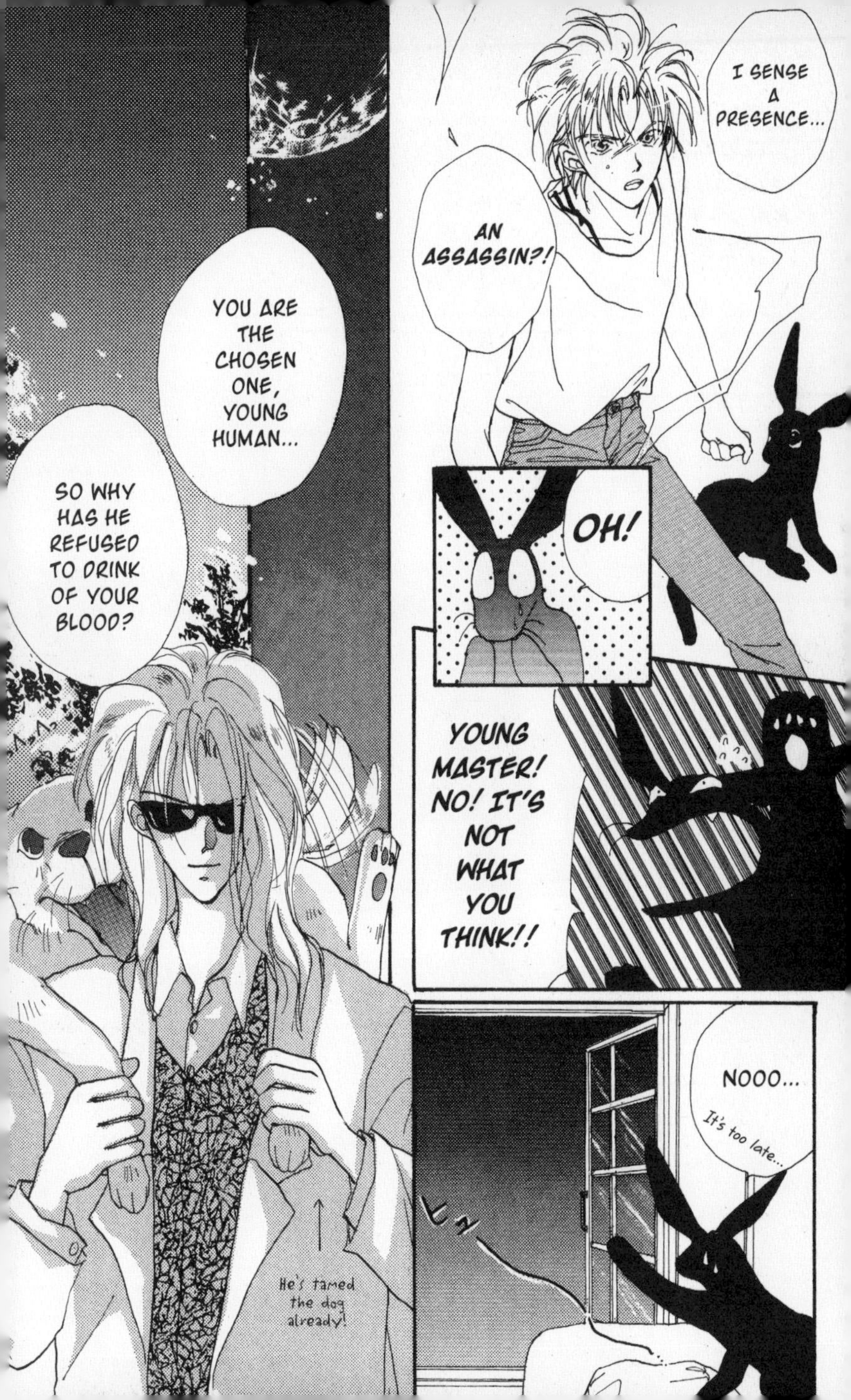
I SENSE A PRESENCE...
AN ASSASSIN?!
OH!
YOUNG MASTER! NO! IT'S NOT WHAT YOU THINK!!
NOOO...
It's too late...
YOU ARE THE CHOSEN ONE, YOUNG HUMAN...
SO WHY HAS HE REFUSED TO DRINK OF YOUR BLOOD?
He's tamed the dog already!

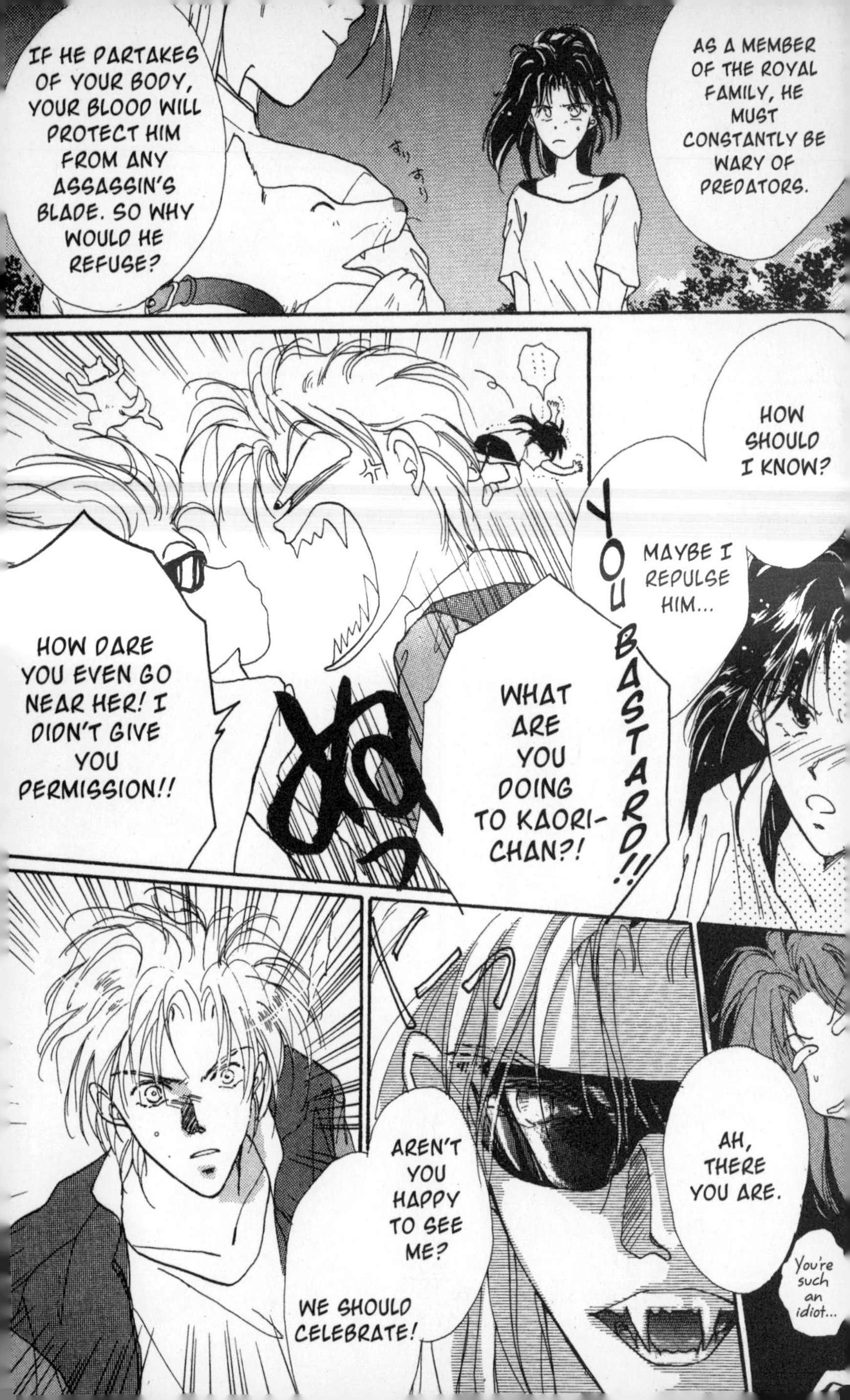
AS A MEMBER OF THE ROYAL FAMILY, HE MUST CONSTANTLY BE WARY OF PREDATORS.
IF HE PARTAKES OF YOUR BODY, YOUR BLOOD WILL PROTECT HIM FROM ANY ASSASSIN'S BLADE. SO WHY WOULD HE REFUSE?
HOW SHOULD I KNOW?
MAYBE I REPULSE HIM...
YOU BASTARD!!
WHAT ARE YOU DOING TO KAORI-CHAN?!
HOW DARE YOU EVEN GO NEAR HER! I DIDN'T GIVE YOU PERMISSION!!
You're such an idiot...
AH, THERE YOU ARE.
AREN'T YOU HAPPY TO SEE ME?
WE SHOULD CELEBRATE!

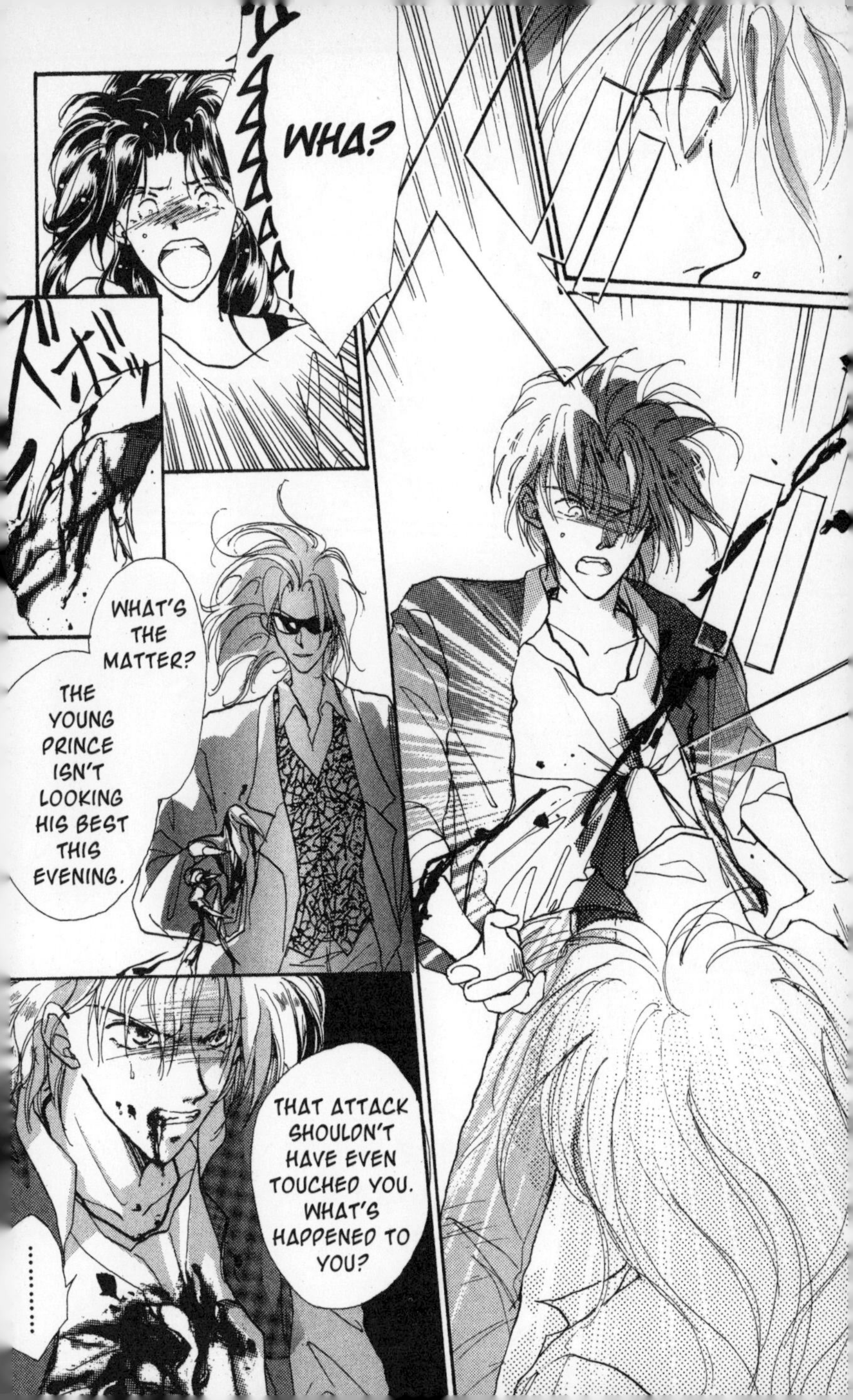
YAAAAAP!
WHA?
ズボッ
WHAT'S THE MATTER? THE YOUNG PRINCE ISN'T LOOKING HIS BEST THIS EVENING.
THAT ATTACK SHOULDN'T HAVE EVEN TOUCHED YOU. WHAT'S HAPPENED TO YOU?
......

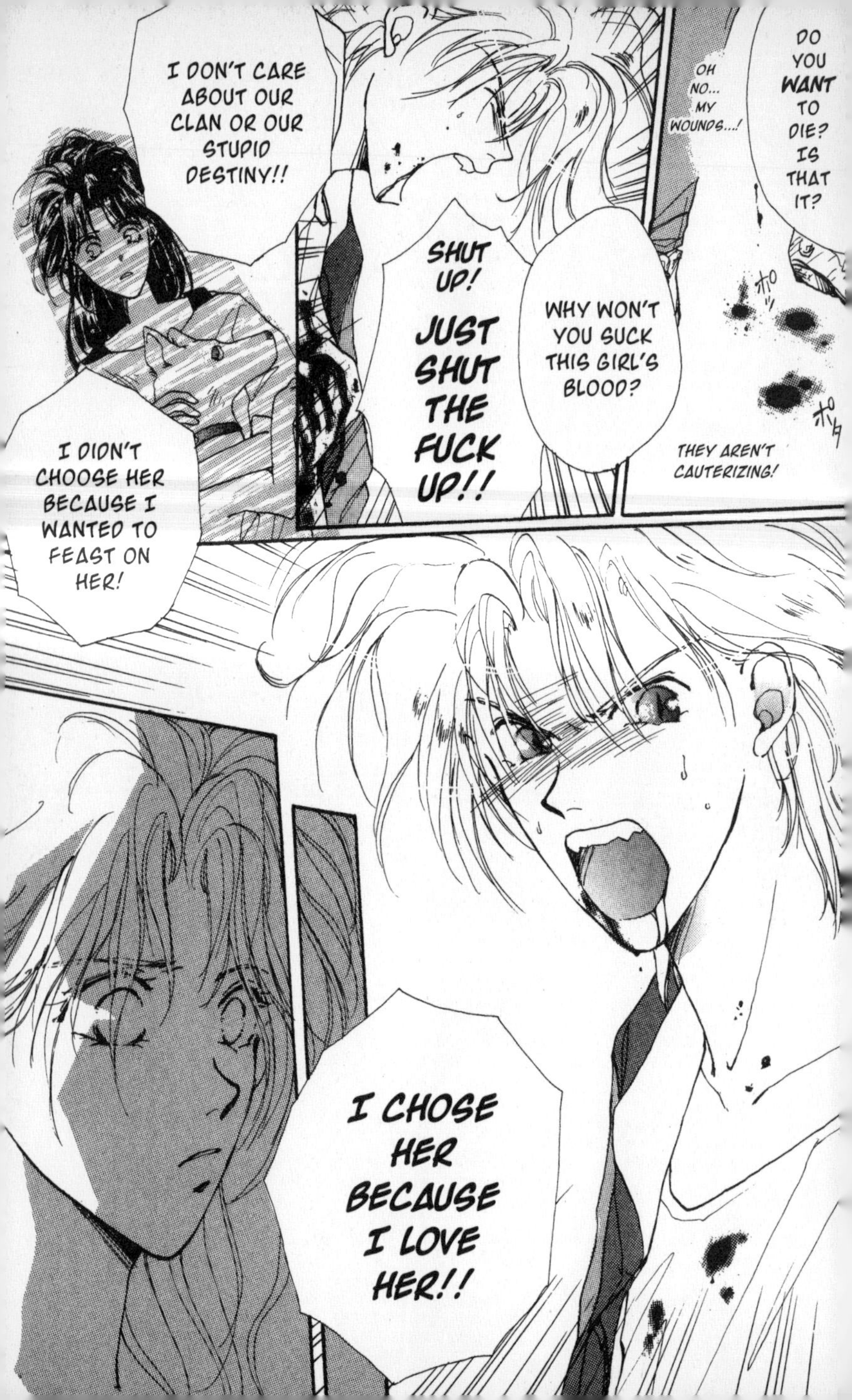
DO YOU WANT TO DIE? IS THAT IT?
OH NO... MY WOUNDS...!
ポタ
THEY AREN'T CAUTERIZING!
WHY WON'T YOU SUCK THIS GIRL'S BLOOD?
SHUT UP! JUST SHUT THE FUCK UP!!
I DON'T CARE ABOUT OUR CLAN OR OUR STUPID DESTINY!!
I DIDN'T CHOOSE HER BECAUSE I WANTED TO FEAST ON HER!
I CHOSE HER BECAUSE I LOVE HER!!

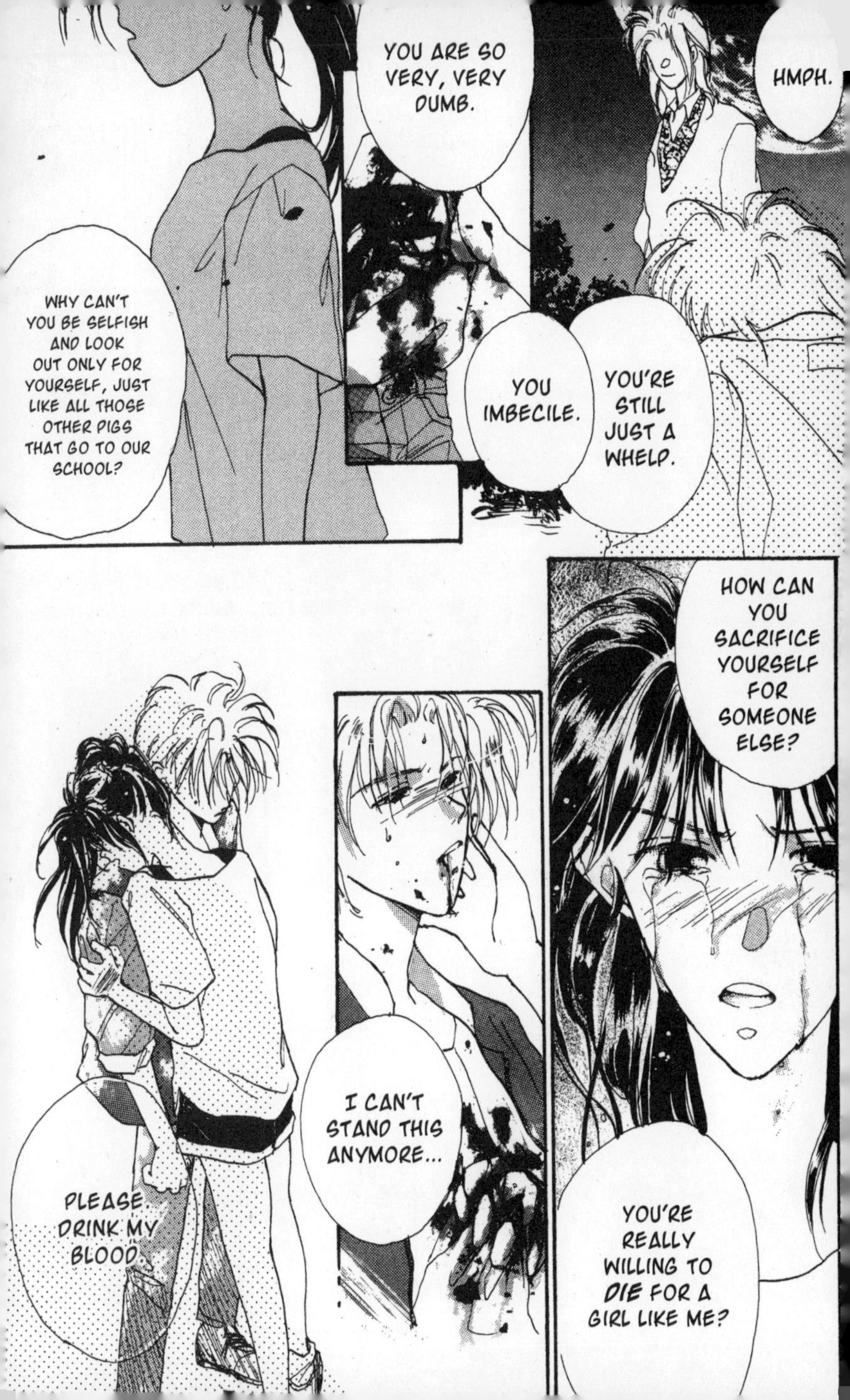
HMPH.
YOU'RE STILL JUST A WHELP.
YOU IMBECILE.
YOU ARE SO VERY, VERY DUMB.
WHY CAN'T YOU BE SELFISH AND LOOK OUT ONLY FOR YOURSELF, JUST LIKE ALL THOSE OTHER PIGS THAT GO TO OUR SCHOOL?
HOW CAN YOU SACRIFICE YOURSELF FOR SOMEONE ELSE?
YOU'RE REALLY WILLING TO *DIE* FOR A GIRL LIKE ME?
I CAN'T STAND THIS ANYMORE...
PLEASE. DRINK MY BLOOD.

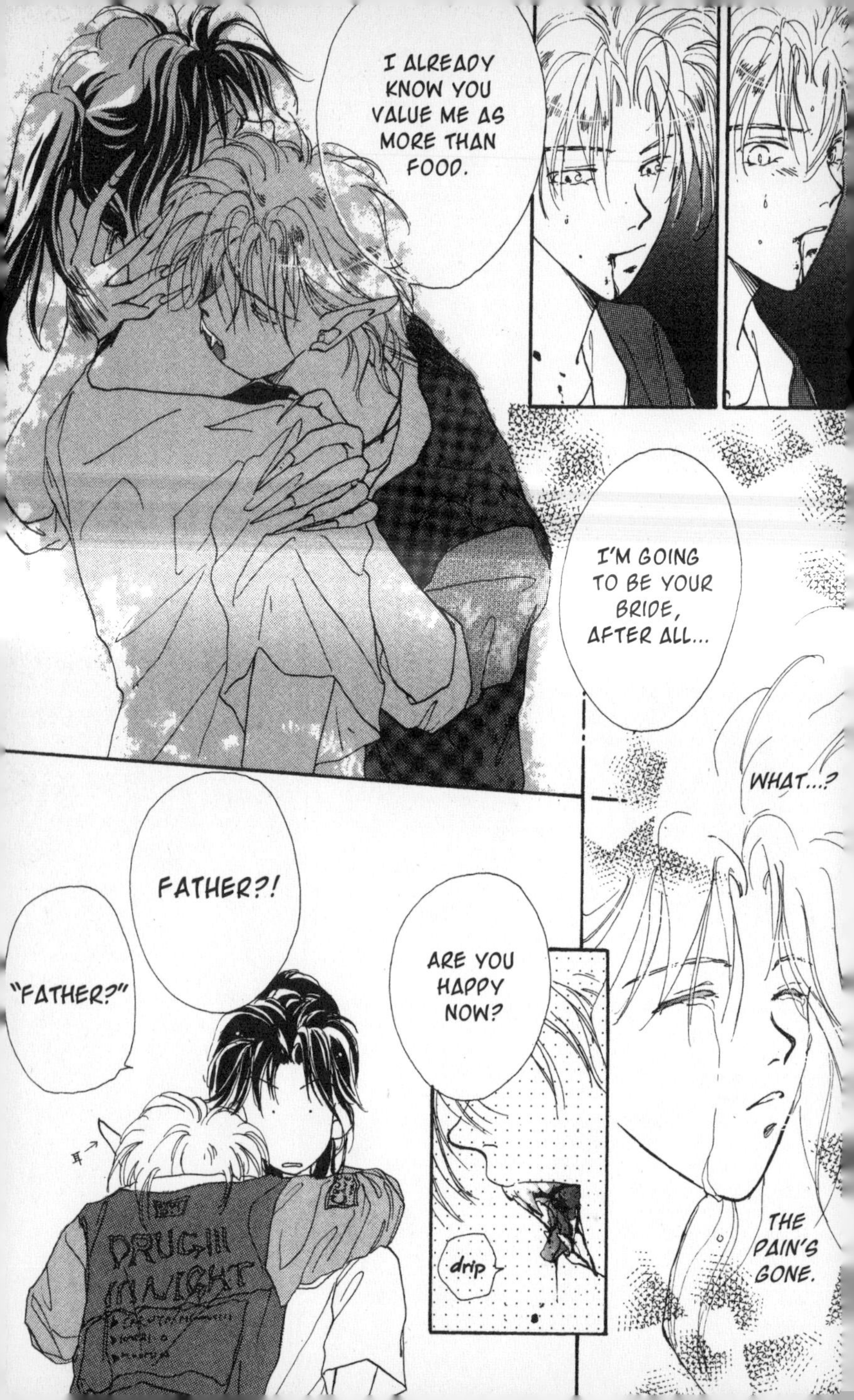
I ALREADY KNOW YOU VALUE ME AS MORE THAN FOOD.
I'M GOING TO BE YOUR BRIDE, AFTER ALL...
WHAT...?
THE PAIN'S GONE.
ARE YOU HAPPY NOW?
drip
FATHER?!
"FATHER?"

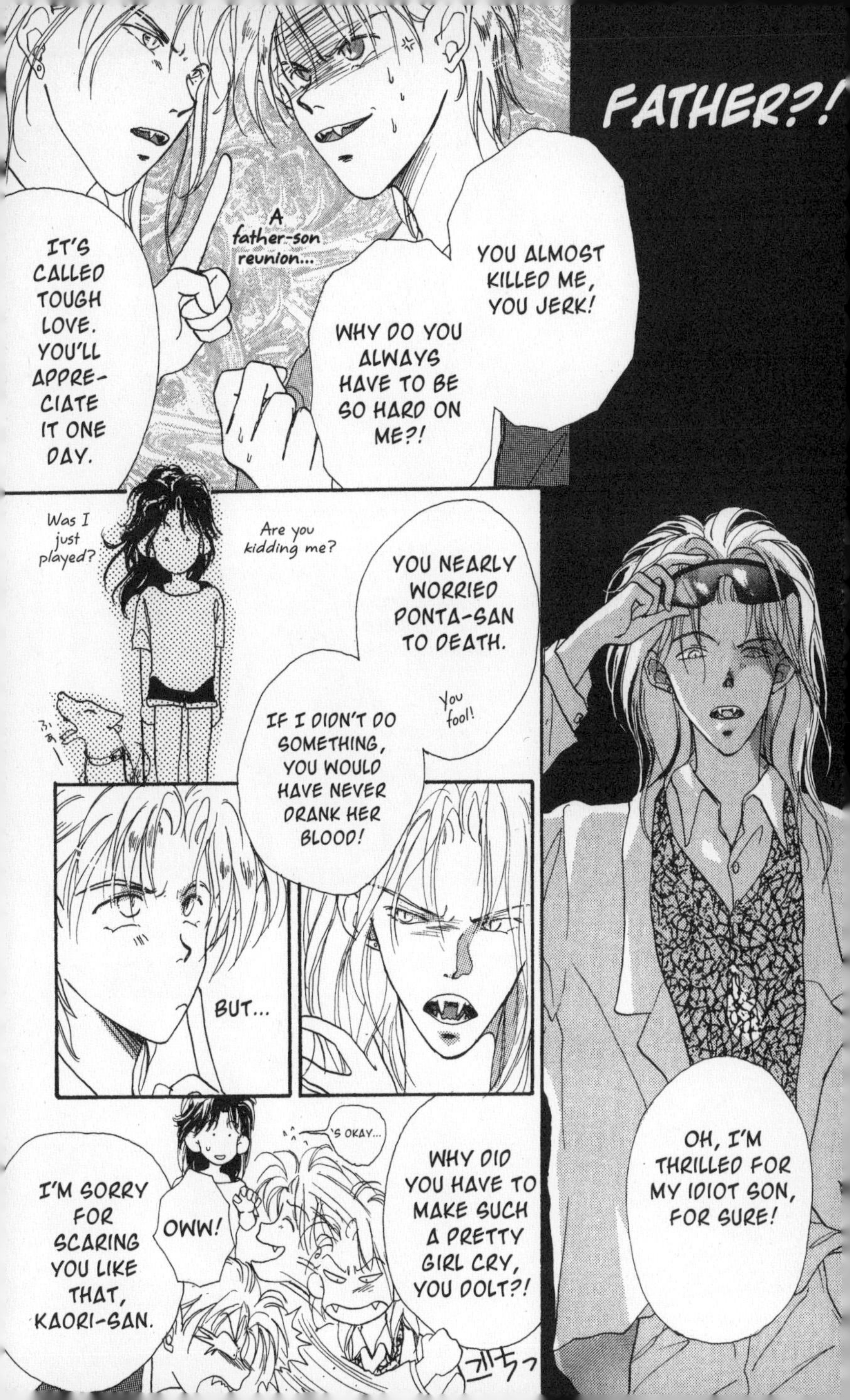
FATHER?!
OH, I'M THRILLED FOR MY IDIOT SON, FOR SURE!
YOU ALMOST KILLED ME, YOU JERK!
WHY DO YOU ALWAYS HAVE TO BE SO HARD ON ME?!
A father-son reunion...
IT'S CALLED TOUGH LOVE. YOU'LL APPRE-CIATE IT ONE DAY.
YOU NEARLY WORRIED PONTA-SAN TO DEATH.
Are you kidding me?
Was I just played?
You fool!
IF I DIDN'T DO SOMETHING, YOU WOULD HAVE NEVER DRANK HER BLOOD!
BUT...
WHY DID YOU HAVE TO MAKE SUCH A PRETTY GIRL CRY, YOU DOLT?!
'S OKAY...
OWW!
I'M SORRY FOR SCARING YOU LIKE THAT, KAORI-SAN.

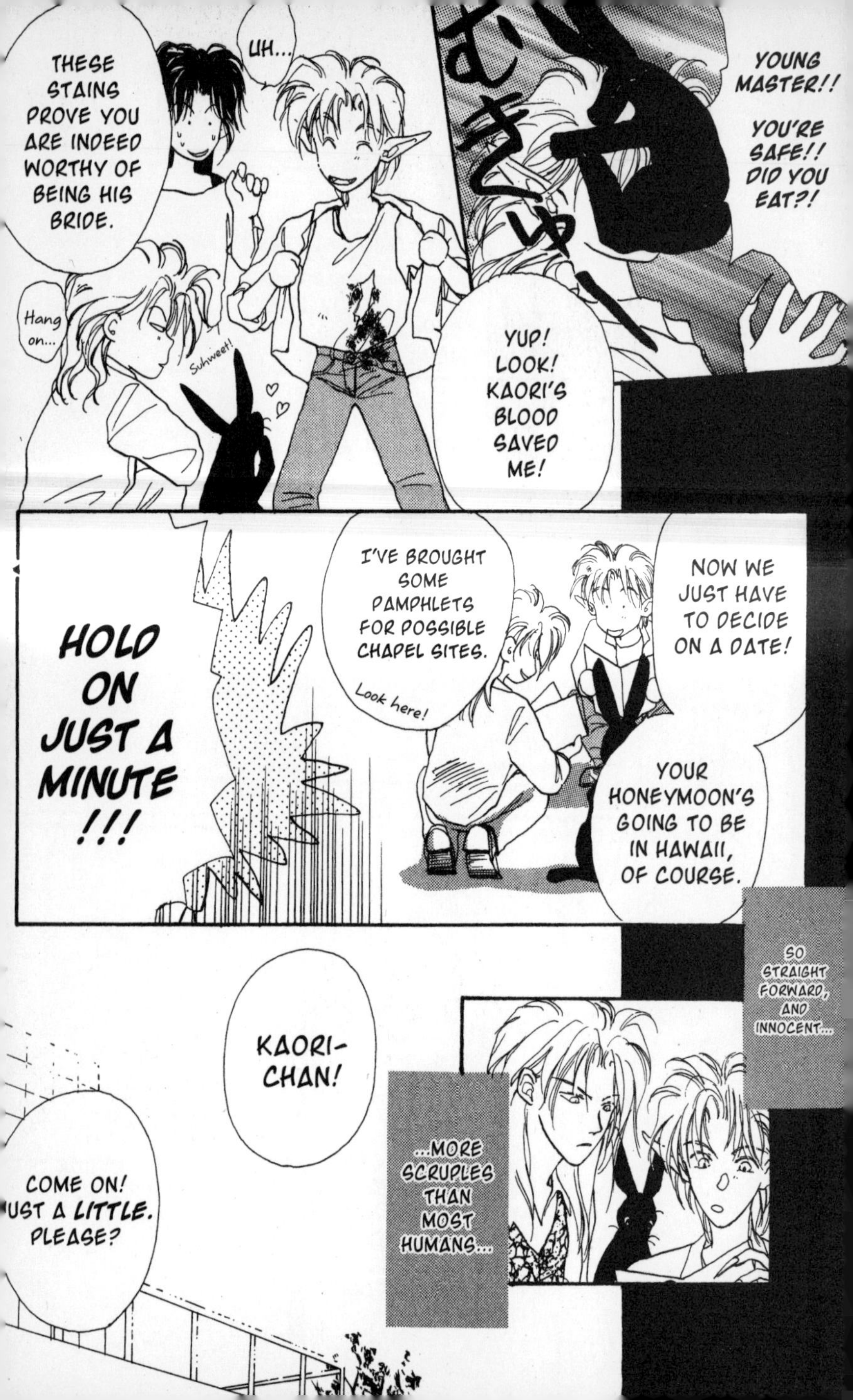
YOUNG MASTER!! YOU'RE SAFE!! DID YOU EAT?!
YUP! LOOK! KAORI'S BLOOD SAVED ME!
UH...
THESE STAINS PROVE YOU ARE INDEED WORTHY OF BEING HIS BRIDE.
Hang on...
Suhweet!
NOW WE JUST HAVE TO DECIDE ON A DATE!
I'VE BROUGHT SOME PAMPHLETS FOR POSSIBLE CHAPEL SITES.
Look here!
YOUR HONEYMOON'S GOING TO BE IN HAWAII, OF COURSE.
HOLD ON JUST A MINUTE!!!
SO STRAIGHT FORWARD, AND INNOCENT...
...MORE SCRUPLES THAN MOST HUMANS...
KAORI-CHAN!
COME ON! UST A LITTLE. PLEASE?

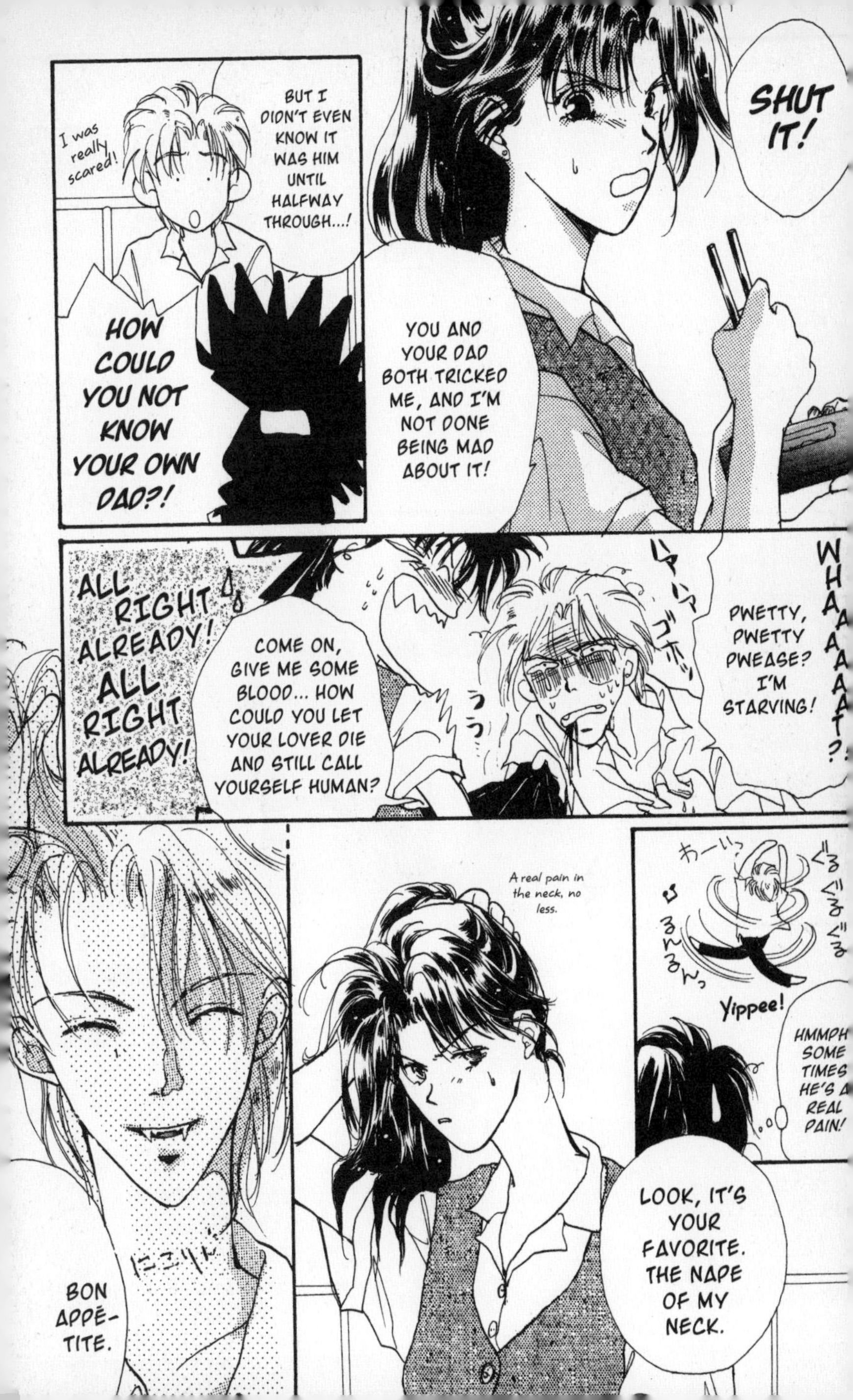
SHUT IT!
YOU AND YOUR DAD BOTH TRICKED ME, AND I'M NOT DONE BEING MAD ABOUT IT!
BUT I DIDN'T EVEN KNOW IT WAS HIM UNTIL HALFWAY THROUGH...!
I was really scared!
HOW COULD YOU NOT KNOW YOUR OWN DAD?!
WHAAAAAAAT?!
PWETTY, PWETTY PWEASE? I'M STARVING!
COME ON, GIVE ME SOME BLOOD... HOW COULD YOU LET YOUR LOVER DIE AND STILL CALL YOURSELF HUMAN?
ALL RIGHT ALREADY! ALL RIGHT ALREADY!
Yippee!
HMMPH SOMETIMES HE'S A REAL PAIN!
A real pain in the neck, no less.
LOOK, IT'S YOUR FAVORITE. THE NAPE OF MY NECK.
BON APPÉ-TITE.

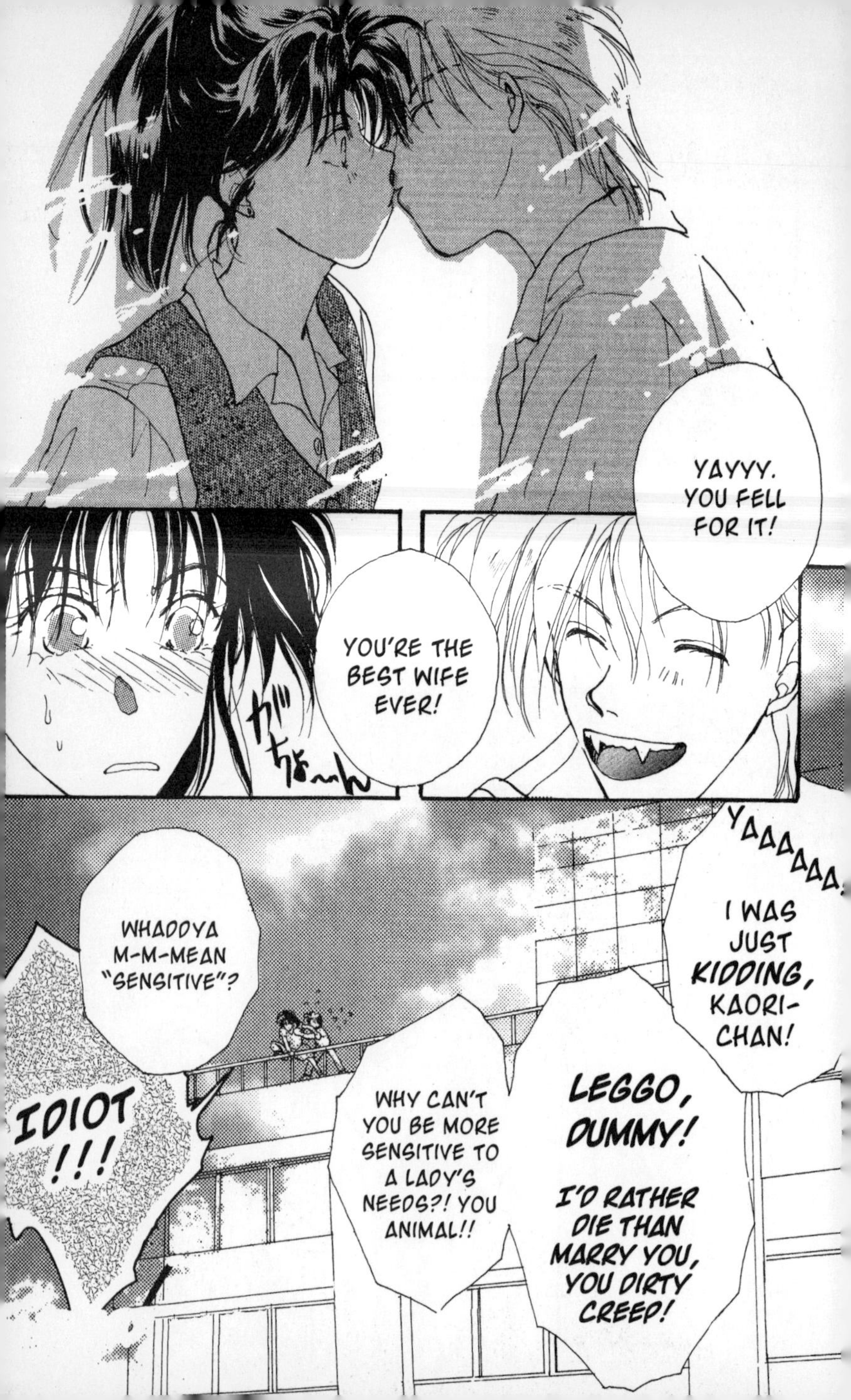
YAYYY. YOU FELL FOR IT!
YOU'RE THE BEST WIFE EVER!
YAAAAAA!
I WAS JUST KIDDING, KAORI-CHAN!
LEGGO, DUMMY!
I'D RATHER DIE THAN MARRY YOU, YOU DIRTY CREEP!
WHY CAN'T YOU BE MORE SENSITIVE TO A LADY'S NEEDS?! YOU ANIMAL!!
WHADDYA M-M-MEAN "SENSITIVE"?
IDIOT!!!

Gravitation

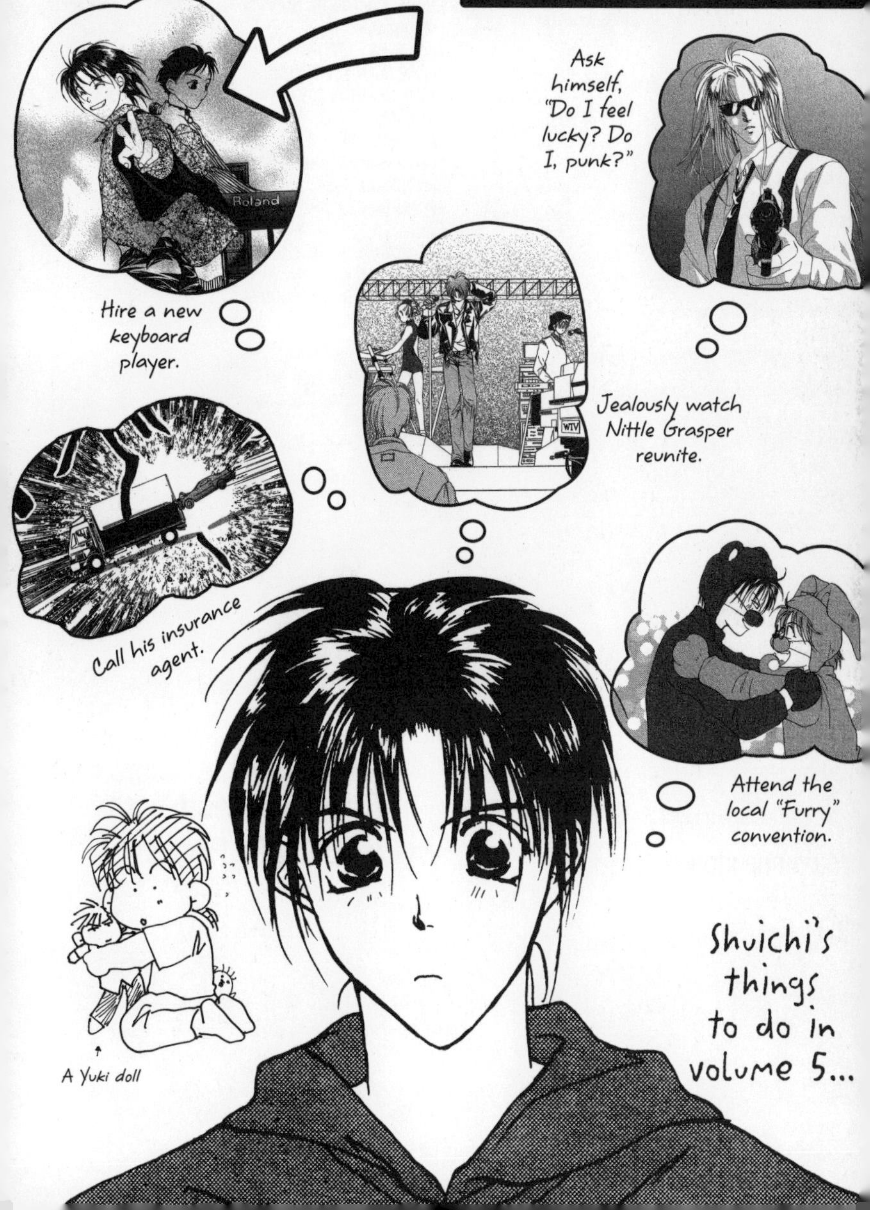
Ask himself, "Do I feel lucky? Do I, punk?"
Roland
Hire a new keyboard player.
WTV
Jealously watch Nittle Grasper reunite.
Call his insurance agent.
Attend the local "Furry" convention.
Shuichi's things to do in volume 5...
A Yuki doll

ALSO AVAILABLE FROM 🐾 TOKYOPOP®

**For more
information visit
www.TOKYOPOP.com**

11.20.03 T

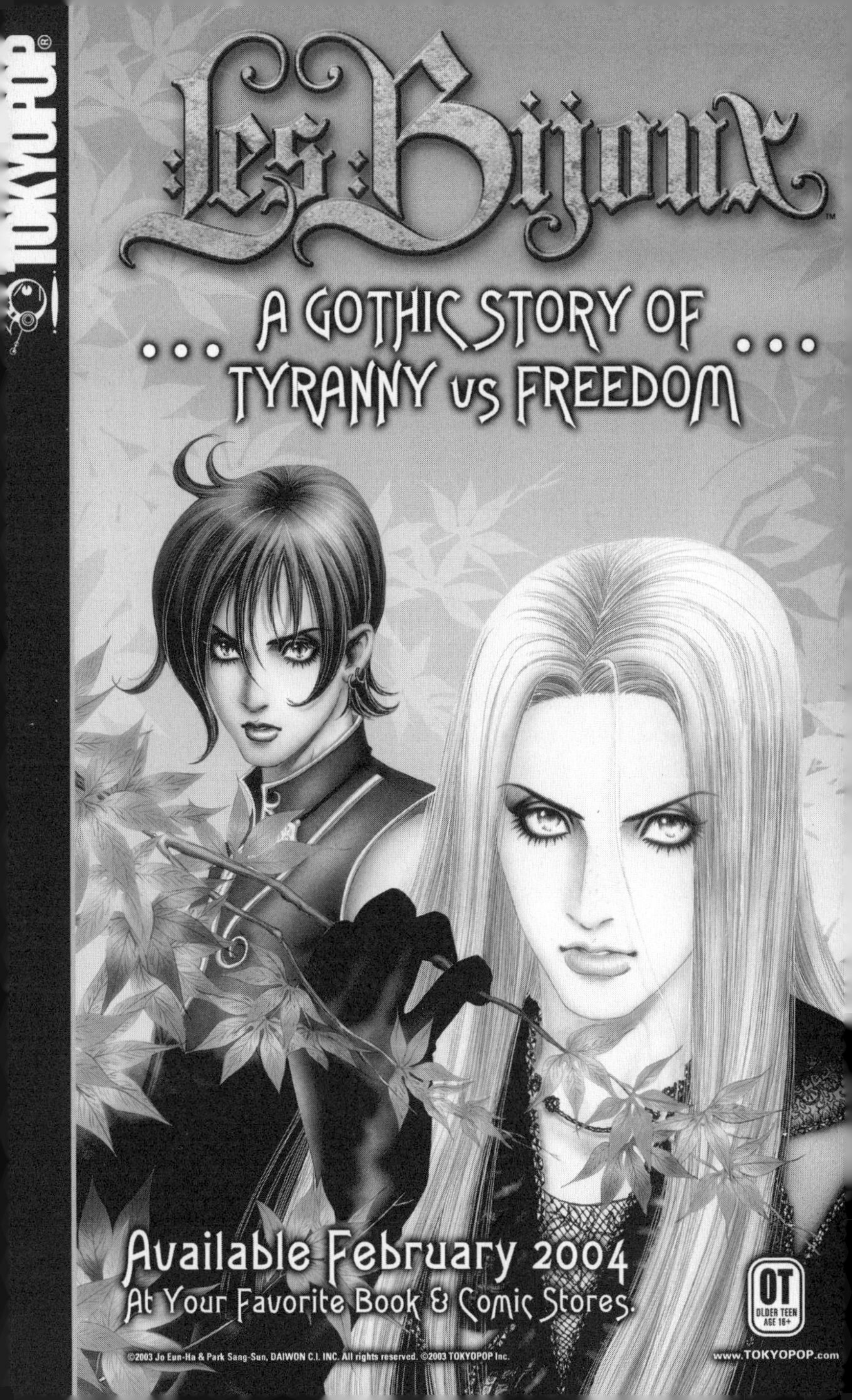

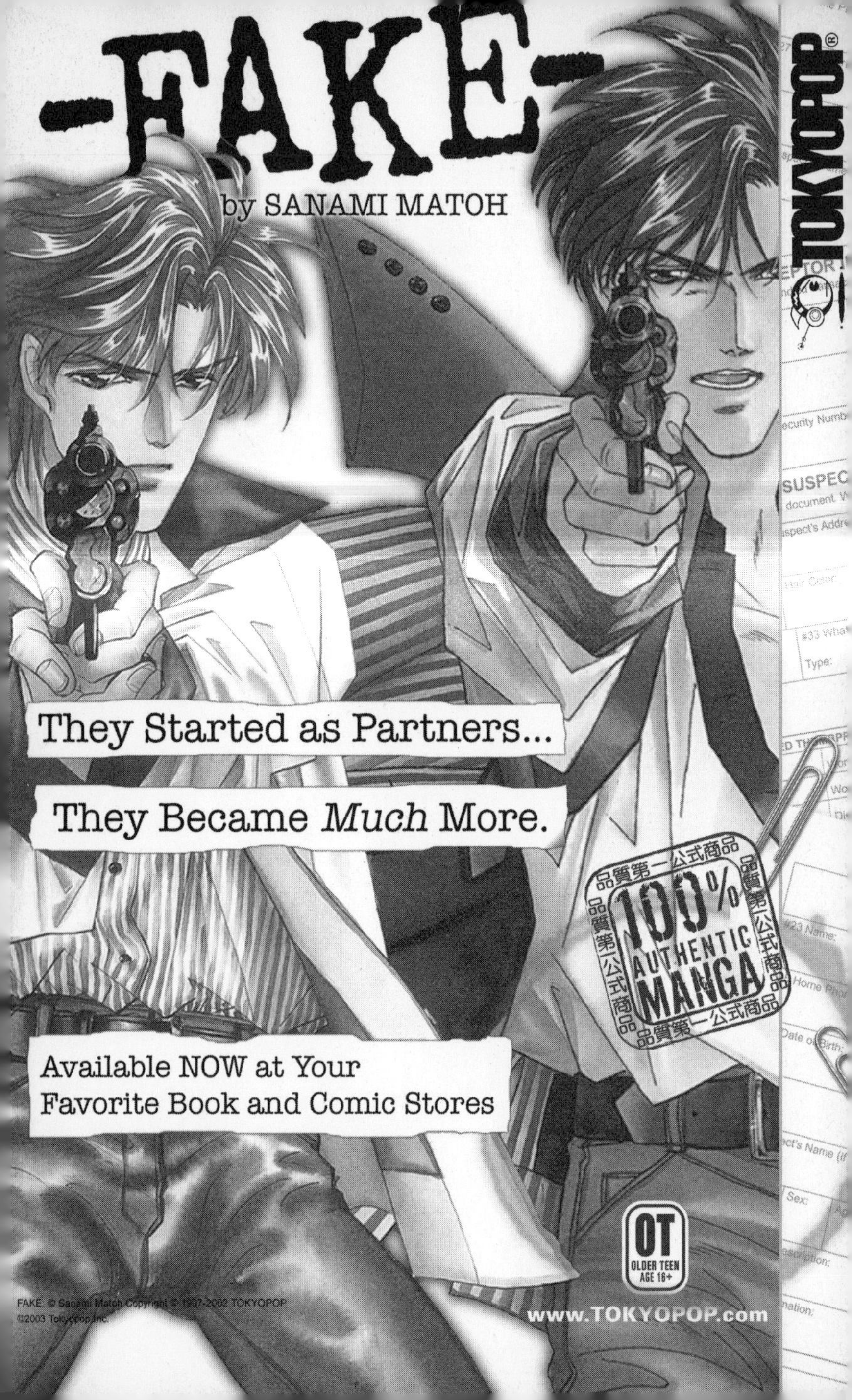
-FAKE-
by SANAMI MATOH
TOKYOPOP®
They Started as Partners...
They Became *Much* More.
100% AUTHENTIC MANGA
品質第一公式商品
Available NOW at Your
Favorite Book and Comic Stores
OT
OLDER TEEN
AGE 16+
FAKE © Sanami Matoh Copyright © 1997-2002 TOKYOPOP
©2003 Tokyopop Inc.
www.TOKYOPOP.com

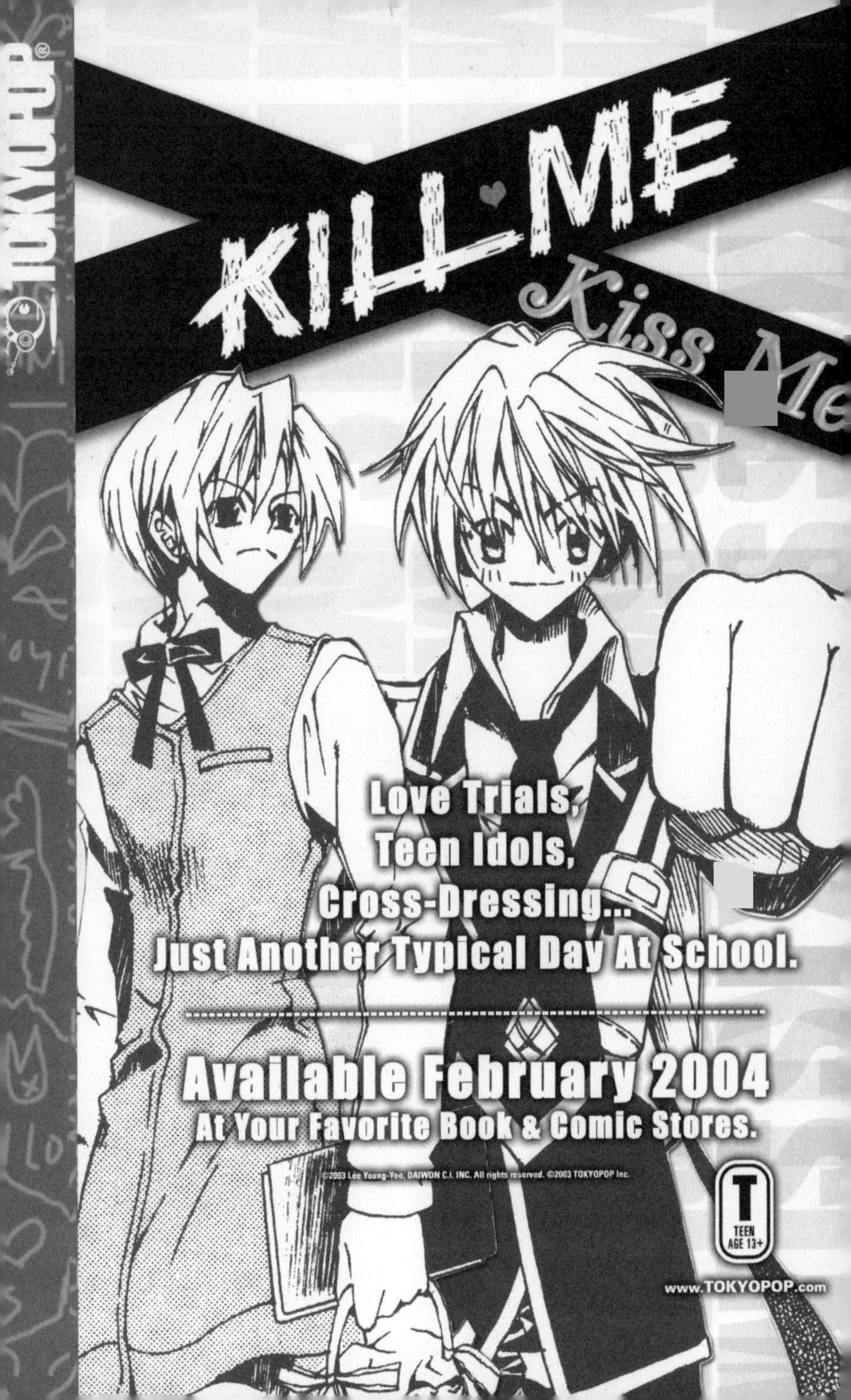
TOKYOPOP
KILL ME
Kiss Me
Love Trials,
Teen Idols,
Cross-Dressing...
Just Another Typical Day At School.
Available February 2004
At Your Favorite Book & Comic Stores.
©2003 Lee Young-Yoo, DAIWON C.I. INC. All rights reserved. ©2003 TOKYOPOP Inc.
T
TEEN
AGE 13+
www.TOKYOPOP.com

STOP!

This is the back of the book.
You wouldn't want to spoil a great ending!

This book is printed "manga-style," in the authentic Japanese right-to-left format. Since none of the artwork has been flipped or altered, readers get to experience the story just as the creator intended. You've been asking for it, so TOKYOPOP® delivered: authentic, hot-off-the-press, and far more fun!

DIRECTIONS

If this is your first time reading manga-style, here's a quick guide to help you understand how it works.

It's easy... just start in the top right panel and follow the numbers. Have fun, and look for more 100% authentic manga from TOKYOPOP®!

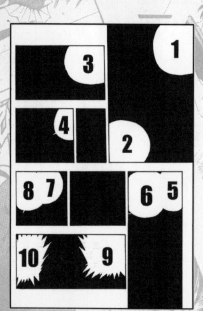